The Early Novels of Naguib Mahfouz

THE EARLY NOVELS OF

Naguib Mahfouz

IMAGES OF MODERN EGYPT

UNIVERSITY PRESS OF FLORIDA

Gainesville / Tallahassee / Tampa / Boca Raton

Pensacola / Orlando / Miami / Jacksonville

Copyright 1994 by the Board of Regents of the State of Florida
Printed in the United States of America on acid-free paper
All rights reserved
00 99 98 97 96 95 6 5 4 3 2 1

Library of Congress Cataloging-in-Publication Data

Moosa, Matti.
  The early novels of Naguib Mahfouz: images of modern
Egypt / Matti Moosa
p. cm.
Includes bibliographical references and index.
ISBN 0-8130-1309-7 (alk. paper)
1. Maḥfūẓ, Najib, 1912– —Criticism and interpretation.
I. Title.
PJ7846.A46Z713   1994
892'.736—dc20   94-22095

The University Press of Florida is the scholarly publishing
agency for the State University System of Florida, comprised of
Florida A & M University, Florida Atlantic University, Florida
International University, Florida State University, University of
Central Florida, University of Florida, University of North Flor-
ida, University of South Florida, and University of West Florida.

University Press of Florida
15 Northwest 15th Street
Gainesville, FL 32611

For Søren

Contents

Preface

IN 1988 an unprecedented historical event occurred: Naguib Mahfouz became the first Arab writer to receive the Nobel Prize in literature. A wave of jubilation spread among the Arabs, who were proud that one of their own had been recognized for his literary achievement. Like other Arab writers, including Taha Husayn and Tawfiq al-Hakim, whose works had been translated into several European languages, Mahfouz was known in the West but only to a limited reading public. The Nobel Prize, however, brought him instant fame and worldwide recognition as a respected novelist.

Until the 1940s little was known about Mahfouz even in his native Egypt. Originally an essayist who wrote extensively about a variety of subjects, he was overshadowed by writers like Taha Husayn, Tawfiq al-Hakim, Abbas Mahmud al-Aqqad, and Ibrahim al-Mazini. But through fortitude, consistency, and industriousness, Mahfouz began to clear a steady path for himself in the field of literature. He gained some fame in the early 1940s when he published three historical novels; among these, *Radobis* brought him the Qut al-Qulub Prize and *Kifah Tiba* (The Struggle of Thebes) the Ministry of Education Prize. But he first won undisputed acceptance as a literary practitioner with his contemporary novels, in which he portrayed realistically many aspects of life in Cairo. The *Thulathiyya* (Trilogy), published in 1956–57, was his most monumental work, the crowning achievement of his career and the first to bring him recognition in literary circles outside Egypt. Today Mahfouz is known as one of the leading novelists not only in Egypt but throughout the world. Students of literature, both in the Arab world and in the West, have produced doctoral dissertations, articles, and monographs about his life and work. Writers and journalists have flocked from all over the world to interview him. By the time Mahfouz won the Nobel Prize, he already was an established novelist in his own right, and the prize was but a manifestation of the universal appeal of his work.

The portrayal of life in Egypt through fiction is not Mahfouz's exclusive province; many Egyptian writers, including Husayn, al-Hakim, Yusuf Idris, and Adil Kamil, have done the same thing very successfully. But what distinguishes Mahfouz from them is his dedication to his craft: while others forsook their literary efforts for more lucrative mundane careers, he persisted in writing fiction, producing more than thirty novels and several anthologies of short stories and plays. Mahfouz may be considered the contemporary Arab Egyptian novelist par excellence. Moreover, he was more eclectic in his choice of themes, which range from social realism to psychoanalysis and metaphysics. He is sometimes described as the Dickens or Balzac of Egypt because social realism dominates his choice of subject and style. In essence, however, he is the Mahfouz of Egypt; his realistic style, his interest in social issues, indeed, his whole ethos are genuinely Egyptian. He should be claimed by all Arabs because most of his novels reflect Arabic and Islamic traditions.

In this book I concentrate on the early works of Naguib Mahfouz up to *Awlad Haratina* (Children of Our Quarter), beginning with a discussion of his nonfiction writings, especially those which shed light on the formation of his literary career. I then deal with the historical novels and a series of contemporary novels, including *al-Sarab* (The Mirage), which offers a psychoanalytic view of the Oedipus complex and portrays many aspects of Egyptian social life. Nearly half the book is devoted to the *Thulathiyya*; with this work, actually completed in 1952, Mahfouz apparently had said all he wanted to say about his society up to the outbreak of the Egyptian revolution in that year. He produced nothing more until 1959, when *Awlad Haratina* was serialized in *al-Ahram*. I conclude with a highly critical but independent discussion of this controversial novel, which the Muslim establishment in Egypt vehemently criticized as a vilification of religion and the prophets, especially Muhammad. Though published in a slightly expurgated edition at Beirut in 1967, it has never appeared in book form in Egypt.

My aim in this book is to introduce to the Western audience Naguib Mahfouz and his principal works, examining his treatment of social, political, and religious themes against the background of twentieth-century Egypt. I approach Mahfouz from a historical rather than a literary viewpoint, showing how he reflects the ethos of the Egyptian society as he lived in it and witnessed it. His novels, especially the *Thulathiyya*, accurately portray the rising spirit of nationalism, the corruption of politicians and the political process, and the fragile relationship between the Coptic Christian minority and the Muslim majority, while offering abundant insight into the social and religious attitudes of Egyptians from all walks of life. In this respect, this book should be of great benefit to those who seek a deeper understanding of Arab and Islamic thought and institutions, and particularly to those who would understand the long, tortuous course of Egypt's relations with the Western world and the Egyptians' struggle to escape British hegemony.

Mahfouz writes in a classical and lucid Arabic style, interspersed with colloquial Egyptian and proverbs known throughout the Arab world. Some of these proverbs, which he uses to accentuate his key points, utterly defy translation. He writes not only to entertain but to treat profoundly social, political, and religious issues and their impact on his society. His overriding purpose is clear: to give a true picture of the human condition as he sees it. If his ideas are sometimes controversial, they are nevertheless stimulating and must be understood in the context of Mahfouz's effort to treat the cultural trends of his society as they affect his own life.

Because much has been written about Mahfouz and his works, it is impossible to examine all of the secondary source materials. Moreover, the ideas expressed about Mahfouz are so varied and conflicting that I find it difficult to reconcile or utilize everything that has been said. Thus, I consider it more appropriate to rely on the original Arabic texts of Mahfouz's novels to determine his ideas and intentions, although on some occasions I have consulted authors who have offered controversial ideas about Mahfouz.

The completion of this book would not have been possible without the assistance of friends and institutions. I would like to thank the Research Committee at Gannon University, whose grant enabled me to begin this project. My longtime friend and colleague George Welch, Jr., of Laredo (Texas) Community College, edited the original manuscript and raised many points about Mahfouz's ideas. I am indebted to my friend and colleague, the late Jack E. Tohtz, Department of English, Edinboro University of Pennsylvania, for his observations regarding characters and plots in Mahfouz's novels, and to Frank Angotti of Gannon University for his invaluable assistance. I should mention with gratitude Ragai N. Makar, head of the Middle East Library, University of Utah Libraries, who has been indefatigable in acquiring necessary sources about Mahfouz and who graciously offered me a copy of his bibliography, *Najib Mahfuz: Nobel Prize Laureate For Literature*, 1988 (Salt Lake City: University of Utah Libraries, 1990). Likewise, for their assistance in obtaining secondary source materials, I am indebted to Fawzi Tadros of the Eastern Section, Library of Congress; Alice Diyab of Harvard College Library; Salwa Ferahian of the Library of McGill University, Montreal, Canada; and Susan Smith, acquisitions librarian, and John Pennsy, interlibrary loan reference assistant, at Gannon University. I thank Ralph Boyles, Academic Computing Specialist at Edinboro University of Pennsylvania, for helping me to organize the final copy of this book on computer. My sister Najeeba Moosa and my friend Nimat al-Amir have graciously assisted in providing texts of Mahfouz's novels. Philip Stewart of the Pauling Human Sciences Centre, University of Oxford, provided the slightly expurgated text of *Awlad Haratina* (Beirut: Dar al-Adab, 1967), together with information about the changes. I would be totally remiss if I did not recognize with special gratitude my sister-in-law Wafa Lamy Moosa, who in a variety of ways has assisted in almost all of my research projects, whether by purchasing books, arranging interviews with men of letters in Iraq, or introducing me to people who could facilitate my research. I also thank Joann Marinelli and Deborah Liegl for typing the manuscript.

Last but not least, I am grateful to my brother-in-law Claus J. Jensen for motivating me to write about Mahfouz. I cannot sufficiently thank my wife, Inge Jensen Moosa, for her understanding and patience while I was writing this book.

Matti Moosa

One

The Formative Years

TODAY NAGUIB MAHFOUZ is perhaps the most celebrated novelist in the Arab world, the result of winning the Nobel Prize in literature in 1988. His output includes more than thirty novels, along with a number of short story anthologies and plays. Several of his novels have been made into movies, and many have been translated into foreign languages, especially English. His winning the Nobel Prize has undoubtedly catapulted Mahfouz into a position of international literary renown.

Mahfouz was born into a middle-class family in December 1911 in the Jamaliyya quarter of old Cairo, not very far from the shrine of al-Husayn, the martyred Shiite Imam. His mother, after the difficult birth, gratefully named him for the obstetrician who delivered him. In 1924 his family moved to the Abbasiyya, a modern quarter of Cairo, where he grew up. Our knowledge of his childhood is scanty; Mahfouz offers only occasional glimpses of it in scattered interviews. He calls his childhood normal, meaning that he grew up in a solid, cohesive family undisturbed by the various ills he associates with broken homes. His parents were happily married, and he loved and respected them. His father, who died in 1937, was a strict Muslim who asserted his patriarchal authority, and the home's atmosphere was strongly religious. Yet this normal childhood was marred by a light and temporary attack of epilepsy, from which

Mahfouz quickly recovered. The youngest child in the family, Mahfouz laments that he spent most of his childhood alone, deprived of the companionship of his two brothers and four sisters, who started careers, married, and left home while he was growing up. Much younger than his siblings, he looked upon them as if they were his parents. He says that he never had the joy of playing with them, going with them for a walk, or confiding his secrets to them. This led Mahfouz to seek friends among the children of the neighborhood. He says he always liked to watch those of his friends who were brothers in order to see how they related and reacted to each other. Would they love each other, beat each other, or gang up against other children?

Mahfouz's father appears to have been a disciplinarian who ruled his household with an iron hand, yet he was compassionate and considerate. In his spare time he took the family to visit the Egyptian Museum to see the relics of Pharaonic, Coptic, and Islamic Egypt. On other occasions Mahfouz accompanied his mother to the same museum. Such visits must have interested him in the ancient history of Egypt, to which he devoted three historical novels.

The young Mahfouz heard much about Egyptian nationalism from his father, a patriot who revered the names of leaders like Mustafa Kamil, Muhammad Farid, and Sa'd Zaghlul. Mahfouz says that his father talked constantly and enthusiastically about these men, whom he regarded as heroes for defying the British authorities. Like many Egyptian men of his time, the elder Mahfouz took politics seriously and talked about different politicians as if they were personal enemies or friends. As we shall see later, the religious and political influences on his childhood are evident in most of his writings. Mahfouz seems not to remember a great deal about his elementary school years, apart from a vague recollection of the 1919 Egyptian revolution against the British, which is reflected in his *Thulathiyya* (Trilogy). (The Trilogy was not published with the title *Thulathiyya*, but it is commonly known by this name in both the Middle East and the West.) He says that he saw the British soldiers open fire on the demonstrators and saw the bodies of the dead and wounded in the Bayt al-Qadi Square. This extremely violent incident disturbed his peaceful childhood and affected the view of the world reflected in his writings.[1]

As did many Muslim children, Mahfouz began his formal education learning the recitation of the Quran at a *Kuttab* (Quranic school) run by a certain Shaykh al-Buhayri. Afterward he attended the Husayniyya Elementary School, graduating in 1925, and the Fuad I High School. He was a diligent student, proficient in the Arabic language, history, and mathematics but weak in foreign languages. In order to gain proficiency in English, he undertook the translation of James Baikie's book *Ancient Egypt* into Arabic. The translation was published in 1932 under the title *Misr al-Qadima* through the efforts of Salama Musa, a Fabian and intellectual whose socialistic ideas influenced Mahfouz.[2]

Mahfouz was also active in sports, and soccer was his favorite game. According to a friend from his youth, Adham Rajab, M.D., Mahfouz was a remarkably speedy soccer player. He also had a tremendous sense of humor. In the late 1920s, says Rajab, Mahfouz went with some companions to the old Fishawi coffeehouse, where men of humor exchanged jokes, some of which were off-color. Mahfouz overwhelmed them with his quick and extemporaneous wit, making them appear ridiculous. Sometimes he would confront twenty of these joke tellers simultaneously and silence all of them. He was so adept at telling spontaneous jokes that his rivals could not help laughing at themselves. While in high school, Mahfouz founded a society for the protection of morality. Its objective was to instill moral principles in the students and combat the use of foul language. The society was short-lived, however, because Mahfouz found himself using foul language to fight those students who opposed him and his society.[3]

Coffeehouses like al-Fishawi were part of Mahfouz's daily life, places where he could enjoy some relaxation by smoking the water-pipe, drinking coffee, and reading newspapers and meet regularly with several intimate friends, one of whom, Ahmad Muzhir, named their group al-Harafish. This term, used by the eighteenth-century Egyptian historian Abd al-Rahman al-Jabarti, means "common people." These Harafish met weekly in different coffeehouses; even today, they continue to meet every Thursday evening at Casino Qasr al-Nil. It is said that Mahfouz always brought a kilogram of kabob (grilled meat on skewers) to these gatherings. He always sat in the same chair, ever happy and full of laughter. It was at these meetings that one of the group, Salah Abu Sayf, discovered Mahfouz's ability to write screenplays. Thus, Mahfouz began writing scenarios for many movies, including those based on some of his novels. Mahfouz, who is known for his loyalty among his friends, has maintained ties with the group to the present day.[4]

In his early teens, Mahfouz began reading Western detective stories translated into Arabic. He also enjoyed watching adventure movies and was fascinated by the heroism of some of their characters. In the meantime, he read the sentimental writings and Western adaptations of Mustafa Lutfi al-Manfaluti and Arabic translations of Western historical novels.

During 1925–26 Mahfouz began to compose Arabic poetry, following traditional meters and rhyme. But he discovered it was difficult to achieve perfect rhymes and decided to break away from the rigid traditional form. He began composing free verse and credits himself with being the pioneer of the Arabic free verse movement.[5] But he never neglected to read major Arabic classics, such as *al-Bayan wa al-Tabyin* (The Book of Eloquence and Exposition), by al-Jahiz, and *al-Iqd al-Farid* (The Unique Necklace), by Ibn Abd Rabbih. In the 1930s Mahfouz began reading the works of prominent Egyptian writers like Taha Husayn, Tawfiq al-Hakim, Abbas Mahmud al-Aqqad, Muhammad Husayn Haykal, and Ibrahim Abd-al-Qadir al-Mazini and lesser-known writers like Yahya Haqqi and Mahmud Timur. He must have been greatly impressed by Husayn's autobiographical novel *al-Ayyam* (The Stream of Days), which he calls "my life story written according to Taha Husayn's manner."[6] But more than any other Egyptian book, two works by al-Hakim, *Awdat al-Ruh* (The Return of the Spirit) and *Yawmiyyat Na'ib fi al-Aryaf* (The Diaries of an Inspector in the Country), left an indelible imprint on his mind. Their influence, especially in arousing the ancient Egyptian spirit, which al-Hakim thought had been resurrected in the revolution of 1919, can be seen in Mahfouz's historical novels.[7]

In his youth, Mahfouz's reading was not systematic; he read haphazardly to satisfy his inquisitive nature. But after graduating from college in 1934, he became more selective in his reading, concentrating mostly on masterpieces of Western literature. Having no one to guide him to the works he should read, he turned to books on the history of world literature, especially the works of the English dramatist, critic, and biographer John Drinkwater (1882–1937). After reading Drinkwater's works, Mahfouz says, he began to look upon world literatures as one, and not the literatures of different peoples.[8] The masterpieces of English literature he read were chiefly those of Shakespeare, Dickens, Wells, Galsworthy, Shaw, Joyce, Aldous Huxley, and D. H. Lawrence. Among the French writers, he read Flaubert, Anatole France, Emile Zola, Stendhal, Proust, Mauriac, Sartre, and others. Of the Russians he read Gorki, Tolstoy, Turgenev, Dostoyevsky, and Chekhov; in German literature he read Goethe, Mann, and Kafka. Of the American writers, he read Melville, Hemingway, Faulkner, Dos Passos, and O'Neill; of the Scandinavians, he read Ibsen and Strindberg. He states he read most of the works in English or French or in Arabic translation.[9] Although Mahfouz names many writers, he points out that he did not read them in toto; he says, "I have not read the complete works of Tolstoy. But when Drinkwater selected *War and Peace*, I read it."[10]

It would be interesting to know Mahfouz's thoughts in later years about his early reading and its impact on his writing. Interviewed by Sabri Hafiz in 1973, Mahfouz mentioned the Western writers who had most influenced him. To him Shakespeare, whom he loved dearly, was like a dear friend talking to him in the coffeehouse. His majestic ideas and humor were so blended with Mahfouz's soul that he could say, "I felt that Shakespeare was the son of my own country, not of another." After Shakespeare he liked Ibsen and Strindberg, but he was unenthusiastic about the theatrical works of Chekhov, which he found sluggish and boring. He was fascinated by Joseph Conrad's *Heart of Darkness*, whose broad and comprehensive outlook on life affected his late novels. He also liked Proust and Kafka but claims he found Joyce unpalatable, considering his ideas and style an experiment that requires meticulous exploration.

"What crazy man," Mahfouz comments, "is able to read *Ulysses?* It is an awful novel. Nevertheless, it has created a trend. It is like the one who points to love, but asks those who desire to attain it to use their own way."[11] Mahfouz saves most of his praise for Melville's *Moby Dick*, which he considers perhaps the greatest novel in the world. Although Hemingway and Dos Passos were fine writers, he says, their work could not reach its level. Mahfouz notes that he did not like Faulkner, considering him unnecessarily complex.

In sum, Mahfouz says that in one way or another he was influenced by these Westerners and their works. In writing his novels, he used such diverse techniques as internal monologue, naturalism, and realism, but with modifications.[12] Realism was his favorite technique, and he chose it courageously after some deliberation. Mahfouz notes that Virginia Woolf had attacked the realistic technique, saying European novels were oversated with it. But realism was not known in Egypt nor the Arab world, and Mahfouz felt eager to use it. If he had not done so, he would have been merely one among many writers who followed what he calls "modern" techniques.[13] In many of his novels, he uses situations and characters drawn from real life. In *Khan al-Khalili*, for instance, the character Ahmad Akif is based on a real person of that name. The protagonist of *al-Sarab*, Kamil Ruba Laz, is actually Husayn Badr al-Din, a law school graduate. The central figure of *al-Liss wa al-Kilab* (The Thief and the Dogs), Said Mihran, symbolizes the notorious thief Mahmud Sulayman, who was sought by the police for his crimes. And Mahfouz states that *Bidaya wa Nihaya* (The Beginning and the End) is based on the actual story of a family he had known. The story of this family had a happy outcome, says Mahfouz, but he preferred to end it with a tragedy in order to arouse the sentiments of the readers.[14] Likewise, his vignette "Hanan Mustafa" is said to be based on the true story of his first love for the young woman of that name.[15] We can thus readily understand why Mahfouz did not like Faulkner and Joyce; they did not suit his taste for realism because Faulkner was a myth maker and Joyce was a symbolist. He felt more comfortable with Galsworthy, Dos Passos, and Thomas Mann.

Mahfouz began his literary career while still a high school student, writing essays on different subjects in philosophy and literature. He also wrote short stories. (In fact, as an elementary school student, he experimented with rewriting short fiction works by H. Rider Haggard and others and adding a few details from his own life. He would put his own name on the cover, as if he were the author, and invent the name of the publisher.)[16] He seemed to favor writing about philosophy, but he never neglected writing short stories. His interest in philosophy led him to seek a government scholarship to further his study in France. Mahfouz states that after his graduation with a B.A. degree from the University of Fuad (the present Cairo University) in 1934, he applied for the scholarship, but for what seemed to be trivial reasons he was turned down. The scholarship award was influenced by sectarian considerations between Muslims and Coptic Christians, and the Copts were allowed only one candidate. The screening committee mistook Mahfouz for a Christian Copt, dropped his name from the list, and chose another candidate who in fact was a Copt.[17] Mahfouz's inclination toward philosophy was the dissertation he chose for his master's degree, entitled "Mafhum al-Jamal fi al-Falsafa al-Islamiyya" (The Concept of Aesthetics in Islamic Philosophy), under the Islamologist al-Shaykh Mustafa Abd al-Raziq. He collected the necessary sources to write this dissertation for two years, but he did not complete the project.[18]

For many years Mahfouz experienced a mordant internal conflict over the choice between philosophy and literature until finally he opted for literature, specifically the writing of fiction. That he chose philosophy first and then switched to fiction shows not only the perplexed state of mind of a young man trying to make his way through a literary world dominated by towering writers like al-Manfaluti, Husayn, al-Aqqad, al-Mazini and others, but also the whole intellectual ambience of Egypt in the 1930s, when Mahfouz began writing.

In several interviews Mahfouz has revealed his reasons for choosing at first to write on philosophical topics. Studying philosophy for several years, he says, had encouraged his affinity for it. He also had concluded that philosophy was more important than literary genres like fiction because it had a definite and concrete objective, the quest for truth, while fiction was meant only to amuse and entertain. In other words, young Mahfouz was seeking a pragmatic objective to which he would devote his life and pen. To him, writing fiction was for idealists and dreamers, not for practical men who strove not only to transform society but to make a decent living, as well. He also realized that his countrymen were more inclined toward politics than toward literature, including fiction. They held fiction writing in low esteem; some of them considered such activity a matter of shame, not pride. Mahfouz admits that when some of his early short stories appeared in periodicals like *al-Risala* and *al-Riwaya*, he denied authorship in order to escape the ridicule of his friends.[19]

Another reason for Mahfouz's vacillation between philosophy and literature is, he says, that many of his early short stories were rejected, while his articles on philosophical themes were accepted for publication. This convinced him that the reading public was more interested in serious subjects than in fiction. The conflict between philosophy and literature continued to obsess him until he finally reached a point where he had to choose between them. He decided in favor of fiction after his short stories began to be unreservedly accepted for publication, a fact that convinced him the reading public had become more appreciative of fiction.[20]

But when did Mahfouz discover that he had a literary talent, and who first alerted him to it? He states it was his close friend Adham Rajab, himself a voracious reader, who introduced him to modern English literature and gave him free access to his own substantial library. Two years after his graduation from college in 1934, Mahfouz decided that he was a writer and devoted himself to that calling.[21]

Although he eventually opted for fiction, he spent the years from 1930 to 1945 writing mostly essays, and his first short story anthology, *Hams al-Junun* (The Whisper of Madness), did not appear until 1938. But his various articles on philosophy are worth noting, because traces of philosophical concepts can be detected in many of his novels and short stories.

To the best of our knowledge the first of Mahfouz's philosophical articles was "Ihtidar Mu'taqadat wa Tawallud Mu'taqadat" (The

Death and Birth of Doctrines), which Salama Musa published in October 1930 in his periodical *al-Majalla al-Jadida*. In it he states that life is subject to constant change and evolution, and such change is inevitable and in itself a necessary evil. Given the choice between change and permanence, he would definitely choose permanence, which is conducive to the tranquillity of the soul and clearly preferable to the frightful results of change that affect life and civilization. Nonetheless, we should not lament that constant change spells the end of time-honored concepts but accept it as the natural result of human civilization, the true criterion of the evolution and progress of the intellect. Because of the sometimes brutal and painful results of change, which yield pain and perplexity, the concepts that should provide us with peace and serenity of soul can lose their aura of sanctity. Mahfouz complains that the age in which he lives is characterized by unprecedented skepticism and turmoil; concepts men have accepted and cherished for generations have been shaken to their foundations. One reason for consolation, however, is that man is by nature a believer. Man is made up of matter (body) and spirit, and faith alone can fulfill his spiritual half. Without it, he must find something else to which he can surrender his heart and mind. Thus, people who have no religious beliefs espouse social or political ideals; they must surrender themselves either to God or to Caesar.

But where did young Mahfouz stand with respect to this constant change and evolution, and what doctrine, in his opinion, were his people inclined to espouse in order to ensure tranquillity of mind and happiness? New ideas and doctrines like socialism and communism were being imported into Egypt and finding some acceptance among the intelligentsia. Such doctrines ran counter to a traditional Islamic society like Egypt's. They also contradicted the political structure of the Egyptian regime, whose monarchical-parliamentary system the British had fashioned after their own. (Indeed, the British had occupied Egypt in 1882, following Ahmad Urabi's rebellion, and for all intents and purposes treated it as a colony, controlling it until the officers' revolution in 1952.) Moreover, Egypt's economy, like that of Britain, was capitalistic. So what doctrine did young Mahfouz believe his countrymen should adopt to supersede the existing political and economic system? He desired an egalitarian system that would benefit the majority but would not antagonize faithful Muslims and cause them to reject it, a system midway between capitalism and communism. His choice was socialism, which he believed could ultimately triumph over other doctrines, although he realized it was far from perfect. Socialism can fulfill some of man's material needs but not his spiritual needs: it cannot help him redeem his soul. The material fulfillment brought about by socialism is worldly, while man's spiritual happiness is otherworldly. Because socialism (like other doctrines) cannot realize fully its promises of a perfect life, many of its adherents will eventually desert it; nevertheless, Mahfouz concludes, we must accept the fact that what it offers is better than our present condition.[22]

Over a decade later, Mahfouz attacked communism as a dictatorial ideology that advocates revolution to preserve its dictatorship and eliminates political freedom by its one-party system. Mahfouz favored a peaceful democratic socialism with a reformed parliamentary system.[23] In the late 1960s, Mahfouz finally defined the type of socialism he felt would eventually dominate. In an interview, Raja al-Naqqash somewhat cunningly suggested that Mahfouz apparently sympathized with Marxism yet was hesitant to advocate it in his writings. Asked why, Mahfouz answered that he was inclined not toward Marxism but toward moderate socialism. While he respected Marxism, he detested the materialistic tenets upon which it is based and remained suspicious of the feasibility of implementing it. He stated that society should be liberated from class privileges like inheritance and from exploitation in every form, that social status should be based on the individual's natural and acquired talents, that wages should be set according to need, that the individual should enjoy freedom of thought and belief under a law that extends to both the government and the governed, that democracy should be implemented in its fullest meaning, and finally that the function of government should be confined to the protection of public safety and defense. This, Mahfouz said, is his overview of a Marxist society where individual freedom and happiness prevail. It is a society where everything depends on science, which eventually leads to the discovery of the highest truth and the creation of knowledge.[24]

This is, to be sure, not the scientific socialism of Karl Marx, but a mixture of the theories of eighteenth- and nineteenth-century classical economists. It reflects not so much Marxism as the theories of Adam Smith, David Ricardo, and John Stuart Mill, tempered perhaps by Fabianism. Mahfouz himself admits that he came under the influence of Salama Musa, who, he says, "directed me to two important principles, science and socialism, and once these two principles entered my mind, they never left it."[25]

Mahfouz's penchant for moderate socialism sheds some light on his political predilection. Early in life he sympathized with the leftist wing of the Wafd party but refrained from partisan activity. He believed that the Wafd was the people's party, truly a national and democratic body. While it played a significant role in giving Egyptian nationalism a definite form, there was a need for a more decisive ideology to ensure the full rights of the Egyptian people. Socialism was still in its infancy in Egypt, and there was no organized socialist party. So to whom would Mahfouz turn in his political predicament? Surprisingly, he turned to the Wafd, praising it and some of its leaders in a few articles in the Egyptian newspaper *al-Ayyam* in 1943, while realizing that it was powerless in facing the British authorities. In one of these articles he praised the minister of education, Najib al-Hilali, as a great founder of true democracy in Egypt, a genius whose talents would light the path for the Egyptian people. Apparently, having read al-Hilali's program for public education, Mahfouz had seen in its light the Egyptians as a progressive people and not as the powers of iniquity and oppression (meaning the British imperialistic authorities) wanted them to be. In another article he extended his flattery to other political leaders then advocated the right of the government to interfere in the national economy of Egypt in order to ensure the freedom of the individual from want and hunger. In a third article, he vehemently attacked communism and again advocated moderate socialism.[26]

We do not know Mahfouz's frame of mind when he praised the Wafd party, although he was not politically active. Was it his despair about his literary life or the difficulty of publishing substantive work during the war that motivated him to flatter the minister of education in order to win an audience? According to the Egyptian writer Abd al-Muhsin Badr, such flattery was tantamount to hypocrisy.[27]

Mahfouz's early articles on different topics, especially philosophy, reveal the inchoate ideas of a young man who was probing his way through the myriad of Western concepts that had invaded Egypt. They show the perplexity of a young Muslim Egyptian with a keen and curious mind trying not only to make sense of these concepts but to reconcile them with his own traditional beliefs. Such perplexity can be detected easily in Mahfouz's novels, as shall be seen in following chapters. Suffice it to say at this juncture that Mahfouz had read Western philosophy, especially that of the French antirationalist Henri Bergson. Mahfouz's idea that life is an inexorable sequence of change and revolution that causes man anxiety echoes Bergson, who maintains that the nature of the universe is revolutionary; that everything in it is moving, growing, becoming, and living, so that both the knower and the object of knowledge are changing. There is an infinite variety and change of forms, and in the presence of life, change, and movement, the conceptual thinking of man stands helpless. Mahfouz devoted several articles to the philosophy of Bergson, especially his *Laughter*, *Élan vital*, and *Consciousness*.[28] But despite his respect for philosophy, he does not seem to be enthusiastic about its role in life. He seems to consider our modern age one not of philosophy but of science, technology, and practical activity. He maintains that science and philosophy differ only in form, not in content. Both are of the same essence because they emanate from the same knowledge inherent in the human soul and life.[29]

Mahfouz is equally obsessed with the metaphysical subject of religion, especially the concept of God. To him, religion is an essential element of life. In an article on the philosophy of love, he equates love with perfection, because God is the source of both, and asserts that love is holy because God is holy.[30] In two related articles, he discusses the importance of religion and recounts how since ancient times people have tried to fathom the nature of God. His survey takes him from the maze of Greek philosophy down to the modern age. But the arguments and the proofs philosophers offer, whether moral or logical, do not satisfy the person who is seeking something more concrete. Mahfouz presents two concepts of God: one from the sociologist Émile Durkheim, who maintains that the concept of God has been inherent in the human collective society since it began, and one from the mystics.

Mahfouz criticizes Durkheim for confining God to a narrow social perspective. Such ideas do not satisfy his desire to know about God, and he seeks an answer (or perhaps consolation) in the mystics, whose precept is to know God by sense rather than through reason. To the mystics, he says, God is not a simple idea that can be fathomed by logic nor a complex idea that can be understood by deduction, but rather a transcendental essence that we feel in the depth of the soul, attaining knowledge of it through meditation and sublimation.

After sifting through these ideas about God, Mahfouz emerges with a skeptical outlook. To the question of what will be their effect on those who seek to know God, Mahfouz's answer is that in confronting them, man stands helpless. Indeed, he finds himself more distressed and more perplexed than ever because they do not lead man to a true and decisive belief in God.[31] At this stage of his life and later, as some of his novels and short stories show, Mahfouz's stance on religion and especially the concept of God is doubtful if not unorthodox in the Islamic context. He is ever tormented by the ambiguity of faith and skepticism. Such torment is most evident in the person of one of his characters, Kamal, in the *Thulathiyya*. Kamal wants to believe in God, but he is not sure of God or religion. Religion, as practiced by his Muslim countrymen and his family, does not make much sense to him. The only religion he confesses to is science, which he considers the key to the mystery and majesty of the universe. Kamal is sure that if the prophets of old were resurrected today, they would choose science as their message for mankind.[32] The fact that after the appearance of *Thulathiyya* in 1956–57 Mahfouz identified himself with Kamal allows us to better understand his religious skepticism and faith in science.[33]

In the early 1970s, however, he seems to have repudiated his total identification with Kamal, calling it only partially correct. He further states that he will never again identify himself with his characters, because this is the most egregious mistake a writer can make.[34] A decade later, he seems to have dissociated himself from the actions of some of his characters, leaving readers and critics to their own speculations. But whether he identifies himself with some of his characters or not, the fact remains that in many of his novels Mahfouz appears to be a perplexed person who has not yet found a satisfactory answer to the complex realities of life in this world and beyond. Indeed, he keeps reiterating his position on Marxism, socialism, and religion. In the mid-1970s, he made it clear once more that although he rejects the materialistic ideology of Marxism and the dictatorship of the proletariat, he admires its advocacy of social justice and reliance on science. Moreover, he maintained that he is a Muslim believer who sees no contradiction between Islam and socialism, and in fact that Islam calls for socialism. He made his position clear when he stated in March 1973 that in his heart he has combined an aspiration for God, faith in science, and a predilection for socialism.[35] Indeed, after the abrogation of the Anglo-Egyptian treaty in 1951, Mahfouz hoped that a new socialist party would emerge from the Wafd's left wing to effect a genuine popular revolution. This did not happen, however, and the Egyptian revolution of 1952 was effected by the military, not through the political process. Although the revolution's leaders advocated socialism, Arab nationalism, and democracy, he says true socialism and democracy have not been realized in Egypt. In order for these objectives to be achieved, it is imperative that freedom first be established and respected.[36]

While still a student at the College of Arts, Mahfouz attended music classes at the Arab Music Institute and chose the zither as his favorite instrument. He believed then that the study of music was essential to the knowledge of aesthetics and the philosophy of beauty. But after one year, despite having acquired some proficiency, he concluded there was no connection between playing the zither and the philosophy of beauty, dropped his music classes, and turned toward the reading of science and literature.[37]

Mahfouz did not confine himself to philosophy and science, but wrote on a variety of other subjects, including psychology, music, and literature. Most of these articles were superficial, although some of the articles on literature show some literary acumen. As do most Arabs, he appreciated Arabic music. He was fascinated by the voice of the Egyptian singer Salih Abd al-Hayy. His friend Adham Rajab relates that in the early 1930s, Mahfouz gathered regularly with friends in the evenings at a coffeehouse in the Sakakini quarter of Cairo to listen attentively to the radio broadcast of al-Hayy's three courses of singing. Likewise, he idolized Umm Kulthum, the Egyptian singer who captivated Arab audiences with her miraculous voice. Perhaps because of his love for her voice, he named one of his daughters after her. Although he appreciated singers like Salih Abd al-Hayy, Asmahan, and Muhammad Abd al-Wahhab, he reserved his affection for Umm Kulthum.[38]

Mahfouz wrote about Molière, Ibsen, Shaw, and Chekhov in an informative rather than critical manner. The importance of his treatment of some works by these writers lies primarily in what it reveals of their impact on his writings. Discussing Shaw's play *Back to Methuselah*, Mahfouz states it was intended to depict the process of the creation, beginning with the story of Adam and Eve, and man's eternal quest to obtain the philosopher's stone and overcome death. Furthermore, Mahfouz says, in its political aspect, the plot portrays the shortcomings of civilized life. The story of the creation, the dialogue between Adam and Eve, and man's eternal quest to overcome death are reflected in many works by Mahfouz, especially *Awlad Haratina*.[39]

Mahfouz wrote several articles on Arabic literature and Arab writers, two of which are of great significance. One of these is about three Egyptian writers, Abbas Mahmud al-Aqqad, Taha Husayn, and Salama Musa, who have left their mark on Arabic literature, and by whose work he has been greatly influenced. He classifies them according to their literary ideas, placing al-Aqqad at the top, Husayn second, and Musa third. But before examining Mahfouz's opinion about these writers, we must ask why he is influenced by them, given the great intellectual, ideological, and literary disparity among them. Mahfouz states they share the common bond of an intellectual literary revolution, symbolized by the literary acumen of Husayn, political and literary thinking of al-Aqqad, social and

scientific precepts of Musa.[40] Al-Aqqad has the highest rank because he is by nature a talented and intuitive man of letters. Like a
sufi, or mystic, he probes the very essence of literature and attempts
to lift it to the highest stage of perfection. He is a literary maverick,
a self-made writer whose great trait is that he does not imitate other
writers and embraces no specific literary doctrine. We shall see
shortly, however, that despite his praise of al-Aqqad, Mahfouz was
one of his severest critics.

Mahfouz places Taha Husayn after al-Aqqad because his literary
perception is that of the intellect, calling him a man of intelligence
whose writing combines simplicity, humor, and intellectual acumen conducive to skepticism. In fact, he says skepticism is the
foundation of Husayn's literary investigation, which has become a
model for other writers. As to Salama Musa, who occupies the third
place in Mahfouz's literary hierarchy, Mahfouz calls him a pragmatic thinker, obsessed with social reform, to whom literature is a
means to an end, not the end in itself. Mahfouz considers al-Aqqad
the soul of the Arab literary *nahda* (awakening), Husayn its intellect,
and Musa its will.[41] Of course, not everyone agrees with Mahfouz's
classification of these writers, reflecting as it does his own literary
predisposition.

Mahfouz had great respect for al-Aqqad, whom he considered
preeminent among Egyptian writers, but disagreed with his ideas
about fiction as an art. In his little book *Fi Bayti* (At My House),
al-Aqqad converses with a friend in his private library about a
variety of subjects. His friend, admiring the library, notes the small
number of books of fiction compared to other voluminous collec-
tions in it. Al-Aqqad responds that there are few such books in his
library because, truthfully, he would not read a story if he could
read a book of essays or an anthology of poetry. Indeed, he would
not consider fiction as the best product of the intellect. His interlocu-
tor asks whether the writing of fiction is not an art, like poetry or
any other. Al-Aqqad answers that a practitioner of fiction may have
a more fertile imagination or sharper wit than a poet or nonfiction
writer, but storytelling (fiction) still occupies a place beneath that
of poetry, prose, or literary criticism. Although we read the novels
of writers like Dickens, Tolstoy, Dostoyevsky, and Proust and

recognize their genius, he adds, "We should not place fiction at the top of the literary genres and relegate others to a secondary place."[42]

Al-Aqqad goes on to justify his opinions on style, the quality of fiction, and the reading public. Whenever the output of fiction increases, its quality diminishes, he says, noting how plentiful stories and novels are and how puny their quality is. To prove that a fifty-page story will not provide the same quality or substance as a piece of poetry, he recites these lines: "My eyes turned back to cast a look at the ruins of the abode of the beloved. But as these ruins faded in the distance, my heart, rather than my eyes, turned to cast a last look at them."[43] Al-Aqqad quotes more poetry to support his belief that writers of fiction cannot express deep meaning in a few words, except by using introductions and a mass of details. As to the reading public, he contends that it is easy for semiliterate people to develop a taste for fiction, which they can absorb, but it is difficult for them to develop a taste for poetry or exquisite pieces of literature. Fiction, he argues, is for everybody, but it is difficult even for the educated elite to acquire a taste for poetry.

Finally, al-Aqqad comments on the uproar some men created at the turn of the century by the exaggeration of the importance of fiction, leading people to believe no one can be rightfully considered a genuine writer unless he produces fiction. He says this was the result of introducing psychological studies into schools and many writers' belief that psychology was the only means of understanding human behavior and communication. But there were other reasons for the popularity of fiction: the ability of the semiliterate public to read and absorb cheap types of fiction, and the emergence of the moving pictures, which made it easier for the reading public to appreciate fiction without actually reading it. Al-Aqqad adds yet another reason, the rise of communism, which became especially popular among students. The communists, he says, regard fiction highly because it is written for the ignorant and serves as a suitable means to disseminate their ideology. They particularly emphasize the kind of fiction that deals with social problems such as inequality and poverty, knowing that such sensitive subjects appeal to the poor and the oppressed.[44]

In a 1945 article, Mahfouz sharply disagrees with al-Aqqad. He says that predicating the preference of one art form over another merely on considerations of technique and substance is futile. Art, regardless of its style, technique, or form, is an expression of life. It has one objective, to promote happiness, peace, and cooperation among people. No one should venture to disturb people's happiness and peace of mind, as al-Aqqad does, by telling them that one kind of art is high and the other low, one noble and the other ignoble. Perhaps, says Mahfouz, al-Aqqad means no harm by classifying the arts as he does. As a critic, he has the right to do so, but in this case al-Aqqad has in fact turned into an antagonist. Mahfouz says that the person who would not read a story if he could read a book or an anthology of poetry cannot be a fair judge of fiction. If criticism is a criterion for the evaluation of art, how can al-Aqqad prefer one type of art to another? And how can one accept his judgment, knowing beforehand that he denigrates fiction? Mahfouz adds that he does not understand how al-Aqqad can apply the same standards of form, style, and substance to poetry and fiction, unless he has arbitrarily decided that a full-length story with a moral can be summarized in one line of poetry. This is difficult to achieve because the story is a portrayal of life and thus must be comprehensive and detailed. Each part of it reflects some aspect of life. Poetry or literary prose cannot usurp the position fiction has gained. Let not al-Aqqad believe, says Mahfouz, that the purpose of details in fiction is merely to fill empty pages, because their use is one of the characteristics that differentiate the short story from other literary genres. Fiction writers' attention to detail did not develop arbitrarily, he says, but came about as a result of the constant scientific evolution of our generation, which focused attention on the study of particulars, whereas philosophy was confined to the study of universal principles.

Mahfouz also challenges al-Aqqad's low opinion of the reading public as a justification for his preference of poetry over fiction. Al-Aqqad means, he says, that because fiction is popular only among a group of readers who cannot absorb poetry, the latter is the nobler art. Mahfouz contends that the popularity of an art among a group of people is meaningless unless we investigate the reasons for its appeal. For example, music is popular among all kinds of people, literate or illiterate. How then can one say that music occupies a higher status than sculpture because the latter is appreciated by those who go to museums? And in comparing poetry and fiction, what kind of story is al-Aqqad talking about? Is it not the story of crime, adventure, and cheap sex? Certainly he does not mean the artistic story, as defined by those who study the art of the story. The artistic story is not a cheap tale; it reveals values and character, offering an analysis of the human soul and human traits, philosophical themes and social ideas. Without these characteristics, it becomes merely a tale. Mahfouz concludes that the story is more popular in our time than poetry. Though al-Aqqad may read fiction only because he feels he is forced to do so, others read it at their leisure for entertainment. Thus, he argues, we can readily say that the story is more popular than poetry because its technique is easier, and because it is meant to entertain.[45]

Oddly enough al-Aqqad, who places fiction as an art beneath poetry, tried his own hand at it. His so-called novel *Sarah* (1938) revolves around a beautiful, warm, and licentious female ruled by her instinct rather than by her mind. She is the image of femininity yet is so completely an abstraction that her name is not even mentioned until sixty pages have gone by. The subject of the novel is the renewed relationship of Sarah and men who had loved her in their youth, but their relationship is dominated by suspicion, with the result that the characters lack freedom of action. In essence, *Sarah* is a series of disjointed sketches rather than a coherent, plausible novel.[46] Mahfouz alludes to it as an analytical story but says no more about it or about al-Aqqad as a fiction writer, since he was predisposed toward other types of literature, especially literary synthesis.[47] Although he disagrees with al-Aqqad over the artistic value of fiction, Mahfouz never deprecates his eminent role in the realm of Arabic literature.

In conclusion, the literary career of young Mahfouz shows him writing on different subjects, especially philosophy, before discovering that his talent lay in the realm of fiction. He began writing at the tender age of nineteen, when most of his schoolmates could not even understand philosophical themes, let alone write about them.

No one expects young Mahfouz to have been a philosopher with mature ideas. He was an intelligent young man with a keen, inquisitive mind, trying to fathom the world around him. He was fascinated by philosophy and literature, hoping to find in them some answers to the eternal questions about God, humanity, and the universe that have obsessed the minds of human beings since the world began. His interpretations of the ideas about the writers he had read became firmly fixed in his mind and were later reflected in his writings. In fact, his lonely childhood, his Islamic upbringing, and the influence of his authoritarian father and loving mother are symbolized in many of his characters. His early reading of Arabic classics, masterpieces of Western fiction, and the fictional works of the preceding generation of Egyptian writers played a decisive role in shaping the literary career of this future Nobel Prize winner.

Two

The Historical Novels

AS WE HAVE SEEN, Mahfouz began his literary career when he was in high school, producing essays on different subjects together with short stories. He began to write novels while in college, but these first efforts were not publishable. Through the effort and encouragement of Salama Musa, however, he eventually had several historical novels published. Mahfouz relates how this happened. During one of his visits to the office of the magazine *al-Majalla al-Jadida,* Musa asked him whether he thought that there was a chance for the novel to succeed in Egypt. Musa believed that since most Egyptian fiction writers were influenced by Western ideas and techniques, it would be difficult to produce a genuine Egyptian novel. Perhaps, he thought, a student from the Azhar (an Islamic religious institute, now a university) could write an authentic Egyptian novel, because Azharite students were not influenced by Western culture. Mahfouz responded that although the novel in Egypt was still in its infancy, he himself had ventured into the genre. Surprised, Musa asked him whether he really wrote novels; Mahfouz answered that he did. Had they been published? No, he said, adding that he was not sure they were worthy of publication. Musa asked him to bring the novels along on his next visit. On his return, Mahfouz presented him with three novels, one of which was entitled *Ahlam al-Qarya* (Village Dreams). After reading them, Musa told him that although he had a gift for writing fiction, the novels were of poor literary quality and unfit for publication. But, by constantly reminding Mahfouz of his talent, Musa motivated him to write a novel of better quality.

Mahfouz found his subject matter in the ancient history of Egypt, which, he says, he aspired to recreate in fictional form as Sir Walter Scott had done with the history of his country. To achieve this aim, he chose forty themes for historical novels that he hoped to complete in his lifetime, but he finished only three before discovering that he was more interested in social realism. He brought Salama Musa the manuscript of his first historical novel, entitled *Hikmat Khufu* (The Wisdom of Cheops). Musa found this title unappealing, retitled it *Abath al-Aqdar* (Ironies of Fate), and published it as a separate issue of *al-Majalla al-Jadida* for September, 1939. Two more historical novels followed, *Radobis* (1943) and *Kifah Tiba* (1944).[1]

Some writers have exaggerated Mahfouz's importance as a writer of historical novels. Ahmad Haykal says that *Abath al-Aqdar* is considered "the true beginning of the nationalistic historical novel. It does not teach history, but tends to glorify it. Its objective is to deepen the feeling about the glorious Pharaonic past."[2] In fact, this work was not the beginning of the nationalistic historical novel nor of the Egyptian historical novel; yet Mahfouz deserves a prominent place among the writers of the historical novel in Egypt, especially those who, as he did, graduated from the Egyptian University.

To the best of our knowledge, the first Arab writer of historical novels was Salim al-Bustani (d. 1884), whose novels *Zenobia* and *Budur* took their themes from Arab history.[3] But the writer who more than anyone else in the Arab world popularized Islamic history through fiction was Jurji Zaydan (d. 1914), a Lebanese Christian who lived most of his life in Egypt. A prolific writer, he produced more than twenty novels whose themes came from Islamic history, from the time of the Prophet of Islam to the Ottoman coup d'état of 1908, including several dealing with Egyptian history.[4] His purpose was not only to popularize Islamic history, but to teach it. Subordinating history to fiction, he made his characters vehicles for what he considered his most important task, portraying the historical events of their time.[5] Nevertheless, he cleared the field for those who succeeded him, affording them the opportunity to concentrate more on their characters' behavior in the context of different historical situations.[6]

This trend toward human analysis in the historical novel reached a high point in the works of Muhammad Farid Abu Hadid, Ibrahim Ramzi, Ali al-Jarim, Muhammad Said al-Uryan, and Ahmad Bakathir. More than Zaydan, these writers concentrated on the development of characters and the extensive analysis of their social, political, and cultural milieu. For example, al-Uryan's *Ala Bab Zuwayla* (At the Zuwayla Gate, 1945), which deals with the Mamluks' struggle for political power, analyzes the behavior of the common people in the context of historical events and compares favorably with Zaydan's *al-Mamluk al-Sharid* (The Escaping Mamluk), which relates the escape of a Mamluk from a plot devised by Muhammad Ali Pasha (d. 1849), viceroy of Egypt, to eliminate the Mamluks.[7] Writers like al-Uryan used the historical novel not for teaching history, but for a dynamic examination of complex social and political issues underlined by a human message.

This trend in the Egyptian historical novel took on another dimension in the writing of a new generation of novelists like Muhammad Awad Muhammad, Adil Kamil, Jamal al-Shayyal, Ibrahim Jalal, and Naguib Mahfouz. Most of them were university graduates who had been greatly influenced by the trends of the Western historical novel and by the Egyptian novelists already mentioned. They were deeply concerned with portraying social and political movements and the various problems of their time. More important, they sought similarities between events in the ancient and contemporary history of Egypt, offering the historical novel a new nationalistic connotation. They tried to analyze the different aspects of individual personality and human nature. To them, relating a historical story was a way to inculcate a moral lesson. They strove to unravel the mysteries of the human soul in a historically objective and faithful manner. Prominent among them was Mahfouz, who more than any of the others used the historical novel to study human nature. He gave it a new dimension by tackling vibrant themes from Egypt's ancient history, some of which were reflected in the surge of nationalism, whose aim was to liberate its people politically, socially, and culturally from foreign domination. For this reason, some Egyptian critics maintain that Mahfouz's *Abath al-Aqdar* (Ironies of Fate) condemns and ridicules kings for their despotism while it praises the common people for their fortitude.[8]

Abath al-Aqdar

Abath al-Aqdar, Mahfouz's first historical novel, draws its theme from an ancient Egyptian legend. As the title indicates, fate plays a central role in the novel, manipulating the characters like puppets. The novel revolves around the struggle between the powerful will of the pharaoh and omnipotent fate and ends with the victory of indomitable fate over the recalcitrant pharaoh.

Khufu (Cheops, 2680 B.C.), king of Egypt during the fourth dynasty of the old kingdom, builder of the great pyramid at Giza, had been told by the renowned soothsayer Dedi that after his reign the throne would pass not to one of his sons but to Dedef, the newborn son of the high priest of the temple of the god Re. Disturbed by this prophecy, Khufu led a contingent of his palace guard to urge the high priest to vow loyalty to himself and, placing the state above his love for the newborn child, to kill him. But the high priest, having received the same prophecy, attempted to save the child by arranging for him to escape with his mother and Zaya, a faithful maidservant, and killed himself just as Khufu arrived. Meanwhile, Khufu had killed another newborn child and his mother, erroneously believing that they were the ones intended by the prophecy, and returned to his capital, Memphis, feeling pleased that he had saved the throne for his sons.

Unluckily, Dedef, his mother, and Zaya lost their way in the desert. Zaya, who could not have children of her own, abducted Dedef, leaving his mother alone in the desert, but was soon captured, first by rebel tribesmen who carried her and the child to Sinai, then by the pharaoh and his men, who took them back to Memphis. Claiming that Dedef was her son, she began looking for her husband and was told she would find him among the workers who were building the great pyramid. On reaching the site, she learned that he had died but was assured that the compassionate Khufu had ordered that she and her son should receive state support. Eventually she married the construction superintendent and moved to his palace with Dedef, who grew up among Khufu's household.

Dedef entered the military academy, where he won the confidence of the pharaoh and the crown prince, who later made him an officer in his private bodyguard. Meanwhile, he had fallen in love with a beautiful girl, supposedly a peasant, who he discovered was the pharaoh's daughter, Princess Mer Si Ankh, already (to his dismay) engaged to the governor of Sinai. After saving the crown prince from an attacking lion, Dedef was promoted and commissioned to lead an expedition to Sinai to subdue some rebellious tribesmen. Dedef invaded Sinai and brought back many captives, including an old woman who claimed to be an Egyptian, not an enemy. Feeling sorry for her, he successfully entreated King Khufu to give her freedom and took her into his own household. When the captive woman reached the palace, she recognized her old servant Zaya, who had kidnaped her son; she recognized Dedef, for in fact she was his mother. She related to her son the old prophecy that he would succeed the pharaoh on the throne.

Meanwhile, the crown prince was plotting to get rid of his father, who he thought had occupied the throne for too long. Dedef got wind of the plot, set himself to guard the old pharaoh, and killed some of the would-be assassins, among them the crown prince. The pharaoh showed his gratitude by designating Dedef as his successor, to the exclusion of his own sons, and giving his daughter, Mer Si Ankh, in marriage. When the pharaoh learned that Dedef was the child designated by the old prophecy to succeed him, he did not feel angry but rather submitted to the irresistible power of fate. The prophecy had been fulfilled, in spite of his power and authority. The novel ends with the pharaoh on his deathbed, observing that more than twenty years ago he had declared ferocious war on fate and defied the gods. At last, he confesses, he has been humbled by the gods.[9]

From this summary, it seems clear that *Abath al-Aqdar* is based on an ancient legend, most likely derived from James Baikie's book *Ancient Egypt,* which aimed to inform the reader about daily life in ancient Egypt by describing the journey of a ship that sailed over the Nile to Thebes. Mahfouz used some of the same Egyptian names appearing in it, and in fact, some of the descriptions of the pharaoh's family and his personal character are almost identical in both works.[10] But he altered the old prophecy about the pharaoh's successor to make the action more dramatic. In Baikie's book, Khufu was succeeded by his son the crown prince, then by the latter's son; after that, power was transferred to the three sons of the priest of Re, who successively fell heir to the throne. Furthermore, the legend as related by Baikie does not show whether Pharaoh Khufu attempted to get rid of the priest's three sons. Baikie's account of this folktale is similar to that given by the Egyptologist James Henry Breasted. According to Breasted's account, based on the papyrus original, Khufu felt bored one day and asked to be entertained by his sons, who related to him tales of past times. One of the sons, Prince Harzazef, told his father that there was in his kingdom a magician who could do even greater marvels than the men of the past whose wondrous works the sons were relating. Summoned by Khufu to appear before him, the magician performed miraculous deeds. In response to a question by the pharaoh, the magician said that the three children soon to be born by the wife of a certain priest of Re had been begotten by Re himself, and that they would become kings of Egypt. Upon hearing this prophecy, Khufu became sad. The magician, who thought that there was no reason for the king's melancholy, assured him that his son would reign, then his grandson, and after that one of these three children.[11]

In essence, *Abath al-Aqdar* is a conflict between man and fate. No matter what man does, he is subject to an inexorable and mysterious external power controlling his actions. It defies his will and manipulates him like a puppet. In this context Khufu represents man, trying unsuccessfully to defy fate and subjugate it to his own will. He was the omnipotent ruler of Egypt who tried to achieve a great miracle by building a massive pyramid that symbolized not only the will of divine Khufu but also the collective spirit of Egypt, an extension of his own omnipotent will. He was sure of his majestic power, which no man could defy. But he was not aware of that mysterious external power, fate, until he discovered that whatever he intended

could be foiled by events for which there was no logical explanation. He learned belatedly that it is futile to defy fate.

Thus, when Khufu first heard from the soothsayer Dedi the
prophecy that a stranger, not one of his sons, would succeed him, he
began to investigate the relation of man with fate. He asked the sage
Khomini whether fate could be avoided if man acted beforehand to
protect himself. Khomini's answer was that according to the Egyptian wisdom transmitted from times of old, man's precaution cannot dispose of fate. This sounded pessimistic, and Khufu, not convinced, turned next to his crown prince, who responded with a
serious look that indicated that he, too, believed man cannot defy
fate, no matter what precautions he takes. Khufu smiled and told
the men, in effect, if fate is what they say it is, then there can be no
meaning to the creation, life, and the dignity of man. In fact, there is
no distinction between work and idleness, strength and weakness,
rebellion and subservience. But, the pharaoh said, fate is no more
than a false belief, not to be held by mighty men.[12]

Events proved Khufu wrong, however; despite his might, he
could not prevent fate from determining his life, and on his deathbed he acknowledged the futility of his actions. More than twenty
years ago, he said, he had commanded a contingent of soldiers to
kill an unknown infant who he believed was to succeed him to the
throne. Instead, he killed another infant by mistake. Ironically, he
found himself protecting the stranger infant, whom he allowed to
marry his daughter and proclaimed as his successor. He thought
that he had overcome fate and secured the throne for his sons, but
now found himself humbled by the gods, who "slapped my
pride."[13] This last statement by Khufu is significant, for it raises the
question of whether fate is mere coincidence, that is, sheer luck, or
the determinant action of a divine power operating beyond man's
will.

Since Mahfouz is a Muslim, raised in a strongly religious family,
it is most likely that fate here has an Islamic connotation. According
to Islamic tradition, man's actions, both good and evil, are absolutely decreed and predestined by God, and everything that has
been or ever will be depends on his divine will and foreknowledge.
Yet one cannot overlook the biblical and mythological parallels in

Mahfouz's novel. In the book of Exodus, the pharaoh tried to get rid of the newborn Hebrew males by ordering them to be thrown into the Nile. Moses would have met the same fate had his mother not placed him in a basket and floated it on the river, from which it was lifted up by the pharaoh's daughter; even more ironically, he became her adopted son. He might well have become pharaoh if God had not called him to save his own people. In Mahfouz's novel, Dedef not only escaped the pharaoh's effort to destroy the male child prophesied to occupy his throne but was raised by the pharaoh, married his daughter, and succeeded him. In Greek mythology, of course, the legend of Laius and Oedipus has some similarity, however remote, to the theme of this novel. But the manner in which Mahfouz tackles the theme and portrays his characters, indeed his whole outlook, is essentially Islamic. He even uses Islamic terms in a pre-Islamic setting, for example, *sahaba* (companions) for Khufu's retinue, and the Quranic term *hawari* (apostle) to describe his army commander.[14]

In fact, the novel abounds with detailed descriptions of situations and dialogues that reflect the author's ideas and imagination, particularly when he discusses the pharaoh's family gathering, his library, his hunting party, and the educational system in Egypt. Much of this description may seem redundant and puerile, but Mahfouz intends it to endow the events of the novel with a sense of authenticity. We should remember, however, that he is writing a historical romance, not a reconstruction of the ancient history of Egypt.[15] Even if he should intend to represent the historical facts in fictional form, he faces great difficulty in placing them in their proper perspective. The theme of this novel derives from a myth handed down from the time of Khufu in the old kingdom, but there is little specific information about how this pharaoh lived, thought, or communicated. Thus, it was inevitable that Mahfouz should inject his own ideas into the narrative through the different characters and the events they experience, cloaked with a veneer of historical facts.

Khufu is not only the divine ruler of Egypt whose authority no man may contradict, but a warm and considerate person who loves his family and cares for his friends. At the outset of the novel,

Mahfouz presents him as a fully developed character, relating his different traits and characteristics. We first see him reclining on his golden sofa, in a room overlooking the spacious orchard at Memphis. He wears a silk gown whose golden hem shimmers in the rays of the setting sun. He seems relaxed, supporting his back with a cushion stuffed with ostrich feathers and resting his arm on a silk cushion embroidered with gold. A halo of pharaonic glory graces his forty-year-old features. Khufu enjoys family gatherings, in which he feels relaxed after the toil of the day. His eyes roam among his sons and companions as he contemplates the progress of the building of the pyramid, which he intends to be a miracle for his people.[16]

One writer suggests that Mahfouz is describing the Abbasid Caliph Harun al-Rashid of *The Arabian Nights* rather than the divine pharaoh.[17] If this is true, he has utilized one ancient fantasy to represent another. In fact, his vision of the pharaoh's life is similar to those provided by other twentieth-century writers about the ancient civilization of Egypt, although somewhat embellished. According to Egyptologists, the pharaoh lived in a royal palace surrounded by pools and lakes, which provided coolness and recreation, and graced with pleasure gardens where he could enjoy some relaxation. Although he was considered a god, he often became tired and bored and had to be entertained; in Mahfouz's novel, Khufu is diverted by his sons and the old soothsayer Dedi. Apart from the daily business of the state and the strict official etiquette, the pharaoh did have some private life. He enjoyed the company of his closest advisors, sons, and courtiers. He often relaxed beside one of his favorite wives while slaves anointed their feet. Despite his luxurious life, Breasted writes, the pharaoh was not a despot like the Mamluks of Muslim Egypt.[18]

Mahfouz describes a conversation between Khufu and his chief architect Mirabo, in which the pharaoh asserts that divinity is nothing but power. The chief architect responds that divinity is also mercy and love.[19] It seems doubtful that Khufu conversed with anyone about divinity or even tried to define it. According to historical accounts, the pharaoh believed himself to be the sublime god of both state and people. One of his titles in the old kingdom was the *good God*, and he was so reverenced that no man dared refer to him by name.[20]

Mahfouz seems also to inject his own ideas about art and woman's nature into this dialogue between Dedef and his step-brother Napha:

> Napha: Do not make an effort to explain or apologize, I know what you mean. This is the third time today that I was likened to a woman. This morning my father told me that I am unpredictable like a young woman. Likewise, an hour ago the priest Shelba told me that I am like a woman, easily overcome by emotion. And here you tell me that I am just like your mother. What am I, then, a man or a woman?
>
> Dedef (laughing): You are a man, Napha, but with tender soul and feeling. Do not you remember that Kheni said once that the artists are a cross between males and females?
>
> Napha: Kheni believes that art requires a borrowing from femininity. But I don't doubt that woman's sentiment greatly contradicts that of the artist. For by nature woman is selfish and seeks only what will fulfill her vital ambitions. But the artist has no objective except to fathom the essence of things, which is beauty. For beauty is the unraveling of the essence of things, which brings it into conformity with the rest of created beings.
>
> Dedef (laughing): Do you think that by this philosophizing you can convince me that you are a man?
>
> Napha (with a defiant look): You still need proof? If you do, then know that I am going to be married.
>
> Dedef (surprised): Is it true what you say?
>
> Napha (laughing): Would you deny me marriage?
>
> Dedef: No, Napha, but I remember that you once made our father angry because you showed no interest in marriage.[21]

This cannot be the conversation of two people in the old kingdom. There is little doubt that Mahfouz, who was greatly concerned with subjects like art and beauty, is speaking here. As we saw in chapter 1, he had written about the nature and philosophy of aesthetics, and his ideas are reflected in this dialogue.

Mahfouz's description of the construction superintendent's quarters at the pyramid site makes it sound like a government office in

Cairo or any other modern city. After the maidservant Zaya, who had kidnapped the infant Dedef, returned to Memphis, she sought out her husband and was told that he could be found among the workers who were building the great pyramid. She reached the site and found the office of the superintendent in an attractive building of moderate size. After the sentry at the door admitted her, she entered a large hall where various officials sat behind their desks. The walls were covered with bookshelves filled with papyrus scrolls. When the soldier motioned, she passed through another door to a smaller room, more beautiful and richly furnished; in the corner the superintendent sat behind a magnificent desk. He was plump and of medium stature. He had a noticeably large head and a short, fat nose, a large mouth, and fat cheeks like two small waterskins. His bulging eyes were covered by heavy lids. He looked arrogant as he was doing his business. He sensed that someone had entered his office, but did not raise his eyes to see who it was. When he had finished what he was doing, he finally raised his eyes and looked haughtily at Zaya, asking:

"What do you want, woman?"
Frightened and perplexed, Zaya answered in a disturbed and feeble voice, "I have come looking for my husband, my lord."
He asked her, in the same tone, "Who is your husband?"
"A worker, my lord."
The superintendent struck the desk with his fist and said sharply, while his words echoed as if in a vault, "What is the reason that he is not working and causing us trouble?"
Zaya became more frightened and did not answer. He kept looking at her round, bronze-colored face, her honey colored eyes, and her tender youth. He found it painful to see fear come over that lovely face. He may have acted arrogantly to demonstrate his authority, but he had a kind heart and tender feeling.[22]

We leave the reader to decide whether this can be accepted as an imaginative description of an ancient Egyptian office and the behavior of a superintendent under the pharaoh Khufu. To me, it seems more appropriate to a modern Hollywood movie. In fact, the novel abounds with similar examples of inappropriate and outlandish descriptions that contradict the notion that Mahfouz has taken his account from the ancient history of Egypt. Even the writing of a historical romance like this one requires a certain degree of perspective.

Mahfouz presents the educational system under Khufu, for example, as almost identical to that of his own youth. At the age of five, the male child enters elementary school, where for seven years he is taught reading, writing, arithmetic, geometry, religion, ethics, and patriotism. Then he is transferred to an institution equivalent to the secondary school in modern Egypt. According to the novel, when Kheni and Napha finished their secondary schooling, Kheni entered the University of Ptah to further his studies of religion, ethics, and political science, hoping to find a religious or judicial position, while Napha joined the Khufu Institute of Fine Arts because he liked to draw; other students, like Dedef, joined the Military Academy to specialize in the art of war.[23] Fantastic as it may seem, the most obvious historical inaccuracy in this novel is the mention of horses and chariots, unknown in Egypt during the time of the old kingdom. The horse was introduced into Egypt by the Hyksos (shepherd kings), who invaded Egypt in 1788 B.C. and were expelled in 1580 B.C. It was during this period that the Egyptian armies began to use chariots on a large scale. The reference to people using gold and silver coins provides another example of Mahfouz's carelessness about historical facts.[24] In the old kingdom, barter was the primary means of exchange, although gold and copper rings of fixed weight were used in some transactions and circulated as money. We shall not mention here other historical inaccuracies in the novel, for Mahfouz is not being judged as a historian; but, as we have said earlier, the writing of historical fiction requires careful attention to the known facts.

Mahfouz's central theme is that man's actions are subject to an omnipotent fate. It is in this context that we must understand both the prediction about the stranger who would succeed to the throne and Khufu's ultimate failure to overcome fate. Ironically, he found himself protecting and supporting the very man he tried to kill after hearing the prophecy. The novel has many shortcomings in both form and content; indeed, Mahfouz himself called it "kid stuff."[25]

Nevertheless, it marks the end of his obscurity as a novelist and the beginning of a long, busy career during which he refined the writing of the Egyptian novel and gradually won recognition as a leader in his craft.

Radobis

Mahfouz's second historical novel, *Radobis*, focuses on a love that is totally subject to fate. Whereas in *Abath al-Aqdar* fate is depicted as a strong external power opposed to the will of man, in *Radobis* it is an uncontrollable force emanating from the very depth of man's soul.

In essence, the novel is a romance whose theme, the love between Pharaoh Mernere II and Radobis, is not coincidental but determined by fate. The setting is the southern city of Abo; the occasion is the festival of the Nile, which attracts crowds from every corner of Egypt. Mahfouz describes in detail the people awaiting the pharaoh's arrival; their conversation previews the events and characters of the novel. Looking over the crowd, a man whose appearance shows his upper-class status dolefully remarks that many such festivals have been celebrated and many pharaohs have attended them, but all have gone as if they never existed. They have gone to rule another world better than the present one, he adds, and all people will one day follow them to that world. He wonders aloud whether future generations will remember him and the crowds celebrating the festival of the Nile, as those present remember others who have come before. He wishes that death did not exist. Another says philosophically that death is as natural as life and questions the value of immortality when people cannot satisfy their hunger, stop growing old, or even attain love. Such statements may reflect the skepticism of Mahfouz, who apparently could not find an answer to the whole question of existence. The pessimistic view taken by this character reflects the innermost sentiments of a perplexed soul.

The people then talk about the pharaoh, observing that he is tall and handsome like his grandfather Mehtemsauf. He is a valiant warrior, expected to invade the north and south to bring them under his dominion. He is young and rash and indulges in carnal pleasure. He is a spendthrift who loves luxurious living. He has always been in need of gold, silver, and other valuables to satisfy his taste for luxury. Inevitably, he has come into conflict with the priests, as he coveted the temples' wealth in order to build more palaces, plant more groves, and gratify his sensualities. The priests oppose his confiscation of this property on the grounds that the temples' land had already been appropriated by his forefathers. In the pharaoh's opinion, the priests wrongly regard the temples' large estates as their personal property, and he is entitled to use them to build palaces and mausoleums as his forefathers did. The conflict has polarized relations between the pharaoh and the priests, especially the priest of the city of Memphis and the high priest and prime minister Khnum Hotep, and rebellion appears imminent.

Suddenly there appear four Nubians carrying a magnificent litter worthy of nobles and princes. In it the beautiful Radobis leans on a cushion, carrying in her right hand a fan made of ostrich feathers. Her eyes glow with a soft and dreamy look, cast at the far horizon. The crowd, apparently spellbound, seems about to forget the pharaoh and the celebration of the festival of the Nile. In a passage which recalls *The Arabian Nights*, Mahfouz introduces the sorceress Dam, whom he describes as old, stooped, and toothless, with unkempt white hair, a long hooked nose, and long yellow nails. Leaning on a heavy cane, her eyes flashing with terror, she plows through the crowds to reach the litter, seeking to tell Radobis her fortune, but is stopped by a slave. Thus, we are left temporarily in suspense as to what fate has in store for this beautiful woman.

The events of the novel begin to build after the celebration of the festival of the Nile and culminate in the pharaoh's meeting with Radobis—by sheer coincidence, according to an Egyptian legend. After returning to his palace, the pharaoh decides with his prime minister to solve the question of the temples' estates by adding them to the possessions of the crown. With this vexatious matter settled, he begins to relax, walking through the royal garden. Radobis likewise returns home after the festivities, totally enthralled by the young and handsome pharaoh, and takes off her clothes to cool herself in her private pool. Suddenly, an eagle flying over her palace snatches her gold-rimmed sandal and drops it in the lap of the pharaoh, who wonders about its owner. His chamberlain, Sofkhatep, knowing Radobis and her captivating beauty, encourages the pharaoh to seek her out, while his army commander, Taho, tries to dissuade him because he himself is desperately in love with her. Eventually, the pharaoh meets Radobis, and they fall madly in love.

The eagle's snatching the sandal is based on Egyptian folklore, according to which eagles, liking beautiful young women, snatched them up and flew them to the top of the mountains. In Radobis's case, the eagle snatched her sandal instead. That this event leads to the pharaoh's meeting and falling in love with her is not accidental. Fate in this case is not, as most people in Egypt think, a coincidence or sheer luck, but action predetermined by the gods. In essence, it is an expression of an Islamic concept, much like what we have seen in *Abath al-Aqdar*. Mahfouz's concept of fate is clearly expressed by the royal chamberlain, who tells the pharaoh that the term *coincidence* has been misused by people who, like a blind man, probe their way in the dark. Every happening in this world, whether trivial or significant, is undoubtedly associated with the will of the gods. They do not create events for their own amusement but have a definite purpose in mind.

Thus, the political destiny of the young pharaoh becomes connected with his love adventures, as designed by the gods. On the surface, this love story appears to be no different from many others occurring throughout history, even down to the present day. But the political fate of Pharaoh Mernere II, and indeed the fate and the well-being of the Egyptian state, hang in the balance. Not only does the pharaoh love Radobis to the point of losing his sanity, he is willing to sacrifice himself and Egypt to make her happy. His love overwhelms his will. There is an unfathomable force within him that drives him mad and, in spite of himself, toward this woman. He is so infatuated that he cannot even accept the fact that Radobis is a high-society prostitute; he cannot believe that when she was young she fell in love with a sailor who later deserted her, or that she habitually sold her body until their fateful meeting. Consumed by passion, the pharaoh lavishes everything on Radobis.

At the same time he abjectly neglects his wife Nitocris (also his sister), who has swallowed her pride and suffered silently from the pharaoh's love affairs. The priests are no less angered by his behavior, feeling he has deprived them of their possessions and neglected the affairs of the state to cater to his mistress. The priests and the prime minister, unhappy at seeing the divine pharaoh in the clutches of a cheap woman, begin to spread detrimental rumors about him. The prime minister, having lost favor, approaches Nitocris, pretending to hope that she may be able to alert the pharaoh to the growing resentment against him. The pharaoh meets with her, but on discovering that her purpose is to discuss his relations with Radobis, he becomes furious, accusing his wife of jealousy, and refuses to change his ways.

He dismisses his prime minister and appoints the chamberlain Sofkhatep in his place, preparing for a showdown with the priests. But the only forces he can rely on to crush them are the royal guard and an insignificant garrison at Beja. Egypt has no regular army, and the pharaoh cannot form an army except in case of war. He and Radobis concoct a plan to solve this problem: they contact the governor of Nubia, asking him to send a message indicating that the Me'sayu tribes have rebelled. Thus, he can prepare for war against the alleged rebels, though in reality he has found a pretext to overcome his opponents.

Pharaoh tries to implement his plan during the festival of the Nile the following year. Reading the message from the governor of Nubia, he orders all governors to return to their provinces to marshal military forces. But the priests discover his plot and invite the chiefs of the supposedly rebellious tribes to offer their allegiance to the pharaoh. Believing he has been betrayed by his own messengers, he continues with his plan, but the priests instigate the people, now in full rebellion, to attack his palace. Not wishing to shed the blood of his guards, he goes out alone to meet the crowd with great courage and dignity. One of the leaders, fearing the people may lose their mettle and retreat, wounds him fatally with an arrow. The pharaoh asks to be moved to Radobis's palace; Nitocris assents, and he breathes his last in the arms of his beloved Radobis, who then ends her life by taking poison.[26]

As in *Abath al-Aqdar*, Mahfouz does not strictly follow history; he is writing a romance, not a historical novel. At first, he sets the time of the action as "four thousand years ago." Later he says that the events of the novel took place toward the end of the sixth dynasty, which marked the end of the old kingdom. But in fact, the sixth dynasty ended in 2475 B.C., while the old kingdom lasted until 2300 B.C.[27] Moreover, the history of ancient Egypt reveals nothing about Mernere II beyond the fact that he reigned for only one year near the end of the sixth dynasty. There was a Queen Nitocris toward the end of the sixth dynasty, but she had no connection with Mernere II. Her name appears in the Turin papyrus and in Greek sources, but the stories about her beauty and the assertion that she was the builder of the third pyramid are most likely apocryphal.[28] Further, there is no evidence of a priests' rebellion throughout more than a hundred years of the sixth dynasty, a period of relative peace. Mahfouz appears to have used historical figures and events out of context in order to create a framework for his novel.

The love between the pharaoh and Radobis is heartfelt, characterized by complete commitment and devotion. It is a purified love, made impeccable by the gods, even though Radobis lived in luxury and offered her body to men of high position, among them the army commander Taho. When she could no longer submit to him, he called her worthless and ugly, adding that she was merely a frigid woman with a beautiful body. Likewise, the crowds who had been spellbound by her physical beauty, knowing she had had many lovers, doubted she knew true love. They were wrong. Radobis had kept her true and pure love for the only man worthy of it. Thus, when she met the handsome pharaoh, she refused to come to his palace, lest she become simply another of his concubines. She preferred to remain in her palace to offer him her soul, having given only her body to other men. To demonstrate her complete spiritual metamorphosis, Radobis visited the temple of the god Sotis to be purified from her former carnal life and to devote her love to the pharaoh and surrender her heart, which no other man had possessed. Fate finally tied her to her true love.[29]

The pharaoh, no less a paragon of sublime love, looks like Shakespeare's Romeo rather than a divine Egyptian monarch. Although at first he is portrayed as a reckless young man who relishes sensual love and luxury, there is no indication that he is an out-and-out philanderer; he seems to lead a quiet family life, and to be devoted to his wife/sister Nitocris. In fact, only after he meets Radobis does he begin to act as a supreme lover, forgetting (or perhaps Mahfouz himself forgot) that he is divine. He does not even find it demeaning to return her gold-rimmed sandal and confess that he had thought her portrait, drawn inside it, was only a fantasy until his eyes fell upon her face. Only then, he says, did he learn the awesome truth that beauty, like fate, takes man by complete surprise.

Shocked by the pharaoh's sudden appearance at her palace, Radobis cannot believe her eyes. She rises, bows to him with utmost respect, and motions to him to sit on her couch. From that moment on, he submits his entire will and being to her, saying that henceforth madness shall be his emblem.[30] This is the manifestation of absolute love, transcending his divine status and his throne. Yet it is tainted by selfishness on the part of the pharaoh, who is so blinded by love that he abdicates his responsibility to his people and his state in order to lavish the resources of his kingdom on the woman who has captivated his heart.

To some people, this kind of love may seem highly sentimental and exaggerated. But only a few decades ago Edward VIII of England gave up the throne for a twice-divorced commoner who was not even an English citizen, and he lavished on her whatever he could get from his friends, his royal estate, or the British government. Whether or not he claimed to be divine, Pharaoh Mernere II was after all a mortal who like other men in Egypt craved love and companionship. He may have been rebelling against the Egyptian tradition that had forced him to marry his sister Nitocris, or perhaps, unhappy in this marriage of convenience, he had found in the ravishingly beautiful Radobis an answer to his unrequited love.

Whatever the reason may be, love is the theme to which Mahfouz devotes the largest portion of this novel. He portrays Radobis as the happiest woman in Egypt, the one who captures the heart of the pharaoh. Although she has no title, she rules him. On finally meeting Queen Nitocris, she asserts confidently that the real queen is not the woman who marries a monarch and sits on the throne, but the one who occupies the throne of his heart. Nitocris must have felt great pain to have such a woman as her rival; she must also have felt weak and embarrassed.[31]

The reader who expects to learn something about the history of Egypt in the sixth dynasty will be disappointed. The setting and characters in the novel are subordinated to Mahfouz's real purpose, the analytical study of man's nature and his reaction to his circumstances. This is why at the beginning the Egyptians appear occupied with the questions of life, death, and especially life after death. This interest is also manifested in the prayers of the priests, the sermon the pharaoh gives at the altar, and the songs of the people in the street. Mahfouz expresses in great detail how the Egyptian people lived and behaved. He seems concerned more with Pharaoh the man than with Pharaoh the monarch, more with Radobis the true female than with Radobis the high-society prostitute.

Here they (and we) face an extremely tense situation, marked by psychological conflict. Most conspicuous is the pharaoh's conflict with himself as he succumbs to an irresistible love. He is also at odds with his national duty, which must be sacrificed if he is to pursue adventurous love with a woman of questionable worth. It is the conflict between the pharaoh's private and public lives that leads him to a tragic end. And through it the characters become vibrant, looked upon more as complex beings whose behavior reflects the good and evil sides of man's nature. They seem to express their innermost sentiments with no dissimulation or duplicity.

Thus, when the pharaoh faces Nitocris, he acknowledges his behavior and his love for Radobis, while the queen advises him to act more prudently. He responds that prudence in the present instance would be a sham, worthy only of a weak person. But no matter what justification of his actions he offers, still he realizes that he has let down the very faithful wife who stood by his side during hard times. When the crowds surround and attack the royal palace, the pharaoh refuses the protection of his private guards and withdraws to offer his last prayers before the statues of his parents. In his hour of agony, the human pharaoh turns to his wife and apologizes for having wronged and humiliated her. He feels sorry that he has foolishly made her life miserable. Then, in great astonishment, he asks how all this could have happened. Could he have followed a different course in life and avoided falling in love with another woman? He realizes that he has been overwhelmed by an extraordinary madness, and that he no longer has the will even to repent what he has done. He goes on to philosophize that reason can remind men of their insignificance and stupidity but it cannot remedy their defects. Finally, he asks Nitocris whether she has seen a more tragic state than his. In his agony, he cannot find words to express his misfortune. He concludes that madness is and will ever be, as long as there is life.[32]

Here stands Pharaoh the man, frail, weak, and sorrowful. This is the way Mahfouz wanted him to be, in order to depict vividly the shortcomings of human nature, the deficiency of human reason, and the futility of man's actions. Here stands man, face to face with fate, over which he has no control. Here also is the pharaoh whose false claim of divinity is destroyed by circumstances that transcend his will and expose him as an ordinary man who, although a king, has become a captive of his own nature.

Like Mahfouz's earlier novel, *Radobis* has some historical inaccuracies, such as references to the use of horses and chariots. Mahfouz provides an interesting but lame excuse for these lapses. He states that he submitted *Radobis* to a literary contest for an award established by the lady Qut al-Qulub al-Damardashiyya. The award committee liked the novel, but had found historical inaccuracies in it. A member of the committee, the prominent Egyptian writer Ahmad Amin, summoned Mahfouz and, questioning him, found that he knew a great deal about the pharaonic history of Egypt. Noting that the novel described chariots pulled by horses, which had been introduced into Egypt by the Hyksos long after the sixth dynasty, he asked, "Why did you make this historical error?" Mahfouz says he offered only a generalized rationale: he had thought the chariots and horses would offer the royal procession he portrayed a touch of grandeur and glory, which he felt the dramatic situation required. He closes by saying that he ignored this simple historical fact in order to create some artistic persuasion.[33]

Finally, let us note that some analysts believe that in this work

Mahfouz meant to criticize the condition of Egypt under the monarchy through the medium of a historical novel. Some have even suggested that the profligate and irresponsible King Farouk is the model for Pharaoh Mernere II. As the ancient people of Egypt under Mernere II revolted against him for his dissolution and extravagance, they argue, the Egyptians in our time revolted against Farouk.[34] Although Mahfouz wrote this novel during Farouk's reign, he denies that he had in mind any such analogy to the contemporary situation.[35] Evidently these analysts have read too much into the novel, which on its face contains nothing to suggest a comparison between Mernere II and Farouk.

Kifah Tiba

Kifah Tiba (The Struggle of Thebes, 1944), the third and last of Mahfouz's historical novels, is essentially an epic portraying the struggle of the southern city of Thebes against the Hyksos, whose eventual expulsion gave Egypt independence from foreign domination and set it on the way to becoming an empire. Unlike his earlier novels, in which history is subordinated to the philosophical treatment of fate, *Kifah Tiba* is focused more directly on events set in a specific time and place, while the love story between Pharaoh Ahmose and the daughter of the Hyksos king seems to be of secondary importance. Nevertheless, Mahfouz does not strictly adhere to the historical facts and even finds himself forced to manipulate them in order to support his own convictions about certain matters, such as Ahmose's distribution of land, which has no basis in fact. He may be forgiven for not following history precisely, however, because the original source materials on the Hyksos and the Theban dynasts who fought against them are deficient and confusing. For example, the novel has Apophis as the Hyksos king and Sekenenre as the ruler of Thebes; but the Hyksos had more than one King Apophis, and the Thebans had more than one Sekenenre. (As we shall see later, Mahfouz is writing an epic of ancient Egyptian nationalism that prefigures the struggle of the Egyptians in modern time against British imperialism.)

It is interesting to note that Mahfouz once said he was inspired to write *Kifah Tiba* when he saw the mummy of Sekenenre full of wounds at the Egyptian Museum.[36] Thus, he tries to portray an Egyptian king who heroically fell in battle while defending his country against foreign occupation forces. The king lost the battle, but not the war. Although Mahfouz does not identify this Sekenenre, he must be Sekenenre Ta'o II (the Brave) who suffered a violent death. While fighting the Hyksos, he was hit with an ax and club and fell to the ground. His enemy struck him on the head, fracturing his skull and jaw. Looking at his distorted face, one wonders what tremendous pain this valiant monarch endured. No doubt Mahfouz was moved by the ghastly sight of his mummy, which may well have inspired him to write this novel.

In 1788 B.C., toward the end of the middle kingdom, Egypt was suffering internal political and social chaos. As the nobles gained more power, the pharaoh lost a great deal of authority and prestige. Whatever progress the Egyptians had made in the past was by now lost. With no central government to exert power, Egypt became vulnerable to foreign invasion. About 1750 B.C. certain hordes of Asiatic origin, commonly called the Hyksos, invaded the Nile delta. By about 1675 B.C., they had brought the whole country under their domination, except for Thebes in the south. After almost two hundred years of struggle, the Thebans under Pharaoh Ahmose I finally managed in 1580 B.C. to expel the Hyksos. Thus, Egypt regained its sovereignty and started on its way to becoming an empire.

Mahfouz's novel is divided into three parts. The first deals with the occupation of Egypt by the Hyksos, who under King Apophis reduced the native rulers, the Sekenenres, into mere vassals and took over their capital, Thebes, in the south (upper Egypt). By way of asserting his authority, the Hyksos king Apophis sends a messenger to Sekenenre II, ordering him to get rid of the hippopotami in his pool because they are disturbing his sleep. He further warns Sekenenre to replace the worship of the god Amon with that of the Hyksos god Set, and to recognize his authority over Thebes. Sekenenre refuses and leads his army northward to fight Apophis. The Theban army is defeated, Sekenenre is killed in battle, and the enemy mutilate his body. Sekenenre's family escapes to Nubia, and the Hyksos become the lords of all Egypt.

The second part begins ten years after the defeat of Sekenenre. Sekenenre's son Kamose is busy marshaling a huge army to fight the Hyksos and regain sovereignty over Thebes. The crown prince Ahmose is sent on a reconnaissance mission to explore the situation in Egypt. Disguising himself as the merchant Asphenis, and using every possible means, even bribery and deception, he manages to reach the governor of Thebes and finally the court of the Hyksos king. He succeeds in recruiting men who support his family and carries them in the lower deck of his ship to Nubia to join the army in exile. While carrying out his mission, however, Ahmose falls in love with Amenerdis, the beautiful daughter of King Apophis. In token of his love, he gives her a heart-shaped emerald with a white chain, which the princess greatly cherishes.

In the third part of the novel, the Theban army under Kamose invades upper Egypt and liberates its cities, but his family refuses to enter Thebes until all Egypt has been freed. The Hyksos retreat to the north, and men from the liberated cities join his army. Kamose loses his life in battle, and Ahmose succeeds him as commander. Among the captives taken by the Egyptians is the Hyksos princess Amenerdis. Brought before Ahmose, she treats him with contempt and threatens to kill herself. Meantime, Ahmose attacks Avaris, the Hyksos capital in the delta, and cuts off its water supply. The Hyksos negotiate an agreement with Ahmose by which they are to evacuate Avaris, leave Egypt, and hand over thousands of Egyptian captives in exchange for Amenerdis. Ahmose agrees, but he visits the princess before releasing her. When she learns that she must decide whether to stay or leave, she confesses her true love to Ahmose, but they both realize it is a hopeless love. Finally, she chooses to depart, placing her national duty over her love. She takes with her the heart-shaped emerald from her lover, leaving only the white chain in his hands. With her departure the saga of an unrequited love comes to an end.[37]

In *Kifah Tiba* Mahfouz does not treat the abstract concept of fate as either an external force controlling man's will or an internal force emanating from man's inner being. Rather, he concentrates on the Egyptians' struggle against their oppressors, the Hyksos. In his previous novels, historical events appear only in outline and are of

secondary importance; in this novel, the historical material constitutes the central theme, while the love story between Ahmose and
the Hyksos princess occupies a secondary place. Indeed, this love
episode is superimposed on the central theme, and it could be
dropped without affecting the structure of the novel.

Mahfouz admits that while he was writing *Kifah Tiba* (1937–38),
his major concern was the Egyptian national question, that is, the
Egyptians' struggle to overthrow the British, who had occupied the
country in 1882.[38] The British had proclaimed Egypt a protectorate
during World War I but rescinded the protectorate in 1922 and
recognized Egypt as an independent sovereign state, though they
kept it tied to their own interests. Thus, when Mahfouz wrote this
novel, Egypt was no longer under direct British control, but it was
weak, governed by a dissolute, irresponsible king and a band of
self-seeking politicians. There was, however, a minority of national
leaders who wanted to free their country from the grip of the
British. The Egyptians' national struggle culminated in the revolution of 1952, when young army officers overthrew the monarchy
and took control of their country. It is in this context that *Kifah Tiba*
should be read and understood.

Mahfouz explains that when he was writing the novel Egyptian
nationalism was ablaze, and there were many people who saw a
real continuity from the pharaonic period to the modern history of
Egypt. The pharaonic age, he says, was the brightest spot in the
history of Egypt, in contrast to the present age of decadence,
humiliation, and indignity caused by British imperialism and the
control of the Turko-Egyptian aristocracy. Some members of this
aristocracy could trace their heritage back to the Mamluk period;
others were members of the royal family or descendants of Muhammad Ali, viceroy of Egypt at the beginning of the nineteenth century. Until the revolution in 1952, the Turko-Egyptian aristocrats
occupied high positions in Cairo government and looked upon the
native Egyptians as inferior. Although they became to some extent
Egyptianized, they were not completely integrated into the society;
in race and language they remained alien to Egypt and never
hesitated to collaborate with the British to promote their self-inter-

est. A separate social caste, they looked down upon the Egyptians as subhuman peasants who deserved to be preyed upon.

Mahfouz was aware of the implied comparison between the Hyksos and the British in this novel but says he was unaware of another analogy between the Hyksos and the Turko-Egyptian aristocracy until a non-Arab writer brought it into focus. Apparently, this writer stated that Mahfouz was writing of a utopia in which Egypt would be liberated from the control of the Turko-Egyptian aristocracy and not just from British authority. Mahfouz says that he liked this analogy because "in reality, I was seething with anger against the British and the Turko-Egyptian aristocracy, while I was writing a genuine Pharaonic novel in which the British and the Turko-Egyptians had no part."[39] Be that as it may, the reader who has some knowledge of the contemporary history of Egypt will surely discern the connection between the Egyptians' national struggle and the events of the novel.

What gives more credence to this opinion is that Mahfouz himself was one of those nationalists born before World War I who witnessed the transformation of the national movement into a political cause, represented in the struggle involving the royal palace, the Wafd party, and British imperialism. His generation was able to define and analyze the problem of Egypt's relations with the British but could not resolve it. Apparently, through the medium of fiction, Mahfouz finally found a solution to his political frustration and that of Egypt. As the ancient Egyptians had been able to expel the Hyksos after almost two hundred years of occupation, the modern Egyptians may likewise expel the British and topple the Turkish aristocracy, though heretofore such events had been only a novelist's dream.

This thought, however, does not seem to have been uppermost in Mahfouz's mind. It is not clearly stated in the novel. We can comprehend it when we see how the Hyksos looked upon the Egyptians, who they thought should be treated as a subject people. We can also comprehend it from the manner in which the Egyptian characters thought of themselves, their national destiny, and their attitude toward the Hyksos. Thus, we come to realize the extent to

which the Hyksos symbolized the ideas and attitudes of the Turko-
Egyptian aristocracy toward the indigenous Egyptians. A Hyksos
general tells his king, "Truthfully, lord, the *fallahin* (peasants) have
no stamina. Truthful is he who said that if you want to make use of
the *fallah*, starve and whip him."[40] In another instance Ahmose of
Abana, on meeting his namesake Prince Ahmose (disguised as the
merchant Asphenis), tells him that the Egyptians are slaves who
should be whipped and fed with the crusts cast to them. The king,
ministers, judges, officials, and landowners are all Hyksos. Power is
in the hands of the white people (the Hyksos) who wear dirty
beards; the Egyptians, who formerly owned the land, are now
slaves in their own land. Prince Ahmose asks whether there are
many like him who feel outraged because of the inequities inflicted
upon the Egyptians. Ahmose of Abana answers that there are such
men, but they suppress their outrage and suffer humiliation, like
any weak person who has no means to defend himself.[41]

We learn more about the Hyksos as white lords and the Egyptians as brown-skinned slaves from the confrontation between
Pharaoh Ahmose and the beautiful Hyksos princess Amenerdis.
Enraged when she refers to her people as masters and the Egyptians
as slaves, he tells her that she is arrogant and does not know what
she is saying. If she had lived a century earlier (presumably before
the Hyksos occupied Egypt), he says, her father would not have
become king, and she would not be a princess. Ahmose reminds
Amenerdis that her people came from the cold northern deserts to
seize his country's sovereignty. They fancied themselves masters of
Egypt and regarded the Egyptians as peasants, feeling superior
because they were white and the Egyptians were brown-skinned.
But, says Ahmose, justice will take its course, and the true masters
(the Egyptians) will regain their lordship and shake off the yoke of
servitude. Whiteness will be the mark of those who live in the cold
northern regions, and brown skin will become the emblem of the
true masters of Egypt, who have been purified by her sun.[42] Thus,
the novel is permeated by the racial conflict between the Hyksos
and the Egyptians, whom they hated and despised as inferior.

This contemptuous attitude of the Hyksos toward the Egyptians
resembles that of the aristocratic Turko-Egyptians in modern times.

The Egyptian writer Yaqub Sanu points out that the Turkish officials exacted taxes from the poor, helpless Egyptian *fallah* by the use
of the whip.[43] In Muhammad Timur's short story "Fi al-Qitar" (On
the Train), published in *al-Sufur*, June 7, 1917, as the passengers are
discussing how best to educate the *fallah*, one comments that the
best means is the whip, which costs the government nothing, while
education is costly. Mahfouz, fully aware of the humiliation of his
own people by their foreign masters, seeks through Hyksos characters to show that the Turko-Egyptian aristocrats of his time harbor
similar contempt toward the Egyptians. This theme is further accentuated in his novel *al-Qahira al-Jadida* (New Cairo).[44]

Beneath the portrayal of the characters and the battles the Egyptians fought to liberate their country from the Hyksos lies
Mahfouz's national sentiment. He realized when he wrote this
novel that his people were not the masters of their own country, let
alone their destiny. They lacked the military power to rid themselves of British authority and were even so weak they could not
eliminate the Turko-Egyptian aristocracy who preyed on them.
Thus, he used the medium of fiction to vent his gripping frustration
and release his nationalistic sentiments, for he could say about the
Hyksos what he could not say about the British or the Turko-
Egyptian aristocracy without exposing himself to retribution.

In fact, both the Hyksos and the Egyptians are stereotyped, and
so is the conflict between them. In Mahfouz's mind, they represent
an absolute dichotomy between good and evil. The Egyptians stand
for light and truth, the Hyksos for darkness and falsehood. The
Egyptian army is the army of truth fighting a holy war against the
forces of falsehood. Although in numbers and equipment it is no
match for the Hyksos, it prevails because truth is on its side. Indeed,
if the god Amon is with the Egyptians, who then can defeat them?
Realizing that his enemies are stronger, Sekenenre appeals to the
god Amon for help, in words that parallel those of the Prophet of
Islam before he fought against his enemies the Quraysh at Badr:
"Worshipped lord, help us overcome this adversity and grant your
children victory. If you fail them today, your name will never be
mentioned in your resting place, and the doors of your holy temple
will forever be closed."[45]

Mahfouz portrays Egyptian kings as god-fearing, noble, brave, civil, just and peace-loving. They are the moving spirit of their people. Their subjects are likewise brave; seldom is a coward found among them. They are also tall, handsome, brown-skinned like their predecessors, and very proud of their heritage. In brief, they are paragons of every human virtue (8,11,26). Not so the Hyksos. They are white-skinned, short, pudgy, cowardly, ignoble, unjust, barbarous, and bloodthirsty. Mahfouz cannot see anything aesthetic about the statue of the Hyksos king which has replaced the statue of Sekenenre; it looks lifeless, representing a short, pudgy person with a massive head, hooked nose, and long beard (92). The Hyksos are avaricious men who love gold enough to betray their national cause for it. When Ahmose goes into occupied territory disguised as the merchant Asphenis, he finds the borders tightly guarded and the gates closed before him. The chief guard responsible for the safety of the borders refuses to let him pass. But when Ahmose offers him gold, the guard lets him pass safely, and the whole northern country is opened to him. Even the Hyksos princess takes a precious necklace from Asphenis, ostensibly to buy it, but does not pay for it (92–95).

In war the Hyksos are depicted as more savage than courageous, killing innocent women and children mercilessly and indiscriminately. When Ahmose tightens the siege against Thebes, they inhumanely use Egyptian women and children as shields. The valiant Egyptian soldiers, shocked beyond belief at seeing the bare bodies of women and children tied to the city walls while enemy soldiers stand behind them, sarcastic and defiant, determine to storm the city knowing that some of the women and children will be killed but thinking it better for them to die than to become slaves to Apophis. As they begin their attack, they can hear the loud and desperate cries of the women begging them to strike and avenge their humiliation by the Hyksos and praying that the lord will give them victory (143–45). In contrast to the savage Hyksos, they treat their avowed enemies with magnanimity and tolerance. When they retake the city, appearing determined to kill the invaders who have usurped their land—especially the chief of police who whipped the Egyptians, and the unjust judge of the city—Ahmose advises his men not to do so, because killing is against their sacred traditions. He reminds them that they are well known for their respect of women and for not punishing helpless captives of war. "The truly virtuous man," he says, "is he who adheres to virtue while he is in a state of outrage and anger" (151–53).

Further evidence of the savagery of the Hyksos is their killing of the Pharaoh Sekenenre. In the heat of battle, he is hit by a spear and falls to the ground, seriously wounded. Instead of taking him captive, the Hyksos soldier strikes him on the head with an ax, then others gang up against him and mangle his body with their spears (35–36). At the Egyptian Museum in Cairo the contorted face and jaws and the deep holes in the mummy's skull betray the brutal manner in which this valiant pharaoh was killed. This Hyksos savagery is contrasted with Egyptian magnanimity, represented in the duel between Ahmose and Khinzir, the bravest of the Hyksos, who had killed Ahmose's grandfather. Before their combat, each boasts of his own prowess and the bravery of his people, mocks his enemy, and threatens him with death. The actual conflict demonstrates their skill and dexterity. When Khinzir hits Ahmose's head with the tip of his sword, the Hyksos joyfully shout victory slogans. But when Ahmose strikes Khinzir's shield and knocks him to the ground, no cries of victory are heard in the Egyptian camp. Declining to take advantage of his foe, he magnanimously casts aside his own shield to fight Khinzir on even terms. Surprised, Khinzir shouts that such an act is worthy only of noble kings. The fight continues and Khinzir falls to the ground, having suffered two mortal blows. Ahmose and his men are now in a position to mutilate the body of their fallen enemy, as the Hyksos did to Sekenenre. Instead, he draws near and praises the strength and bravery of Khinzir, who, breathing his last, says that King Ahmose has spoken the truth, and that no Hyksos man will ever be able to challenge him again. In a final act of compassion, Ahmose picks up Khinzir's sword, places it beside his body, mounts his horse, and returns to camp (131–34).

In portraying the Egyptians and the Hyksos as symbolizing the strife between good and evil, civility and savagery, reverence and tolerance, Mahfouz perhaps inadvertently injected his own sense of values into the novel. Human history, both ancient and modern, is full of savagery and inhumanity. One has only to skim the pages of the Old Testament to realize how ancient people treated each other in time of war. Neither the history of the Arabs, before or after Islam, nor the history of Western countries is free from atrocities. The absolute dichotomy between good and evil permeates most of Mahfouz's novels. Perhaps it is a manifestation of his frustration and that of his generation because of the power of their British and Turko-Egyptian masters, who like the ancient Hyksos regarded the native Egyptians with utter contempt. He finds no redeeming virtue in those who preyed on his own people, whether in ancient or modern times.

Mahfouz also injects his own understanding of socialism into the Egyptian society under Ahmose, describing his distribution of land to the peasant farmers in something like a sharecropping transaction. Although there is no historical evidence to support it, he superimposes this socialistic idea on the narrative as part of his vision of the utopian city of his dreams. Quite possibly he was not sufficiently courageous to openly embrace the idea of land distribution at a time when the British grip on Egypt was strongest, and when most of the land was owned by wealthy aristocrats. After he wrote *Kifah Tiba*, however, his proclivity for social reform became stronger.[46]

In the light of Mahfouz's dogmatic moral dichotomy, setting forth the Egyptians and the Hyksos as symbols of good and evil, the love episode between Ahmose and Amenerdis appears pale and tenuous, and it cannot be expected to mitigate the long hatred between the Egyptians and the Hyksos. It is from the very beginning illogical and indeed impossible, given the circumstances that surround it. That Ahmose, disguised as an obscure Egyptian merchant, and the Hyksos princess should fall in love at first sight is absurd. And how are we supposed to believe that Ahmose, of the divine blood, could ever think of loving an enemy princess, unless he has forgotten about his own royal status and the Egyptian tradition that deified him?

Mahfouz makes this love relationship even more implausible when Amenerdis stands before the newly crowned Pharaoh

Ahmose as a prisoner of war. Instead of appealing to him in the name of love to show mercy, she turns arrogant and hostile, even threatening to kill herself if he should touch her. During this unemotional dialogue, they both recite the glorious deeds and traits of their people. Their talk, more a diplomatic negotiation between the representatives of two sovereign peoples than a passionate, tender declaration of love, ends with an agreement by which the Hyksos are to release the Egyptian prisoners of war in exchange for the princess. Thus, this contrived and implausible love relationship ends with the lovers' separation. The only consolation for Ahmose is the recognition that he has put responsibility to his country above love.[47]

The novel teems with historical characters, most important of whom are the three pharaohs, Sekenenre, Kamose, and Ahmose, and the old queen Tetisheri, mother of Sekenenre. The three pharaohs personify Egypt and its people. They are the very soul of Egypt; without them the Egyptians can accomplish nothing. They possess sublime traits and are preeminently suited to lead their people. The Hyksos characters, in contrast, possess no redeeming virtues; in fact, Mahfouz does not even give names to the Hyksos minor characters and refers to them only in the third person.

Of all the women in the novel, Tetisheri is most important. She appears as a lovely and charming lady, the proud matriarch of the line of kings and queens who inherited her dainty features. To the royal household and the Egyptian people, Tetisheri was called the Holy Mother, a symbol of the pharaonic traits of solemnity, courage, and fortitude. In Mahfouz's portrayal, she is the collective consciousness of the Egyptian nation, a second goddess Isis. After her husband's death, she left the throne to her son and his wife but retained some influence, acting as a counselor to her son Sekenenre the Brave, whose mutilated body she may have seen being carried from the battlefield to the palace. She was the moving power and spirit behind the war of liberation, and it was on her advice that Ahmose launched his final assault against the Hyksos. She was, as Mahfouz portrays her, in her sixties, yet still beautiful and active. She possessed all the dainty features of the pharaonic royal family, especially the slight protrusion of her front teeth, which fascinated the people of southern Egypt. She was a highly educated woman who read much about history, especially the accounts of Khufu and the *Book of the Dead*. In brief, she was the symbol of the indomitable spirit of Egypt. It is no wonder that the inhabitants of southern Egypt deified her, calling her the Holy Mother. She appears throughout the novel as the symbol of fortitude and determination, showing no sign of human weakness until Thebes is finally liberated from the enemy. Upon hearing the news of victory, she becomes excited, and her heart begins to beat rapidly. Carried in her litter to the palace, she rests in great serenity, surrounded by the female members of the royal family. After she regains some strength, she manages to sit upright and looks compassionately on the ladies, apologizing to them in a feeble voice for her show of weakness. She asks to kiss each one of them, as if she has a premonition that her end is near.[48]

As in the two earlier novels, Mahfouz describes the events in *Kifah Tiba* with so much detail that it diverts the reader's attention from the central theme. Some of these details are superfluous and boring. The army's march to the front, for example, is portrayed as if it were a hunting expedition (28). When Sekenenre meets with Tetisheri to seek her advice about the demands of the Hyksos king, Mahfouz even notes that he sits at her right hand, while his wife sits at her left, and that Tetisheri kisses him on the left cheek and his wife Ahotpe on the right (18). There are also lengthy, often repetitious dialogues between Ahmose and the Hyksos princess, most of which turn into disputes between the pair, who brag about the noble traits of their own people. Finally, there are meticulous descriptions of battles, soldiers, armaments, and the manner in which these battles were fought, down to how many chariots and horses and captives were involved (118–21).

From a historian's point of view, Mahfouz appears to have adhered more closely to the facts than he did in the previous novels. He uses pharaonic and Hyksos names the same way as Egyptologists. Given that the available historical evidence, especially about Ahmose, is meager and confusing, Mahfouz has succeeded in giving the common reader a fictionalized picture of the struggle between the Egyptians and the Hyksos. Yet the main question here is not historical integrity so much as plausibility. Does present-day Egypt resemble that of the pharaonic period? Are the Egyptians of today similar to the people in the time of Sekenenre and Ahmose? Naguib Mahfouz seems to believe that they are, and that the passage of time and the many foreign invasions have not affected them greatly. Not even the Arab conquest could affect the pharaonic features of Egypt; the conquerors imposed their religion (Islam) and their language on the Egyptians but could not convert them to Arabism. They were and are still pharaonic Egyptians, with the traits of the ancient culture. Indeed, Mahfouz so firmly believes that the two cultures have mingled that in his address to the Nobel Prize Committee, he called himself the product of two civilizations: pharaonic and Islamic. He explicitly avoiding saying that the latter is the exclusive civilization of Egypt.[49] In brief, Mahfouz, like a number of Egyptian writers, is a leader of the movement that has claimed that by history and culture Egypt is more pharaonic than Arab. This movement was very lively and strong until the rise to power in 1954 of President Jamal Abd al-Nasir, who propagated Arab nationalism in Egypt and gave it a great impetus in the Arab countries. It is in this pharaonic context that Mahfouz's historical novels should be read and appreciated.

Three

The Contemporary Novels

AFTER COMPLETING *Kifah Tiba*, Mahfouz began to concentrate more on portraying contemporary life in his native Cairo. Why he dropped historical themes in favor of the contemporary novels, which deal with social realism, is not clear. The only explanation he gives is that historical fiction was an inadequate vehicle to convey his impressions about contemporary life in Egypt. "To me," he says, "history lost its charm. There was a time when I wanted to write more historical novels, but I could not."[1] True to his word, Mahfouz devoted his time and energy to the domestic scene in Cairo. He never went back to the historical novel.

Between 1940 and 1951, Mahfouz produced five novels dealing with social themes, beginning with *al-Qahira al-Jadida* (New Cairo) and ending with *Bidaya wa Nihaya* (The Beginning and the End). These were not his only novels about contemporary life in Cairo; they were followed by many others, especially his *Thulathiyya* (Trilogy), published in 1956–57. In this chapter we shall deal with the first five novels, in chronological order.

Al-Qahira al-Jadida

In *al-Qahira al-Jadida* (New Cairo), which appeared in 1945, Mahfouz attempts to portray the life and mores of a group of university students in Cairo over a nine-month period, from December 1933 to September 1934. The central characters are four senior students, Ali Taha, Mamun Ridwan, Ahmad Badir, and Mahjub Abd al-Dayim, all in their early twenties. Because they graduated from the College of Arts in the same year as Mahfouz, and like him the first two were philosophy majors, we may conclude that their attitudes and actions reflect his view of his own society. Mahfouz also portrays the life and influence of the upper middle class, mostly of Turkish origin, their corruption, and their control of power in the Egyptian government and society. Underlying this portrayal of Egyptian society is the strife between good and evil, between principles and lack of them, and the reaction of different people to this struggle.

Mahfouz's choice of 1934 as the time of his novel has significance beyond his graduation from the university in that year. It reflects the rise of an Egyptian intelligentsia; since the establishment of an Egyptian university in 1908, many students had been exposed to a variety of intellectual concepts that were mostly Western and included materialistic philosophy and socialism, both of which were alien to the indigenous Islamic culture and traditions. While they were being taught about the democracy of the West, especially British democracy, they found to their utter frustration that the British, who considered the Suez Canal vital to the defense of India, controlled their country's institutions, denied them independence, and manipulated the political process for their own interests. Although the British had recognized Egypt as an independent sovereign state in 1922, they still held responsibility for its defense and for the protection of minorities and foreigners. The constitution of 1923, which ostensibly offered the people more freedom, in fact gave the king more power. The situation was aggravated by widespread corruption. Connections, bribes, and prestige were the primary means of finding government employment—the only hope of college graduates in an unindustrialized country where agriculture was despised and left completely to the *fallahin*. Egypt was almost a caste society. At the top were the minority aristocrats, especially the Turko-Egyptians, at the bottom stood the *fallahin,* and in the middle were small businessmen, professionals, and craftsmen.

Education was varied; one could easily perceive the influence of the conservative religious learning at al-Azhar or the secular education at the university. As a result, Egyptian society since the turn of the century had witnessed the growth of divergent, even contradictory ideas and attitudes. On one hand, Muslim groups called for the restoration of Islamic ideals, which (let us not forget) have played a great role in the life of the Egyptians. Opposite them stood the Western-educated Egyptians who adopted secular ideas, some even embracing atheism. There were also zealous patriots who advanced the notion that Egypt is for the Egyptians. And there were the opportunists who could not care less about moral or national ideals as long as they could attain their own interests. The conflict of these ideas was intensified by one of the worst constitutional and economic crises Egypt had ever suffered. An important sign of change was the admission of women to the university, a phenomenon unprecedented in an Islamic society. It is against this background, the Cairo of 1934, that Mahfouz wrote *al-Qahira al-Jadida*.

The novel opens with the four friends engaged in casual conservation about the new female students, commenting scathingly on their physical appearance and discussing whether they are ambassadors of learning or love. When one asserts that God created them to be ambassadors of love, another admonishes him that they are at the university, a secular institution where God and love should not be mentioned. The students debate whether woman is man's partner, with equal rights and obligations, then discuss human principles and whether they are necessary for man and society.

Mahfouz uses this conversation to reveal his characters' moral and intellectual tendencies. Mamun is a true Muslim who believes there is nothing but God in heaven and Islam on earth, while Ali Taha believes in science and socialism; Ahmad Badir, a journalism student, believes that man should stand as a mere observer and never get involved, and Mahjub Abd al-Dayim, a cynical opportunist, believes religion and principles have no meaning. Having introduced the four, Mahfouz provides a full report about each, covering his life, family, moral behavior, relations with women, and even his job opportunities.[2] Thus, we are faced from the beginning with nondimensional, fully developed characters whose actions have been predetermined by the author; there is no room for them to grow and manifest their changing attitudes. Even more striking is that after presenting them, Mahfouz suddenly abandons Mamun Ridwan, Ali Taha, and Ahmad Badir, to concentrate on Mahjub Abd al-Dayim, while the other three appear only intermittently in connection with him. Years later, he acknowledged the serious drawback of starting with fully developed characters, controlling their actions, and concentrating on the life and career of only one of them.[3]

Mamun Ridwan, a conservative young man and a true Muslim believer, seems to have learned a great deal about religion and morality from his father, a teacher in a religious institution. He is conscientious, honest, and very serious about putting his religious beliefs into practice, so much so that some of his friends call him the anticipated Mahdi or the Muslim Imam. He shuns participation in political activities and, unlike his classmates, denies the existence of an "Egyptian question," that is, the problem of throwing off the British authority and achieving full independence. For him there is only one question, that of Islam in general and Arabism in particular. The three pillars of his belief are God, virtue, and Islam. Mamun is not influenced by the trend of secularism at the university nor by the concepts of psychology, sociology, and metaphysics. He is delighted to find that the teachings of philosophers like Plato, Descartes, Pascal, and Bergson always point to God, his God. Perhaps because of a childhood illness that caused him pain and loneliness, Mamun has developed a hot temperament that in some instances drives him into fits of irrationality. Also, he tends to do everything passionately and thus appears as a fanatic. Yet he is kind, loving, and simple. He is engaged to a relative who, like him, has been raised in a conservative home which adhered to Islamic traditions. He visits her only in the presence of members of her family and in fact has never even thought of attempting to meet her alone. Much to his disappointment, his fellow students do not heed his call for Islam or Arabism; instead, they are concerned with the Egyptian question, the 1923 constitution, and the boycott of foreign goods.

His colleague Ali Taha is similar in character, but not in ideology.

He is a handsome young man with a noble countenance—intelligent, sociable, well-read, articulate, truthful, and, like Mamun, firm in his principles. But he is also an atheist who has adopted the philosophy of materialism; he believes that the essence of existence is matter, and that life and spirit are complex interactive materialistic forces. To be sure, the devout Mamun often tells him that this philosophy cannot solve a single problem, but Ali Taha will not change his mind. He finds himself drawn to Auguste Comte and accepts his view that there can be only one God—society—and one religion—science. He contends that, like the religious believer, the atheist too has principles and ideals, and that good is more deeply rooted in human nature than is religion. It is good that created religion, and not the opposite. He often says that he once was a virtuous believer without reason, but now is a virtuous rationalist who does not believe in fables. This implies that Ali Taha had acquired faith in his youth but after being exposed to the ideas of great European philosophers, he relinquished it for rationalism. Yet despite his having grown up in an Islamic society, surrounded by religious men, this faith must not have been deep because he lost it so easily.

Moreover, Ali Taha dreams of social reforms, looking for an earthly rather than a heavenly utopia. He attempts to interest his colleagues in socialism but fails. Mamun argues that Islam contains a reasonable kind of socialism because it imposes the *zakat* (religious tithe), which could guarantee social justice if fairly implemented. If Ali Taha desires a universal order based on true happiness, justice, and brotherly love, he says, he should try Islam. The nonchalant Ahmad Badir answers that he is a member of the Wafd party, which has capitalistic aims, and therefore he cannot be a socialist. Abd al-Dayim counters with his standard vulgar assertion that everything is *tuzz* (in this context, crap). Ali Taha describes himself as a socialist, an atheist, an honorable man, and a platonic lover. It may seem unusual that he is a socialist, for in fact he comes from a well-to-do family. His father gave him a hundred pounds to start a weekly magazine calling for social reform; he has even deserted his job at the university library and stopped working for his master's degree (as Mahfouz did), in order to devote his time and energy to the struggle for Egypt, to transform it from a nation of slaves to a nation of free men.

He is in love with Ihsan, a high school senior who is aware of her captivating beauty but no less aware of her poverty. Her father, Shihata Turki, operates a small cigarette shop but could not support the family without the extra income her mother brings in. Yet perhaps her biggest problem is her parents' loose moral principles. Indeed, they unscrupulously sought to marry her to an immoral but rich man, offering their daughter for his money. But Ihsan avoided this disgrace and apparently found true love when she met Ali Taha. Her parents oppose him, feeling he cannot support her, but she ignores their objections. Unfortunately, her love for Ali Taha does not last, and eventually she leaves him to further her own selfish ambition.

After briefly describing Ahmad Badir, who takes the attitude that as a journalist he should act only as an observer, reporting the problems of his society without getting involved in them, Mahfouz turns to the fourth student, Mahjub Abd al-Dayim, who is the focus of the novel from chapter 5 onward, while his classmates are reduced to secondary roles, appearing only to interact with him. Tall and thin, he is neither handsome nor ugly, but one notices above all the look of defiance in his face. He has many concerns, especially sex, which he considers the only reason for women's existence. From the moment he sees Ali Taha's fiancée Ihsan, he lusts after her. Indeed, he does not even find it unpalatable to engage in sex with a dirty-looking young woman who makes her living by picking up cigarette butts; she is simply an available female. His philosophy means license, and his motto is *tuzz* (could not care less), the term he applies uniformly to values, ideals, principles, and traditions. He sums up life in an equation: religion + science + philosophy + character = *tuzz*. Often he says sarcastically that his family bequeathed him nothing to make him happy, and it is not fair to inherit anything that will make one miserable. Mahjub is a solipsist. He always twists Descartes's dictum, "I think, therefore, I exist," to mean that the self is the most important thing in existence. He is extremely selfish, believing that his own happiness is of primary importance. At best, he is a cynical, sarcastic young man who has no use for religion or science; his ultimate objective in life is to attain pleasure and power through any and every means. In brief, he is a degenerate scoundrel, a nihilist destitute of moral values. But he keeps his morbid, immoral ideas to himself, revealing only interests he believes are fashionable, like atheism and free expression.[4]

Mahjub is also envious, rebellious, and self-destructive, blaming his misery on his poverty. His father is a mere clerk who earns eight pounds a month yet manages to send him three pounds a month for his tuition and living expenses. What a good and loving man this poor father is, taking food from his own mouth to support a profligate and ungrateful son. But Mahjub Abd al-Dayim always appears short of money, able to afford only the cheap common Egyptian meal of fava beans. What grieves him most is that he does not have money to spend on his sensual lusts. Thus, he is always rebelling against society, with its values and moral principles. He cannot understand why he was born poor while others were born rich. He laments the inequality of wealth in his own town, al-Qanatir. He is ready to sell his soul to the devil, if the devil will help him attain the niceties of life and reach the top of the social ladder. Eventually he meets the devil, who leads him to the top and then causes him to fall, ending his career in a catastrophic scandal.

The devil's disciple is Salim al-Ikhshidi, a native of his home town and secretary to the cabinet minister Qasim Bey Fahmi, who is due to become the director of the minister's bureau. Mahjub meets him at the railway station while on his way to al-Qanatir to see his father, who has been half-paralyzed by a heart attack. He learns that when al-Ikhshidi was a student at the university, he was active on campus in politics and student affairs and even distributed leaflets against the 1923 constitution. Suddenly, he stopped his extracurricular nationalistic activities on the premise that "learning is only for the students." There were rumors that he would be arrested for his activities, but nothing of the sort happened. Instead, as soon as he graduated, he was appointed secretary to Fahmi, having been chosen over many more qualified graduates. How did he obtain this position? By using connections and even immoral means. Utterly without principle, he discovered that he could achieve his ends by selling his soul to the devil. What aggravates Mahjub's sense of deprivation is that al-Ikhshidi is well enough off to travel first-class, while he can hardly afford a third-class ticket.

On seeing his sick father, Mahjub is less concerned about his condition than about the possibility that his father may not return to work, and that he will lose his monthly allowance. His father's assurances that he will get some gratuity from the government give him no comfort. Seeking relief from his financial situation, he turns to a distant relative of his mother, Ahmad Bey Hamdis, who enjoys both position and wealth. Much to his disappointment, Hamdis ignores his request. Indeed, why should a man who has risen from the ashes of poverty to become a member of the upper middle class care about Mahjub and his needs? Frustrated, he plans to take advantage of Hamdis's pretty daughter, Tahiyya, as an act of revenge. He leads her to a lonely spot near the site of the pyramids, intending to attack her, but she becomes furious at his improper behavior, and he retreats in discomfiture.

Things go from bad to worse for Mahjub. Lack of money reduces him to one meal a day, leading him to fear that he may starve, yet he finds it demeaning to ask his friends for a loan. Since Hamdis will not help, he seeks out Salim al-Ikhshidi at his office at the ministry. Mahjub relates his problems, and al-Ikhshidi responds that since he knows English and French, he should seek work as a translator for the magazine *al-Najma* (The Star). The editor is his friend, and Salim will prevail on him to give Mahjub a job. But Mahjub needs money now, not later. Furious at himself and the world, he shouts, "The world shall pay for the agonies I am suffering!" Desperate, he turns to his classmates and is relieved when Mamun Ridwan lends him some money.

Mahjub has yet to face real life in a corrupt society where dog eat dog seems to be the dominant principle. If Hamdis and al-Ikhshidi could rise from poverty to power, he thinks, why should he not do the same? So, after his graduation, Mahjub goes to seek al-Ikhshidi's help in finding a government job and is told that there is a price for everything if he is willing to pay. Mahjub needs a connection, al-Ikhshidi says, and there is none better than the powerful businessman Abd al-Aziz Bey Radi, but the job will cost him half the first two years' salary. If Mahjub is unwilling to pay this bribe, he should contact Dawlat, the famous songstress, who enjoys widespread influence in government circles but is more expensive than Radi. If he cannot pay to get a job, his best chance is to meet with Ikram Niruz, a very rich and influential high-society woman, the founder of the Blind Women's Society. She has strong government connections but is also extremely egotistical, adoring publicity and prestige. Since she is to host a party for blind women, Mahjub should interview her; an article for *al-Najma* praising her achievements on their behalf may be the magical key to his dream of obtaining a government position.

At the party, Mahjub comes face to face with the world of the aristocracy, a world of money, power, and luxury, miles apart from his own. He is surrounded by high-society women wearing beautiful, expensive dresses and exotic perfumes. They not only flaunt their luxury but openly show disrespect for their traditions by conversing in fluent French rather than Arabic. The party teems with men who have climbed the social ladder through unscrupulous means, including gambling and pandering. One of the guests reportedly once lost a wager in which his wife was the stake; another, on discovering that his wife had taken their chauffeur as a lover, asked her to choose between them, whereupon she chose the chauffeur. Here al-Ikhshidi and people like him fit right in. The only one out of place is Mahjub's colleague Ahmad Badir, who is present to cover the party. Eventually, Mahjub meets the hostess, who addresses him in French and tells him that his hopes of a bright future depend on the article he intends to write about her. But what surprises him most is that the party turns out to be merely a beauty contest, with girls paraded on the stage. As he soon discovers, the contest is rigged, and the sole purpose of the party is not to help the blind women, but to entertain the members of high society.

At this point, instead of allowing the narrative to flow naturally, Mahfouz introduces a rather contrived plot twist to lead the protagonist to his downfall. Al-Ikhshidi tells Mahjub to forget about the article he is supposed to write about the socialite Ikram Niruz; he has a new plan for him. He promises Mahjub an appointment as secretary to the cabinet minister Qasim Bey Fahmi, provided he will marry Fahmi's mistress and allow him to continue their relationship. The minister, in return, will provide a luxurious apartment and all expenses for the newly married couple. Mahjub, opportunistic and unprincipled, readily agrees, not knowing that the bride-to-be is none other than Ihsan Shihata Turki, the former fiancée of his friend Ali Taha. That she has become mistress to a rich and powerful cabinet minister is a surprise for which Mahfouz offers the reader no motivation. Early in the novel she informs Ali Taha that she is through with him, but only later do we learn why. Apparently, Fahmi had long had an eye on Ihsan. He chased her day after day, taking her for rides in his car and buying her beautiful clothes. Finally, she succumbed to his advances, largely because of her unprincipled parents, who, knowing that Fahmi was rich and could alleviate their poverty, deceived themselves into believing that he would marry their daughter. Clearly Ihsan, like Mahjub, had the disposition for immoral behavior; she was ambitious, selfish, and indecent, with a totally twisted sense of values. Like him, she detested her poverty and low social status and believed that the only way out of misery was to attain luxury and prestige, even at the expense of selling her soul to the devil.

Thus, Mahjub and Ihsan pay the price for satisfying their greed and ambition to join the corrupt upper class—he by becoming a pimp, and she a whore. He occupies a large, well furnished office at the ministry, has a private telephone, and is addressed with all respect by minor officials as Mahjub Bey. He and Ihsan move into a luxurious apartment in an exclusive district, enjoying the status they so longed to attain, while Fahmi takes care of all their expenses. In return, on certain weeknights Mahjub has to leave the apartment to allow Fahmi to enjoy the company of his wife. Ironically, he is soon rewarded with a promotion as director of the minister's bureau, practically outranking al-Ikhshidi himself. Alas, poor al-Ikhshidi! He thought that by arranging Mahjub's marriage to Ihsan he could win promotion to the highest rank at the ministry, but he has been outmaneuvered by the very man he tried to use to achieve his selfish needs. Mahjub, now a member of the rich and influential upper class, considers himself successful, for he equals Ahmad Bey Hamdis in wealth and status. He moves in the circle of the aristocrats, mostly of Turkish origin, and enjoys their sumptuous parties, often aboard yachts on the Nile. As for the principles of ethics and morality, they are to him nothing but *tuzz*. At the zenith, he gives no thought to the possibility of downfall, even forgetting that his parents need his help.

In the end, however, a surprising sequence of events shatters Mahjub's dreams and brings him down. His father unexpectedly visits, rebuking him for neglecting his parents and marrying without the courtesy of informing them. Their argument is interrupted by the persistent ringing of the doorbell, after which Fahmi's wife dashes in, demanding furiously to know where her husband and Ihsan are making love. She raps at the bedroom door, telling her "honorable minister husband" to "come out of this brothel." When Mahjub interferes, she yells, "Shut up, you dirty pimp!" Finally the door opens and Qasim Bey Fahmi comes out, showing no sign of shame or remorse. He pleads with his wife to lower her voice and behave appropriately. She responds angrily, "You dare, Excellency, to tell me what is appropriate and what is not? You think it is appropriate to be caught red-handed in the bedroom with the wife of this insolent pimp. Would you be pleased if your son and daughter knew about your appropriate behavior?" (212). Then she leaves, warning her husband not to try to make up with her. Mahjub's father, totally dumbfounded by what he has heard and seen, realizes that his son has lost everything. He turns his back on his son and, leaning on a cane, drags himself out the door. When Ihsan comes out crying and asks what has happened, Mahjub says that their dreams are shattered, but he does not show remorse or admit his fault. Outwardly, he seems unaffected by his tragic fall, which he dismisses with his eternal response of *tuzz*; this time, however, it is an attempt to conceal his utter despair and defeat. His rise and fall becomes a public scandal; Qasim Bey Fahmi resigns his position in the cabinet, while Mahjub is demoted and transferred to Aswan. Since scandal forms the major event of the novel, it is worth noting that it was printed in 1953 by the Story Club in Cairo under the title *Fadiha fi al-Qahira* (Scandal in Cairo), perhaps for more lucrative marketing.

Essentially, Mahfouz seeks here to portray the contrasting mores of the upper and lower middle classes in Cairo in the 1930s. The upper class enjoyed power, wealth, and prestige but was morally corrupt. The lower-middle-class poor struggled to improve their lot but found that all avenues to success were closed unless they compromised their principles and emulated the upper class. From the outset, Mahfouz confronts us with an absolute moral dichotomy between these two classes: one adheres to traditional societal principles of ethics; the other is devoid of moral principles, totally depraved. At one end of the social spectrum stands the upper class, represented by the cabinet minister Qasim Bey Fahmi and others; at the other end are hapless men like Mahjub Abd al-Dayim. But many members of the lower middle class, including Mahjub, Salim al-Ikhshidi, Ahmad Bey Hamdis, and even Ihsan Shihata Turki, have no qualms about violating accepted moral principles, which they see as a hindrance to their ambition to get ahead in society.

Mahfouz would have us believe that Mahjub and Ihsan fall into immoral behavior because of their poverty. This is rather lame rationalization. People behave immorally not because they are poor, but because they are unprincipled. Indeed, Mahfouz points out that Mahjub's parents are poor, but they are also moral and decent. Surely there were other students like Mahjub who came from poor families and struggled for whatever job they could find. He and Ihsan have no right to use poverty as an excuse for depravity.

We see here the moral dilemma of Egyptian society in the 1930s, which Mahfouz attempts to resolve. The moral climate is changeable, and in seeking answers to their social and moral problems, the members of the lower middle class are beset by different and contradictory concepts. The Muslim believer Mamun Ridwan maintains that lack of faith in God is the root of evil. The true believer, with God as his guide, will never behave like Mahjub. The socialist Ali Taha argues that society tempts people to commit crimes, and that it protects criminals like Qasim Bey Fahmi, who resigned his cabinet position but was not brought to justice or punished. Mamun seems to believe that Fahmi escaped justice because the laws of

Islam are no longer enforced; in ancient times, he would have been stoned to death. The nonchalant journalist Ahmad Badir comments cynically that society tolerates crime, and that someday Fahmi will be offered another government position, in which he will continue his corrupt actions.[5]

As a believer, Mamun poses the whole serious question of man's responsibility for his actions. This question preoccupied ancient and modern philosophers, who tried to determine whether there are absolute truths of justice, beauty, and goodness and whether man is responsible for his actions, good or bad. To the Sophists, man is the measure of all things, which means there are no absolute truths or standards of right and wrong. Man becomes the ultimate judge of his actions, responsible only to himself. To the more conservative Greeks like Socrates and Plato, such dogmas could lead only to atheism and anarchy. They argued that if goodness and justice are left to the whims of man, then religion, morality, and even the state and society cannot be sustained. Absolute truths do exist, and man is responsible to a higher power for his actions.

Moreover, says Mamun, since God has revealed these philosophical and theological truths in the Quran and has given man laws based on them, he alone determines what is right and wrong. Man's actions become subject to God's laws, and if he violates them, man must answer not to himself, but to God. He cannot avoid judgment by blaming everything on his personal misfortune or on society. Mamun says that Mahjub has abandoned the criterion of right and wrong, and that *tuzz* has become the ultimate measure of his actions, which run counter to faith in God. He has a similar view of Ali Taha, who has replaced God with socialism. Both of them have lost sight of what is sacred, and their only salvation is to return to faith in God, the foundation of a stable, moral society. Although Mamun believes that Islam is the remedy for the ills of Egyptian society, including poverty and crime, he gives no practical example to show how it can serve as a tool for reform or social justice. Islam, as he presents it, appears to be only a slogan. Although he criticizes the Friday *khutbas* (sermons) because of their traditional form, which appeals to ignorance and superstition rather than enlightenment, he offers nothing in their place.[6]

Likewise, socialism, which Mahfouz presents through Ali Taha to counterbalance Mamun's religious beliefs, remains merely an abstraction, rather than a viable ideology offering specific solutions to Egypt's problems. Ali Taha is as committed to social reform and as idealistic as Mamun, the only difference being that he is a nonbeliever. Both men dream of a utopian world free from evil. Mamun imagines an earthly heaven where faith and the spirit can combat evil. Ali Taha, pragmatist that he is, maintains that under the conditions prevailing in Egypt in the early 1930s, such a society depends on fate and divine decree.[7] It is interesting to see the nonbeliever socialist speak of such forces in a manner tantamount to saying God's will be done.

Thus, Mahfouz reveals the hopes and dreams of the lower middle class through these university students, who are fully aware of their own problems and those of their society. Each of them proposes a solution that reflects his personal convictions, but the attitudes and proposals of these bright young men are idealistic rather than pragmatic. The novel demonstrates their confusion and their lack of positive direction. They complain, criticize, and diagnose the maladies of their society, but none appears to have a practical plan to combat its ills. The real problem is to change the corrupt political regime controlled by unprincipled, rich, and powerful men whom these students consider an impediment to reform and progress. It is interesting that nowhere in the novel does Mahfouz suggest violence as a method of change. He has placed great hope in the educated class to effect the change but offers no practical solutions.

As his characters, Mahfouz came from a small middle-class family; as they, too, he graduated from the university in 1934. It is likely that some of these students reflect his own hopes, dreams, and frustrations regarding the conditions in his country. When the events of this novel took place, Egypt was in the grip of not only the British, but of a group of aristocratic officials, mostly Turks and Circassians. These Turko-Egyptian aristocrats, whom an Egyptian writer calls "the new Hyksos," were rich and powerful and occupied key positions in the government.[8] Like the ancient Hyksos, they were alien to Egypt in appearance and character. These foreign parasites ruthlessly exploited the hapless and subservient poor *fallahin,,* whom they considered slaves, and used their quasi-Egyptian status as a pretext to control both the people and their government.

Mahfouz displays their evil attitudes and their contempt for the Egyptian people in depicting a yacht excursion, on which Mahjub and Ihsan join members of the aristocracy. After a dance, some guests sit down to chat about the political situation in Europe, talking about the rise of Hitler and the possibility of war between Germany and France. When they proceed to discuss the internal situation in Egypt, Mahjub hears someone say that Egypt can be ruled by any tyrant without serious problems. Another guest comments that any political regime would turn into dictatorship if implemented in Egypt. A third guest adds that this is a country where the beating of a member of the poor class by an effendi is considered honorable. In this case, Ahmad Asim laments, Egypt will never gain its independence. Another guest, Ahmad Iffat, says laughingly, "Why should Egypt want to be independent? The leaders are quarreling to attain governmental power, while the people are not worthy of independence" (192).

Mahjub asks, "Does not it bother you to say such a thing about your own people?" Iffat responds, "Not one single drop of Egyptian blood runs in my veins," evoking a storm of laughter. Suddenly enraged, not from any national feeling but because of his own sense of pride, Mahjub asks Iffat what he thinks of the speech at the Egyptian senate in which his father gloriously defended the *fallah.* Iffat chuckles and says, "That was at the Senate. But at home my father and I agree that the best way to treat the *fallah* is by using the whip." Everyone laughs. Mahjub, thinking he has defended his "Egyptian nationalism," wonders to himself, "How can Ali Taha reform this noble people or realize his high ideals?" (193). Clearly, the new Hyksos aristocracy is little different from the old one and even seems more barbaric. They are degenerates, hypocrites who, like Iffat's father, pretend in public to defend the *fallah,* while in secret they propose to whip him like an animal. To them, the Egyptian is only prey. They are corrupt and dissolute—the cabinet minister Qasim Bey Fahmi, the socialite Ikram Niruz, and even Ihsan's parents, whose family name betrays their Turkish origin.

Members of the aristocratic class, the novel shows, lived in a society all but closed to members of the middle class, to say nothing of the peasants. If someone aspired to enter this aristocratic society, he had to play the game by its rules. He had to sacrifice his own soul and moral principles to the interests of the powerful, like Salim al-Ikhshidi and Mahjub, who acted as pimps, and Ihsan, who became Fahmi's whore. In brief, it was not easy to emulate the aristocratic class unless one not only had the disposition for corruption, but was totally corrupt.[9] What is surprising is that one seldom finds a truly decent character in this novel. The Egyptian aristocratic class was corrupt, but could the whole upper class have been as morally bankrupt as Mahfouz suggests in this novel? Perhaps in the back of his mind was the concept of the struggle of good versus evil, which he acquired from Islamic tradition and from his study of philosophy and applied to his own society.

Some final observations are in order before we move to the next novel. Mahfouz's characters are all Muslims who reside in certain communities of Cairo. They are decidedly urban, belonging to the upper or lower middle class. They move and act in a very specific place and time, a fact which narrows the scope of their actions. In fact, in many of Mahfouz's later novels Cairo remains the primary setting. To the present generation, this novel's value is chiefly historical; many landmarks and streets it mentions, like Rashad Pasha Street, are gone, as is the Giza train. Economic realities have likewise changed; no Egyptian student today could rent an apartment or buy a meal as inexpensively as did Mahjub Abd al-Dayim.[10] Life has changed in Cairo, especially for the university students, and Mahfouz himself is certainly aware of this change.

Khan al-Khalili

Mahfouz's second contemporary novel, published in 1946, bears the name of an old quarter of Cairo with long, narrow streets and cross alleys packed on both sides with shops offering a variety of wares. Teeming with people in different attire and of different origin, the quarter appears more like a carnival than a business district. There are watchmakers' shops, a tea-seller's shop, rug shops, and brassware shops, next to a small kabob restaurant and a coffeehouse. The Khan al-Khalili quarter has an aura of solemnity because it lies next to the famous Azhar Mosque (a present-day university) and houses the holy shrine of al-Husayn, the second son of the Imam Ali, who was martyred in Karbala, Iraq in A.D. 680. According to tradition, when al-Husayn was murdered, his head was cut off to be trans-ported to the Umayyad Caliph Yazid in Damascus, but it later was moved to Cairo, where a shrine was built over it.

The events of *Khan al-Khalili* cover twelve months during World War II, from September 1941 to August 1942. During this period, the German forces commanded by Field Marshal Rommel reached al-Alamayn and were almost at the gates of Alexandria. With British forces occupying Egypt, the people found their country the arena of a conflict not of their making. Yet Mahfouz's intention was not, as some writers have maintained, to portray the vicissitudes of the war in Egypt,[11] but to show its effect on the social and economic conditions in Egypt and on the attitudes of the common people. The novel appears to focus upon the love of two brothers, Ahmad and Rushdi Akif, for the same young woman, Nawal, but in fact Mahfouz is concerned as much with the quarter of Cairo where they live as with these individuals. He provides a true picture of the lives, hopes, and frustrations of middle-class Egyptians in the early years of World War II. The main character is undoubtedly Ahmad Akif, who serves as a link between his family and other characters whom he meets frequently at the Zahra coffeehouse in Khan al-Khalili.

As the novel opens, Ahmad and his parents have moved from the Sakakini quarter to Khan al-Khalili, whose inhabitants believe their quarter is sacrosanct because of the holy shrine of al-Husayn, and that the Germans, who are seeking the Muslims' support, are reluctant to bomb it.[12] Their new residence is an upstairs apartment in a building whose ground floor is occupied by different shops. From the window of his room, Ahmad can see the flat roofs of similar buildings, and behind them the tall, majestic minaret of al-Husayn's shrine. The apartment is just large enough for him and his parents; his younger brother Rushdi, meanwhile, is employed by a bank in Asyut, in southern Egypt.

Ahmad Akif's personality makes him an interesting and even sympathetic subject for psychoanalysis. According to Mahfouz he is modeled on an actual person, an employee in the administrative office of the Egyptian university. Although he had a college degree, Ahmad Akif was a silly, shallow braggart who pretended to be the fountainhead of knowledge and was mentally unstable. Despite reading *Khan al-Khalili* and seeing his own name in it, says Mahfouz, he did not realize he was the model on whom the character was based.[13]

The fictional Ahmad Akif has a variety of psychological problems that set him apart from the other characters of the novel. He has an inferiority complex (later a superiority complex), a persecution complex (if not paranoia), and a libido complex and imagines that the whole world is against him. He is a minor official at the Ministry of Public Affairs, drawing a meager salary, still unmarried in his forties. His peculiar physical appearance and slovenly dress reflect his eccentric character. His head is narrow and bald, his face long and thin; his teeth are yellow from smoking. He would give more attention to his appearance, were it not for his belief that great men usually do not care about how they look. He is always nervous and restless and at times depressed.

Yet Mahfouz exposes a rather admirable side of this unfortunate character: Ahmad Akif is a responsible person who has sacrificed his personal happiness and even his career to support his family. Indeed, his selflessness may be one of the reasons for his eccentricity. In this respect, he is different from Mahjub Abd al-Dayim in *al-Qahira al-Jadida*, who because of his poverty became rebellious, dissolute, and irresponsible. Ahmad has great respect and love for his family. At times he laments his bad luck and the opportunities he has lost because of his family, but he never deserts them or acts irresponsibly toward them.

His father, a clerk at the Archives Department in the Ministry of Public Works, was forced to retire while still in his forties, charged with negligence and defying administrative investigators. Ahmad had to abandon his law studies abruptly and take a minor position at the Ministry of Public Works to support his family. Leaving school was a severe blow that shattered his dreams of a bright and successful future. He became angry and depressed, believing that he had been wronged and persecuted. He developed a superiority complex, believing that he was a genius who would have become a cultivated lawyer or a leader like Sa'd Zaghlul.

What grieves him even more is that he has lost many opportunities since he interrupted his study to support his family. During those twenty years he might have become a cabinet minister, like some of his schoolmates who were fortunate enough to continue their studies. Every day he reads in the newspapers about one of them who holds a high position in the government and then condemns the circumstances that thwarted him. He attempted to continue his law studies by correspondence but failed two subjects in the final examination. Instead of admitting his failure, he rationalizes it, claiming that he did not study hard enough. He tried business, but failed again. He thought of devoting his energy to science and invention but abandoned the idea on the pretext that Egypt had no place where he could conduct his scientific experiments. Though he imagined that he could emulate Newton or Einstein, he was making no progress toward his goal. Undaunted, he turned his hand to literature, began to read the works of old and modern Arab writers, and convinced himself that he was a belletrist. He wrote several articles and submitted them to periodicals, but none saw print. This time he blamed his failure on vicious publishers who did not understand his ideas and literary genius.

Ahmad Akif began to question the meaning of greatness and what Egypt knows about it but quickly concluded that in Egypt, greatness means the right connections and expediency. After all, he reasoned, Sa'd Zaghlul reached the top through proper connections. Ahmad became more angry at his adversities but comforted himself with the thought that life is futile. What good is it, he asked himself, if people die like beasts? What is the use of knowledge, writing, or invention if men will be consumed by death? Like Solomon, Ahmad could say, "Vanity of vanities! All is vain." His pessimistic view of life did not discourage him from reading in search of knowledge, but increasingly he favored *yellow books* (so called because of the paper they were printed on) that treated a variety of religious, literary, historical, and philosophical subjects.

He read so much and argued on so many subjects that his semiliterate friends at the Ministry of Public Works called him the Philosopher. About this time, Ahmad was attracted to magic and began reading books on the subject. This new pursuit was another manifestation of his superiority complex, for he believed that through magic he could find the keys to knowledge, gain power, and control the universe. He would become almighty God. His infatuation with magic, however, almost drove him to insanity and death; so he abandoned it. Thus Ahmad Akif, who imagined himself a man of many talents, developed a persecution complex. He felt that he had been wronged by men who could not understand or appreciate him. Yet like a masochist, he enjoyed suffering. He could visualize himself in the place of the political leader who suffers because of his principles or because of his support of the defeated party.

Mahfouz blames Ahmad Akif's eccentric behavior partly on his childhood. As the first-born child, he was overloved and pampered by his parents, and thus unprepared to bear the responsibility of supporting the whole family at the early age of twenty. Life was neither propitious nor kind to him, and from its vicissitudes sprang all his different complexes. It seems likely also that he inherited some of his erratic behavior from his mother, Dawlat. Although she appeared to be cheerful and sociable, her life was not free of sorrow. She was a hypochondriac and blamed her imaginary sickness on *Ifrits* (demons), whose control she believed could be overcome only through exorcism. Forbidden by her husband to hold a session to exorcise demons (the Egyptian term is *Zar*), she attended sessions held by women friends. Ahmad, who knew of his mother's activity, said in obvious bewilderment, "Truly our family is the victim of Satan." Not only had his father enticed him to study magic, driving him close to insanity; now he was antagonizing his mother, leading her to destroy the family.

Ahmad Akif also suffered from a serious sexual problem. Though past forty, he had never managed to meet the woman who could share his life. Timid in nature, he was a misogynist; he hated and feared women, especially if they were beautiful, believing that his physical appearance made him unable to attract them. Whether founded or not, such beliefs must have contributed to his sexual complex. Furthermore, his upbringing as presented by Mahfouz fostered the development of his psychological problems. He feared his father because he was strict and loved his mother because she spoiled him. He remained his mother's baby when he grew up and expected the world to pamper him as she had done. At the age of forty, Ahmad still could not face life as a man. "Could his parents believe," Mahfouz writes, "that this bald, failed son was their own victim?"

As a teenager, Ahmad Akif appears to have been quite normal. When still in high school, he fell in love with a beautiful young Jewish woman, a neighbor in the Sakakini quarter. She knew that Ahmad cared for her, but she flirted with him instead of reciprocating his feelings. Their relationship was based on childish sentiment rather than on true, committed love and ended abruptly when the young woman became engaged to a man from her community—an event that left Ahmad heartbroken. Later he was attracted to the daughter of a widow who was his mother's friend. He wanted to marry her, but her mother objected that she was still a young woman, and he had a long way to go to finish school and support a wife. Ahmad's hopes were once more shattered, and the wounds to his psyche deepened. Unable to stand rejection, he lost faith in love, women, and the whole world. Yet twenty years later, after a life of loneliness and frustration, he tried his luck again. He asked for the hand of a merchant's daughter in marriage, but her mother objected because he was old and his salary was trifling. Beaten down again, he began to vilify women as dirty animals without souls or brains. He could see no difference between true love and sex, and threw himself in the arms of prostitutes, hoping to find the love he eagerly sought. In his sick mind, be believed that prostitutes were the only true women, although he recognized that they sell their bodies to men to make money, or perhaps to satisfy their sensual cravings. Ahmad, decidedly lacking in sexual prowess, was again disappointed, and his sexual complex worsened.[14]

Ahmad's misfortunes continue when he falls in love again, this time with Nawal, a vivacious sixteen-year-old high school student, the daughter of Kamil Khalil, an official in the Department of Surveys and a patron of the Zahra coffeehouse, which Ahmad frequents. He is acutely aware of the difference in their ages, realizing that if he had married twenty years ago, he might have a daughter her age. A forceful conflict develops between his heart and his reason, but he continues to deceive himself into believing that he is in love. He continually watches her from his window and contrives to meet her on her way to school, in the streets, and when her family comes to visit with his. He becomes infatuated, like a teenager, and is distressed to learn that a young attorney, Ahmad Rashid, may be in love with her. But his dreams are totally shattered when he finds out that he is losing Nawal to his younger brother Rushdi, who returns to Cairo from his job in Asyut. Ahmad, having given up his studies to support the family, is pleased that Rushdi has become financially independent. Rushdi, on his part, loves his brother Ahmad and appreciates the sacrifice he has made for the family. He seems convinced of his brother's broad knowledge and literary ability, and most likely he has no idea of his psychological problems. Surely he has no knowledge about Ahmad's suppressed emotions and his latest imagined love affair with the vivacious Nawal.

Unlike his older brother, Rushdi is suave, cheerful, and sociable. He is also profligate—like his closest friends, fond of wine, women, and song—and a compulsive gambler. In fact, his dissolute life forced him to interrupt his study at the School of Commerce and seek a minor position at a bank. At one time he decided to swear off his life of dissipation, get married, and settle down, but he did not do so. One day soon after his return, he sees a beautiful girl in the opposite building—none other than Nawal, his brother's dream girl. He is fascinated by her beauty and eager to learn more about her. For the first time, he intends to build a true and lasting love relationship. He pursues Nawal until he meets her, and the two soon fall in love. Poor Ahmad! As if his problems were not enough, his whole imaginary world collapses when Rushdi ecstatically tells him that he intends to marry Nawal, the daughter of his friend Kamil Khalil Effendi. Ahmad feels as if he has been stabbed in the heart, but he has no choice except to control his emotions and congratulate his brother.

But fate has something else in store for Rushdi, who shows signs of ill health that nobody else considers serious. He even has a premonition that his end is near. One day, as he and Nawal stroll past his family's cemetery, she remarks that every time she passes by it, she recites the Fatiha (the opening chapter of the Quran) for the souls of the departed members of his family. He casts a doleful look at the graves and wonders whether his beloved Nawal will soon recite the Fatiha for his own soul. Ahmad appeals to him to lead a more sober life and save his health, but to no avail. When his coughing becomes worse and he begins to spit up blood, Rushdi is finally taken to a doctor who says that he has tuberculosis and should be admitted to the sanatorium at Hulwan. Everyone is shocked (in 1942, tuberculosis, for which there was no known treatment, was usually fatal). To make things worse, Nawal's parents prevent her from visiting him, lest she become infected. Rushdi never mentions her again, and asks to be moved home, where he dies within a few days. Shaken by his death, the family moves to a new residence in the Zaytun quarter, leaving behind the memories of the past. The novel ends with the phrase, "Farewell, Khan al-Khalili."

It seems ironic that Rushdi, who wins the struggle for Nawal's love, turns out to be more of a failure than his brother as his life is cut short.[15] Is it fate, luck, or sheer circumstance? Or is it because Mahfouz, who frequently appears unsympathetic to his lively and dynamic characters, chooses to end their lives tragically? One writer has lamented that Mahfouz does not want to see such characters live.[16] It is difficult to pass judgment on the course taken by a novelist; after all, he is free to end his work in a way befitting his objectives. One may speculate that if Mahfouz had ended the novel with the marriage of Rushdi to Nawal, the eccentric Ahmad would have become insane or committed suicide in a fit of jealousy—a tragic outcome in either case. That so many of his characters meet tragic endings reflects his frame of mind before the Egyptian revolution of 1952. He was sad and frustrated over the condition of the lower classes, who were manipulated by unprincipled politicians and the omnipresent British authorities. In such a morbid and melancholic ambience, says Mahfouz, it was difficult to write cheerful stories. He claims that his characters appreciated life and strove to live it abundantly but found themselves beaten down by uncontrollable circumstances.[17]

On the surface, Mahfouz apparently seeks to portray through Ahmad Akif the disadvantaged status of Egyptian government employees, whose livelihood was subject to the whims of corrupt, selfish, powerful men who occupied key positions in the government. These minor officials had no laws to protect their jobs and no equitable merit system to ensure their advancement. Many Egyptians sought government employment only because of the lack of economic opportunities such as exist today. The lower middle class was squeezed in between the upper middle class, which controlled wealth and land, and the *fallahin*, who owned no land and simply worked for their landlords. Yet, beyond simply portraying Ahmad Akif as a symbol of the lower middle class in Egypt, Mahfouz attempts also to show the rise of a semiliterate class in the 1940s, comprised neither of university graduates like the students in *al-Qahira al-Jadida* nor of literary figures such as Taha Husayn. The great majority of these semiliterates dabbled in a variety of disciplines but mastered none. They were dilettantes, acquiring only a smattering of literary clichés, which they proudly used to impress the illiterate.

Ahmad Akif is a perfect example of the semiliterate; he has read ancient Arabic yellow books and the works of contemporary Egyptian writers, but his knowledge remains sketchy and shallow. He has no direction, no methodology. Worse still, he cannot comprehend the concepts or appreciate the depth of what he has read. He is one of those effendis who think that by reading a few books they can become literate, even educated. He can impress only the illiterate or the barely literate, like Nunu the calligrapher, who cannot comprehend the words he inscribes. On first meeting Ahmad, Nunu invites him to his shop, where he offers him tea and the *nargila* (water pipe). When Ahmad, who fancies himself superior to his host, declines to smoke the water pipe, he asks why; after all, it merely offers smoke purified by water, and its shape has "sex appeal." Nunu, plainly trying to show that he is as knowledgeable as Ahmad, asks whether he considers the *baladi* (common countryman) like himself ignorant. Ahmad cannot comprehend that in social status and knowledge, he is no better than Nunu, who belongs to a circle of effendis who meet at the Zahra coffeehouse. When Ahmad is challenged there by the socialist attorney Ahmad Rashid, who asks his opinion about Nietzsche, Marx, and Freud, he is stunned because he has never heard of these men.[18]

Nunu the calligrapher, a jovial, carefree soul who lives for today and leaves tomorrow to care for itself, is the epitome of the common Egyptian *baladi* (native) in his way of life and social conduct. His motto, *mal'un Abu al-Dunya* (cursed be the world, or to hell with the world) epitomizes his happy-go-lucky attitude and is not meant as an insult to believers. He symbolizes the great majority of the simple Muslim folk of Egypt, who have faithfully resigned themselves to God's will, and above all embodies the fundamental Islamic concept of total reliance on God, which tends toward fatalism. Because the world belongs to God and the providential act and command are his, man should not worry; man either must accept and submit to the total order of life or be miserable. He tells Ahmad that he cannot curse life with actions as he does with words, nor can he mock the world if he is poor, naked, sorrowful, or hungry.

Then Nunu delves into the sensitive subject of Muslim marriage, telling Ahmad that he treats life the same way he treats his wives: "The world, like a woman, loathes the man who bows to her and appreciates the man who beats and curses her. Thus, my policy in dealing with the world and women is one and the same."[19] When Ahmad asks how many wives he has, Nunu replies that he has four wives and eleven children. This response is not surprising, for the Quran states, "Marry women of your choice, two or three or four" (4:3, the Sura of Women). As a Muslim, Ahmad does not object to the practice of polygamy, but he is concerned about the condition God attached to it in the second part of the same verse: "But if you fear that you shall not be able to deal justly (with several wives), then marry only one." Asked how he can treat his four wives justly, Nunu explains that he keeps them in a four-room apartment, one room for each and her children. Whatever he makes he distributes among his wives, telling one to buy meat, another vegetables, another melon, and so forth, and asking them to eat with their children and thank him. As Nunu sees it, the essence of fair and just treatment consists of satisfying the needs of the body, chiefly for food, without regard for spiritual consideration. Polygamy is a means to satisfy his sensual desires, which are extraordinary. When Ahmad asks why he cannot be satisfied with one wife, Nunu answers that a whole city filled with women is not enough to satisfy him. After all, he is master Nunu, who relies on God.

Ahmad Akif, who has never been married, cannot understand how four wives can be cooped up in a small apartment and yet not fight with each other out of rivalry or jealousy. Nunu provides an answer that would be shocking to the educated class but probably not to the lower middle class or the *fallahin*. In full confidence, he asserts that the reason for the bad traits of women, such as jealousy, is man's weakness. He explains that a woman is like a piece of dough that man can shape the way he wants to. She is an animal lacking both reason and religion and should be treated either with care or with the stick. He brags that because of such treatment, his wives are happy and peaceful, always trying to please him. But Nunu the Muslim, who relies completely on the providence of God, sees nothing wrong with having a concubine; they may also know that he has an illicit relation with Aliyyat, wife of Abbas Shafa, but have not indicated their displeasure. A strong man like himself, he says, can make a woman do his bidding and does not resort to divorce unless it suits his whim.[20]

Nunu is plainly more honest than many of the novel's upper-middle-class characters, who commit sinful acts and then try to conceal or justify them. He has no feeling of guilt or shame about his sexual behavior. His reliance on God seems to be not so much a spiritual or mystical commitment as a resignation to fate. In his view, fate is associated with *qada* (the divine decree of God), in conformity with the Islamic view that God is the author of good and evil, and that He guides as He misleads. The Quran states, "God rightly guides those whom He will, but those whom He leads astray shall surely be lost" (7:178). Whether he is rightly guided or lost, this is how Nunu understands God's will and dispensation. In keeping with this understanding of fate and divine decree, he tells Ahmad, he has not gone to the shelter to seek refuge from air raids. "What shelter?" he asks. Can Nunu evade fate or postpone God's divine decree of death? After all, the duration of life is one, God is one, and "whatever is written on man's forehead" shall happen to him. Nunu is pragmatic and aware of man's foibles. He believes that despite the sanctity and blessedness Khan al-Khalili enjoys because of the presence of the shrine of the Imam al-Husayn, it can accommodate both vice and virtue, obedience and disobedience of God (45).

Twisted as his views on religion and morality are, Nunu stands in sharp contrast to Ahmad Akif, a timid introvert who suffers from many psychological problems. Ahmad lacks self-confidence and tries to conceal his inferiority complex through erratic behavior, as is clear from his infatuation with a sixteen-year-old to whom he cannot confess his feelings. Nunu, on the other hand, is an extrovert, happy, convivial, and lecherous, unashamed to brag about his sexual prowess. He truly symbolizes the Egyptian *Ibn al-Balad* (common countryman) in his joviality and love of life.[21]

Invited by Nunu to the Zahra coffeehouse, Ahmad Akif for the first time faces the reality of life. He meets a peculiar mixture of lower- and middle-class people, among them the literate and the semiliterate. Besides Nunu these include Abbas Shafa and his heavyset but nice looking wife Aliyyat, who invite the Zahra group and others to their home to smoke hashish and enjoy her sexual favors; Sulayman Bey Atta, inspector of elementary education, an ugly, middle-aged man who managed to marry a very beautiful young woman because he was rich; Sayyid Effendi Arif, a colleague of Nawal's father at the Department of Surveys, obsessed with his problem of sexual impotence; Zifta, the owner of the coffeehouse and a drug addict; and the attorney Ahmad Rashid, who moved to Khan al-Khalili from Hulwan after his family was ordered to evacuate its home for military purposes. The words and actions of these characters, who are all connected with Ahmad Akif, reflect the attitudes and behavior of the majority of the Egyptian people.

Coffeehouses in Egypt, in fact all over the Middle East, are not like the present-day cafés in Western Europe or the United States. They are places of social gathering for men only; the patrons, who usually share common interests, meet after working hours or on the weekends (Thursday and Friday in the Muslim countries), to enjoy rest and relaxation. They drink tea or coffee, and some smoke the *nargila*. Some groups include writers, artists, or other professionals who want to discuss and promote their craft. The coffeehouses, social centers for the exchange of ideas, formed an integral part of Mahfouz's life and career. Often he met with a group of writers while the police chased them from one coffeehouse to another, accusing them of holding illegal meetings. Mahfouz, who says smoking the water pipe activated his thinking, admits that the plot of his novel *Al-Karnak* (1974) was invented at the Fishawi coffeehouse in Cairo.[22]

When he first visits the Zahra coffeehouse, Ahmad Akif considers himself superior to the other patrons because of his extensive knowledge and even feels that joining them is a gesture of humility on his part. He is uncertain about how to approach these men, apprise them of his intellectual strength, and win their respect. As he scans their faces, he is sure that none of them can match his intellect—until his gaze falls on Ahmad Rashid, who more than the rest evokes his concern. Rashid, a young lawyer with a massive head, his round face and eyes concealed behind large dark glasses, asserts that socialism is the only means to reform Egyptian society. Ahmad Akif, who sought a law career but failed, looks at him enviously and senses that he is faced with an educated person who clearly is different from the others. When Rashid condemns the Khan al-Khalili quarter as so dirty and dilapidated that it ought to be demolished and replaced by a modern one offering a better, healthier lifestyle, Ahmad replies that Khan al-Khalili is a historical part of old Cairo, built by the Fatimids in the tenth century, and that destroying it means destroying part of the city's glorious past. He uses this opportunity to impress the men with his extensive knowledge, telling them that he has spent twenty years studying history. When asked whether he did so to obtain a diploma, he retorts that he sought knowledge for its own sake, and that a diploma means only that its holder has memorized the subject matter and passed a test.

The showdown with Ahmad Rashid comes when Akif starts reciting ancient Arabic poetry to support one of his arguments. Rashid says he does not like to cite ancient poetry as evidence because he hates to return to the past. He wants to live in the present, where there are many wise men qualified to guide the people. Ahmad Akif, who knows little about modern thinkers, asks how an educated man can overlook the glory of the past, with its prophets and apostles. Rashid retorts that the present age has its own apostles, like the two geniuses Sigmund Freud and Karl Marx. Ahmad Akif, unfamiliar with these names, asks rather indignantly whether they are a match to the geniuses of ancient times. Rashid seizes this opportunity to elaborate on the psychoanalytical ideas of Freud, the socialistic ideas of Marx, and their benefit to mankind. Still not satisfied, Ahmad Akif tells him that he is young and inexperienced and needs to learn about the past and its wisdom. Rashid denies that there is any wisdom in the past; if there were, he says, the past would not be the past.

"And what about our religion?" asks Ahmad Akif. "Isn't it from the past?" To this Rashid answers, "What credulity!" Ahmad Akif, who has read the religious ideas of the Brothers of Sincerity, tries to refute Rashid's idea that religion is mere blind faith or superstition. He explains that religion contains emotional sentiments for the simple people and intellectual concepts for the thinkers. There are eternal truths like God, divine law, and active reason (nous) which should satisfy the educated believer. Rashid shakes his head to show his contempt, saying that modern scientists know the elements contained in an atom, and they assert that besides our galaxy there are billions of others. Where, then, is God? Because religion is founded on fables, there is no point in contemplating problems that cannot be settled, while there are countless problems in the real world which demand solutions. Rashid then changes the subject, telling Akif that they should not let the others share in their conversation because they cannot comprehend the subject. Ahmad Akif agrees, adding, "Don't forget that the beginning of science is always unbelief."[23]

A few days later, as they resume their discussion in the coffee-house, some young boys and girls pass by, singing and asking for donations. The socialist Rashid, offended by this, tells Ahmad Akif, "We are a nation of beggars—and a handful of millionaires."

There is no option for the people except to beg or do menial work, he says, adding that there is nothing more evil than a regime that dehumanizes people. He does not understand how wise men can allow the majority of their countrymen to remain sick, hungry, and ignorant, or why, if the *fallahin* are aware of their rights, they do not demand them. Rashid responds vehemently that the *fallah*, oppressed and dehumanized, cannot demand anything because he is not free and reminds Ahmad, "In the past free men, not slaves, fought against slavery." Ahmad Akif says that if the *fallah* deserved more than what he has, he would have obtained it—by force, if need be. Rashid nervously asks, "Are you a follower of Nietzsche?" Ahmad Akif is dumbstruck, for he does not know the name. When Rashid asserts that Egypt is drifting aimlessly, Ahmad charges that his effort to save the *fallahin* from their misery would kill the humane spirit of the educated people. The lawyer chuckles, saying that science alone allows the individual to obtain his rights and emancipate his soul from the shackles of self-delusion and humbuggery: "As religions delivered us from paganism, by the same token science ought to deliver us from religions" (85–89). He has deep faith in socialism as the basis of an ideal society, in which human and aesthetic values will transcend materialistic values. Later on, hearing that the ugly, deformed Sulayman Atta is to marry a beautiful young woman, Rashid laments that money can subjugate beauty and sublime values, reducing them to animalistic levels, and says that such a crime could not be committed under socialism (104).

Khan al-Khalili first reveals Mahfouz's concern over the condition of the *fallahin*, although his portrayal of them is rather shallow and trivial, presented only through the words of the socialist Ahmad Rashid, opposed by the equally superficial conservative Muslim Ahmad Akif. One cannot help noticing their reiteration of the ideas of some characters in *al-Qahira al-Jadida*. Like Ahmad Akif, Mamun Ridwan is a believing Muslim, but his understanding of Islam is sounder. More literate and better educated, he can defend his Islamic principles and religious beliefs, whereas Ahmad Akif, who lacks the knowledge and intellectual capacity to refute Rashid, simply condemns him to hell (64). The abstract socialistic and atheistic ideas of Ali Taha are merely restated by Rashid, although he is more of an iconoclast.

Ahmad Akif and Ahmad Rashid epitomize the conflict of conservative and liberal ideas in Egypt in the 1940s. The conservatives cherished their values and especially their religious beliefs as the foundation of society. Many of them could not comprehend ideologies imported from the West, like socialism. As does Ahmad Akif, they recognized that the *fallah* was wronged and oppressed but could not identify with him or his misery. Members of the lower middle class were as much the victims of an undemocratic and oppressive regime as were the *fallahin,* but they were busy looking out for their own interests. Ahmad Akif blames the *fallah* for his misery, Rashid blames the regime, and both end up creating a lot of ineffectual sound and fury.

Rashid's ideas should be of great concern to us because they are presented without any serious challenge from other characters. It is not clear whether Mahfouz's primary intent is to demonstrate through Rashid the new and daring leftist ideology of the 1940s, or to show the lack of public response to it. Here we see an educated lawyer amid a circle of illiterates and semiliterates discussing with them an ideology they cannot comprehend, although they accept him as their friend.[24] Rashid, who rejects the idea that the past had any wisdom, lives only for the present and finds guidance for the future in the teachings of Freud and Marx, whom he regards as the apostles of the modern age. Not being an historian, he does not understand that the past is an existential part of every human being, as much a reality as the present. We know the past, but suffer the present. If the teachings of Marx and Freud are relevant to our age, Mahfouz implies, so are the teachings of the prophets and sages of old, particularly those of Muhammad, the Prophet of Islam.

Rashid believes that science is the only solution to the problems of mankind, and that belief in God is sheer superstition. As we have seen earlier, Mahfouz believes that science is "pure good," and that those who think otherwise should instead direct their attack against social and political institutions.[25] He is skeptical about religion, although he seems to be a believer. Whether the ideas Rashid voices about science are those of Mahfouz himself is not the point; science, Mahfouz implies, is not the answer to man's problems, social or otherwise. Science and its handmaiden technology, which belong to the realm of material consequences and conditions, should never be the means to justify our values or decisions. Our world is not simply a material phenomenon but a civil ethos of substantial cultural complexity. It is distressing that Mahfouz uses the general term *science* as if it were eternal and unchanging and without explicitly defining it, although from his use of the term one may infer that he means that body of practical knowledge (and the method of obtaining it) which is contrary to metaphysics. He often appears to equate science with pure technology, which paradoxically has contributed to both war and peace, construction and destruction. It is largely responsible for the evils and blessings of the industrial age and it is both good and evil. The idea that science is the solution to man's problems and can emancipate us from religion is as futile as Rashid's belief in the redemptive power of socialism. Indeed, this belief raises some very serious questions. Are God and his teachings mere superstitions? Is religion so detrimental to society that it must be destroyed and replaced by science? The ultimate question is whether science contradicts or conforms with religion, specifically the belief in God as the creator of the universe.

Unfortunately, Mahfouz leaves these questions unresolved, thus creating serious flaws in the novel. He lets the socialist Rashid harangue the semiliterate Ahmad Akif, who is no match for him. He should instead have created an educated and intelligent adversary who could meet Rashid on equal ground and at least betray the weakness of his propositions (and perhaps refute them). I find it difficult to accept Rashid's ideas as those of Mahfouz himself. As a product of a predominantly Islamic society whose culture is based largely on religious tradition, Mahfouz is too prudent and intelligent to believe that the past is void of wisdom, that God and religion are sheer nonsense, and that science can liberate mankind from the bondage of metaphysical superstition.[26]

Through the habitués of Zahra coffeehouse and some other anonymous characters, Mahfouz depicts the effect of the war on the common people of Egypt. According to Nunu the calligrapher, the war has turned the world, that is, Cairo, upside-down. In Khan al-Khalili, poor young women have become prostitutes; they hang around the British troops and learn some English jargon. Moral corruption, however, was not confined to Cairo; in Asyut, where Rushdi worked, the Allied troops were draining the markets of meat and fruits and seducing the local women. Domestic servants deserted their employers to work in the cabarets—that is, to sell their bodies. Prostitution was not exclusively for Arab women; Nunu recalls hearing a young Jewish woman, on being accosted, say ruefully in a twisted Scottish accent, "Behave like a gentleman, please."[27] The war has also created among the lower classes a group of profiteers who are rising to become members of the aristocracy and who will soon enjoy prestige and countless privileges. Mahfouz suggests that there is no longer a demarcation between the upper and lower classes; the new aristocrats are the dregs of the past (62).

More interesting is Mahfouz's presentation of the common Egyptians' view of the war and their attitude toward the Allies and their adversaries. During a German air raid, Ahmad Akif and his family go to an underground shelter where many others from the lower classes also seek refuge. When Ahmad says, "The bombing was a mistake. It will not be repeated, God willing," someone responds, "The place that houses the head of al-Husayn shall not be harmed," and another adds, "If God is willing."

The conversation continues:

> "Everything is bound by God's will."
>
> "Hitler has deep respect for Islamic countries."
>
> "It is even said that he believes in Islam, but conceals his faith."
>
> "That is not far-fetched. Did not the righteous and pure Shaykh Labib say that he saw in a dream the Imam Ali Ibn Abi Talib investing Hitler with the sword of Islam?"
>
> "How then was Cairo bombed in the middle of this month [Ramadan]?"
>
> "The Sakakini quarter, most of whose inhabitants are Jews, is the one that was bombed."
>
> "What do you think the Muslim nations expect of Hitler?"
>
> "When he is through with the war, he will restore Islam to its past

glory, create a great union of Muslim nations, and strengthen its ties with Germany through friendship and alliance."

"That is why God supports him in his wars."

"God would not have made him victorious if it were not for his good intentions." (71–72, 74–75, 97–98, 104)

Ahmad listens intently to this dialogue but does not realize how gullible the people are or how deeply they are influenced by sheer propaganda. Elsewhere in the novel people talk about the landing of Rudolf Hess in Britain and the British bombing of Tripoli, like Cairo, a Muslim city. Some of these people support the Germans, some the Allies, and some, like the socialist Ahmad Rashid, even the Russians.

Mahfouz vividly exposes the credulity of common Egyptians about the war. As Muslims, they regard the omnipotent will of God as the cause of everything in life, including the early German success in north Africa. Some of them may genuinely believe that Hitler reveres Islam or has in fact secretly become a Muslim, and that his victory is consequently a victory for Islam. We cannot expect these ignorant people to know that Napoleon tried the same tactics, proclaiming himself the defender of Islam in order to win the Egyptian's support when he invaded their country in 1798. Likewise, before World War I Kaiser Wilhelm II, eager to win the Ottoman Empire to his side, visited the provinces of the Middle East and declared that he was the friend of Islam. Some gullible Muslims even called him Muhammad William. While German propaganda was trying to portray Hitler as the friend and defender of Islam, the British tried to expose him as its enemy. I shall never forget the British propaganda in Iraq during 1939–41, when Germany's successes were stunning, intended to arouse the people against Hitler as the archenemy of Islam and the Muslims.

Thus, life goes on in the time-honored Khan al-Khalili quarter, some of whose denizens fantasize or escape reality by taking opium and hashish, while others seek diversion at the home of the whore Aliyyat and her pimp husband. Many no longer distinguish between right and wrong. They celebrate Ramadan but lament that the war has deprived them of various niceties. The women of the quarter have their own gatherings where they smoke, gossip, and brag about their men. Ahmad's mother, for example, says her husband is an inspector in the Awqaf (religious bequest) Department, and her son is a bureau chief at the Ministry of Public Works, even though he is only thirty-two. She seeks to impress Tawhida, Nawal's mother, so that she will accept Ahmad as a prospective husband for her daughter. And why should they not brag? Do not politicians, businessmen, and religious men lie too? They know that as women they are wronged and degraded, but they do not seem to do much about it (63, 68). While the men and women of Khan al-Khalili are busy with their lives, hopes, and frustrations, the quarter stands as it was in the time of the Fatimids, a timeless historical monument to medieval traditions. Not even the newcomers from more modern quarters like Ahmad Akif, who loathes it, or the socialist lawyer Ahmad Rashid, who wants to demolish it, can change its character or the way of life of its inhabitants.

Before leaving *Khan al-Khalili*, we should note the strong similarity between Ahmad Akif and the character Abd al-Rahman Effendi in Mahfouz's short story "Hayat li al-Ghayr" (Living for Others), which appeared in 1938 in his anthology *Hams al-Junun* (The Whisper of Madness). Abd al-Rahman Effendi is an anonymous minor government functionary, drawing a meager salary after being forced at an early age to work in order to support his family. He intends to ask for the hand of the sixteen-year-old daughter of a neighbor but finds to his disappointment that she is in love with his younger brother Dr. Anwar, who asks him to arrange his engagement to the young woman. Mahfouz, of course, expands this plot in *Khan al-Khalili* and ends it with the untimely death of Ahmad's brother Rushdi.[28]

Zuqaq al-Midaqq

In *Zuqaq al-Midaqq* (Midaqq Alley, 1947), which takes its name from an alley in old Cairo, the locale again plays a significant role. Indeed, the interaction between the alley and its inhabitants is so intense that it is difficult to separate the two without destroying the structure of the novel. Midaqq alley becomes the protagonist, defiant and changeless, while its inhabitants hate it, curse it, leave it, and return to it. Something mysterious ties its inhabitants to it despite its dreariness and squalor. Perhaps its status as a relic of the Fatimid and Mamluk periods makes it a unique monument to antiquity and its people a continuation of its tradition. They live in semi-isolation, with little concern about outside events.[29] The timelessness of the alley seems to be the dominant theme as Mahfouz opens the novel with a graphic description of its features, including Kirsha's coffeehouse, Uncle Kamil's sweets shop, Husniyya's bakery, Abbas al-Hulu's barbershop, Salim Alwan's retail store, the dental clinic of the quack Dr. Bushi, and the apartment of the middle-aged Saniyya Afifi.[30]

The events of the novel occur during 1944 and 1945, but the war affects the lives of only a few inhabitants of the alley who, dissatisfied with their lot, leave to seek their fortune by working in the British military barracks or entertaining British troops. The conflict between their traditional values and those imposed upon them by the war is obvious. No matter how aberrant some of their traditional values may seem, they are better suited to the inhabitants of the alley than the values of the Allied troops. The alley loses two of its people: the beautiful young Hamida, who becomes a prostitute entertaining British troops, and Abbas al-Hulu, who loves her but dies trying to convince her to leave her dissolute life and marry him. Yet the war cannot violate this closed world or disrupt the daily activity of its people. As soon as each crisis is over, the alley returns to its normal life, with all its joys and sorrows. It remains as it has been since Fatimid times, omnipotent and impervious to change. As Mahfouz states, "Its doors and windows would creak as they were opened, and then creak again as they were closed."[31]

This changelessness in the alley is not fortuitous but rather the natural reflection of the behavior of its people, whose lives are inextricably intertwined with it. Thus, its varied shops and stores are an integral part of their lives, and the absence of any one of them would leave a noticeable vacuum. Above all, Kirsha's coffeehouse is central to the life of the alley. It is the meeting place where the men gather, whether only to gossip or to seek solutions to their problems. It is a virtual microcosm and the only outlet the alley's inhabitants have to the outside world of metropolitan Cairo. The human action in the novel begins and ends here.

After summarizing the history of the alley and describing its shops, Mahfouz moves immediately to Kirsha's coffeehouse to set the stage for the interaction of the people with the alley and show the impact of modern civilization on traditional customs. The coffeehouse becomes the scene of intense conflict between old and new values and reflects whether the people are amenable to change. There we meet a variety of people; in addition to Uncle Kamil, Abbas al-Hulu, and Dr. Bushi, there is Sayyid Darwish, a half-witted character who once taught English in a high school. Disillusioned, he tries constantly to explain Arabic words by their English equivalents. There is also an old, debilitated bard who enters with a young attendant, takes a seat in the middle of the coffeehouse, sets down his *rababa* (a one-stringed fiddle) and book, and calls for a cup of coffee. For twenty years he has entertained the patrons by playing his fiddle and singing the traditional epics of Arab folklore. (Indeed, for decades, throughout the Middle East, including my native Mosul, bards were the major source of entertainment in the coffeehouses.) No sooner does he begin playing his fiddle and singing the epic of Abu Sa'dat al-Zanati and Abu Zayd al-Hilali, than Kirsha yells at him to stop. The poor bard is perplexed; why, of all the inhabitants of the alley, is he singled out for condemnation? Kirsha tells him that the clients' minds are satiated with the tales he relates, and that today the people have no use for a bard. They want a radio, and since one has already been installed in the coffeehouse, he should look elsewhere to make a living. The bard retorts that ancient Arab folklore has its special appeal; since the time of the Prophet of Islam in the seventh century, generations have listened to these epics, and the radio cannot replace them. Kirsha becomes furious and hits the desk with his fist, shouting that everything has changed.

Not even the decent and devout Muslim Sayyid Ridwan al-Husayni, the moral conscience of the alley, can help the bard. He tells him to accept his destiny and rely on God, since man's livelihood stems from God's bounty. The half-witted Sayyid Darwish says that the bard's role as entertainer is over, and now it is the time

of the radio. In a resigned philosophical manner, he explains that
what has happened to him is the predetermined will of God. The
bard, however, finds little consolation in their words. Casting a
contemptuous look at the radio, he leaves on the arm of his young
assistant.[32] For the first time, some modern amenities have managed to penetrate the traditional quarters of old Cairo, but they do
not seem to have transformed the lives of the inhabitants of the
alley. The radio offers the coffeehouse patrons a mixture of music
and news that appeals to them more than the monotonous, stale
singing of an old bard, but his expulsion does not affect their mores
or disturb life in the alley.

Zuqaq al-Midaqq has no formal plot and no dominant character.
The alley, which permeates and influences the lives of its inhabitants, is in an allegorical sense the protagonist. The appearances of
several characters are evenly distributed and orchestrated by the
author so that none of them commands a principal role. They differ
from one another only in the nature and intensity of their reactions.
Perhaps the liveliest character is the young woman, Hamida, who
interacts with several suitors in the alley. Although the author did
not intend her to be a heroine, without her the novel would collapse.
Whereas most of the characters in Mahfouz's earlier novels are
drawn from the upper middle class and the intelligentsia, the
characters of *Zuqaq al-Midaqq* are common folk from the lower
middle class. Except for Darwish, the former English teacher, and
Sayyid Ridwan al-Husayni, who once attended the Azhar but could
not finish his studies, they are semiliterate or illiterate. The only
common bond among them is the alley itself.

As in the earlier novels, Mahfouz presents his characters fully
developed at the outset, but he is careful to keep some of their
actions unrevealed to the end, thus heightening the reader's antici-
pation. These actions can be viewed only in the context of life in the
alley and would be vitiated by any substantive change in it. We can
appreciate the interaction of time and place in this novel only when
we realize how dexterously Mahfouz makes his characters an essential part of the locus. Uncle Kamil cannot be seen except through his
sweets shop; he always sits in his enormous chair at the entrance,
flyswatter in hand. Obese and dull, he spends most of the time

dozing, awakening periodically to sell some confection. He is indifferent to his obesity and the risk that it may kill him someday. His business is as dull as his disposition. In fact, he would fail to close his shop at the end of the day without being reminded to do so. In contrast stands the barber Abbas al-Hulu, a handsome, neat, well-dressed young man. His shop, although small, is clean and neat, reflecting the personality of its owner. The nearby bakery is dominated by the rowdy Husniyya, who constantly abuses her husband Jaada, sometimes physically.

The most lively and vibrant character is the twenty-year-old Hamida, whose situation Mahfouz presents so as to evoke our sympathy and compassion. After her natural mother died, Umm Hamida adopted her and brought her to the wife of Kirsha, the coffeehouse owner, to be nursed with her son, Husayn, who according to Islamic law became Hamida's foster brother. Hamida is young, beautiful, and full of life. But she is also poor, and this fact, together with her growing awareness of her beauty, causes her to be disgruntled and rebellious. It is not surprising that she is pugnacious and foulmouthed. Like Mahjub Abd al-Dayim and Ihsan Shihata Turki in *al-Qahira al-Jadida*, Hamida blames her misery on poverty. Her chief desire is to enjoy material things; she especially envies the young Jewish working women, who wear beautiful dresses and enjoy a great deal of individual freedom. She is also eager to marry, but among the men of the alley the only one she finds desirable is Husayn Kirsha, whom she cannot marry because he is her foster brother. Though others court her, they do not suit her taste. Abbas al-Hulu seems earnest, but he is not her type. Salim Alwan, the shop owner who follows her constantly with his eyes, is a married man and too old; although he is rich and could satisfy her material needs, he too is not for her. Uncertain of her desires, she feels she has no place in the alley. She laments her position in life and resents the fact that she has been raised by an adoptive mother who does not know the difference between earth and gold.[33]

We soon discover that Mahfouz not only has set the stage for Hamida's downfall but has deliberately facilitated it. In chapter 5, he details her background and character, in order to demonstrate that this beautiful young woman is driving herself to the abyss.

Unjustifiably setting himself up as judge and jury on her behavior, he portrays her as rootless, quarrelsome, and thoroughly materialistic, without presenting substantive evidence that she is really a bad person. As he did with Mahjub Abd al-Dayim and Ihsan Shihata Turki in *al-Qahira al-Jadida*, he cites poverty as the reason for her eventual fall. He not only passes judgment on the behavior of this unfortunate girl without regard for her circumstances but also uses other characters in the novel, especially women, to criticize her. Because she is quarrelsome, the women of the alley hate Hamida, charging that she hates children and lacks feminine grace; even Kirsha's wife, her foster mother, wishes that she were a mother nursing children, subjected to the authority of a cruel husband who would beat her day and night.[34] Poor Hamida! Mahfouz has already pronounced his verdict, and she is doomed to perdition. Twice he has an opportunity to redeem her, but he declines because doing so would damage his effort to portray the social and moral degradation of the Egyptian society, due partly to the impact of the war.

At one point it appears Hamida will marry Salim Alwan, who has prospered during the war and could satisfy her material desires. But he is thirty years older, already married to a good woman from a respected family, and has grown sons and daughters. Alwan's great weakness is his insatiable sexual appetite, which he stimulates with a special meal of cooked green wheat filled with pigeon meat and nutmeg, prepared for him daily at Husniyya's bakery. At first the recipe was a secret, but after Husniyya tried it on her husband and found it successful, it was used throughout the alley. It is not surprising that he should lust after young Hamida, sensing that she is an easy target. His urgency is heightened by the fact that his wife, no longer able to tolerate his sexual demands, is about to desert him. He accuses her of being frigid and unreceptive and considers her disobedience a sufficient reason to marry another woman. Unable to control his lust for Hamida's seductive body, he even justifies it on religious grounds, saying he should not deprive himself of something made lawful by God, meaning that the Quran allows him more than one wife. In his view the only problem is their age difference, which he believes he can overcome with his aphrodisiac meal; so he tells Hamida's mother that he wants to marry her adopted daughter. But with Hamida already engaged to the barber Abbas al-Hulu, her mother seeks advice from Sayyid Ridwan al-Husayni, who warns against the marriage, saying it would create many problems. Nevertheless, she finally convinces Hamida to marry Alwan for his prestige and wealth. But Mahfouz concocts a means to foil the prospective marriage and drive Hamida to the calamitous end he has planned for her. Before her mother can deliver the happy news that Hamida has agreed to marry him, Alwan is hospitalized with a severe attack of angina; he later recovers but loses Hamida, who quickly forgets about him (chapters 17 and 18).

The second opportunity to redeem Hamida is through marriage to Abbas al-Hulu, a gentle and kind young man—peaceful, tolerant, and content with his modest lot in life. He is a good Muslim who observes prayer and fasting and never misses the major Friday prayer at the Husayn mosque. Abbas al-Hulu is truly in love with Hamida and is friendly with her foster brother, Husayn Kirsha, even though he is an amoral, dissolute, unscrupulous, greedy person who indulges in wine, sex, and drugs. Husayn works for the British military authorities and traffics in goods stolen from the British army depot by his partner, Corporal Julian. He encourages al-Hulu to leave the alley, which he feels offers nothing but death, and find lucrative work with the British army.

But al-Hulu, though not averse to leaving the alley in which he has lived nearly a quarter of a century, cannot go without Hamida. One day he finds her walking with a group of girlfriends and asks her to follow him to the Azhar Street, where he begins to pour out his heart, declaring his love and his desire to marry her. Their dialogue is so natural, sweet, and unpretentious that we must feel a great sense of compassion toward this couple as they try to define their relationship. But in chapter 10, after they exchange greetings in a manner that suggests an extended conversation, Mahfouz inexplicably interrupts their dialogue to speculate at length on Hamida's emotions and attitude toward Abbas al-Hulu. She was undoubtedly expecting him, but does not know how to react. She neither loves nor hates him. She does not want to reject him harshly, because he is the only young man in the alley suitable for her, yet she realizes the great difference between his gentle modesty and her own boundless ambition, kindled by her instinctive desire for power and reflected in her pugnacity. If it were not for her belief that marriage is the solution to her problems, she would doubtless reject him out of hand. But she chooses to go along with him and fathom his innermost secrets, in the hope of escaping her perplexing difficulties. To satisfy her desire for a better life, he tells her, he will work for the British military authorities at Tall al-Kabir and then return to open a bigger and better barbershop. When Hamida shows contempt for living in the alley, he even agrees for her sake to leave and live wherever she chooses (86, 92, 95). Their discussion continues until Hamida and her adoptive mother agree that she will marry al-Hulu. Overcome with joy, he delegates Dr. Bushi to ask Hamida's hand in marriage. Then comes the celebration of the engagement, with Uncle Kamil preparing a luscious tray of sweets for the occasion. Hamida appears very happy and even brags to her friends that each of them would consider herself happy if she could find a comparable suitor. In fact, however, she is distressed because al-Hulu is leaving the alley but is consoled by the thought that he loves her and can provide her with a better life. She wishes him good luck and the blessing of al-Husayn. To show his sincere love, al-Hulu steals a kiss while they are climbing the back steps leading to the house. Hamida has never felt the warmth of love as at that moment in the arms of Abbas al-Hulu. She is exhilarated at the thought that their lives are bound together forever (111, 116).

Soon after al-Hulu leaves for Tall al-Kabir, the beauteous Hamida catches the eye of an effendi, Faraj Ibrahim, apparently a man of some means, who follows her to Kirsha's coffeehouse. His behavior seems normal as he continues to frequent the coffeehouse, occasionally flashing large sums of money. When he encounters Hamida during her daily stroll, she warns him not to chase after her, but he is resolute and insistent. He tells her not to be angry with him because he desires her; she is made to be possessed by men, and he is determined to possess her. He adds that she is special and does not belong in the alley. Hamida interprets his words to mean that he wants to marry her. She is attracted to the effendi, who lures her on by depicting a life of expensive clothes and other luxuries, like that of movie stars. In fact, however, he is a pimp who induces girls like her to become prostitutes to entertain the British and American troops. Angered, she leaves his apartment, declaring he is not a real man. He answers that a pimp is also a man, the agent of happiness in this world, and voices confidence that she will be back; after all, she is good-looking and was born to be a whore. Mahfouz seems to contradict himself, portraying Hamida as happy to have Abbas al-Hulu as a prospective husband and then making her forget him and succumb to the deceitful stratagem of a pimp. But this is what he has planned, and he justifies her sad end by having Kirsha's wife state that she is beautiful but not good (210, 212, 221, 229).

As Faraj Ibrahim predicted, Hamida returns to him. He gives her a new name, Titi, has her trained in dancing and music, and teaches her some garbled English phrases to allow her to communicate with English soldiers. She is not the only one to lose her human dignity; many others like her have already fallen into his hands, thanks to the war, which has altered the fabric of Egyptian society by inducing once-innocent people to act immorally. But Mahfouz, apparently unwilling to let the unfortunate Hamida speak for herself, keeps bombarding us with his own judgment on her conduct; for almost a third of chapter 31 he doggedly tries to show that she has chosen prostitution of her own free will and finally surrenders because of her material desires. Persuaded by Faraj Ibrahim, she concludes that to wallow in gold, she must first wallow in dirt; thus, she opens her heart willingly to the new life of luxury. Surprisingly, Mahfouz does not attribute her downfall to sexual aberration or dissolution but rather to her pride, her desire to control others, and her bellicose nature. Yet later in the same chapter he implies that it is human weakness that leads Hamida to succumb to the pimp. Abbas al-Hulu has been away for a long time, and she has had no communication from him, no indication that he will ever return. She thinks that Faraj Ibrahim, who is after all rich and available, loves her and intends to marry her. Too late, she realizes that this is not the case, and she becomes angry and uncertain about what to do when she sees that there is no escape from her predicament.

Not even the gentle, sincere, loving Abbas al-Hulu can save

Hamida. He returns to the alley with money and a necklace for her but is shocked to hear that she has gone off with a wicked man. After a long search he finally spots her entering a flower shop but cannot believe his eyes, since she has changed so much. Asked why she has left her home and mother to end up in such a miserable state, she answers, "Don't ask me anything, for I have nothing to say. This is the irrefutable *qada* (divine decree or predestination) of God" (287). Al-Hulu, not satisfied, rebukes her, but she tries to convince him that he has planned one thing while fate planned something else. (We shall return to the question of predestination and fate later.) Plainly he still loves her and wants her back, but she has passed the point of no return. She confesses that her actions were wrong and that she is a miserable creature, misguided by Satan. She cannot return to the alley, where everyone will look upon her as a whore; she alone must pay for her mistake (289, 292).

Enraged, al-Hulu determines to avenge his honor against Faraj Ibrahim; he discloses his intention to Husayn Kirsha, who argues that Hamida is the real criminal. But al-Hulu, having made up his mind, goes to the nightclub where she works. He is shocked to find her among a group of British soldiers, with her legs stretched out in the lap of one sitting opposite her while another, standing behind her, offers her a drink. He yells at her and she sits bolt upright, telling him to leave the bar. Infuriated by her words, al-Hulu picks up an empty glass and strikes her on the face, drawing blood. The soldiers strike back, kicking and beating him to death. We are left with the impression that no one will dare prosecute them, for they are the imperial masters of Egypt, beyond the reach of the law. It is sad and ironic that al-Hulu, who worked for the British in order to fulfill the desires of his life by marrying Hamida, loses not only his life dream but his life at their hands. Everyone in the alley feels sad at his death, including Hamida's mother; as soon as Hamida recovers from her wounds, however, her mother renews relations with her, regarding her as a precious source of material gain. The novel closes with Hamida as a common prostitute and al-Hulu dead in his effort to save her, but life in the alley goes on as usual, as if nothing significant has happened. There will be a new barber, and the pimp will one day find another girl to follow in Hamida's footsteps, unless the people of the alley do something to avert further calamity. In sum, her fall is but one instance of the social degradation and exploitation of women in Egyptian society. It is tantamount to spiritual suicide.

Let us make one final observation about Hamida. Does she mean, by saying that what has happened to her is "the irrefutable divine decree of God," that he has foreordained that she should become a whore? Exactly. Her answer touches upon the very complex concept of predestination as understood by Muslims in the Middle East. According to Islam, God has, since eternity began, decreed and predestined good and evil, and everything that was, is, or will be depends on his divine prescience and sovereign will and is fixed on the *preserved tablet* in heaven. The Prophet Muhammad is reported to have said, "God foreordained the destinies of men fifty thousand years before He created the heavens and the earth."[35] It is not surprising, then, that Hamida tells al-Hulu that her becoming a prostitute has been foreordained by God, whose judgment is final and irreversible.

While Hamida rebels against the alley and seeks to escape it, others leave it but return, and still others, content with life there, choose to remain. For better or worse, the alley becomes the focus of the characters' actions, and their experience determines their attitudes regarding the quality of life there. The rebellion of a few residents cannot destroy the alley and its tradition, nor can the introduction of modern gadgets and ideas alter its essential being. Meantime, its inhabitants carry on their lives as usual. Through them Mahfouz is able to portray the vagaries of the life of common people who are ensnared in the alley and cannot leave it unless they compromise their traditional values and way of life.

Beside Hamida stands her foster brother, Husayn Kirsha, who like her rebels against life in the alley, which he says harbors only death. His father, Kirsha, is a drug addict and a pederast, squandering his livelihood to support his aberrant conduct, which leads him into constant quarrels with his unpleasant spouse. Coming from such a background, Husayn Kirsha is unconcerned with moral issues; unable to endure the drab alley, he is determined to seek a different life elsewhere and enjoy some modern amenities—to be a gentleman, as the English say. Despite the entreaties of his mother and the violent opposition of his father, he leaves the alley, spitting at it and cursing it and its people. He thinks he can manage without his family's assistance but learns otherwise when he loses his job soon after marrying and is forced to return home, bringing not only his wife but her brother as well. The modern life Husayn sought outside has come to naught, and he finally takes refuge in the same alley he has cursed and detested.[36]

Perhaps the most morbid of all the characters is Zita, who lives (apparently happily) in squalor at the dingy outhouse near Husniyya's bakery. His profession is as evil as his character. He inflicts physical deformities on men in order to provide them with a reason to beg. Melancholic and sadistic, he enjoys causing others pain and wishes the world were full of beggars. He is utterly devoid of human feeling or values. He takes pleasure in peeping through the keyhole to see Husniyya beat her husband; in fact, he hates Jaada but lusts after his bovine wife. In his sadistic imagination, he pictures Jaada being cut to pieces by axes, Salim Alwan flattened by a steamroller, and Kirsha torn apart beneath train wheels, with his remains placed in a dirty rag and thrown to the dogs.[37] But what is Zita's function in this novel, and why does Mahfouz give him such a repugnant role? An isolated character who has lost touch with humanity and has no sympathy for others, he serves to personify the social conditions that reduce people to desperation, deprive them of human dignity, and force them to accept beggary. He becomes the vehicle for Mahfouz's vehement protest against the social abuses of the Egyptian lower class by the government, which he feels has been indifferent to their plight. When men feel the pangs of poverty and believe that their government and society do not care for them, they will resort to the meanest measures to make a living, and the easiest of them all is beggary. They are ready even to sacrifice their physical well-being to achieve their objectives. Zita's evil actions are a manifestation of his rebellion against society. Because he cannot change the attitude of government and society toward the poor, turning healthy men into maimed beggars is an easy way out. But it perpetuates rather than solves the problem of poverty. His desire to hurt other people apparently gives him a sense of being, an identity.

The social degradation of the lower middle class in Egypt is also personified by Zita's partner in crime, the quack Dr. Bushi, who makes his living by robbing graves, stealing gold dentures, then selling them to his unsuspecting patients. He has been left to his evil devices, without supervision or scrutiny from the government. Although they end up in jail, imprisoning them does not solve the social problem of beggary, nor does it mean that the government and society have taken any measures to mitigate the plight of poor people or improve their lot.[38] Among the victims of their fraud is Saniyya Afifi, probably the most docile and gullible of all the female characters. A woman of some means, she owns a three-apartment building in the alley, living in one apartment and renting the others to Umm Hamida and Bushi. Long ago, she married the owner of a perfume shop, but the marriage failed; now in her fifties, she is very lonely. Umm Hamida, a shrewd marriage broker who knows how to manipulate the emotions of this naïve woman, promises to find a suitable husband for her. Naturally, Saniyya Afifi welcomes the idea and agrees to let Umm Hamida live in the apartment rent free. Feeling a new sense of life and hoping that Umm Hamida will find her the right man, she begins to take more care of her physical appearance, and especially her decaying teeth. She visits Dr. Bushi, who advises her that she needs a gold denture, and gladly agrees. As it happens, Bushi recently made a gold denture for Abd al-Hamid al-Talibi, a flour merchant who died soon afterward. He and Zita go to the cemetery, open al-Talibi's grave, and steal his gold denture, but they are caught red-handed by the police. When Saniyya Afifi hears of their arrest, she throws away her denture, realizing that it was probably made from stolen materials. Yet her fortune is not all bad; the marriage broker, Umm Hamida, finds her a husband much younger than herself.[39]

Since Mahfouz aims to depict the nature of Egyptian society in his time, it is no surprise that he also treats political corruption and the futility of the parliamentary process. Politics is a shortcut to power and prestige but can also lead to ruin. Thus, when the war profiteer

Salim Alwan voices his ambition to become a member of the Egyptian parliament, one of his sons, an attorney, advises him to stay away from politics, which will eventually destroy their family and devour their business. He tells his father that he may find himself spending much more on his political party than on his own interests, and if he seeks a seat in the parliament, he will gamble a lot of money on a position he may not win: "Is not the parliament in our country like a person with heart trouble, threatened at any moment by an attack? Furthermore, what political party would you choose? If you choose a party other than the Wafd, you will weaken your position in business. If you choose the Wafd, you will not be able to trust a prime minister like Sidqi, who will turn your business into chaff winnowed by the wind" (71).

Mahfouz's attempt to show the futility and the abuse of the parliamentary process, which ended in the Egyptian revolution of 1952, dominates chapter 19. The people of the alley arise one morning to see a pavilion set up in a deserted lot in al-Sanadiqiyya, across the way. Uncle Kamil, the dull, obese sweets seller, obsessed with death and dying, assumes it is intended to honor someone recently deceased but is told that it is set up for the parliamentary election. He typifies those Egyptians who have no idea about politics and know little about politicians except their names. Although a picture of Mustafa al-Nahhas Pasha hangs in his shop, he considers its presence a matter of traditional deference rather than evidence of his support for the political ideas of al-Nahhas. And when some supporters of the candidate for parliament, Ibrahim Farhat, want to hang a campaign poster in his shop, he objects that it is a bad omen that will jeopardize his livelihood. Farhat is a consummate campaigner, adept not only at shaking hands and conversing with the people, but also at offering bribes. He is especially eager to win the support of Kirsha, the coffeehouse owner, but when he offers a bribe, Kirsha angrily rejects it because it is less than what Farhat has offered to those who sell broad beans. Kirsha represents another segment of Egyptian society—one that is motivated by opportunism rather than genuine political conviction. In his youth, he participated in the 1919 revolution. It is said that he set fire to the cigarette company building in al-Husayn's square and engaged in the bloody skirmishes between the revolutionists and the Jewish and Armenian minorities. Ever the opportunist, he is reported to have taken a bribe from the government's candidate in the 1925 election and then offered his vote to the Wafd party candidate. In 1936 he condemned political corruption and abandoned politics for the life of pleasure, but he is still popular among his customers and could win votes for Ibrahim Farhat. At an election rally attended by different kinds of people mostly out of curiosity, Farhat gives a speech repeating slogans and familiar political clichés, full of the usual promises any candidate would make. Some people like Uncle Kamil are so ignorant of the election process they do not know that they need a registration card before they can vote. The whole event turns into a big party with singing and dancing, and a female dancer appears half-naked to praise Farhat as the best candidate (157–58, 166). Measured by the standards of American political campaigns, the activity Mahfouz describes seems normal. But in the strictly conservative Egyptian society of the 1940s, it constitutes a moral abomination and a travesty of the political process.

Zuqaq al-Midaqq is overshadowed by pessimism, gloom, and misfortune. On finishing it, the discerning reader must ask why Mahfouz is so obsessed with portraying the dark side of life. Is it because of his natural tendency, his home life, or Egyptian society? Or perhaps he wants the reader to feel sorry for the characters. We know from the sketches of his early life that he was a loner who did not have a truly normal youth, despite his claim to the contrary. The tragic gloom that overwhelms most of his fictional characters reveals pessimism, if not outright despair. Indeed, there is hardly anything cheerful about the characters of this novel, nearly all of whom have been touched by some sort of calamity. The one slightly bright spot is Sayyid Ridwan al-Husayni, who represents the moral conscience of a society plagued with wickedness and sin. His deep faith and cheerful outlook on life reveal his belief in the omnipotence of God and the impotence of man.

Al-Husayni is an optimist who cherishes life and believes that it is worth living for its own sake. His optimism emanates from his religious convictions. Since God is good, all his creation is absolute goodness. Evil is only a disease, an impediment to the understanding of the goodness of God and his creation. Though others are skeptical about God and his benevolence toward mankind, al-Husayni maintains that those who suffer and blame God for their suffering are rebelling against his wisdom. Their attitude, he says, shows man's ignorance of the correlation between God's wisdom and man's suffering; the "afflicted in this life are the beloved of God, whom He has chosen to see whether they are worthy of His love and mercy" (57–58, 98, 103, 296). One is tempted to say that al-Husayni is echoing the words of Solomon in Proverbs 3:11–12, "My son, despise not the chastening of the Lord; neither be weary of His correction; for whom the Lord loveth He correcteth." He rejects the idea that man's suffering, including his own inability to have children, is the result of divine retribution and sees God as far from being vengeful. In the end, he maintains, suffering leads to perfection. Calamities can be conquered only by love, which is the best medicine. In the depth of misfortune dwells happiness, like gems in the heart of the ground. Therefore, says al-Husayni, "let us teach ourselves the wisdom of love" (57, 296).

Mahfouz also uses al-Husayni to deal with the complex question of the perfectibility or depravity of human nature, which has preoccupied religious and lay scholars for centuries, with one side holding that human nature is inherently good, and the other asserting that man is totally depraved. When al-Husayni visits the businessman Salim Alwan, recovering from his heart attack, he points out that Alwan could have died and his recovery is a miracle, adding that the lives of men are divine creations for which they should thank God. Alwan, who realizes that he has lost the joy of life and is especially depressed because he has lost Hamida forever, is not impressed by this philosophy. He believes that sickness is an evil that should afflict only the wicked, and angrily asks, "What have I done to deserve such punishment? . . . Don't you see that Kirsha is as healthy as a mule?" Al-Husayni answers that he knows Alwan is a good man, righteous, generous, and observant of his religious duties. But, he reminds him, God tested his servant Job, and he should not grieve or despair because God has likewise tested him. Still unimpressed, Alwan suggests that he has been afflicted because of his wealth and position in society (192–94).

By asking why he deserves such punishment he accentuates his goodness and moral rectitude in a subtle attempt to cloak his sin of self-righteousness with righteousness. Indeed, there is no popularly perceived sin of "goodness," only the sin of moral self-sufficiency. Salim Alwan takes the optimistic view that human nature is inherently good and that a good man should not be subject to sickness, which he deems an unjust punishment. Al-Husayni, unfortunately, by affirming that he is good, righteous, and faithful in observing religious duties, inflates Salim Alwan's egocentric pride and convinces him even more of his moral perfectibility, for which he believes he should be rewarded and not punished. Is he really good and righteous? Mahfouz has already presented Salim Alwan as a war profiteer who made his wealth on the black market and who uses bribery to advance himself. Morally, he is contemptible not only for coveting the voluptuous Hamida but also for giving high priority to his sexual performance. In short, he is simply lecherous (68–77). Thus, what Mahfouz presents through al-Husayni as his goodness and righteousness is at best sheer hypocrisy.

Moreover, Mahfouz should have realized that al-Husayni's comparing Alwan to the righteous Job of the Old Testament does not stand up. God does not punish Job for some evil that he has done but rather allows Satan to test his faith. Satan believes that Job is true to God only because God is good to him, and that if God stops being good to him, he will certainly blaspheme. But when Job is afflicted with calamities he neither blasphemes nor blames anyone for them. Salim Alwan is not tested by God for his faith, nor is Satan the source of his affliction. The story of Job reveals that God regards him as blameless, while there is nothing to indicate that Alwan is blameless. The fallacy of Salim Alwan's asking what he has done to deserve such punishment lies in the fact that he does not realize that God's knowledge, his intention, and providence are unlike those of man. Calamities should be considered not as acts of divine revenge but as tokens of God's eagerness to have man tie himself more steadfastly to his creator. Al-Husayni is correct only when he admonishes Salim Alwan not to despair and always to remember God, because "true happiness deserts us as much as we desert our faith" (194).

Sayyid Ridwan al-Husayni is unique among the alley's inhabitants, a true Muslim believer whose spiritual life is exemplary. Yet even when he decides to perform the solemn duty of pilgrimage to Mecca, he gives a long sermon on its spiritual benefits—in his house, rather than at the mosque—and then visits the coffeehouse to bid farewell to his friends, vowing to make his journey on their behalf. Like many of his neighbors, he suffers misfortunes, but he never loses faith in God's providence. While others leave the alley to seek money or pleasure and are lost, he leaves only for Mecca, to atone for his own sins and those of his fellow men. When he returns, they show their understanding and appreciation with a joyful celebration, covering the floor of the alley with sand, lighting candles, and hoisting banners in his honor (293, 298, 309, 313).

While misfortunes befall the inhabitants of the alley, life goes on as usual. They remain in their self-contained world with little or no concern for life outside it. They are captives of their inner souls and feel content with the little they have in their self-imposed isolation rather than with all the ephemeral gain the outside world can offer. In the final analysis, *Zuqaq al-Midaqq* is about individuals. The alley is the stage of their hopes and suffering, and life itself the reason for their joy or bitterness, whether or not they feel attached to it. We must keep this perspective in mind, for it would be easy to mistake the Midaqq alley for another insignificant and obscure locus in a city like Cairo, teeming with alleys.

Al-Sarab

Al-Sarab (The Mirage) appeared in 1948, although some writers maintain that Mahfouz finished it before *Zuqaq al-Midaqq* and then withheld it from publication. When the response to *Zuqaq al-Midaqq* was highly favorable, they say, Mahfouz felt sufficiently encouraged to have *al-Sarab* published.[40]

Whereas Mahfouz's other contemporary novels deal primarily with social aspects of life in Cairo, *al-Sarab* fixes on the Oedipus complex of its protagonist, Kamil Ruba Laz. Kamil's character is based on an actual person, Husayn Badr al-Din, an educated man who had wealth but squandered it on his drug habit, became homeless, and slept the nights at the Fishawi coffeehouse. He was a drug addict and was jailed for drug use. Because of his relationship with his mother, he developed a severe psychological problem; although friendly with many women, he could not develop sexual relationships with them. Mahfouz calls Badr al-Din aberrant and evil, adding that when the latter learned he had been used as a model in this novel, he insulted Mahfouz and wanted to shoot him. Because of its subject matter, some writers consider al-Sarab a purely psychological novel, standing apart from the sequence of social novels Mahfouz had designed.[41] Although the plot revolves around Kamil's psychological complexes, however, Mahfouz seems chiefly concerned with the behavior of different groups in Egyptian society. The novel reveals his strong interest in the social activity not only of Kamil's family, but of other characters who touch upon his life. It vividly shows the relationship between men and women in a conservative Muslim society, family ties, and the influence Islam as a religion and a way of life has even on a neurotic deviate like Kamil. Finally, it explicitly demonstrates the social chasm that separates the Turkish aristocracy from the common Egyptians. The similarity between Ahmad Akif in *Khan al-Khalili* and Kamil Ruba Laz in *al-Sarab* is striking. Both characters suffer psychological problems that render them unable to adjust to society or brave living outside their insulated world. Thus, some writers rightly consider *al-Sarab* a continuation of Mahfouz's contemporary social novels, but with a different technique and emphasis.[42]

In essence, the novel deals with psychological rather than social realism, concentrating on the personality and conduct of Kamil Ruba Laz. Our insight into his nature is strengthened because Mahfouz, using a technique he has not tried before, makes him the first-person narrator, leaving us with the impression that he intends to let his protagonist reveal his conduct without interference. But let us not forget that his intention is not to write a solely psychoanalytical novel or a study of the Oedipus complex; his main concern is to show another aspect of Egyptian society, from the viewpoint of a man who belongs to a Turko-Egyptian family and happens to suffer from an Oedipus complex. The setting of the novel is the city of Cairo, and the major events cover nearly thirty years—the age of the protagonist when he begins to narrate his life experiences.[43]

The Oedipal elements appear in explicit detail in the novel. At the outset of his narrative, Kamil surprisingly indicates he has been fully conscious of his feelings toward his mother since early childhood. He was so attached to her that their lives were inseparable. His open sexual curiosity was manifested when they bathed together. She would sit opposite him in the tub while he sprinkled her naked body with water and scraped the soapy foam from her body to rub it on his own. He slept in the same bed with her until he was twenty-five, and when his maternal grandfather rebuked him and told him to sleep in a separate bed, Kamil bought a new bed but placed it in the same room with his mother's. As a child, he never left his mother alone, even when she was working in the kitchen. He spent most of the day either clinging to her shoulders or nestling in her lap. Often he had strong yearning for the days when he nursed at his mother's breast. She was his whole life.[44]

There is no doubt of the erotic nature of Kamil's attachment to his mother. His narrative reveals the great role she played in stimulating his unnatural desire after her own unhappy marriage. She lived with her dissolute, irresponsible husband only briefly after having her first child, a daughter, Radiya. After almost seven years' separation, she reconciled with him for a week, during which she conceived their second child, a son, Midhat. Her third child, Kamil, was born in the house of his maternal grandfather, a retired army colonel. His father took custody of the first two children, and Kamil grew up knowing nothing about him except what he heard from his mother. In fact, he did not meet his father again until he was an adult, and then only briefly. Thus, Kamil spent his childhood with his mother and his grandfather and was prevented by his father from seeing his brother and sister. His mother, likewise forbidden to have contact with Radiya and Midhat, concentrated her love and attention on Kamil. She became possessive, fearing she might lose him to her husband, who could legally claim custody of him. Consequently, she spoiled him and did not punish his childish actions, even when they were destructive or dangerous. Perhaps because she had been deprived of her daughter, she dressed Kamil in girls' clothes and made him wear long hair (18–19). Her sad married life and lack of true conjugal and filial love may have motivated Kamil's mother to use him as a substitute for the emotions she had never experienced.

Kamil did not enjoy a normal childhood. Because his mother wanted him for herself alone, he had no playmates. When his aunt and her family came to visit one summer, Kamil was overjoyed to play with his cousins, much to his mother's chagrin. No sooner did they leave, however, than she reasserted her possessive attitude. It is not surprising that Kamil grew up timid, neurotic, and fearful. His mother filled his mind with morbid tales of genies, ghosts, thugs, and thieves until he began to believe he lived in a world possessed by demons. Anxiety became his natural state and contributed to his misery. He suffered from a variety of phobias. He feared animals, darkness, school, and appearing in public. Above all, he feared death—especially the death of his mother, which meant eternal separation from her. This fear was magnified one day when, as a student, he had to recite the following verse from the Quran: "And when the last shouts come on the day when man flees from brother, mother and father . . ." (20–21, 39). Yet despite his anxiety and immaturity, Kamil was aware that his mother was the source of his emotional problems. Grieving over her separation from his brother and sister, she had no consolation except Kamil, to whom she devoted her life. Kamil, recognizing his mother's attachment to him, laments, "I realized too late that her compassion was excessive and could become destructive" (18).

Indeed, her possessiveness destroyed him emotionally and impeded his intellectual development. She kept him out of the elementary school until he was seven, and even then she took him to school every day and waited to take him home. Kamil says he hated school and learned nothing there, not even how to write his own name. Extremely shy and timid, he became the object of ridicule by both teachers and classmates. Afraid to ask permission to go to the bathroom, he kept quiet and urinated in his pants. One time, instead of addressing the teacher as "Sir," he called him "Nina," that is,

"Mom." His grandfather's decision to transfer him to another school apparently did him little good. He managed to pass the tests but was still mocked by his teachers and schoolmates. Because he was a slow learner, he was called "the excellent imbecile." It is not surprising that he shunned all intellectual and athletic activities and became more introverted. He finished elementary school at seventeen and high school at twenty-five. His grandfather pushed him to enter the law school at the Egyptian University, but Kamil, too timid even to deliver a speech in front of his classmates, left before the end of the first semester. Later his grandfather used his connections to find Kamil a minor position in a depot at the Ministry of Defense, but when his coworkers discovered that he was neurotic, they began to exploit his weakness. They became his new enemies, as students and teachers had been his old enemies. He developed a persecution complex and came to the view that life was a barren desert, a mirage. In brief, he was unable to cope with real life (40, 62, 79, 97–98).

While Kamil had a strong love for his mother, his primary feeling toward his father was not jealousy but a powerful rage, due largely to his mother's instigation. Kamil grew up with his father absent and did not meet him until he was seventeen. Reportedly his father was thoroughly dissolute—a drunkard, a gambler, an irresponsible parent. But Kamil knew only what he had heard from his mother: that his father was the cause of her misery, the one who had shattered the family unity. Thus, his hatred of his father was the natural outgrowth of his mother's hatred, and he realized that in this predicament he was as much her victim as she was his father's victim (7, 11, 16, 112, 175). Indeed, she created in him a sense of guilt that demanded he share her misfortune. When she learned he was thinking of marriage, she tried everything in her power to dissuade him lest he repeat her unhappy situation. She urged him not to forget her experience or the fact that she sacrificed her married life for his happiness (108–9, 111–112). Kamil's mother forbade him to see his father, believing it was more honorable not to acknowledge such a man. When he was seventeen, however, her father insisted that Kamil should meet his father, and she agreed, reminding her son that his father was the cause of his tragedy and hers. When they finally met, Kamil's father questioned the purpose of this visit; the grandfather said simply that he thought they should know each other. The father craftily asked whether Kamil would like to stay with him permanently, knowing he could hardly agree to such a proposition. Kamil sensed that both he and his father harbored a deep-seated hatred toward each other. His father suggested that the real purpose of Kamil's visit was to seek support and funds for his education, but his grandfather insisted that it was to establish a compassionate relationship between father and son. Kamil's father called the old man mad and told him to either leave the boy or take him back. The grandfather, disgusted by this rude outburst, took the young man by the hand and left. As they left, Kamil began crying, but he was consoled by the thought that he was returning to his mother; he belonged to her, not his father (62–63, 71, 124).

Kamil's attitude toward his father cannot be viewed in a strictly Oedipal perspective, for there is no evidence that his attachment to his mother is accompanied by jealousy of his father. His effort to mend fences with his father was motivated by need and not a sense of filial affection, as is made clear by the fact that he did not contact his father again until he was thirty and needed money to marry and start a new life. But this visit was even more disappointing than the first, for his father told him that he had no money and many expenses (most related to drinking). His father mocked him, saying that marriage is a terrible disease that causes people to spend enormous amounts of money and advised him not to marry. After all, he said, a wife would dominate him and exhaust his money and energy, and if he died, she would immediately marry someone else. Unable to believe what he had heard, Kamil left, bidding his father a cool farewell. All the way home, he thought of his mother, asking God to bless her. When he arrived, he regained his composure and kissed her warmly on the forehead (139, 150).

Such open affection as Kamil physically displayed toward his mother is often an expression of psychological love. As we have already seen, there was an erotic attachment between Kamil and his mother that continued into his adult life, but whether he had an incestuous intention to seduce his mother is uncertain. His sexual drive is manifested by his yearning for that time in his childhood when he could devour the nipple of his mother's breast. This suggests that Kamil had a strong sexual desire for his mother but lacked the will to fulfill it. This sexual desire shaped his adult life and caused most of his problems, ranging from schizophrenia to abulia to emotional paralysis.

The novel is very clear on the matter of Kamil's first sexual encounter. His mother employed a homely young maid who, besides doing household chores, served as his playmate. She taught him the fundamentals of religion, beginning with the concepts of paradise and hell, thus adding more phobias to those already haunting his mind. In the meantime, whenever she found an opportunity to be alone with Kamil, she awakened his sexual desire. She was his first sex partner, and despite his innocence he found the experience quite pleasurable. His mother caught them in the act and expelled the maid. More significantly, she warned him of the divine punishment he would receive in this life and the hellfire in the life to come (25, 45).

This was the beginning of Kamil's sexual malaise. Made to feel guilty for his actions with the maid, he spent the rest of his life suffering from shame and self-abasement. He was torn between the enjoyment of sex and the notion that sex is evil. While he had no will to engage in sex with his mother, whom he idolized, at the age of fourteen he resorted to masturbation to relieve his inhibited sex drive. Greatly influenced by his childhood experience, he came to appreciate and enjoy ugly women. They aroused him sexually, while beautiful women did not. The dichotomy between beauty and homeliness, personified by his mother and the maid, dominated his thoughts. He had become schizophrenic yet was conscious of his emotional predicament and tried to find a solution for it. He seems to have lost confidence and self-esteem and considered life worthless. Drawing an analogy between people and trees, he reasoned since we prune trees to rid them of deformed branches, why can't we do the same to people? Why help worthless people to live and impose them on life or impose life on them by force? This, Kamil thought, is why such people live as outsiders who in their prime of life roam aimlessly, trampling innocent victims. This melancholic analogy reveals his morbid state of mind: going beyond natural selection and the survival of the fittest, he wants to eliminate by force all those people who like himself suffer from mental disturbances or psychological maladies. This idea demonstrates the intensity of his internal emotional conflict, which almost drove him to madness and suicide. In fact, he contemplated drowning himself in the Nile but changed his mind at the last moment because he did not want his death to add to his mother's misery. That evening he returned home, began to pray, and went to bed holding his mother's hand. He gave up entirely the idea of suicide and began to write his life story, as evidence of his determination to live (5, 7, 57–60).

Kamil continued to agonize over the conflict between his spiritual beliefs and his life of sin. Although he undoubtedly believed in God and the resurrection, he suffered a spiritual abulia, which indicates that his faith was not deep or dynamic. Kamil felt more concern about God's punishment in the afterlife than about obeying God in this life. One dialogue with his mother reveals how superficial his concept of God is. He says he believes in God and wants to know more about him but wishes that God would give his servants the believers (Muslims) the grace to see him and his glory. He asks his mother, "Where is God?" She answers, "Everywhere." "Is He in this room too?" he continues. "Yes, in this room," she replies, adding that he should ask God's forgiveness for asking such a question, meaning that he should simply surrender his will to God. Kamil says that he asked God's forgiveness, with the full knowledge that he was sinning while God was watching. He felt guilty and remorseful, but in the end his internal conflict, too strong for his will to overcome, caused him to experience a spiritual paralysis (7, 56–57, 107).

Kamil was unable to resolve this painful conflict because he had not experienced true altruistic love. Maternal love had become an abnormal obsession with him, and masturbation was destroying his self-image. But a bright spot appeared on the horizon of his desolate and dark life one day when he spotted a beautiful young woman, Rabab. He fell in love at first sight and determined to marry her, though he had not yet even spoken with her. Enraptured even by the prospect of seeing her, he was wild with dreams about love and a happy, settled married life as the solution to his problems. In fact, however, these fantasies aggravated his internal emotional conflict; the mere thought of loving Rabab established her in his mind as a rival to his mother. Indeed, when his mother learned of his intentions, she tried to dissuade him by making him feel guilty, suggesting that he wanted to marry in order to be rid of her. Since he had decided against suicide and religion offered no relief, Kamil sought solace and release for his emotions elsewhere. Frequenting a bar in al-Alfi Bey Street, he discovered that a few glasses of beer dispelled his fears and concluded that drinking was the key to finding the young woman of his dreams. He left the bar to see a prostitute but could not have sex with her and went home burdened with guilt. His mother told him that what he had done was evil and demanded repentance, but he did not alter his ways (110, 115, 126, 137–38, 163–64).

His grandfather's sudden death from a heart attack left him with financial responsibilities he was not prepared for, worsening his mental anguish. His grandfather left no money nor property, and his own meager salary was barely sufficient for a modest life-style. How could he take care of a wife or family? His mother warned him that if he married, his financial condition would become worse. He appealed unsuccessfully to his father for assistance, and for the first time the prospect of poverty frightened him. As an immediate solution, he and his mother moved to a humble, less expensive apartment (102, 132, 135, 139). Finally, after a long period of anguish, daydreams, and hesitancy, Kamil found the courage to visit Rabab's family and ask for her hand in marriage. Her father approved, and Kamil appeared overjoyed by his prospective marriage, although his mother began to make life more miserable for him.

Kamil's problems were far from over, however; in fact, they worsened within the first few nights after his wedding. He was unable to consummate the marriage. He went through the ritual of foreplay but failed to achieve physical union with Rabab. He felt totally impotent in her presence. He could feel his soul mingle with hers, but their bodies were apart. He wanted to tell her the truth about his attachment to his mother and his practice of masturbation but did not have the courage. He began to fear her body as much as he craved it, and whenever he saw her lying in bed naked, his sexual drive immediately vanished. He found no relief for his agonizing failure except crying. Although his mother was in fact the major cause of his complex, he unconsciously attempted to put the blame on his habit of masturbation. He asked himself whether his "decent and immaculate beloved wife" could engage in beastly lust as he did and concluded that she could not (chapters 40–43, especially 226, 238, 240). Here is the key to Kamil's sexual impotence with his wife. He saw in her the image of his chaste and immaculate mother, a redeemer who had sacrificed her life for him. To him, Rabab was a sacrosanct object, a holy temple. How could he consciously have sex with her and defile this holy temple? Whenever he went to bed with the woman he loved, he immediately identified her with his mother and saw her as an untouchable sacred symbol. As a result, he became sexually crippled.

Soon, however, he became involved with an older woman, Inayat, with whom he became virile and aggressive and enjoyed the thrill of sexual relations. Although she was not attractive, she was physically seductive. A widow in her forties, she had more sexual experience than the callow and innocent Rabab, and she knew how to please a man. Like the maid who first awakened Kamil's sexual desire in his childhood, Inayat unleashed his repressed sexual drive and catered to his primordial animal instinct without remorse or restraint. Thus, he surrendered his will to her and enjoyed the sensual physical contact he could not have with his wife. Kamil was conscious of the dichotomy between his pure love for Rabab and his lust for Inayat but seemed to enjoy life. Inayat was the only defense mechanism he had against his agonizing anxiety and weakness, his lack of self-confidence and the will to act. Most of all, she was a defense against the Oedipus complex that had tied him so long to his mother. It was time to regain his virility and self-confidence, and Inayat was the only woman who could restore to him what he had lost (312–13).

Once Kamil begins his sexual relationship with Inayat, he is no longer the abnormal person we met at the beginning of the novel. There is no evidence that he is timid or aberrant or that he continues to masturbate. He seems to suffer only from the contradiction of his dual roles; he is simultaneously a timid impotent husband and a virile lover. While he clearly enjoys his relationship with Inayat, he suspects Rabab of having sex with another man because he has failed to satisfy her sexually. This suspicion contradicts the notion that he is the timid, impotent man she married. He believes that Rabab misled him when she said that she had no interest in sex and thinks that by blaming her for his impotence, he can justify his own extramarital affair (356). Indeed, we learn, Kamil's wife has become pregnant by the young gynecologist Amin Rida, but when he performs an abortion to conceal the fact, she dies. Kamil is shocked by her death and again soon afterward by the death of his mother. He grieves for them both but appears in full control of his emotions (367). We hear nothing more about Kamil's complexes, anxieties, and neurotic life, for he has finally overcome his long-standing psychological problems.

The novel, however, is not merely about Kamil's Oedipus complex. It portrays in detail a Turko-Egyptian family and the social behavior of its members. Although Mahfouz dealt with the Turko-Egyptian upper middle class in his earlier novels, this is the first time he has concentrated on that segment of society. The protagonist, Kamil Ruba Laz, comes from a dysfunctional family whose utter disintegration is summed up by his grandfather: "God created this family as a miracle for mankind. Every family forms a cohesive unit except this one, which is a fragmentation of individuals"(74).

Ruba, Kamil's father, was an ignorant and dissolute man, alcoholic, devoid of fatherly love, indolent and irresponsible. He came from a rich Turko-Egyptian family and relied more on his family's wealth than on his own achievements. When he asked to marry Kamil's mother, her father was warned that he was a worthless person, unsuitable for his daughter. But the father, thinking Ruba's wealth would be enough to assure her happiness, gave his consent. The result was an unsuccessful marriage that left the family's unity totally shattered, with Radiya and Midhat living with their father and Kamil living in his grandfather's house with his mother. Anxious to receive his share of the inheritance, Kamil even tried to kill his father by poisoning his food, but his plan was discovered and foiled by the cook (13). Another time Kamil's grandfather saw Ruba, after leaving a bar dead drunk, being kicked and beaten by a gang of lower-class youths. When the old man managed to save him, he asked, "Did you see how these ruffians beat me, how they injured my dignity? I am Ruba, who comes from an ancient family" (15). Proud of his Turko-Egyptian heritage, he could not even believe that he had been assaulted by a gang of hoodlums for whom he had utter contempt, much like that of the aristocrats toward the Egyptian peasants in Mahfouz's earlier novels. The best that can be said about him is that he was egotistic and selfish. While his son Kamil was struggling with his fears and complexes, Ruba was obsessed with pride and his heritage. Lonely and forlorn throughout his life, he eventually dropped dead of a heart attack at a bar (171, 173).

The other members of Kamal's family likewise behaved in less than exemplary fashion. His grandfather, the retired army colonel Abd Allah Bey, spent more time at the gaming club than at home. One day, desperately short of money, he sold his carriage and horses and extorted money from his old cabman to settle his gambling losses (61). His sister Radiya, finding her opportunity for marriage blocked by her selfish and uncaring father, eloped with Sabir Amin, a minor government employee in the city of Banha, even though he came from a family socially beneath her own. Midhat ran away to marry his cousin without his father's consent, and neither of his parents attended his wedding.

In addition to revealing the broken unity of Kamil's family, *al-Sarab* presents a picture of Egyptian customs pertaining to male-female relations and courting, usually carried on within the confines of the family. It shows how parents exercised their traditional authority to dominate their children even after they were grown. It offers glimpses into the affluent life of the Turko-Egyptians, who were conscious of their high social status and had little respect for members of the Egyptian middle class. Thus, when Kamil's mother learned that her son intended to marry a teacher, she contemptuously told him that girls from decent families do not become teachers, adding that a woman teacher is usually homely, uninhibited, or lacking in femininity. Kamil disagreed and thought that her ideas were morbid (187–88). But the truth is that the wealthy classes in Egypt in the 1930s looked down on young women who took up professions. The prevailing attitude was that a woman should wait at home until a man came seeking her hand in marriage, and that it was disgraceful for her to work outside. Thus, Kamil's mother ruled out Rabab as a suitable wife for her son on the grounds that she did not have the proper social status.

Bidaya wa Nihaya

Bidaya wa Nihaya (The Beginning and the End, 1949) covers the period from November 1935, to the end of 1939, filling the gap between the events of *al-Qahira al-Jadida* and those of *Khan al-Khalili*. Whereas in his earlier novels Mahfouz sought to portray the interaction of the upper and lower middle classes in Cairo, in this novel he portrays the members of a lower-middle-class family, discussing their hopes and fears, their ambitions, and their brave struggle against the hardships caused by the death of the family's head and sole breadwinner.

The period Mahfouz chose as a setting for this novel was perhaps the gloomiest in the modern history of Egypt. British imperialists controlled the country's political, economic, and military institutions by manipulating a group of subservient politicians who indulged in rhetorical squabbles rather than useful action. The so-called political parties were generally headed by feudal lords who placed their own interest above that of the people. The lower middle class and the peasants, who constituted the bulk of the population, were at the mercy of the wealthy landholders and politicians. In one sense the peasants were better off than the lower middle class, which suffered from a stagnant economy and thus had no hope of bettering its life-style. For years the government employees had no salary increments or promotions but survived with moderate difficulty thanks to the relatively cheap prices of food and basic materials. There were, moreover, no social welfare programs to alleviate the financial burden of the lower middle class. The political situation was no better than the economic one. After years of political unrest and demonstrations against its authority, the

British government, which had signed several treaties with Egypt, began in the mid-1930s to reconsider its position in the Middle East. The result was a new treaty, signed in 1936, which Egyptian politicians called the treaty of honor and independence. But many people, suspecting that Great Britain intended simply to tie Egypt to its empire and legitimize its control of the nation, considered the new treaty of little avail. It is in this turbulent period of political uncertainty and economic hardship that the action of *Bidaya wa Nihaya* is set.

The novel opens with the death of Kamil Ali, a minor official at the Ministry of Education. His family, like those of many government employees, lived modestly on his monthly salary of seventeen Egyptian pounds; after his death they find it difficult to live on his five-pound pension. Beside his widow there are three sons, Hasan, Husayn, and Hasanayn, and a daughter, Nafisa. Hasan, the eldest, drops out of school to join a gang of drug dealers and live with a prostitute. Husayn and Hasanayn, still in high school, badly need financial support to continue their education. Eventually they manage to have careers, Husayn becoming a minor government employee at a secondary school in Tanta, and Hasanayn a cavalry officer in the Egyptian army (though his end is unhappy). Nafisa, a seamstress, becomes a prostitute and ends up drowning herself in the Nile. The mother tries with patience, fortitude, and sound management to keep the family together but fails. At the age of fifty she is a broken woman, totally crushed by her family responsibilities, the problems of her children, and the ever-present specter of poverty. She is a nervous and physical wreck, looking much older than her real age.[45]

Thus, Kamil Ali's death marks the beginning of the family's misfortunes and leads to its final destruction. As in his earlier novels, Mahfouz uses a plot structure based on the illness, incapacitation, death, or absence of a major figure in the family, generally the father, which confronts the family members with hardship and tests their moral strength. In *al-Qahira al-Jadida*, the anomalous conduct of Mahjub Abd al-Dayim is attributed partly to his father's illness; the problems of the family in *Khan al-Khalili* stem from the forced retirement of the father; one cause of Hamida's tragic end in

Zuqaq al-Midaqq is the fact that she is fatherless; and Kamil's psychological complexes in *al-Sarab* are caused partly by his father's desertion of the family.

The death of Kamil Ali coincides with the national demonstration staged by the Wafd Party after Samuel Hoare, British foreign secretary, rejected Egyptian demands for the restoration of the constitutions of 1923 and 1930, arguing that they did not fulfill the national aspirations of the Egyptians. Denouncing this declaration on the grounds that the British government's real intention was to place Egypt's resources and military facilities under its direct control, the Wafd called for anti-British demonstrations on November 13, the national Jihad day. Hasanayn, a student at the Tawfiqiyya High School, participates in the demonstrations. Shortly after, the school's principal summons him and his brother Husayn to inform them that their father has just died. Shocked by the sad news, they rush home to console their mother as the family faces an uncertain future.[46]

The three brothers' response to their father's sudden death reveals some aspects of their character. Hasan, the eldest at twenty-five, is pragmatic and believes that life is a matter of survival. He shows no interest in formal education, contending that school does not teach real life. To him, life is the only school. Hasan was a source of frustration for his father, who once called him a "street boy" and told him that since he had left school, he would have to fend for himself. His relationship with his father was based on self-interest rather than genuine filial love. Although his father spoiled him and thus was partly to blame for Hasan's waywardness, we are led to believe that if he had not died so suddenly, he would have given Hasan better parental guidance. Primarily concerned with his own security, Hasan shows less sadness at his father's death than his brothers because he is more experienced in life than they.[47] He has no religious faith, and the idea of death does not provoke his curiosity. He is too preoccupied with the present to think of eternity. Although he appears selfish, irresponsible, and rebellious, in the end it is he who helps his brothers attain their careers.

Husayn is gentle and idealistic, a true believer who unquestioningly accepts his father's death as an act of God's will. He asks God to have mercy on him and his father on that day when both of them shall stand in his presence. Strengthened by his faith, he refuses to blame God for the family's misfortunes, declaring, "If God is responsible for our father's death, yet He is not responsible for our meager livelihood."[48]

Hasanayn, the youngest son, whose faith is more hereditary than heartfelt, is led to question the nature of existence. The very idea of death baffles him, leading him to ask, "Is death the end? Will nothing remain of my father except his dust, beyond which there is nothing?" In this regard, he is not very different from his elder brother Hasan, except that Hasan accepts death as an unpleasant reality and does not bother to ask questions about it. Hasanayn, a materially ambitious young man who cherishes social prestige more than human values, laments the fact that his father is to be buried in a humble, obscure grave, rather than in a mausoleum signifying his family's lofty status (16).

His questions touch upon the fundamental issue of life and death, which has occupied the minds of philosophers since the beginning of civilization. They evoke the existential philosophy of Sartre's *Being and Nothingness*, though they appear to spring from sharp emotion rather than deep thought. To be sure, this is a novel, not a philosophical treatise on life and death, but Hasanayn's questions reveal his thoughts and attitudes, which eventually lead him and his sister Nafisa to disaster. If death is the end, he asks, then what is the meaning of life? Indeed, what is the meaning of the whole history of humanity, with all its tragedies and glories? Death is the ultimate tragedy, the inescapable fate that awaits the whole human race. Because he sees only this aspect of the nature of death, he is unable to make sense of his father's death. Lacking spiritual faith and an eschatological outlook, Hasanayn looks upon death merely as a biological event that touches men the same way it touches animals. To him, death is a burden, a problem, an unfathomable mystery that renders life meaningless. While Husayn recognizes man's finitude and sees death as a step to an everlasting life in the presence of God, Hasanayn views it as a vast, senseless void. This outlook leads him to make material gain and social prestige his priorities, which thus shapes his whole career.

Nafisa, Kamil Ali's only daughter, is the child most affected by his death. At twenty-three, she is considered a spinster in a country where most girls marry at sixteen. She has no formal education and is physically unattractive; worse still, she is slightly hunchbacked, which makes marriage unlikely. But she is a proficient seamstress who makes clothes for friends and relatives—not for profit, but out of friendship. (To make a living as a seamstress was considered undignified in Egypt in the 1930s. Moreover, by tradition her father was solely responsible for the family's livelihood; thus, she did not dare work while he was living lest she disgrace the family.) After his death, however, she realizes that she must assist in alleviating the family's need and begins charging customers for her work, albeit with obvious reluctance and a sense of shame (17, 23–24).

Kamil Ali's funeral reflects the family's social status. Apart from relatives and neighbors, most of those attending are, like the deceased, minor employees at the Ministry of Education. But there is an unexpected mourner, Ahmad Bey Yusri, who is rich and socially prominent because of his position as inspector at the Ministry of the Interior. His arrival in a sumptuous car, with an attendant who opens the door to help him out, is a striking symbol of his high social status. The prestige-conscious Hasanayn is especially pleased to see such a dignitary at his father's funeral. Many evenings Kamil had gone to Yusri's villa to entertain him by playing the *ud*; though they were friends, Yusri never considered Kamil Ali his equal. Nevertheless, Hasanayn takes his presence as a sign that Kamil Ali "was a great man, and like him his funeral was great too" (13–15, 17–18).

Mahfouz is not alone in portraying the predicament of the Egyptian lower middle class; other novelists have plowed the same field. What is unique about Mahfouz is his minute and faithful description of characters and situations so that they become highly believable. He sets the stage dexterously, revealing each family member's reaction to Kamil Ali's sudden death and its effect on the entire family. Their conversation makes it apparent that poverty is their major concern. Poverty, Mahfouz would have us believe, is the scourge of the lower bourgeoisie in a brutal capitalistic society where wealth is controlled by a handful of landowners and politicians; it threatens the cohesiveness and the moral fabric of the family. No sooner is Kamil Ali buried than the family members begin to discuss how they can manage without him. He left only a meager pension, and the money found in his wallet after his death is not even enough to pay for his funeral. His widow realizes they have no relative who can help in their hour of need, and there is no one outside the family to whom she is willing to explain their problem. She entrusts the family to God's care, saying that they have no one else, and he will not forget his created beings. Nafisa shows even more reliance on God's providence, declaring that he will take care of the family and that no one should die of hunger in this world. Comforted by the thought that many families have survived similar misfortunes, the mother urges her children to understand their situation and bear their loss with dignity and fortitude with God's help (18–19).

This total reliance (*tawakkul*) on the omnipotent will and providence of God brings into focus the concept of God in Islam. God is the almighty, the indisputable master who stands far above his creation, and no man dare challenge his authority. God is considered an almighty will, and as such he determines everything in this universe. Man, on the other hand, is a servant (*abd*), whose supreme duty is to obey and submit to the will of God. To challenge or question it is blasphemy, and if God wills, he can destroy mankind. Muslims believe that God is the supreme source of the livelihood of men, but this does not mean he will put food on every Muslim table. Rather, it means that God determines whether and how he wills men's livelihoods.

The pages of the Bible are likewise filled with exhortations to rely on God's providence, particularly in the Book of Psalms. But such reliance on God has often been misinterpreted to mean that God is ready to bear man's burden to do what man asks him to do, with little or no effort on man's part. Some Westerners see this absolute reliance on an omnipotent God as an abdication of responsibility. In reality, however, it reveals that Western man has put God aside and proclaimed himself the master of his own destiny; he feels no need for a supreme metaphysical power to help him secure his livelihood. In essence, to secularistic Western man, poverty is a failure of the economic and social system, and not an act of God associated with his will.

When Nafisa and her mother urge reliance on God, they are in fact affirming the traditional Middle Eastern belief that God has the power and the will to lead the family out of its predicament. Of course, not all the children agree with their mother or take her utter reliance on God seriously. The wayward Hasan, a school dropout who cannot hold a job, remains unconvinced. He tells his mother that if, as she says, God does not forget his created beings—and he is one of them—then the whole family should wait to see how God will remember them. After all, Hasan asks, why has God taken his father, and why should he exercise his will at the expense of this family? Convinced of his ability to find his own way, he tells his mother that life abounds with opportunities, although just now he depends on her for his needs. He considers himself an optimist and not greedy. All that he wants is food, shelter, a glass of brandy, some hashish, and a few women—nothing more. He believes that these demands are modest and within reach. If he can find a job, and he believes he will, then he can attain all his material desires, and he trusts that God will help him achieve his goals (22–23, 29, 35).

As Hasan leaves to make his way in the world, his two brothers candidly discuss their situation. Their talk indicates that Mahfouz is concerned not only with poverty as the cause of the Egyptian lower middle class's discontent, but also with the ability of religious faith to relieve that feeling. He strikes a balance between faith and skepticism, between hope and despair. They both realize the family is facing a difficult situation, but they disagree over their mother's response to it. Husayn, an optimist, believes God will help the family out of its predicament but adds that patience and fortitude are needed. Hasanayn, not convinced, asks why if, as his brother so deeply believes, God is the source of livelihood, the world has so many poor and so much misfortune. Husayn answers that his brother is mistaken in holding God responsible for their misfortune. He asserts that faith in God is conducive to hope, without which there is no point in living. Hasanayn suddenly shifts his position and blames the family's difficulties on fate, which Mahfouz has presented in earlier novels as an extraneous formidable force beyond the control of man (29, 35). But blaming fate and rebelling against it could not solve social problems, and because the Egyptian lower middle class was not a unified political force in the 1930s, its members—including Hasanayn, as we shall see shortly—sometimes sought to better their lot by resorting to unscrupulous means, which was tantamount to committing moral suicide.

Poverty, then, is Mahfouz's central theme; he balances the spiritual attitude of some family members toward their problems against the pragmatic resolve of Kamil Ali's widow. She shocks the children by moving the family to a cheaper apartment, tells Hasan to find a job and fend for himself, cuts off the allowances of her younger sons, and seeks ways to cut food costs. Nafisa, she says, should charge customers for her work and stop working free for friends and relatives. The very thought alarms the prestige-conscious Hasanayn, who declares angrily that his sister will never become a seamstress, nor will he be the brother of a seamstress. The more practical Hasan retorts that there is no shame but shame itself, while Husayn feels very sad about his sister's situation but leaves the whole matter to the will of God. Nafisa, feeling helpless, is convinced she must accept her future as a professional seamstress but feels a sense of shame (20–23, 37–38, 47, 51).

Mahfouz's presentation of poverty as the cause of the problems of the Egyptian lower middle class in the 1930s should be regarded with caution. Although their lot was not enviable, it was not unmanageable. According to the Egyptian writer Abd al-Muhsin Badr, the five-pound monthly pension Kamil Ali left was meager, yet many Egyptian families of that time lived on smaller incomes.[49] Thus, Kamil Ali's family was not so destitute as to be totally devastated by his death, as Mahfouz implies in presenting the condition of the lower middle class, to which he and his family belonged.

It is not just want per se that Mahfouz dramatizes in this novel but its impact on the moral fiber of the lower middle class. *Bidaya wa Nihaya* is about problems of individual morality aggravated by a corrupt, impotent, and indifferent political system. Mahfouz is a serious novelist interested in universal issues such as truth and falsehood, good and evil, belief and unbelief. He skillfully portrays them in operation as he slowly unfolds the actions of his characters. There are highly intense moments of moral conflict, especially between Hasan and his brothers or between the brothers and their sister, all intended to show what influences shape the moral consciousness of Egyptian society.

Hasan's name, which connotes excellence, misrepresents his real nature, although his actions reveal he is not completely devoid of human compassion. As we have seen earlier, he was spoiled as a child and had dropped out of school. He could not hold a job because he always quarreled with his employers. He rebels against any authority, spiritual or temporal, and contends the distinction between morality and immorality is a false measure devised by man. He maintains that the so-called moral, decent life most people live is only a veneer concealing their basest actions. He challenges his brother Hasanayn not to question his conduct but rather to contemplate his own immorality.[50]

Though he lacks professional training and moral guidance, Hasan believes that the world is waiting to be conquered. To him, the smartest man is the one who can make a living in the shortest time, regardless of the means. This twisted philosophy leads him downward to a life of crime. He becomes involved in gambling and robbery. He joins the musical band of a certain Ali Sabri as a singer—not because he loves music, but because being with the band allows him to enjoy wine, women, and drugs. Night life in Ali Sabri's coffeehouse is not all rosy, however, and Hasan finds himself one day in a brawl with Mahrous, an enormous black man. Later, at a brothel, he meets an attractive prostitute named Sana who has sufficient means to live in a nice apartment on Clot Bey Street, and he moves in with her. His life goes from bad to worse, and he is hunted by the police. We hear little more about Hasan until the novel's end, when we find him attacked by hoodlums, who fracture his skull and leave him for dead. Some friends find him and bring him to his family's apartment. Fearful of falling into the hands of the police, he refuses medical attention but eventually recovers and decides to try to flee the country, although Mahfouz leaves his fate unclear. Having taken a shortcut to better his lot in life, Hasan slides into the abyss of crime and is condemned to live without hope or future.

Despite his distorted sense of morality, Hasan possesses some redeeming traits, most notably compassion and responsibility toward his family. This wayward person, who makes his living through drug traffic, provides his family with some necessities, especially food. On one occasion he surprises them with a leg of lamb and a can of lard; the others, who expect nothing from one they consider worthless, are overjoyed. The ensuing dialogue reveals Hasan's sense of morality and his anger against the political system. He asks when the family last tasted meat. Husayn answers that like (the vegetarian poet-philosopher) Abu al-Ala al-Ma'arri, they have stopped eating meat. Hasan sarcastically asks whether Husayn knows why the government opens schools. It does so, he says, to make people like his brothers abhor meat, in order to have it all for itself.[51] He means that those in power deceive the people by pretending to serve their interest, while in reality they are robbing them of their livelihood and getting rich at their expense. Moreover, he says, schools teach nothing about real life, for he has learned more about the world through experience than his brothers, who despite their education cannot afford a luscious piece of meat.[52]

With the aid of Hasan's ill-gotten money, Husayn is able to secure a government position, and Hasanayn enrolls in the military academy and graduates as an officer. At one point, Hasan offers to let Husayn sell the gold bracelets of Sana, the prostitute he is living with, to cover his expenses until he receives his first pay. Furthermore, if it were not for Hasan's important connection with the inspector of education, Husayn could not have found a government position. In sum, if this family had adhered strictly to considerations of honor and morality, Husayn would never have become a government employee, nor Hasanayn an army officer. Perhaps Mahfouz intends to suggest that the morality of the Egyptian lower middle class differs little from the Western attitude summarized in the adage, You scratch my back, and I'll scratch yours. The whole family recognizes that Hasan's life is ignoble and his use of connections to obtain a desired end is opprobrious, yet Hasanayn praises his gangster brother as noble and benevolent, for morality is in the eye of the beholder.[53]

Although Husayn seems to possess a deeper sense of morality than his brothers, he does not shy away from selling Sana's bracelets to meet his expenses until he receives his first paycheck. Torn between need and honor, he reasons that he must avert poverty or follow the same path that has led his brother Hasan to destruction. Unlike Hasanayn, he considers using illicit money or the property of a prostitute a matter not of honor, but of self-defense and survival and believes he has done nothing improper. With his family in need, he thinks he must choose between its survival and the considerations of honor and repute that obsess his brother Hasanayn (304). Like Ahmad Akif in *Khan al-Khalili*, he puts the family's interest above his own, sacrificing his ambition to further his education and accepting a minor position at a secondary school in Tanta to help support the family until Hasanayn finishes school and Nafisa is married (177, 190, 203, 223). He even refuses to condemn Hasan's conduct, instead regarding his brother as his father's victim, just as his father was the victim of want (302). Moreover, despite other defects of character, Husayn takes love and marriage seriously, placing them above carnal pleasure. Thus when Hasanayn, after being temporarily infatuated with young Bahiyya, abandons her to marry a girl from the upper middle class, Husayn immediately marries her himself (329, 330, 340, 342).

Husayn represents the moderates among the Egyptian lower middle class who were aware of the social, economic, and political problems of Egypt, particularly poverty and its consequences. Although Hasanayn blames the British occupation for his family's problems, Husayn realizes that the Egyptians have striven unsuccessfully against poverty for thousands of years, and that changing the status quo requires great individual sacrifice. He regards his family as a microcosm of Egyptian society. Having become used to hunger like the rest of the people, they seem to be devouring each other. He is surprised that while the country destroys its sons mercilessly, some maintain that the Egyptians are a contented people. To Husayn, to be poor and contented is the ultimate misery, tantamount to death (199, 226). He marvels at the joy his family expresses because his gangster brother Hasan lavishes on them a leg of lamb, his seamstress sister Nafisa provides them with a dry morsel, and he himself forgoes his opportunity for higher education so that his rebellious, selfish brother Hasanayn can continue his schooling. "What kind of brutal life is this?" he asks. Although Husayn is well aware that the social and economic disparity in Egyptian society is perpetuated through hereditary rights, he is not despondent or vindictive, simply sad for himself and the millions of Egyptians like him. He objectifies his agony, seeing himself not merely as an unfortunate individual but as part of a "wronged nation." Resigned to the problems facing his family, he finds solace in the belief that misery and poverty affect countless other families as well. Thus, his family's predicament symbolizes that of all Egypt (184). But he can only accept the status quo, make the best of life, and wait until things get better.

Husayn reads constantly, seeking a solution to the problems of his family and country. He finds in Ramsay MacDonald's *Socialism: Critical and Constructive* a political philosophy that reinforces his humane, egalitarian outlook and his hopes for a better society that is ruled by the principles of equality and the just distribution of wealth but does not contradict his views on religion and morality. Yet the moderate socialism of MacDonald, deeply rooted in Fabianism (which Mahfouz learned under Salama Musa) is far different from the scientific socialism of Karl Marx. Although it does not contradict the Islamic principles he has held since childhood, it cannot fulfill his dream (302).

Husayn is somewhat passive, a mystic who endures the blows of life, totally resigned to his fate. He does not seek to overcome poverty pursuing a life of crime, as Hasan did, or fantasize about climbing the social ladder and joining the upper middle class, like Hasanayn. He accepts his lower-middle-class status and thus survives while his brothers and sister come to grief, but in the end he pays dearly for his choice. By abandoning his dreams and accepting his role as a minor government functionary, he accepts the premise that members of the lower middle class like himself are doomed to stay within the perimeter of their class or face destruction.

Hasanayn represents the segment of the lower middle class that is constantly striving to climb the social ladder, but the means he chooses to achieve this goal are as twisted as those of his brother Hasan. Measured by universally accepted human values, both brothers are found wanting. Hasanayn reminds us particularly of Mahjub Abd al-Dayim in *al-Qahira al-Jadida*. He is ambitious, impetuous, and dissatisfied with his lot in life and thus rebels against God, fate, and society. Especially self-conscious about his lack of social status and prestige, he experiences feelings of inferiority. He is untrue to himself, his friends, and his family. Totally selfish, he never hesitates to take advantage of his own family to further his ambition.

Hasanayn receives the news of his father's death with despair because it makes his life unbearable. He is concerned chiefly about the impending loss of money to pay for his pleasures, such as the movies, soccer, and boxing matches, and complains that God has deprived him of these pleasures by taking away his father (29, 32). He also worries about the kind of funeral his father will have and where he will be buried, considering a humble funeral as much a catastrophe as death itself. He is disturbed to see that most of the mourners are common working people and makes every effort not to let them accompany his father's body to the cemetery lest they see him buried in an obscure grave in what looks like a potter's field. His inflated ego blinds him to the fact that his father, who migrated from Dimyat to Cairo, was a minor government employee who could not afford (and did not need) a magnificent tomb. Thus, Hasanayn sees his father's departure from this world as a symbol of the shameful social decline of his family in a megalopolis like Cairo (13–14, 16, 24). When his mother suggests that Nafisa should charge customers for her work as a seamstress, Hasanayn protests angrily and proudly, although he and Husayn otherwise may have to leave school. Thus, this hypocritical and ungrateful young man has to swallow his pride until he graduates from the military academy. No sooner does he become an army officer, however, than he insists that she stop her work immediately, not because he cares about her welfare, but because it is unseemly for the sister of an army officer to be a lowly seamstress (184).

Hasanayn's ego and his concern about his family's image often cause him to lie. When he first returns to school after his father's death, his schoolmates offer him and Husayn their condolences. When one of them voices the hope that their father left an estate, Hasanayn answers quietly that he did. His lie outrages Husayn, who is not sure how they should behave now that their schoolmates think they are rich. He looks his brother in the eye as if to warn him, but Hasanayn ignores him and goes on exaggerating his late father's social position (32, 34).

Hasanayn is a pitifully unhappy character, so self-centered that he sees nothing in life as worthwhile unless it serves his own interest. It is no wonder that his concept of love is sordid and selfish. Hasanayn is obsessed by the sensual, drawn to the carnal and the vulgar. He thinks he is in love with Bahiyya, the fifteen-year-old daughter of Farid Effendi, the neighbor and friend of the family, though in fact he feels only physical attraction. From the moment he sees her, he begins to fantasize about the sort of male-female relations dramatized in Western movies, widely popular in the Middle East during the 1930s, when dating was almost unknown, and where sex outside of marriage could be sought only in brothels. The sex-starved Hasanayn, aroused at the sight of Bahiyya's bare legs as she leans forward, begins to imagine how beautiful it would be to see a woman taking off her clothes and laments that he is not free to indulge in sex. He even recalls that the Quran allows Muslims to marry four wives and as many slave girls as they can capture (4:3). But, he adds sadly, Egypt no longer respects Islam, meaning that most Egyptian Muslims do not take more than one wife or indulge freely in sex. He is totally entranced by his lustful fantasies, imagining Bahiyya naked before him, throwing herself at his feet and surrendering to his desires; but in reality he is just a poor young man who cannot afford the responsibilities of love and marriage. In his own mind, he is neither an opportunist nor a coward, just someone who wants to enjoy love, that is, sex. He senses that Bahiyya is available and looks to her for instant gratification rather than a long-term relationship (54, 56–57, 60–62). At one point he meets her on the rooftop and declares his love. He seeks only a hug and a kiss, but she fends him off and rebukes him for his improper behavior, whereupon Hasanayn, determined to get what he wants, declares himself engaged to Bahiyya, thinking that as her fiancé he has at least the right to kiss her (57, 84, 88–92, 105, 109).

Bahiyya epitomizes the conservative Egyptian young woman who adheres to the traditional moral standards, which forbid premarital love play or sex. She believes that relations between a man and a woman, even during the engagement, should remain pure, untainted by loose behavior; even kissing is something only immoral women do. But Hasanayn, impetuous and sexually hungry, finds her attitude more than he can understand or endure. Why can he not even enjoy an innocent kiss? The best we can make of his behavior is that like many young men during the 1930s, he is greatly influenced by the displays of affection in Western movies, which began to shatter the traditional strict sexual morality of Egyptian society. After all, he and Bahiyya are teenagers, not yet ready to marry, let alone to start a family. Although she is only fifteen, she shows remarkable restraint and maturity in checking Hasanayn's advances. She knows that her chances for marriage could be damaged if she gives in to him and the engagement later is broken off. Even later, when he graduates from high school and enters the military academy, she remains faithful to her moral tradition, which regards as taboo any physical contact, however innocent, outside marriage (151–54).

Hasanayn may truly love Bahiyya, but such a feeling is incompatible with his unyielding ambition to join the upper middle class. When he seeks to enter the military academy, he calls on his late father's friend Ahmad Bey Yusri, who is rich and influential enough to help him attain his objective. He lives in a sumptuous villa, with a car and a private chauffeur, and enjoys social prestige and amenities that are mere dreams to a lower-middle-class youth. Hasanayn wishes he could have such a life, filled with material pleasures and pomp. His ambition is further aroused when he sees Yusri's sixteen-year-old daughter bicycling on the garden walks. She is not as beautiful as Bahiyya, but her family's wealth and social position make her more attractive. Comparing her with his homely sister Nafisa, he is surprised that two females can be so different, and thinks to himself: "How wonderful to own a villa like this and mount this girl! It is not mere lust, but power and glory. A girl of prominent social status who will strip off her clothes and sleep in my arms with her eyelids half closed, as if every part of her warm body would cry out, 'Master!' This is the real life. If you mount it, you have in fact mounted a whole social class" (245).

At this point, Hasanayn realizes that Bahiyya cannot fulfill his life's dreams. This feeling is reinforced by the sarcastic remarks of his fellow cadets at the military academy, who consider Bahiyya good as a temporary plaything but not a suitable match for a future army officer (266–69). Convinced that she will be a social liability, he forsakes her, hoping to marry Yusri's daughter.

After his graduation, Hasanayn decides that he and the rest of the family must change their life-style to suit his new status. He convinces them to move to a sumptuous new apartment on Zaqaziq Street in Misr al-Jadida district. Everyone is stunned by the contrast—particularly Nafisa, who exclaims, "We have truly become a part of the upper class!" (316). He urges her to stop working as a seamstress, for he does not know that she has already slipped into a life of whoredom. He also calls on Yusri once more, to seek his assistance in arranging the transfer of his brother Husayn from Tanta to Cairo. Next, he seeks to convince Hasan to change his way of living. He has long regarded Hasan's sinful life as a serious problem for the family but now also sees it as a threat to his status. He challenges Hasan to choose a new, honorable, dignified life. How can he ever face people and rise to the upper class while his brother remains a hoodlum, living with a prostitute? Hasan responds by asking whether Hasanayn considers a life of poverty honorable, saying there is little honor in working for minimal wages. Moreover, he says, it was the money he made from drug trafficking that enabled Hasanayn to continue his studies at the military academy. Pointing to a photo of the prostitute he lives with, Hasan tells his brother that he is indebted to this dishonorable woman for the very uniform he is wearing. Indeed, if it were not for his dishonorable life, his family would have starved and their brother Husayn would not have found a government job. He counterchallenges Hasanayn, saying that if he wants him to mend his ways and live an honorable life, he should find another career and calling him a selfish, ambitious person who cares more about the star on his uniform than an honorable life (chapter 71).

Hasan and Hasanayn have one thing in common, a warped sense of morality. Hasan justifies his wicked life and the money he and Sana have made on the grounds that a life of poverty is more dishonorable. Hasanayn, in turn, seeks his brother's financial assistance when he needs it, without worrying about the source of his income. Only after he has become financially independent does he object to his brother's life-style; indeed, he is less concerned about Hasan's immorality than about his own reputation. Deep down, Hasanayn is hypocritical, opportunistic, and self-seeking. He is as wrong as his brother in attempting to excuse his sordid actions. Hasan is not far from the truth when he tells Hasanayn that they are morally alike and have the same blood running through their veins. The best solution is for both of them to forget what has happened and remain on good terms (294–95). Hasanayn accepts this solution, having managed to point out that Hasan's life-style is at odds with his own social ambition and perhaps thinking that their relation is little known outside the family circle.

Hasanayn's main concern now is to break off with Bahiyya and complete his rise to success by winning the hand of Ahmad Bey Yusri's daughter in marriage. Although Bahiyya is physically attractive, he can never accept her as his wife or her parents as his in-laws, for she lacks the proper education (chapter 78). Poor Bahiyya, who has behaved with complete propriety, keeping herself pure for Hasanayn alone, senses that he wants to get rid of her but can find no reason for his negative behavior. How can this decent but callow girl understand that Hasanayn wants a rich, educated wife from a higher social class? For this selfish reason, he finally breaks his engagement, despite the vehement objection of his mother. Soon afterward, however, his brother Husayn successfully seeks her hand in marriage. Apparently he has long loved Bahiyya but avoided competing with Hasanayn for her heart. Although Husayn is outraged by his brother's indecorous treatment of Bahiyya, his decision to marry her is not an act of pity but an expression of love and respect.

With Bahiyya out of the way, Hasanayn calls on Ahmad Bey Yusri to ask for his daughter's hand. But first he concocts the story that his family has inherited a substantial share of a religious bequest (*Waqf*) in order to impress her family with his newly acquired wealth. He does not realize, however, that there are serious obstacles to his success. He is shocked to hear from a fellow officer the rumors that his brother Hasan is a gangster and his sister Nafisa is a common prostitute, and that everyone knows he himself sought the hand of the daughter of the wealthy Ahmad Bey Yusri and was rejected. In utter disbelief, he goes immediately to Yusri's villa, where he confronts his daughter and asks her whether she knows of his marriage proposal. She says she does but adds that a man who asks a girl's hand in marriage should come from a decent family (349–50). Hasanayn is stunned. When he realizes that he has been rejected, his world of dreams comes tumbling down. He felt that the star on his military uniform was evidence of his new social status, but he was wrong. He is still the son of Kamil Ali, a minor government employee whom Yusri never treated as his equal. He scorns Bahiyya as unworthy of him but is rejected by the Yusri family on similar grounds. He thinks that the activities of his siblings have escaped notice but discovers to his consternation that the past is very much alive and he must deal with it.

The second tragic blow Hasanayn suffers is the downfall of his brother Hasan. Some rival gangsters attack him, fracture his skull, and leave him for dead; but friends find him and carry him to his family's house. Hasanayn, who has always considered Hasan a disgrace to the family, is more concerned about his own honor than his brother's being near death. He fears his brother's beating will cause a scandal and lead to his own social death but brings himself to summon a doctor. When Hasan regains consciousness, he apologizes to the family for the trouble he has caused them. Yet this apology cannot mitigate Hasanayn's feeling that his brother has done irreparable damage to his reputation. He will never be able to face himself, society, and the world. He asks his mother, "Why did you bring us into the world and commit such a crime?" (360). His words are not only disgraceful but tantamount to blasphemy. They reveal his spiritual emptiness and despair; he has committed moral suicide.

No sooner does Hasan recover and disappear forever than Hasanayn suffers yet another devastating blow. Nafisa is arrested in a brothel run by a Greek madam in the Sakakini district, and Hasanayn goes to the police station to identify her and take her home. On the way, she says that she has committed a crime and does not ask forgiveness. He turns and slaps her face, driving her to the ground. Nafisa says that she is concerned not about herself but about hurting him. He yells, "Whore! You have already hurt me badly!" She says she plans to kill herself, although this action appears intended not to save her soul and atone for her sins but rather to express her suffering and reproach Hasanayn. When she is vague about how she will take her life, he suggests that she drown herself in the Nile, and she agrees. Although he is pleased with her decision, he feels a certain loss of dignity, for according to Middle Eastern tradition, he should kill her himself rather than suggest the means of suicide. When he asks Nafisa why she has done such a terrible thing, she answers that it was the command and will of God; he retorts that it was rather the command and will of Satan (370–71).

But why should Hasanayn even think of having his sister kill herself, and what gives him the right to do so? In the Western world, few people regard premarital sex as objectionable, let alone dishonorable; the new age that has liberated women has also liberated sex. In the Middle East, however, a woman's honor is revered, and indulgence in premarital or extramarital sex may cost her more than her marriage. A Middle Eastern man has the right to kill any female member of his family if she has engaged in illicit sex. His punishment will be very light; in most cases, he will be acquitted and released because he has washed away his dishonor. This is an exclusively male right in a male-oriented society, however; a woman cannot avenge her honor if she finds her husband with another woman.[54] Thus, it is not surprising that Hasanayn, believing that his sister has dishonored him and the family, boldly declares that death is the best end for her. Too cowardly to kill her himself, he calls a taxicab and takes her to the Zamalik bridge.

Cold-bloodedly, he asks whether she is ready to jump, and she answers that she is. As Nafisa prepares to die, she tells him not to remember the hurt she has done him. He responds hypocritically, "May God have mercy on all of us."[55] These words, however, are commonly used by people throughout the Middle East and should not be taken to mean that Hasanayn truly believes in God or his mercy. Indeed, although the Quran punishes adultery by flogging (24:2), it does not impose this penalty on women alone and let men go free. Thus, Hasanayn embodies the hypocritical and distorted view of sexual morality held by many Middle Eastern men, who absolve themselves of the same acts for which they may even kill their women.

Hasanayn, who has lived in utter delusion and self-deception, cannot realize the enormity of the crime he has committed against his sister. Without shame, he lies to the police officer, saying he did not see her drown. When he sees her body being pulled from the river, he feels no remorse, but rather a deep sense of relief. Satisfied that he has done what is best for her, he thinks not about how much she has sacrificed for him but about how he will face the world. He is mentally exhausted but not penitent, realizing that Nafisa's downfall is a fatal blow to his social ambitions. At first he blames poverty and misery for his sister's death. Later he begins to question what right he had to inflict such punishment on her, wondering whether he pushed her to suicide to avenge the family's honor. Eventually, he castigates himself for setting himself up as her judge, while admitting that he has acted criminally. Although he ultimately accepts his guilt, he seems to blame his crime on human nature. He recognizes that he has destroyed himself and others, and that there is no escape from his predicament. Driven by despair, Hasanayn, like his sister, ends his life by plunging into the Nile. His suicide is an expression of the illusiveness and futility of his existence, and of his alienation from society.[56]

There is a tense conflict in Hasanayn's soul between his makeshift world of dreams and the brutal world of reality. The past scares him because he realizes it is as much a living reality as the present. He thinks his wild dreams and ambitions will assure him a happy and prosperous life and cannot understand why he suffers. He tries too late to forget the past and realizes that his own suffering and that of his family transcend the death of his father. Recognizing that the causes of human misery lie not only in material needs but in human nature, he says philosophically, "There is an essential fault in our nature which I cannot fathom."[57] His words raise the controversial question of whether human nature is inherently good or bad. Perhaps expressing the view of Mahfouz himself, Hasanayn asserts the depravity of human nature, although he cannot understand its cause. In doing so, he expresses a concept that is biblical rather than Quranic. Like the Bible, the Quran mentions that Adam and Eve ate of the forbidden fruit, but it does not explain whether their sin permeated the entire human race, nor does it state that human suffering, misery, and death were the fruits of this original sin.

Despite having caused his sister's death, Hasanayn remains to the end self-seeking and self-righteous. He laments his failure to achieve his social goals, particularly his rejection by the Yusri family as a worthy son-in-law, for which he blames both Hasan and Nafisa. His greatest fault is that he is myopic about himself, his family, and society. Unable to recognize that his problems are intertwined with those of his family, he refuses to shoulder his share of their common burden, and does nothing to preserve the family's cohesiveness or contribute to its well-being. He sees the others only as a convenient means to improve his own social position. Unlike his brother Husayn, who accepts the family's social status and ends up safe, Hasanayn finally drives himself and his sister to perdition.

But why should Nafisa suffer such a tragic end? Mahfouz treats her more harshly than he did Hamida in *Zuqaq al-Midaqq*. While one can argue that Hamida's fall results from her lack of a solid family life, Nafisa's case is different. She comes from a good lower-middle-class family with loving parents, although they live modestly on her father's meager income. Having neither beauty nor wealth, she is especially distraught by the sudden loss of her father. While her mother tries desperately to sustain the family, Nafisa feels an agonizing sense of loneliness and laments that she is as dead as her father, who lies in his grave in Bab al-Nasr Cemetery, while she is buried in her desolate apartment at Shubra.[58] Like other girls of her age and class, she hopes for love and marriage, although she knows her prospects are slim. At the same time, she is sensitive to her family's predicament; while she realizes that being a seamstress is socially degrading, she continues to help the family until Hasanayn forces her to stop working in order to protect his reputation. As Sulayman al-Shatti has suggested, it is her lowly occupation rather than her physical appearance that symbolizes the position of the lower middle class in Egyptian society.[59]

To Nafisa's poverty, unattractiveness, and lowly profession Mahfouz adds another factor, her feminine instinct, to account for her fall into prostitution. Apparently realizing that these disadvantages alone cannot justify the deplorable end he has planned for her, he attributes to her (unlike Hamida in *Zuqaq al-Midaqq*) a powerful sex drive, declaring that she must find a man to quench her thirst or die. She is particularly saddened by making bridal dresses. As she fits a prospective bride, running her fingers over the smooth material, she imagines herself as the bride. But soon she returns to reality, thinking that if her father had not died, she would not have to go through this agony. She feels a burning need for love.[60]

Her one faint prospect for marriage is Jabir, the rather timid and not particularly attractive son of the grocer Salman. When he tells Nafisa that he is in love with her and wants to marry her, her despair turns to hope. Although she realizes that he is not a perfect match, she convinces herself that she is madly in love with him. Temporarily blinded by passion, she surrenders her body to him, confident that marriage is in their future. Sadly, she is wrong. Although Jabir apparently loves her, he is totally controlled by his authoritarian father, who has planned his marriage to the daughter of another grocer. Nafisa feels deceived, but she is powerless. Her future is bleak, and her very life will be in danger if her family discovers their illicit sexual relationship. Worse yet, ironically she is asked to make a bridal dress for Jabir's fiancée. Unaware of her identity, Nafisa chides the bride-to-be for marrying a mere grocer's son, whereupon Jabir's future wife insults her and asks her to leave. Intending to go home and lick her wounds, she falls instead into the clutches of a garage owner, Muhammad al-Full, who sees her walking aimlessly, drives her to an isolated spot, has sex with her, and then pays her.[61]

Thereafter, she prostitutes herself to earn additional money to support her family, and her secret life is not discovered until Hasanayn is told of her arrest. Nafisa's downfall is inevitable. She has no hope of redemption. Like Hamida in *Zuqaq al-Midaqq*, she is destined for prostitution, although there has been nothing in her life to justify this end. Her allegedly uncontrollable sexual drive appears to be a tenuous pretext intended by Mahfouz to justify her becoming a whore. To all intents and purposes, she is a responsible, family-oriented young woman, the victim of circumstances beyond her control. Nafisa's case represents the forceful conflict of perceived values in Egyptian society—or indeed, any society. Most people equate human worth with such material considerations as money and social prestige. Given her other problems, Nafisa has little chance to marry because she comes from a poor family. If she were wealthy, however, she would most likely find a husband regardless of her physical appearance or her morals.[62]

The novel's title, *Bidaya wa Nihaya* (The Beginning and the End) is wholly appropriate, for it opens with the death of Kamil Ali and ends with the deaths of Nafisa and Hasanayn, as well as Hasan's disappearance. Kamil Ali's widow survives but suffers tremendously from the responsibility of trying to keep the family together. The only one who escapes a tragic end is Husayn, a level-headed young man who accepts his lower-middle-class status and makes the best of his situation. Like his mother, he is patient and devoted to the family. During his stay in Tanta, he gives up the chance to marry his superior's daughter, putting the family's interests above his own, and later he marries a girl from his own social class. Yet even he ends up losing, because he accepts his fate and makes no effort to improve his condition.[63] The gap between the lower and upper middle classes remains unbridgeable. There is no chance for Kamil Ali's family to achieve the social level of Ahmad Bey Yusri, either by moving to more fashionable quarters or by gaining professional status or material possessions. One cannot help noticing that Hasan, Hasanayn, and Nafisa all seek through dishonorable actions to improve their lot, and all fail and ultimately meet disaster.

The influence of naturalism is conspicuous in the novel. Mahfouz seems to emphasize heredity and physical drive in determining the characters' destiny. Although the father is depicted as tall and handsome, the name Kamil (meaning perfect) does not suit his character. He abdicates his responsibility to maintain discipline in the family. While he ruins Hasan by pampering him, the mother stops him from doing the same to the other children. Selfishly, Kamil Ali neglects his family to keep up his subservient relationship with Ahmad Bey Yusri, hoping to climb the social ladder. It should not surprise us, then, that with their father as a role model, Hasan and Hasanayn ultimately fail.

The three sons have inherited their father's good looks, yet they differ in appearance. The eldest son, Hasan, is as tall as Kamil Ali; Husayn is shorter, while Hasanayn is taller. Although Hasan strongly resembles his brothers, he is distinguished by the sharp look in his eyes which betrays audacity and recklessness, as well as his thick, slicked-back hair and his manner of dress, which indicate his selfishness and ignoble character. Like his mother, Husayn is short and thin, with an oval face, short and thick nose, round chin, and sparkling eyes. He also shares her most commendable characteristics—fortitude, wisdom, devotion, and belief in God—which finally save him from the tragic end suffered by his brothers.[64] Hasanayn is presented as taller than his father to symbolize his social ambitions. But their sister Nafisa, who is as tall as Hasanayn, is unattractive and slightly hunchbacked. Mahfouz's comment that it is unfortunate that Nafisa is homely like her mother, while her brothers were handsome like their father, may give the impression that he is sympathetic toward her.[65] In fact, however, he robs her of physical beauty in order to drive her to despair, and finally to prostitution. Mahfouz's emphasis on the impact of hereditary traits on his characters' lives indicates that he was influenced by the literary doctrine of naturalism, as exemplified by the French novelist Emile Zola.

Mahfouz's objective is to show the predicament of the Egyptian lower middle class, which he would have us believe lacks the economic and political power to change Egyptian society chiefly because it lacks guidance and unity of purpose. Even the Wafd party, thought to be the people's party, is effete. While the rich swallow the poor in a ruthless capitalistic society, Mahfouz is looking for an ideology that will redeem the lower middle class. Thus, as in other novels, he embraces socialism as a solution to the poverty and social injustice suffered by the lower middle class.

Indeed, after reading *Bidaya wa Nihaya,* one feels emotionally exhausted and dejected. The characters, who reflect Mahfouz's bleak outlook on life, are manipulated toward their inevitable tragic end. The discerning reader can predict the novel's outcome after the first few chapters, which establish Kamil Ali's death as the major cause of the family's problems. The Egyptian writer Fatima Musa attempts to justify Mahfouz's pessimism on the grounds that he is a realist, not a romantic novelist who plans a happy ending for his characters. While many dreamers would like to portray the gardener's son who marries a beautiful princess and inherits her estate, she says, Naguib Mahfouz is a realistic novelist who would not distort his vision by imagining a bright future for lower-middle-class characters like Hasanayn and Nafisa.[66] The Reverend Jacques Jomier attributes the gloom that characterizes Mahfouz's early novels to the fact that when they were written, Egypt, suffering from foreign occupation and tyranny, was plagued by rebellion and social unrest, as well as epidemic diseases that affected almost everybody.[67]

Four

Thulathiyya

THE *Thulathiyya* (Trilogy), published in 1956–57, is the crowning glory of Mahfouz's literary career, undoubtedly his most important work and one of his personal favorites. Our knowledge of the circumstances under which he wrote and published it comes primarily from his own words, in conversations with other writers and reporters.[1]

Mahfouz states that while he was writing his earlier novels, he read many books dealing with the novel as a literary genre. One of them, which he does not identify, treated something called the generations novel. He wanted to write such a novel but hesitated because doing so required a great deal of time and experience. He continued to read major Western novels dealing with several generations, including Galsworthy's *The Forsyte Saga*, Tolstoy's *War and Peace*, and Thomas Mann's *Buddenbrooks*. But only after reading Taha Husayn's *Shajarat al-Bu's* (Tree of Misery, 1944), which he found too short to suit the purposes of a generations novel, did he decide to write one himself.[2]

The trilogy took Mahfouz four years; hampered by sensitive eyes, he wrote only from October to April each year, finishing it in 1952. Fortunately, he was in the prime of life and had great patience and fortitude. He had planned the careers of all the characters—many based on people he knew—down to the most minute detail in order to keep track of their actions. He became preoccupied with them, even while he was working at the Ministry of Awqaf (religious bequests) or writing screenplays. After finishing his novel, Mahfouz titled it *Bayn al-Qasrayn* (Between Two Palaces). Taha Husayn, whom he asked to review it, responded with an article in *al-Ahram* hailing the appearance of a great novelist, a genuine practitioner of modern Arabic fiction.[3]

Filled with pride, Mahfouz took his sole handwritten copy to his publisher, Said Jawdat al-Sahhar, who looked at the manuscript, over a thousand foolscap pages long, and asked with alarm, "What sort of calamity is this?" Shocked to hear al-Sahhar object to the length of his novel, he returned home depressed. He could not sleep that night and felt he was having a nervous breakdown. "After all this gigantic effort," says Mahfouz, "I could not publish my greatest and most valuable work."[4]

One day shortly afterward, Mahfouz was at Nadi al-Qissa (the Story Club), talking about the difficulty of publishing his newest work. The novelist Yusuf al-Siba'i, who was present, asked for a copy, and a few days later Mahfouz took the manuscript to him. Had this copy perchance been lost, he says, the *Thulathiyya* would have been lost forever.[5] In mid-1952, al-Siba'i told him he wanted to serialize it in his new magazine, *al-Risala al-Jadida*. Mahfouz consented, and his work appeared under the title *Bayn al-Qasrayn*. On seeing its success, al-Sahhar expressed his desire to publish it in book form but suggested that Mahfouz divide it into three parts with separate titles.[6] The first part was published in 1956, and the other two the following year. It was soon acclaimed in Egypt as a great literary achievement, earning Mahfouz the State Prize for Literature in 1957.[7]

The trilogy is the saga of three generations of a lower middle-class family in Cairo, stretching from 1917 to 1944. *Bayn al-Qasrayn* covers the period from 1917 to the outbreak of the Egyptian nationalist revolution led by Sa'd Zaghlul against the British authorities in 1919. *Qasr al-Shawq* begins with the British negotiations with Zaghlul's *wafd* (delegation) to London in 1924 and ends with his death in 1927. The final volume, *al-Sukkariyya*, begins with the ardent nationalist Mustafa al-Nahhas addressing a 1935 Wafd party ιference and ends with the 1944 mass arrest of members of a ιigious activist group, the Muslim Brotherhood. *Thulathiyya* offers a broad view of social, political, and cultural events combined with an in-depth analysis of intrinsic human values.[8] It is focused on the character of the Egyptian lower middle class caught in the clash between traditional Islamic ideals and Western doctrines like socialism over the means to solve the country's problems. In this sense it accentuates and expands upon various themes Mahfouz already had tackled in his contemporary novels.

Bayn al-Qasrayn

Bayn al-Qasrayn (literally, Between Two Palaces, although the book has been translated into English under the title *Palace Walk*), takes its name from a street in Cairo, not far from the shrine of al-Husayn.[9] There Sayyid Ahmad Abd al-Jawad lives with his family, including his wife Amina, three sons, Yasin, Fahmi, and Kamal, and two daughters, Khadija and Aisha. Yasin, his child by a prior marriage, has been with his father since the age of nine; his mother has since been married several times. (Although the term *Sayyid* is a title meaning "sir," Mahfouz uses it throughout the trilogy as if it were a proper name. Following Mahfouz, we shall call him *the Sayyid* or *Sayyid Ahmad*, depending on the context.) The household also includes the longtime maid Umm Hanafi, who joined the family's service after she was divorced.

Mahfouz depicts the family's unremarkable daily life in minute detail. Amina rises every night at midnight to await her husband's return from his usual evening parties and attends to him before he goes to bed. She will catch only a few hours of sleep before rising to perform the ablution, pray, and prepare breakfast for the family, while Umm Hanafi is busy kneading dough in the bakery to make fresh bread. Her husband also spreads his prayer rug and, with apparent devotion, asks God to bless him, his children, and his business.[10]

Mahfouz painstakingly describes the physical and spiritual traits of the Sayyid and his family, which are reflected in their actions. Amina is forty years old, of medium height and slender build.

Wisps of chestnut-colored hair escape her brown kerchief. Her tan, longish face is graced with small but beautiful eyes, a fine, flared nose, and a round chin, which make her attractive despite a pitch-black mole on one cheek. The Sayyid is in his mid-forties, tall and broad shouldered, with a bit of a potbelly. His black hair and plump face, with big blue eyes, a large nose, a wide mouth with full lips, and a dark, bushy mustache, indicate a strong, daunting personality. The very picture of virility, he suffers from an old callus which he occasionally scrapes with a razor. His eldest son, Yasin, twenty-one, is larger than he and has inherited his nature. The eighteen-year-old second son, Fahmi, resembles his father, but is taller and thinner. Kamal, only ten, is the favored child of the family. The two daughters, twenty-year-old Khadija and sixteen-year-old Aisha, are a study in contrasts. Khadija, dark-skinned and homely, has inherited her father's temperament, while Aisha is a beautiful blonde. Perhaps because she is self-conscious about her appearance, Khadija seems peevish, quarrelsome, and jealous of her mild-mannered sister.[11]

As was the custom in Egypt and throughout the Middle East, breakfast is served on a big tray, with the men sitting around it. Each in turn breaks off a slice of bread, using his fingers rather than a utensil. The women, whose duty is to prepare meals and serve the men, sit down to eat only after they have left the house.[12] Their eating separately demonstrates the then dominant position of males in Middle Eastern society, transcending religious and ethnic differences. (The Quran, 4:34, however, makes it clear that men are the custodians and caretakers of women because God has made them superior, able to support women from their own means. Thus, good and righteous women are devotedly obedient to their husbands.) It is no surprise that until recently women in the Middle East did not mingle with men, let alone join them at meals. Regardless of their religion, women never worshipped together with men; today, however, Christian women share pews with men in church, while Muslim women still worship in a separate part of the mosque, unseen by men. Men and women no longer eat separately except in some remote places where old ways die hard. Today, in Egypt and elsewhere, women have equaled if not surpassed men in almost every aspect of life. But at the time in which the novel is set, women like Amina and her daughters received no formal education and, by long-standing social tradition, were utterly subservient to men.

After breakfast the men leave—the Sayyid to his grocery on Nahhasin Street, Yasin to the Nahhasin Elementary School, where he is a a clerk, Fahmi to his studies at the law school, and Kamal to the Khalil Agha Elementary School near the shrine of al-Husayn. The women remain behind. Ostensibly, the daughters stay home because there are not enough schools for women, but in fact the Sayyid, like most members of the middle class, takes a dim view of educating women. His position that a woman should leave her father's home only to be married or buried appears based on a saying attributed to the Prophet of Islam: "A woman has two kinds of protection: marriage or the grave."[13] Although women had to perform the daily chores, the home was their exclusive kingdom. Indeed, Amina regards the kitchen and the bakery as her personal domain, where no one, not even her domineering husband, can dare challenge her authority.

The Sayyid's two daughters naturally hope for marriage, but they dare not leave the house against their father's will. (Dating was then unknown in Egypt, and an unmarried young woman could only wait for a suitor to knock at her door.) The *mashrabiyya*, an oriel with latticework enclosure, is their only outlet to the outside world.[14] Through it Aisha eyes a young policeman who passes by every day, hoping to catch a glance at her. Able to show only her face, with the passage of time she gains courage to open the window and expose her full stature, as if to demonstrate her love for this stranger. Khadija, who realizes that her chances for marriage are limited because she is not so attractive as her sister, constantly picks on Aisha, but like her keeps dreaming of a prospective husband.

As in his earlier works, Mahfouz presents his major characters as fully developed, not allowing them to reveal themselves through their actions as the narrative progresses. He discusses Sayyid Ahmad's character, behavior, and feelings thoroughly in the first twenty-five pages. But he introduces secondary characters by name only, arousing the reader's curiosity about their future roles in the action. Among them are Maryam, a neighbor to whom Fahmi is attracted, and Zannuba, a member of Zubayda's female ensemble who catches Yasin's attention.

Mahfouz is also careful to describe the historical background against which the action is set. We learn early on that Sultan Husayn Kamil died in 1917, his son Kamal al-Din refused to succeed him while the British controlled Egypt, and Prince Ahmad Fuad (later King Fuad) accepted the throne with the blessing of the British. Plainly Mahfouz intends to demonstrate the social, political, and cultural trends in Egypt during the latter years of World War I.

The family seems to be conservative and cohesive, dominated by the Sayyid's patriarchal authority. In word and deed he shows himself lord and master of the household. At one point he admonishes Yasin that there is only one law in the house, his own, which he must obey in order to remain at home. When in the first year of their marriage his wife Amina remonstrated with him about coming home late one night, he seized her and said authoritatively, "I am a man and the only one who gives orders. I do not accept any remark about my behavior. You should simply obey. Be careful not to force me to discipline you."[15] Thereafter she knew to obey and fear this man, whom she always addressed as "my lord," with great respect and reverence. Her duty was to make him happy and comfortable and not probe into his private life. She seems totally subservient, helping him dress and undress and fetching water and a basin when he bathes. Out of respect, she does not sit beside him while he relaxes on the sofa and never speaks to him unless asked. In time she learns to suppress her objections to his conduct; although his drinking violates Muslim laws, she accepts it and asks God to forgive him.

Her mother once told her that she should be pleased to have married a man like the Sayyid, a merchant with prominent social standing. Here Mahfouz means that Cairene society, like other Middle Eastern societies, was then exclusively a man's world. The ultimate objectives for a woman were to find a socially acceptable husband, raise a family, and become financially secure. The notion of a meaningful married life based on reciprocal love and sharing did not even cross her mind. A woman was merely the source of man's sexual pleasure. When Amina complains about her husband, her mother replies that he married her after divorcing his first wife, and that if he wishes he may take three more wives; thus, she should thank God that her husband has kept her as his only wife.[16] In fact, Sayyid Ahmad could follow the example of his father, who married more than twenty times. But those marriages brought him only trouble and exhausted his wealth, and the Sayyid does not want to make the same mistake.[17] As a Muslim woman, Amina is in a precarious situation. Her husband can at any time divorce her or exercise his legal right to take other wives. In this century Muslims, especially in urban societies, have tended toward monogamy, mostly for economic and social reasons. Although Mahfouz does not advocate or encourage polygamy, he clearly points out that it is still a religious right that Sayyid Ahmad may claim should he so desire.

Mahfouz treats at length another aspect of patriarchal authority, devoting chapters 27 through 37 to a wife's inability to leave the home without her husband's consent. The Sayyid severely limits Amina's personal freedom. Her leaving the house without his approval would be an egregious act of disobedience, making her subject to his discipline. According to the Quran (4:34, the Sura of Women), men have authority over women and are empowered to discipline them. Muslim jurists and learned men cite traditions of the Prophet, declaring that women's obedience to their husbands is part of their religious duty. Abu Hamid al-Ghazzali (d. 1111), known as Hujjat al-Islam (The Proof of Islam), devotes a whole chapter of his monumental *Ihya Ulum al-Din* (The Revival of the Sciences of Religion) to the rights of a husband over his wife. As a manifestation of obedience, he says, a wife should never leave home without her husband's consent lest she be cursed by the angels until she returns or repents. Even with permission, she should leave secretly, dressed in shabby clothes, in order to conceal her identity. Such traditions are observed by ultrastrict Muslims even today.[18]

While Sayyid Ahmad is very serious about preventing Amina from leaving the house without his consent, the utmost desire of his deeply religious wife is to visit the shrine of al-Husayn and receive the imam's blessing. On Fridays her husband takes his sons to the shrine to pray and hear the *khutba* (sermon); why does he not take her too? One day she seizes an opportunity to visit the shrine without heeding the consequences of her disobedience. No sooner has her husband left for a business trip to Port Said than Amina, wearing her veil, slips out of the house with Kamal, encouraged by the whole family. It is the happiest day of her life as she leaves the house, her great prison, and breathes the air of freedom. Except for a few visits to her mother in the Kharanfash quarter, always in the company of her jealous, possessive husband, she never has left the house during twenty-five years of marriage. When she finally sees the shrine, she feels as if she has discovered a new world; it is no longer something imagined, but a visible, tangible reality. Unable to believe her eyes, she whispers with true devotion, "Our lord al-Husayn." On entering the innermost part, close to the sanctuary, she feels that her soul has been transported to the heavens.[19]

Amina never imagines that her visit to al-Husayn's shrine will end in disaster. On the way home, however, she is hit by a car and suffers a broken collarbone. The whole family is shaken by the accident. Young Kamal cannot believe such a calamity could befall his mother, while the maid Umm Hanafi contends that she could have had a greater disaster if she had not received the blessing of al-Husayn. They both feel that Amina should have been rewarded, not punished for her action. The immediate problem, however, is how to inform the Sayyid about the incident and yet avoid his retribution. The other family members suggest explanations that seem transparent and implausible; Amina decides simply to tell the truth. Expecting a harsh reaction to her confession, she is surprised to hear him tell her to stay in bed until she is well. He continues about his usual routine, by day and night, but she does not object, contented with his occasional inquiries about her health. She naïvely thinks he must regard her suffering as sufficient punishment for her disobedience. No sooner has she recovered, however, than the Sayyid confronts her, saying that he has been deceived by her all these years and should have known better. Although Amina thinks her purpose justifies her action, he shakes his head in disapproval, saying only, "Leave my house immediately."[20]

Poor Amina! After twenty-five years of marriage she is expelled from her home for visiting the shrine of al-Husayn without her husband's consent. Their children are too stunned to contest his decision, while Amina considers it fortunate that her husband merely expelled her; if he had said, "You are divorced," her marriage would be ended. She leaves to stay with her mother, a devoutly religious woman who cannot understand why, after all these years of total obedience, she has rebelled. Here Mahfouz, following the principles of naturalism, implies that Amina, who greatly resembles her mother physically, has apparently inherited her spiritual outlook as well.

Amina's expulsion throws the family into confusion. Aisha is especially resentful, realizing that the responsibility of serving her father will fall to her, and attempts to pass this duty to her sister. The children often discuss their mother's exile, hoping to bring her back. Kamal visits his father at his shop and implores him, "May God protect you; bring back Nina." The Sayyid, at first unrelenting, states that his policy in treating his family is as firm and immutable as a religious doctrine. But eventually, due to the intercession of friends and neighbors and the insistence of his children, he asks his sons to bring their mother back home. In reconciling with her as in expelling her, the Sayyid makes it clear that he is the master of the house, whose word is law. Like the rest of the family, Amina must live on his terms, as she realizes even more after her return.

Mahfouz may have based this episode on a similar case from real life. Opposite his family's house lived the family of Shaykh Ridwan, a venerable-looking man from Syria. Their door was always closed, and the shaykh never allowed his wife to leave the house, not even to visit neighbors. Mahfouz's mother enjoyed relative freedom; she could at least visit the pyramids or the Egyptian Museum apparently without her husband's consent.

Sayyid Ahmad does not trust his wife's judgment nor her handling of the children. When Fahmi decides to seek the hand of the young neighbor Maryam, Amina takes his request to his father. The Sayyid, angry that this boy, still a student, would dare think of marriage, responds harshly: "Only a mother like yourself is capable of corrupting her children. If you were a true mother, this insolent

[Fahmi] would not have dared bring up such a matter with you. But you are a weak mother, from whom no good is expected."[21]

The Sayyid's treatment of his wife makes clear that he regards her as a slave rather than a free woman with dignity. This contemptuous attitude toward women, widespread among Middle Eastern men even today, is apparent in a historic speech delivered by the Caliph Ali Ibn Abi Talib (d. 661) after the Battle of the Camel (December 9, 656), which he fought against Aisha, a wife of the Prophet of Islam, and the two sons of al-Zubayr. Ali, evidently feeling that her place was not on the battlefield but at home in Mecca, gave a speech dispraising women as inferior to men because they lack judgment, reasoning, and religion.[22]

Thus, it is not surprising that when Amina reports the intention of the police officer Hasan Ibrahim to ask Aisha's hand in marriage, the Sayyid says angrily that she should have discouraged Ibrahim and never bothered him with the matter. Amina politely responds she thought it her duty to inform him, as master of the house, of everything that concerns the family. The Sayyid says, "Who knows? You are only a woman, and every woman is deficient of reason."[23] The truth is that his wife is neither stupid nor incompetent. She is awed by her husband's tyrannical authority, fearing that he may expel her from the house forever. Like many men of his generation, the Sayyid feels a sense of superiority and cannot bear to see his authority challenged by a woman. When his first wife Haniyya tried to assert her freedom by leaving the house in defiance of his authority, he resented her audacious act and tried to force her into obedience by beating her. But this tactic did not work, and he finally divorced her, despite his attachment to her (121–22).

The patriarchal authority of Sayyid Ahmad also affects the lives of his children. He constantly monitors their behavior, regardless of their ages. He seems to be especially strict with young Kamal, although Amina protests that he is quite obedient. The young neighbor Maryam tells Kamal, who serves as a messenger between herself and Fahmi, that his father is a strict and frightful man. The Sayyid objects to Aisha's marrying Hasan Ibrahim partly because he may have seen her in person, violating a social taboo. This is a serious offense that can arouse suspicion about the honor of himself and his family and may even destroy his daughter's chances for marrying well. Also, according to custom, she cannot marry before her older sister Khadija. But most of all the Sayyid objects to Aisha's plans because her not consulting with him first is a violation of his patriarchal authority. He tells his wife plainly that he will never allow his daughter to move to another man's house unless the intention of the prospective husband is to be related by marriage to him personally. As time passes, however, he realizes that his continual objections may deprive her of all opportunities. He finally consents to Aisha's marriage to another suitor, Khalil Shawkat, whose brother Ibrahim later marries Khadija. Until then, however, Aisha laments that everything in the house is subject to her father's tyrannical, almost divine authority.

As did many men of his generation, the Sayyid regards a woman as a problem and is quite concerned about his daughters. In a society where virginity is a criterion of honor and respectability, he fears that if they do not marry, they may do something immoral, disgracing himself and the family. (For his sons, especially Yasin, sexual misconduct is objectionable but not condemned. Throughout the Middle East, a man is free to do what a woman cannot.) An unmarried young woman at least enjoys the support and protection of her father; but if she marries the wrong man, he may mistreat her or even divorce her, leaving her to depend on her brothers for support. Unlike a man, she cannot face life alone. A daughter is a social and financial burden on the family. The parents raise her, care for and educate her and then give her to an outsider to treat as he desires. This makes no sense to the Sayyid (301–2).

His attitude about unmarried women is understandable. At the time of the action, women were not economically independent of their families; they had either to marry or to stay at home all their lives. They had few chances for education and training, and their working in the trades was considered socially unacceptable. Their lot later improved as educational opportunities grew, and they slowly began to undertake professions that had been monopolized by men. Today, although the status of the Egyptian woman is far from ideal, it has improved considerably. With the rise of new educated generations, the long-standing dominance of the Egyptian male began to fade. As we shall see in the last part of the trilogy, Sayyid Ahmad, advanced in age and surrounded by his better-educated grandchildren, no longer rules the family.

His patriarchal authority is the accepted norm of a conservative society, not based on any intrinsic human value. Although Kamal believes his father is so powerful that he fears no one, not even God, Mahfouz reveals the more human aspects of the Sayyid's multifaceted personality. At home he is a strict and feared master, while outside he is an amiable person, loved and appreciated by his friends. He is something of an enigma; the members of his household do not know what kind of man he is away from home, nor do his friends know what he is like at home. In essence, he simply keeps his private life to himself, without involving his family. Thus, before returning from his nightly orgies, he tries to sober up and compose himself in order to convince his wife and children that his conduct is above reproach.

The truth is that outside his home he is a hedonist who cherishes wine, women, and song, seeking sexual pleasure with Jalila and Zubayda, leaders of folk ensembles, and Zannuba, who plays the *ud*. But the primary object of his desire is his neighbor Umm Maryam, Bahija, whose invalid husband Muhammad Ridwan has just passed away. She is heavyset and well endowed, and the Sayyid lusts after her. She initiates their relationship and inflates his ego. The Sayyid, who has been involved with Zubayda, tries to find a polite way to get rid of her. Ironically, his son Fahmi is in love with young Maryam, who later marries Yasin. (Odder still, as we shall see in the second part of *Thulathiyya*, Umm Maryam has sexual relations with Yasin before he marries her daughter.) The Sayyid can say little to defend his sense of morality—if indeed he has one.

In fact, his sensual desires are paramount, and he exerts a great effort to keep up his sexual prowess. He loves sumptuous food, including different pastes of walnuts, almonds, and hazelnuts, and his wife is careful to serve him the kinds of meals he loves best. After a big breakfast, he downs a mixture of three raw eggs and milk to replenish his exhausted strength, and he takes a dose of cod-liver oil daily. Some of his friends suggest that he use a little hashish as a stimulant, but he fears that it may destroy his virility. Instead, he uses an expensive narcotic called *manzul*, especially prepared by Muhammad al-Ajami; not wishing to become addicted, however, he takes it only occasionally to heighten his sexual pleasure (27–28).

Mahfouz provides a vivid description of the Sayyid's evening sport in Zubayda's boudoir with a group of intimate friends. Here the quiet, respected merchant becomes a wild merrymaker. He drinks, dances, and plays the tambourine, while Zubayda sings and plays the *ud*. Then the jocund company suggests that they go through a mock wedding. They laugh at first but seem to take their roles seriously. Without hesitating, he takes her by the arm and leads her to the bedroom, amid cheers and congratulations from all (chapter 16, especially 116–19).

The Sayyid's character has yet another major facet, for Mahfouz shows him as a faithful Muslim who fulfills his religious duties. He performs the ablution and prays diligently, asking God to bless himself, his business, and his children and to make them prosperous and successful. He seems to be serious and sincere in his prayer, which he performs with a deep sense of humility. He regularly takes his sons to Friday services, believing that visiting the shrine of al-Husayn itself is a blessing and will protect him and his family from evil. He also reads the Quran but has been able to memorize only the short *suras* (chapters). His religious behavior apparently convinces his children that despite his tyrannical exercise of patriarchal authority, he is not only gentle and graceful but an upright and exemplary man whose moral conduct is impeccable.

What kind of man is Sayyid Ahmad? Jomier maintains that he has dual personalities—one that of a tyrannical father, the other that of an amiable, gentle man. Unlike Molière's Tartuffe, however, he is extreme in his pursuit of pleasure, extreme in his use of patriarchal authority, and extreme in his loyalty to his friends. Jomier concludes that he more nearly fits the image of a man from the distant past than a man from the twentieth century. He is a character straight from the *Thousand and One Nights,* where virility was considered a superlative trait.[24]

The Egyptian writer Yusuf al-Sharuni says Sayyid Ahmad's personality has two facets. Conservative at home, he represents the father figure of the Egyptian middle class of his generation, although Mahfouz exaggerates his patriarchal authority; he is also a libertine, as is shown by his seeking pleasure with his business acquaintances. In this regard, he behavior does not fit the traditional moral standards of the merchant class of his time, characterized by sobriety and temperance. Thus, while the Sayyid is the head of a family in a patriarchal society, he is more like the tribalistic father discussed by Sigmund Freud in *Totem and Taboo*, in that he forbids freedom to his wife and children and allows it only to himself.[25]

Yet another Egyptian writer and critic, Dr. Louis Awad, says that by no standard is the Sayyid an ordinary person. Awad sees him as a massive giant who frightens those around him and whose will is supreme. He is characterized by a unique and peculiar psychological predisposition, and his social behavior is based on contradictions. He adds that those who see the Sayyid as representing the typical Egyptian father of his generation, class, and social ambience in fact imply that Mahfouz has created not a viable and believable character but a caricature, an exaggerated symbol of patriarchal authority. Awad believes that the Sayyid differs from other patriarchal tyrants in that he suffers from a split personality, like Dr. Jekyll and Mr. Hyde.[26]

It seems more accurate to say that Sayyid Ahmad has an unintegrated rather than split personality. He does not even try to connect his life at home with his activities in the marketplace, at the nightly parties in Zubayda's house, or at the mosque where he prays. After describing his religious worship and his dissipation, Mahfouz poses the question whether the Sayyid is two distinct persons in one body. From a psychoanalytical point of view, he is not. At home, he behaves like an authoritarian head of a family in 1917 Cairo. By day he is a typical bourgeois shopkeeper. In the mosque he exhibits complete piety. At night, when he is drinking, dancing, and womanizing, he behaves no differently from the others in his company. Sayyid Ahmad is not especially outgoing or charismatic, nor does he seem imaginative or eccentric. Although his behavior may appear exaggerated, there is nothing extraordinary about his personality. Indeed the world, both East and West, is full of men like him.

The main point is that his behavior in one area is independent of his behavior in another. As Mahfouz rightly notes, Sayyid Ahmad the beast is distinct from Sayyid Ahmad the human being, whose principles insure that no single aspect of his life can overwhelm the others.[27] In other words, the Sayyid has succeeded in combining religious devotion and dissipation without one overlapping the other and without even having to reconcile them except when faced with criticism. His life is compartmentalized. His piety has no effect on his dissipation, his dissipation has no effect on his business. He lives in four mutually exclusive areas, keeping them balanced but not necessarily harmonized. In this sense, Sayyid Ahmad is unlike Dr. Jekyll and Mr. Hyde, where all of the evil is in one personality and all the good in the other; he simply moves from one area of his life to another. His attitude regarding any conflict between them is summarized in his dictum, "Mind your own business, and I mind mine" (51–53).

There is an obvious incongruity in Mahfouz's portrayal of the Sayyid as a moral man, a *hanbalite* (strict Muslim) who takes his religion seriously and is filled with the fear of God at the thought of committing sinful acts. He would never, for example, consider seducing a decent woman or someone close to him; indeed, he declines a friend's invitation to spend a night with a widow because she is the sister of one of his acquaintances. What kind of sense of morality is illustrated by the actions of this man, who abstains from seducing "decent" women but indulges in adulterous relations with those who are considered indecent women? Either such behavior is a contradiction in terms or Mahfouz has missed the mark in assessing his central character. If, as he would have us believe, the Sayyid can distinguish between good and evil, then he must also realize that a sinful act is exactly that, regardless of the intention of the perpetrator. The Sayyid has a twisted sense of morality. His so-called fear of God is a sham, an affront to the majesty and holiness of the being he supposedly fears and worships. It does not prevent him from having immoral relations with Umm Maryam, a longtime neighbor who considers him closer than a brother. He should discourage her efforts to seduce him and not regard her as "another delicious meal" (254–59).

In social realism as Mahfouz uses it here, what is important is the character's typical behavior rather than his unusual actions. In trying to make that which is typical memorable Mahfouz may, as al-Sharuni suggests, have exaggerated some of the Sayyid's traits. But in fact his intention is to show the vicissitudes of a lower-middle-class Cairo family through three generations, and his portrayal of the Sayyid fits this purpose perfectly.

The hypocrisy evident in the contrast between Sayyid Ahmad's dissolute life and his apparent devotion is challenged by Shaykh Mutawalli Abd al-Samad, a saintly septuagenarian who customarily stops at his shop. One day the shaykh asks how he, as a God-fearing man, justifies his avid passion for women. The Sayyid reacts defensively, pointing out that the Prophet Muhammad craved women and perfumes. Shaykh Abd al-Samad retorts that what is legal is clearly distinguishable from what is forbidden under Islamic law. Marriage is different from sensual indulgence. With obvious self-righteousness, the Sayyid lamely responds that he has never violated the honor of a decent woman. The shaykh, calling this a weak man's excuse, reminds the Sayyid that his father had a passion for women but satisfied it by marrying twenty times. Why then does he not follow his father's example in order to avoid sinful sexual relations? The Sayyid points out that his father, virtually impotent, married often in the hope of having many children, yet sired only one son (himself) and squandered his possessions on his many wives. The Sayyid, happy with his three sons and two daughters, has no desire to emulate him. The shaykh says he would never have remonstrated with Sayyid Ahmad except for the fact that he loves him and adds that were it not for his attitude, he would be a perfect man. The Sayyid answers that God alone is perfect; moreover, He is most forgiving, and he offers God his love, obedience, and piety in the belief that *hasanat* (good works) will wash away his sins (50–52).

From this conversation we may deduce that the Sayyid is conscious of his moral weakness but attempts to cloak it with self-righteousness. In this respect he is unlike Nunu the calligrapher in

Khan al-Khalili, who does not seek to conceal or justify his actions. Although the Sayyid declares that God will not punish him for his misdeeds, in truth he relies less on God's mercy and forgiveness than on his own good works. His adultery constitutes a major sin, but worse still is his firm belief in his own rectitude. He is exactly like the businessman Salim Alwan in *Zuqaq al-Midaqq*, who cannot understand why God should punish a good man like him. It is self-reliance that causes the Sayyid to distort the moral rules of his own religion. Though he surely knows the Quran condemns adultery and imposes flogging as the penalty, he contends that he has not violated the honor of decent woman, and that he has done nothing wrong by having sexual relations with loose women.

"Don't forget," he tells the shaykh, "that the women of today are like the *jawari* (slave women of ancient times), whose buying and selling was made lawful by God." In fact, he adds, according to the Quran (4:3) Muslims have the right to own as many slave women as their right hand can hold. Why, then, cannot present-day Muslims like himself possess for their pleasure as many women as they can manage? Of course, the Sayyid does not mention that under Islamic law a slave woman was the property of her master only if he did not marry her or offer her in marriage to another man. If he married her and she bore a child, she was then called *mother of a child* and could no longer be sold. There were many rules that made slave women different from common prostitutes, a fact that the Sayyid may have overlooked in order to justify his sensual indulgence (50).

Sayyid Ahmad's hypocrisy is observed by other people familiar with him. Zubayda, the leader of the female folk ensemble and the Sayyid's sexual companion, tells him on one occasion that he is outwardly righteous but inwardly dissolute. And when Jalila, a member of this ensemble, discovers that he has deserted her for Zubayda, she rebukes him scathingly before his friends and relatives: "Why do you pretend to your family to be righteous, when in reality you are a dissolute person?" (308).

Sayyid Ahmad has no compunction about sin and no understanding of penance. He believes that God will not punish people as long as they do not harm each other. Like many people in our time, he tries to separate God's mercy from his justice and even denies

God's justice to conceal his self-righteousness. He seems to forget that the pages of the Quran are filled with evidence of God's justice as well as his mercy, both immutable and inseparable. God is just in punishing wrongdoers and merciful in treating those who are right in his eyes. But the Sayyid, smug in his sinfulness, does not really want to repent; he loves pleasure too much to part with it. His assertion that God does not punish people for their sins is an excuse for his own actions and a violation of the dictates of the Quran. The truth is that Sayyid Ahmad is a nominal Muslim whose faith is only a veneer. Indeed, he should be considered a *fasiq*, a person who does not meet the requirements of righteousness under Islamic law.[28] He resembles many Muslims (and Christians) who try to combine righteousness and unrighteousness in their lives, and who "have the form of godliness but deny its power."[29]

The clearest evidence that the Sayyid's profession of faith is insincere is that he seeks repentance on his terms, not God's. He thinks God can wait for him to find a propitious time to repent; if not, he can buy forgiveness by doing good works and fulfilling his obligations under Islamic law. In his understanding of repentance, God's mercy does not involve a total change of heart and life. Most Muslims, of course, do not understand what pharisaism is, but Sayyid Ahmad is a typical pharisee. His belief in faith and good works is clearly shared by other characters in the novel. At the bar of Kustaki the Greek, when several patrons are discussing the effects of wine, hashish, opium, and other drugs on man, one customer says that they are beneficial while another objects that wine is forbidden by Islamic law. The first customer retorts, "You talk as if you are at your wits' end. Pay the *zakat* (religious tax), perform the pilgrimage, feed the poor . . . the gates of atonement [for sins] are wide open. One *hasana* (good work) will wash away ten times its equivalent in sins."[30]

From a moral point of view, the Sayyid's eldest son Yasin is little different from his father. He too believes that he can put off repentance until the time is right, and that professing faith is sufficient to prevent God from punishing him. He often says that God is too merciful to chastise a Muslim like himself who has committed only trivial sins without harming other people. But unlike his father,

Yasin tries to justify his sins on the premise that other people do the same things. When he attends the mosque and hears the preacher condemning sins, he looks vainly at his father's face for any sign of contrition and concludes that he too believes God is merciful and will not punish him for some venial sins. Having heard that the preacher is a pederast, Yasin condemns him as a worse sinner than his father. He tries to minimize the Sayyid's misdeeds, believing that if they are less serious than those of others, he will appear just and thus avoid divine punishment (474–75). Yasin makes a travesty of God's holiness and justice.

As the novel begins, Yasin is an elementary school clerk. Now twenty-one, he has lived since the age of nine with his father and stepmother. Although the kind, affectionate Amina treats him as her own son, and although his half brothers and sisters love him, he feels something is lacking in his life. Something inscrutable haunts him, affecting his sense of morality. Mahfouz suggests it is the private life of his mother, who was married and divorced several times after his father ended their marriage.

What must have disturbed Yasin most is that while he was still living with her, she brought men into the house; although quite young, he sensed that there was something unusual in her behavior. An only child, he felt that he was the only person in his mother's life, and she was the only person in his. He must have been disappointed to have strangers sharing his mother with him. He was totally shocked one day to look through the window of her room and see a strange man attacking her like some animal. He could only cry. His mother, sensing his hurt, tried to calm him down, but this disgusting incident wounded his psyche permanently. Worse still, when the stranger did not show up for a few days, she sent Yasin to ask him to visit her at night. The stranger welcomed him eagerly and sent him back with a gift of fruit for his mother. Thus enticed, he volunteered to summon the stranger whenever the occasion arose.

Later Yasin recalled his role with shame, but the thought of his mother with a stranger in the privacy of her home absolutely horrified him. He chose to shun her although his father entreated him to reconcile, perhaps to atone for his own harsh treatment of her. Because of her Yasin distrusts all women, even his loving stepmother, and wishes his mother would go to hell and take the past with her. He assuages his conscience by denying complicity in her actions. He convinces himself that there is nothing pure in this life; everything is polluted, and one has only to open his eyes to see the moral filth. But although he condemns his mother's conduct, it is not so objectionable that he would not accept the old house on Qasr al-Shawq Street and the few shops he stands to inherit from her.

Thus, Yasin is off to a bad start in life. His mistrust of women and his uncontrollable libido lead him to regard every woman as his prey, be she sophisticated or plain, a vegetable seller or a gypsy. Full of lust, he ogles women, especially those with large bosoms or rounded buttocks. Mahfouz portrays him as having an unmitigated sexual desire, as if he were possessed by a demon. He also tries to show through him the adverse effect of divorce on children, its primary victims (81–84).

Yasin also represents the semiliterate Egyptians whose numbers began to grow around the turn of the century. Most were elementary and high school graduates who had had no opportunity to pursue higher education, since the Egyptian University was established only in 1908; before then, only a few young men from the right families could further their schooling in Europe. Many of these semiliterates, like Yasin, held minor government positions. Lacking sophistication, they formed the audience for translations of European detective fiction and some indigenous Arabic works like the historical novels of Jurji Zaydan.[31] Detective stories appeal to Yasin's imagination more than serious literature. He has read part of Zaydan's *Ghadat Karbala,* but cannot comprehend intellectual matters or even write a polished letter. He reads only for entertainment but is considerate enough to share his pleasure with Kamal, who eagerly demands more reading from him.

In many respects, Yasin is the image of his father. Quite dull, lacking charisma and originality, he is a conventional Muslim who hopes to see the Ottomans win the war and restore the caliphate to its former glory.[32] Like his father, too, he is politically uncommitted and makes little notice of the nationalist movement. But he most resembles his father in his unmitigated passion for women; he does not understand true love, only sensuality. His mother likewise indulges freely in sexual relations with no consideration for traditional moral values. Yasin often thinks that if she had been a man, she would have outdone his father in the pursuit of pleasure.

Mahfouz clearly implies that Yasin is as sensual as his parents and that the causes of his conduct are psychological. He suffers from a lack of mother's love, which he tries to offset by self-indulgence. Moreover, his mother's amoral behavior makes him demean women, regarding them only as sexual objects. If he could find a woman with a maternal nature and the ability to satisfy his sexual needs, we are told, he would enjoy a normal life. This may be, but our impression is that he is licentious by nature, with an uncontrollable appetite, and disposed to use force against women who resist his advances.

We meet Yasin at the beginning of the action, dreaming of Zannuba. Infatuated by her at first sight, he follows her to her home, opposite a small coffeehouse in the Sanadiqiyya quarter. He sits in the coffeehouse daily, hoping she will show herself, and when she leaves, he follows her everywhere. Obscenely, he whispers to himself that one of her breasts is enough to destroy Malta, and half of her behind would shatter Hindenburg's brains. He would do anything, even become a donkey pulling her carriage, just to have sex with her. Mahfouz suggests that Yasin becomes infatuated with Zannuba because she offers an emotional release from his frustration; she is a perfect substitute for the mother who left him (80–85, 92–93, and chapter 39). (Indeed, as we shall see in the second part of the trilogy, Yasin eventually marries her, despite the selfish and strenuous objections of his father.)

After waiting impatiently for days, preoccupied with sensual thoughts, Yasin finally succeeds in his pursuit of Zannuba. She agrees to meet him at her home, which apparently belongs to Zubayda. When she greets him at the door, he remarks nervously that he has waited so long for this moment he feels as if his hair has turned gray. When he inquires about Zubayda, Zannuba says she is with a prominent customer. Yasin appears concerned that Zubayda may object to her entertaining men in her house without permission; Zannuba responds that she is not merely an *ud* player in Zubayda's ensemble but also her niece, and there is nothing to worry about. As she leads him inside, he hears singing and music, but his curiosity is not aroused, for he is intent on possessing her luscious body.

But his interest is piqued when Zannuba describes Zubayda's customer as a generous and amiable gentleman who loves pleasure. When he inquires further, she says, "He is a man from our quarter. You may have heard of him. He is Sayyid Ahmad Abd al-Jawad, the shopkeeper in the Nahhasin." Yasin feels shocked. Zannuba, unable to understand his reaction, says, "Did you believe that [he] was infallible? No man can become perfect without passionate love." Yasin asks to see this customer without being observed. Zannuba carries a plate of fruit to Zubayda's room and leaves the door ajar, allowing him to peer inside. He is stunned to see his father with Zubayda, drinking, playing the tambourine, and cracking jokes. Good God! Can this be the same mighty, strict, pious, god-fearing man he knows?

After years of complete faith in the impeccable conduct of his father, Yasin faces a bittersweet reality as his world of idealistic dreams comes apart. He sees in Zubayda's private chamber not a ghost but a man of flesh and bone who, like him, loves pleasure. There his father sits next to his mistress Zubayda, who is playing the *ud* and singing, "O Muslims, O people of God." Yasin needs no further proof; this is the same man who divorced his mother, expelled Amina because she defied his authority, and mocked Kamal when he begged for her return. When Zannuba returns, she notices his bewilderment and, to calm him down, suggests that they do the same things Zubayda and her customer are doing.

"What a coincidence!" he thinks to himself. "I am here with Zannuba and my father is there with Zubayda, both of us in the same house." Yasin realizes that he is the image of his father. He is not at all resentful to see him in a debased state in the company of a whore but rather elated at having discovered his real father, for in him he has found himself. He feels a new sense of genuine love and respect, rather than awe. His father is no longer an inscrutable mystery man but a real person with whom he can identify. They are cut from the same mold, separated only by age and experience. Yasin is so exhilarated that he says with jubilation: "Well done, father. Today I have discovered you. To me, today is your birthday. What a day and what a father, who before tonight was lost to me. Drink and play the tambourine as you wish, not like Ayyusha the tambourine player. I am proud of you. Do you also sing, father?" (288).

Having seen his tyrannical father demand that the family adhere to the highest moral standards, Yasin suddenly sees him as frivolous and dissolute. He could not be more pleased. He can learn from his father how to drink, sing, and make love. As he watches Zannuba standing before the mirror caressing her hair, she looks ravishingly luscious. No longer able to control his lust, he pounces upon her like a beast of prey.

Until the day of Aisha's wedding, Yasin says nothing of what happened at Zubayda's house. At the wedding party Jalila, the folk ensemble leader Sayyid Ahmad deserted for Zubayda, begins to chide him for having ended their long, passionate affair. She does not mind his leaving her, but she resents the fact that he tries to appear as a respectable man in public. The guests are shocked to hear a shady woman like Jalila accuse Sayyid Ahmad of adultery. Yasin, however, is delighted, realizing that she is only one of his father's many conquests. He feels proud about his father's relationship with Jalila, as he did when he saw him with Zubayda.

The one most shocked by Jalila's scurrilous accusation is Fahmi, who thinks that she wants to see his father about some business, or perhaps she is only joking. Yasin reveals the secret of his father's escapade with Zubayda, but the idealistic Fahmi finds it difficult to believe that his father would engage in immoral acts. If what Yasin tells him is true, he reasons, the father he knows at home is not the same man Yasin describes, and virtue has turned completely into vice. Nevertheless, the seed of doubt is planted: Is his father truly moral or hypocritical? Consoling himself with the belief that his father's conduct is above reproach, he refuses to believe Yasin's account. Yasin asks why, adding there is nothing wrong with drinking, singing, or making love. Did not the caliphs do the same? Then his father is at liberty to do whatever he finds enjoyable.

Unlike Fahmi, his mother and sisters receive the news of the Sayyid's adultery with a sense of resignation. Although Amina feels as if she had been stabbed in the heart, she had been aware of her husband's night life and tries to conceal her anger. In fact, she has no choice but to tolerate his conduct, for she faces the prospect of being expelled from the house again or even divorced should she complain about it. Aisha and Khadija likewise show little reaction to their father's misdeeds, for they understand their precarious position in a male-dominated society and may later encounter the same situation with their husbands.

Having caught his father flagrante delicto, Yasin thinks he can justify his own dissolute actions. He regards the Sayyid's patriarchal authority as a social convention with no real impact. He would gladly leave the house if he were economically independent, but for the time being he must submit to his father's strict discipline. Still, Yasin's main problem is his sexual appetite. At Aisha's wedding, after having too much to drink, he craves a woman. It is too late to visit Zannuba. He looks around and spies the maid Umm Hanafi, lying outside the bakery door with her legs bare. She is in her forties, a plain-looking, heavyset woman—but she is a female, and she is there. He attempts to rape her; she pleads with him to leave her alone but to no avail. While she struggles to free herself, Yasin sees his father standing there, seething. The Sayyid curses him and pulls him away, but Yasin manages to free himself and run to his room (318–21).

Yasin's scandalous act shows that the Sayyid's family discipline, based on his patriarchal authority, is incompatible with his own conduct. Feeling that being strict with children ensures they will grow up as decent, moral human beings, he cannot believe that despite his efforts his son has become a dissolute spendthrift. Of course, he does not consider that his profligate behavior has set a bad example for Yasin, who thinks he can have his way with any woman. Indeed the Sayyid is furious not because Yasin has tried to rape Umm Hanafi but because he has shown bad taste. He tells Yasin that like a beast, he has no brains. He wants his son to be like him in every aspect. If he desires a woman, he should choose the best rather than debase himself by attacking a homely, middle-aged maid.

His reaction shows that the Sayyid is not only immoral but selfish. He curses Yasin and even himself, for he never imagined that his children would disturb his peaceful life by their wicked behavior. Like many fathers of his time, he believes as long as he provides material needs for his children and whips them into obedience with his tyrannical authority, all will be well and he will be free to pursue his own pleasures. He is not at all concerned about setting a moral example for his children, nor does he dream that they will one day rebel against his stern rule and hypocrisy. He has no understanding of his children's hopes and frustrations. He demands their respect and refuses to tolerate any behavior that may tarnish the name of the family. Mistakenly believing he can force Yasin to settle down and abandon his profligate life, the Sayyid arranges his marriage to Zaynab, the beautiful daughter of his friend Muhammad Iffat. Given no choice, Yasin marries her and appears to have forsworn his old ways.

But Sayyid Ahmad has greatly underestimated Yasin's sexual appetite, which no marriage can satiate. Moreover, he does not realize that having the newlyweds living in his house will cause great friction between Zaynab and the family. For married sons to continue living with their families was a common Middle Eastern practice, imposed by economic necessity. Few young couples in 1917 were economically independent for job opportunities for men were slim and it was socially disgraceful for women to work outside the home. Thus, Yasin and Zaynab must make the best of a rather difficult situation. The trouble starts when he becomes bored with married life after only a month. He finds nothing rewarding in marriage, not even a beautiful wife. He tries to drag her down to his level by taking her to nightclubs, against his father's objection. Zaynab, who seems to be a decent woman, wants him to stay home and share life with her. But when she objects to his dissolute life, Yasin tells her there is no point in complaining, for since ancient times it has been decreed that homes are for women and the world is for men. Zaynab tries to endure with wisdom and resignation, but as time goes on her situation becomes unbearable.

Except for Fahmi, no one in the family understands her predicament. Amina, who thinks that women are meant to endure and accept their husbands as they are, cannot understand why Zaynab complains. In this respect, she typifies the traditional Egyptian woman, subservient and fatalistic, with no concept of a woman's freedom. Zaynab, however, represents the younger generation of women who have a better understanding of their role in marriage and desire some degree of freedom. Fahmi sympathizes with Zaynab and tries to save her marriage, but without success. He meets with Yasin several times in Ahmad Abduh's coffeehouse (apparently a real place)[33] to tell him of his wife's unhappiness and resentment of his behavior. Yasin calls him simpleminded and tells him now he understands his father and his reasons for pursuing pleasure. What he cannot fathom is how such a man could patiently confine his taste to one meal, that is, one wife, through twenty-five years, while he is already bored. Fahmi retorts that Yasin's attitude is contrary to religion, but Yasin argues that religion is on his side because it allows the Muslim man to have four legal wives besides unnumbered concubines, as the caliphs of old did and rich people still do. Fahmi, unable to convince Yasin of the illogicality of his argument, says he is no different from their grandfather, who engaged in many marriages.[34] The truth is that like his father, Yasin disparages women but needs them to satisfy his sexual desire. He is lecherous by nature as well as unprincipled.

The gap between Yasin and Zaynab widens, and they argue constantly. After one of their quarrels, he takes notice of her black maid, Nur, who lives in a cubicle near the chicken coop on the roof. Fortyish and heavyset, she strikes him as appealing and vulnerable. She tries to thwart his advances but finally surrenders to him. Meantime, Zaynab comes to her quarters looking for Yasin and discovers what he has done. She cannot take any more humiliation and leaves for her father's house, effectively ending their marriage.

When the Sayyid hears of Yasin's scandalous conduct, he angrily accuses his son of defiling the sanctity of his home. Before his marriage, he says, such immoral actions could be tolerated, but now he has no excuse. Sayyid Ahmad has conveniently forgotten that his own life is filled with immoral acts, but as master of the house he allows himself and not his sons the right to indulge. Yasin's actions are objectionable not because they are immoral, but because they constitute defiance of his authority, and they reveal bad taste and lack of finesse. He would have been pleased if his son had been selective, but Yasin, like a beast, merely follows his instinct. The credulous Amina thinks Yasin has defiled the house and sinned against his father but not against his wife. Accustomed to the Sayyid's dissolute behavior, she self-righteously intimates that if Zaynab were really a good wife, she would tolerate her husband's conduct with resignation, as she herself had done (446–48).

Mahfouz uses this episode to illuminate the social position of women and the attitude of men toward them. Clearly Egyptian society, like other Middle Eastern societies, is male oriented and male dominated. Women's freedom is often legally circumscribed by the *shari'a* (Islamic law), especially in regard to divorce. To Yasin and his father, Zaynab, having left the house without her husband's consent, is *nashiz*, that is, a recalcitrant wife who has violated her marital duties. According to Islamic law, a husband has the right to sue his recalcitrant wife in a religious (rather than civil) court, which will force her to return to her husband's home or go to a private home of her choice, called *bayt al-ta'a* (the house of obedience). Yasin cannot hope to force Zaynab into obedience because she has already made up her mind to terminate the marriage. But because divorce is solely the husband's right, she must wait for him to divorce her. When her father, Muhammad Iffat, calls on the Sayyid to discuss the situation, the Sayyid takes the position that Yasin's misdeed should not be grounds for divorce. Although his son has debased himself by sexually assaulting the maidservant, he argues, there is no difference between one female and another. After a long and acrimonious discussion, the Sayyid finally agrees to the couple's divorce on the premise that his patriarchal authority takes precedence over his son's religious rights as a husband. Yasin accepts the decision but voices his resentment: "As you wish, father. Who can oppose your will? You marry me, you divorce me, you give me life and cause me to die. You are everything. But there is a limit to everything. I am no longer a child. I am a man like you, and as a man I will decide my destiny. I can divorce my wife or place her in a different house. To hell with Zaynab, Muhammad Iffat, and your friendship with him"(470).

In the wake of his failed marriage, Yasin begins to realize that he has been influenced by the ruthless discipline of his self-righteous father, who puts up a show of religiosity before his family. Despite his resentment of his father's domination of his private life, Yasin has no choice but to give in to his will, for his meager salary makes it impossible for him to become independent of the family. (After his mother dies, however, he inherits her home in Qasr al-Shawq and goes to live there on his own.) He represents many young men of his class and time who, having only a smattering of education and no hope of advancement, had to make the best of the present. Some of them, like Yasin, must have found in indulgence a relief from their frustration.

In sharp contrast to Yasin stands his half brother Fahmi, who plays a significant role in the novel. He is the best-educated member of the family and the first to attend college as a law student with the promise of a bright future. He is an idealistic, decent young man whose personal conduct appears above reproach. Above all, he is an ardent nationalist. He represents the rising, better-educated generation committed to the liberation of Egypt from the British, the first generation after World War I to take up the national struggle against foreign domination.

Fahmi is a virtual stranger among his own family, related by blood but decidedly unlike them because of his ideas and idealism. He cannot accept Yasin's account of his father's conduct, regarding his father as a moral man whose behavior is exemplary. He respects women, as is shown by his effort to defend Zaynab, although he knows doing so is hopeless. He falls in love with his neighbor Maryam and wants to marry her, but his father objects. He continues to care for her until he discovers that she has a relationship with the British soldier Julian. Then he feels deeply wounded; how could she be so indecent, and how can he forget his dreams of love? The whole family decides that Maryam has deceived them, and she is not the right girl for Fahmi. But ironically Yasin begins to show interest in her; although he had thought of her before, he always shied away because of Fahmi's feelings. Outwardly, he expresses resentment of her dalliance; inwardly, he is exhilarated to have found a young woman who is audacious enough to defy traditional standards. He finds her an image of himself, a like-minded pleasure-seeker, an easy prey within his reach.

The Sayyid's two daughters, Khadija and Aisha, who represent the younger generation, are uneducated and (when we first meet them) homebound. There is an intense rivalry between them, and they even bicker over daily chores—hardly unusual, for conflict between sisters is common in every society. But Khadija complains that her sister is rewarded for her laziness, while she is unrewarded for her work. She prays constantly, but Aisha cannot fulfill her prayer obligations for two days. Khadija fasts the whole month of Ramadan, while her sister pretends to do so but in fact snacks secretly. Aisha is beautiful but thin, she adds, consoling herself with the thought that her own obesity makes her more attractive. All she needs, she thinks, is a little luck and she will outdo her sister.

Khadija is truly her father's daughter, having inherited his physical and personal traits. She has his big nose and, like him, she is domineering, peevish, and hard to please. She criticizes Yasin's wife Zaynab as a dull, arrogant woman who brags about her Turkish origin, moving Fahmi to admonish her to control her sharp tongue. After going to live with her husband in al-Sukkariyya, she fights constantly with her mother-in-law. Nevertheless, she is right in viewing her weight as an advantage, for it is well known that until recently Egyptian men preferred heavyset women like the character Umm Ahmad in old Egyptian movies. Mahfouz projects this point clearly when he states that the duty of the maid Umm Hanafi is to fatten the female members of the Sayyid's family (20). The Sayyid and his son Yasin are captivated by large women, especially those with well-rounded behinds.

Mahfouz devotes much attention to the Sayyid's third son, ten-year-old Kamal. Although it appears there is nothing exciting about his life, he will be the focus of the second part of the trilogy. The first thing that strikes us is that he has no friends his own age—a fact that should not surprise us, for to some extent he appears modeled after Mahfouz himself, who admits that as a child he had no one to play with, and that his home and his family constituted his whole world. Physically, Kamal looks less like his brothers and more like Khadija, having inherited his mother's tiny eyes and his father's big nose. He is especially self-conscious about his massive head, which evokes the ridicule of some schoolmates, who call him the boy with two heads; their taunts goad him into fighting back, and twice he is beaten in brawls. His unshapely appearance annoys him so much that he complains to his mother, who comforts him by saying that the Prophet Muhammad had a massive head, so he has nothing to be ashamed of (57).

Through Kamal, Mahfouz offers glimpses of school life in Cairo around 1917. Many students in Kamal's school are much older that he, and some have even begun to grow mustaches. These students ought to be in high school, not elementary school, but perhaps for economic reasons they have never before had the opportunity to attend. These older pupils often beat the younger ones or snatch pieces of candy from them. A gang of bullies (*futuwwat*) decides to punish Kamal after school, but the principal discovers their plan and calls the police to protect him. Although he is saved from their clubs, he does not escape his father's stick when he gets home (54–55).

Mahfouz portrays Kamal as an inquisitive and intelligent youngster. Like the rest of the family, he is aware of his father's harsh discipline, which at times conflicts with his desire to play. Although the Sayyid knows that young Kamal is a clever and diligent pupil, he seems to place a higher priority on politeness and submission than on knowledge. Islam is part of his school's curriculum, and Kamal waits impatiently for the religion class. The teacher reads aloud Sura 72 of the Quran and elaborates on the *Jinn* (genies) and their hosts, some of whom are believing Muslims and will eventually go to paradise. At home Kamal shares his acquired knowledge with his mother, the only person who has time for him and shows an interest in his learning. She is a devout Muslim; her father was a learned shaykh who memorized the Quran and from whom she learned much about religion. She is suspicious about the manner in which religion is presented in the school but finds no contradiction between her own belief and what she hears from Kamal. She tells him about the miracles of the Prophet of Islam and his companions and about the religious charms used as protection against *Ifrits*, diseases, and harmful reptiles. To her, these stories are the essence of religion. Kamal listens eagerly, but when she insists the earth does not move but sits on a bull's horns, he objects in vain; finally, Fahmi settles the questions by declaring that the earth is lifted by the power and wisdom of God (56, 74–75).

Thus, Kamal's young mind is impressed by religious ideas with which he will wrestle as an adult. This is to be expected of a young Muslim boy raised in a traditional home and sent to a school where religion is taken seriously. Yet Kamal seems to be more curious about ideas than his siblings seem to be. Perhaps Mahfouz has intentionally depicted him as precocious in order to prepare for his significant role in the second volume of the trilogy. Once, Kamal asks his mother whether Muslims will see God with their own eyes in the afterlife. Receiving an affirmative answer, he goes on:

> "Does my father fear God?"
> "Son, your father is a believer, and the believer does fear God."
> "I do not believe that my father fears anything."
> "May God forgive you." (77–78)

This conversation leads the Egyptian writer Ghali Shukri to imply that Mahfouz is predisposed to portray Kamal's father as a God figure; after Amina's accident, he says, "This husband-father-God does nothing but expel his wife as soon as she has recovered."[35] It is very hard to believe that young Kamal ever viewed his father this way; in fact, we have no idea what he thinks about God. Rather, he sees his father as a large, forceful man ruling his family with an iron rod and, not having experienced any such authority outside his home, regards him as the embodiment of absolute power. Mahfouz makes it clear that although Kamal loves his father, his heart is filled with fear of him. When he passes through the dark Qirmiz Alley,

believed to be inhabited by *Ifrits* at night, he recites the Sura of Unity
to drive them away, but he cannot avert his father's wrath even by
reciting the whole Quran. The emotional conflict here is obvious; it
is unusual for a child of Kamal's age to fear his father so much and
love him as well.[36]

Raised in a strong Muslim environment, Kamal evinces the un-
complicated, sincere faith typical of children. He discusses religious
subjects with his mother and accompanies his father to the mosque
on Fridays, and religion is his favorite subject at school. Each day he
passes by the shrine of al-Husayn, whom his family reveres because
of his close blood relation to the Prophet Muhammad. Yet Kamal's
devotion goes further. He grieves for the martyr but is consoled by
the belief that his severed head wandered on until it chose Egypt as
its final resting place. Often Kamal stands before the grave of
al-Husayn hoping to see his fair face, which his mother tells him has
been preserved by divine mystery. But when this dream is not
fulfilled, he is content to express his love and devotion. He recites
the opening chapter of the Quran whenever he passes by the shrine
and asks al-Husayn for help against the *Ifrits* and school examina-
tions and especially against his father's threats. Constrained by his
father's harsh discipline, frightened by his mother's harrowing
stories of evil *Ifrits,* and clearly unhappy at school, he has no one
to turn to. He pours out his soul to this martyred saint and asks
him to solve his problems. The religious myth becomes a reality
he can identify with. He believes al-Husayn's supernatural power
can overwhelm the tyrannical authority of his father, but he cannot understand how the saint could allow tragedy to befall his
mother.

Kamal has a fertile romantic imagination. When Yasin reads
stories to him, he is transported into a fantasy world. On one
occasion, passing by Matusian's shop, he sees a poster of a blonde
woman reclining on a couch, puffing a cigarette with rising curls of
smoke. He fancies himself sharing life with this beautiful female in a
sumptuous room, cruising the Nile with her, or sitting at her feet,
gazing at her dreamy eyes (57–58). He sometimes invents stories;
one concerns a boy who tries to board a carriage and slaps the

driver, who then chases him and stomps him to death. Everyone laughs at his story, not realizing how sensitive and imaginative he is (62–64).

Kamal's imagination is also stirred by the presence of British troops in Cairo. He makes friends with some of them, especially young Julian. He imitates their activities by forming a model of a military camp on the roof of his house. He makes tents out of pieces of cloth, using pencils as poles. Pieces of wood become guns, wooden shoes are trucks, and date kernels are soldiers. Near the camp he spreads pebbles to represent the anti-British demonstrators, meanwhile singing English songs. Then he moves on to the Egyptian camp, arranging the pebbles in an offensive position, and shouts, "Long live Egypt! Long live Sa'd Zaghlul! Down with the British protectorate!" With friends like Julian on one side and his brother on the other, Kamal experiences an intense internal struggle after which he finally declares the Egyptians the victors (501–2).

Kamal also is curious about life around him. His numerous questions, to which he expects answers, irritate others. He wants to know what marriage is and why his sister Aisha is moving to the house of Khalil Shawkat in al-Sukkariyya. He seems overly attached to his sisters and does not want to see marriage snatch them away from him. His mother tells him that when he grows up, he will find a nice woman whom he will bring to live with his family. He asks when Aisha will return home, and he is told she will visit often. Kamal thinks the family is making fun of him. Eager to see for himself why Aisha and Khalil are alone in a locked room, he peeks through the keyhole and see them sitting next to each other, kissing. His mother calls his action shameful; when he asks innocently why Khalil was kissing his sister, she threatens to report him to his father if he asks this question again (314–15). Rebuffed and ridiculed, Kamal keeps his curiosity to himself, for social custom is sufficiently stringent to prevent anyone in his family from answering such impolite (if not impudent) questions. Still he shows some intellectual proclivities, however rudimentary. His desire to know and his penchant to explore life and ideas will leave their mark on his adult life.

But Mahfouz sometimes seems to exaggerate Kamal's curiosity.

On learning that Aisha is pregnant, he asks when the child will come out. She laughs and says, "Very shortly." As her due date approaches, he is most eager to see the baby's delivery. (When Kamal was not yet six, Mahfouz relates, he saw a cat on the roof delivering kittens, mewing and writhing in pain. When he saw a tiny kitten issuing from the cat's body, he became ill and ran away afraid, but he does not make the connection between the cat and Aisha.) He resists skipping school for the occasion, fearing that the principal may report his absence to his father, who will certainly punish him. As soon as school is over, he rushes to Aisha's house, where he hears her moaning and imagines her in pain. Much to his disappointment, however, she has already delivered a baby girl, and he has missed his chance to watch (545–47). This entire episode seems farfetched. Although the ten-year-old Kamal may be as precocious as Mahfouz makes him out to be, it is improbable that an Egyptian youngster in the conservative society of 1917–19 would dare ask about childbirth, which even adults did not discuss openly, much less hope to watch a live delivery.

Although Mahfouz describes the struggle of Egyptian nationalists against British domination, certainly a significant part of the historical background, we should remember that he is not writing a political novel. He seeks to show the strength of nationalism and the effect of the British occupation on the Egyptian people. His characters' actions demonstrate that they are not totally preoccupied with personal concerns. Indeed some, like Fahmi, are deeply involved in the struggle, and all the members of the Sayyid's family have strong national sentiments, unlike the characters of *Zuqaq al-Midaqq*, who are cut off from the outside world.

At the outset Mahfouz offers only a glimpse of political events. The Sayyid complains about the prices that have been driven up by the war and the Australian soldiers who have spread through Cairo like insects, playing havoc with the people, then praises Prince Kamal al-Din for refusing to succeed his father Sultan Husayn Kamil, noting that Sultan Ahmad Fuad (later King Fuad) has accepted the throne with British blessings. Amina, who knows little of events and, seeking to please him, comments, "God is able to restore to us our Effendi Abbas." The Sayyid responds with no little disappointment, "Who knows when Abbas will be restored?" (66–67). (They refer here to the Khedive Abbas Hilmi II, who was pro-Turkish and vehemently anti-British. Shortly after the outbreak of World War I, the British government proclaimed Egypt a protectorate, deposed the Khedive, who was then visiting Constantinople, and installed Husayn Kamil as sultan.)

Elsewhere, Mahfouz sporadically mentions the war and the impact of the British soldiers' behavior toward the people. Fahmi declares the Germans cannot be defeated, while Yasin insists that the Egyptians must rid themselves of the British and restore the caliphate to its past glory. Later Shaykh Mutawalli Abd al-Samad is accosted in the Moski quarter by two Australian soldiers apparently bent on robbery. When he protests that he has only a jug, one grabs it from his hand and smashes it, while the other tears his turban and shawl and throws them in his face. The helpless victim can only ask God to destroy the British as they have destroyed his belongings.

It is not until chapter 48, however, that Mahfouz fixes on the political unrest in Egypt and the outbreak of the nationalist revolution. Fahmi tells Yasin that a delegation (*wafd*) led by Sa'd Zaghlul, with Abd al-Aziz Fahmi and Ali Sha'rawi as members, has called on Sir Reginald Wingate, the British high commissioner, to ask for the termination of the protectorate and the proclamation of Egypt's independence. Yasin, less interested in national politics than in women, has heard of Zaghlul, the president of the legislative assembly, but not of the others. The point is that few young people knew who Zaghlul really was. Although some considered him a great national leader, others thought he was a British lackey. Yasin considers the nationalists' request mere wishful thinking. But Fahmi is more enthusiastic, feeling that the wafd's plan to travel to London and open negotiations represents the first step toward getting the British out of Egypt.

Amina, simple and ignorant as she appears elsewhere in the novel, makes a surprisingly logical comment. She cannot understand why Sa'd Zaghlul and his colleagues should travel all the way to England to ask the British to get out of Egypt. This, she says, is most discourteous; how could someone visit her at home while he intends to expel her from his own home? The British have been in

Egypt for a long time. Thus, it is not at all civil to tell them to get out, especially in their own country. While Yasin and Fahmi do not take Amina seriously, Yasin's wife Zaynab does. She wonders aloud where these men found the audacity to tell the British in their own country to leave Egypt, where their occupation has even made evening walks in the streets unsafe. If they should kill Zaghlul and the others, who would even know?

The mystic Shaykh Abd al-Samad, even more pessimistic, asserts that the British are not so crazy as to leave without a fight, and the Egyptians are not strong enough to force them out. But if the country's leaders could at least get the Australian soldiers out, he thinks, peace would return. Most of Mahfouz's characters appear fatalistic about the British presence in Egypt, but Fahmi and others are optimistic and committed to the cause of national independence.

Mahfouz concentrates especially on Sayyid Ahmad's attitude toward politics and nationalism, which is every bit as ambivalent as his view of vice and virtue. Sa'd Zaghlul and his colleagues have asked the people to sign a petition empowering them to speak for the Egyptian nation in response to the British high commissioner's asking what authority they have. When Muhammad Iffat asks the Sayyid to sign it, he agrees, adding sarcastically that doing so makes him feel as he did after imbibing the eighth glass while lying between Zubayda's legs (377–78). Thus, his priorities are clear; as long as he can have his pleasure, he does not care whether the British stay or go. Mahfouz lamely explains this offhanded remark by attributing it to his sense of humor. He would have us believe that the Sayyid has an astonishing ability to harmonize the serious and lighthearted aspects of his nature, so that neither dominates the other. We are reminded of his effort to balance his religious convictions and his dissolute behavior, which leads to hypocrisy. The Sayyid loves his country, but his family, his business, and his pleasure take precedence over national affairs. For this reason he has never joined any committee of the National Party (founded in 1907 under the leadership of Mustafa Kamil) or attended its meetings, although he believes in its political objectives. He shows his patriotism by donating his money but not his time to the party.

To understand the Sayyid's political outlook, we must understand his background. Perhaps ten years old when Ahmad Urabi's military rebellion against the royal palace was put down and the British occupied Egypt in 1882, he belongs to a generation that has seen the British humiliate and then dominate the country. He remembers well the surge of nationalism inspired by the stimulating articles Kamil wrote in his newspaper *al-Liwa*. And when Kamil died young in 1908, he cried like a child, suffering the ridicule of his companions because he was spoiling their nightly pleasure. Now it is 1918; Turkey is defeated, and Britain victorious. The return of the Khedive is unlikely, yet Zaghlul and his colleagues are determined to confront the British and seek independence. The Sayyid's intuition tells him all this nationalist activity has little hope of achieving its ends; thus, he may as well make the best of life. He shows little interest when his business assistant tells him that people have begun calling Zaghlul's house *Bayt al-Umma* (the House of the Nation). He is like many men of his time who, knowing there was no way to oust the British from Egypt except by force, became passive and fatalistic about the country's political condition. Their hopes could not be rekindled even by a great national leader like Sa'd Zaghlul, and it fell to the younger generation to take the lead in the struggle against the British.

In 1919, after Zaghlul's demand for the termination of the protectorate and recognition of Egyptian independence was rebuffed, disturbances broke out throughout the country. The British retaliated by arresting Zaghlul and three of his colleagues, Hamd al-Basil, Ismail Sidqi, and Muhammad Mahmud, on March 8 and deporting them to Malta. The next day, students from many schools went on strike and protested this action. The British arrested some three hundred of them but could not put down the demonstrations. Lawyers, trade-union workers, and students from al-Azhar swelled the ranks and paraded by the residence of the high commissioner, shouting, "Down with the British protectorate!" British soldiers opened fire on the demonstrators, killing and wounding many. Two days later the scene was repeated, with a great number of casualties consisting mostly of students from the Azhar. The demonstrations persisted, however, and soon spread to Port Said and other cities. With the situation out of hand, the high commissioner eventually had to call British troops from Syria to crush the revolt.

Realizing that force could not settle the Egyptian problem, the British authorities released Zaghlul and his colleagues and allowed them to present their grievances before the peace conference in Paris. From there Zaghlul traveled to London to plead Egypt's case with the British government. In December 1919, the British government delegated Lord Milner to investigate the situation in Egypt. But Milner's commission returned three months later without success, and the next year anti-British demonstrations continued. This time the British deported Zaghlul to Aden, then Gibraltar, and finally to Seychelles. The situation was somewhat eased on February 22, 1922, when the high commissioner issued a unilateral declaration ending the protectorate and promising Egyptian independence. In April of the next year, a constitution was issued and amnesty was granted to Zaghlul, who returned to Egypt and soon became the head of a new political party, the Wafd party. In January 1924, this new party won a decisive victory in the national election, establishing the Wafd and Zaghlul not only as the dominant political forces in Egypt, but as the symbols of Egyptian nationalism.

We should not conclude that Sayyid Ahmad is uninterested in politics. Indeed, he often talks about politics at home and at work, and even hangs Zaghlul's picture in his shop. But, as many Egyptians, he does not act on his professed beliefs. In this respect he reminds us of Mahfouz's father, who, we are told, discussed the activities of Zaghlul and other national leaders but apparently avoided involvement in politics.[37] The outbreak of the revolution, however, affects the lives of all the members of his family, and their reactions constitute a major part of the novel.

Fahmi, like many of his fellow law students, is active in the national movement and often meets with his friends to discuss current events. He contends that the protectorate was imposed by the British government as a wartime measure, without the consent of the Egyptians, and therefore had no legal basis. He is in fact echoing the circular Zaghlul and his colleagues sent to Sultan Fuad after they initially were forbidden to plead Egypt's case at the peace conference. Fahmi is proud that he not only kept a copy of the circular but also helped to distribute it. But his activity alarms his family. Yasin tells him not to keep the circular lest he incur the wrath of the British authorities. Amina cannot understand why her son would jeopardize his life. Fahmi tries to explain that getting the British out of Egypt is the duty of every patriotic Egyptian. His mother, simple and gullible, does not understand why he hates the British so much, since they too have families. "Don't you see, mother," he asks, that they occupy our country, and that there is no life for people under foreign control?" She finally says rather resignedly that while the British have ruled Egypt for a long time, they do not kill people or attack places of worship, and "the Muhammadan nation is all right."[38] Such an answer is to be expected of this woman who, as her husband, has grown accustomed to foreign domination. What does it matter to her who controls Egypt, so long as she has her home and her family, and the Muslim people and their sacred places are left unmolested?

Fahmi is upset that she cannot comprehend the enormity of the situation. He tells her that if the Prophet Muhammad were alive today, he would oppose British rule. Still unconvinced, she says innocently that the prophet was supported by God and his angels. Fahmi retorts indignantly that Sa'd Zaghlul will achieve what the angels of God have not achieved. To a devout Muslim like Amina, his statement is blasphemy. She tells him to ask God's mercy and forgiveness. Arguing that Zaghlul's circular will have little effect, she says emphatically that if the pashas want to evict the British from Egypt, they should do it themselves. Fearing that Fahmi may jeopardize his career and even his life, she says that politics is the business of leaders like Zaghlul, not of ordinary people. She is disturbed when her young son Kamal says that his Arabic language teacher told his class that nations achieve independence only by the determination of the people. If he wants to express such views, she contends, he should do so at home, and Zaynab and Yasin agree with her. Through them Mahfouz appears to voice not only his displeasure with Egyptian politicians, but his lack of confidence in their ability to stand up to the British.

But the situation has gone beyond the mere distribution of nationalist circulars. Sayyid Ahmad and his pleasure companions are saddened but hardly surprised to learn that the British have arrested Zaghlul and other national leaders and deported them to Malta. They wonder whether he will remain in exile forever, and whether the national hopes today will be lost as in the past. They have met as usual to drink and have fun, but the news forces them to face the bitter reality that the British have once more humiliated their countrymen. None of them has even the vaguest idea of what to do; they dare not even express their indignation by joining the demonstrators and can only turn to most merciful God for help. Their sheer fatalism is typical of Middle Eastern people. They seem to have forgotten that God helps those who help themselves, while their adversaries call on the same God to strengthen their foothold in Egypt. After some casual discussion tinged with remorse, they decide to alleviate their sorrow by drinking.

Fahmi is greatly enraged by Zaghlul's deportation. To him the British are villains, answering the Egyptians with threats instead of civility. If the Egyptians do not counter their terrorism, he says tearfully, they will never enjoy peace, and Zaghlul, who has offered himself to ransom the country, will continue to suffer. His mother and Yasin express sadness at Zaghlul's exile, but they care little about politics and the national movement. Zaynab cannot understand why Fahmi rages so strongly against the British, as if Zaghlul were his own relative. She seems to blame Zaghlul and his colleagues for Egypt's plight and their own, contending that if they had held their peace like other people, the British would not have deported them. Although she belongs to the new generation, like Amina she is uneducated and has little understanding of politics. Her utmost desire is to have a loving husband who will share life with her. But Yasin, while declaring he is sad at Zaghlul's deportation, decides it is time to gratify his carnal instincts and leaves the house, most likely for the nearest bar.

Fahmi senses that the situation in the country is abnormal, and that some cataclysmic event is about to happen. Arriving at the law school, he finds some students calling for a strike, excitedly shouting, "Down with the British protectorate!" and "Long live Sa'd Zaghlul!" The British advisor to the Ministry of Justice comes to urge them to mind their own business and return to classes. One shouts back that the country's leaders have been imprisoned, and they will not study the law in a country where the law has been trampled upon. The law students take to the streets, joined by others from the schools of engineering and agriculture. The revolution has begun, and no one feels happier than Fahmi. When the peaceful protests are met with force, he is not afraid of dying. He knows he is fighting for the freedom of his country. To him the demonstrations, supported by Egyptians from every walk of life, represent a new hope, the dawn of a new era that will shake the foundations of the Nile valley.

The revolution has a great impact on Kamal. It affects his freedom of movement between home and school—a trivial thing to grown-ups, but not to a ten-year-old. He used to tarry on the way home, but after some of the demonstrators are killed by British troops, his mother asks Umm Hanafi to escort him to and from school. Kamal realizes the country is in revolt but does not understand why. He has heard Fahmi discuss politics and the deportation of Sa'd Zaghlul. But why should the Egyptians go on strike and confront the British, the mere mention of whom is frightening? He cannot make sense of all the catchwords he hears bandied about and is especially baffled by the conflicting attitudes of his other family members. While Fahmi is indignant and militantly anti-British, Yasin is passive, sympathetic to the popular cause, but unwilling to let the revolution interrupt his pursuit of pleasure. Kamal hears his kindly mother asking God to purify the hearts of both sides and establish peace between them, but he also hears Zaynab pouring invective upon Zaghlul and blaming him for all the trouble in Egypt.

Despite his perplexity Kamal sympathizes with the revolution, although he cannot explain why. For the first time he confronts the idea of death without comprehending it. Whether or not the revolution means something to him, he finds himself marching alongside his schoolmates shouting nationalist slogans. When Azharite students pass by calling them to join their protest, Kamal quickly falls in. He is now part of the revolution, and there is no way to retreat. As waves of demonstrators move down the street near al-Husayn's shrine, the British soldiers open fire. A stray bullet whizzes past his ear, barely missing him. As long as he lives, he will never forget its sound. He is saved from possible death by Uncle Hamdan, who pulls him into his sweets shop. After the situation calms down a little, Kamal runs home. On the way he meets Fahmi, who begs him not to reveal that he was among the demonstrators, for the Sayyid does not want to see his son die for anyone or any cause.

British troops are now everywhere in Cairo, even camped outside the Sayyid's house. From what he has heard at home, Kamal imagines they are devils, but as he looks at them close up, he gains the courage to go out and make friends with them. One soldier gives him a piece of chocolate and asks whether he likes the English. When he answers that the English should release Sa'd Pasha (Zaghlul), another soldier rubs his ear and says, "Sa'd Pasha, no." When the soldiers ask whether there are girls in his home, he says that his sisters are married and there are no women at home except his mother. (We have no idea how he communicates with these soldiers, because he does not know their language.) On arriving home, he rushes to the room where the pictures of Zaghlul and other national leaders are hung and whispers to himself that the English are handsomer than Sa'd Pasha. His brother Fahmi shakes his head, saying, "What a traitor! They have bought you with a piece of chocolate" (463).

This episode demonstrates Kamal's soul-searching nature as well as his state of confusion and indecision. He joins in the demonstrations and shouts nationalist slogans but does not understand the words or why people are shouting them. Kamal is an innocent, perplexed soul. He has within him a seed of altruism and human compassion, manifested in his attitude toward the English soldiers. After meeting them in person, he decides in his childish innocence that they are simply human beings. Kamal does not seem to view life in absolute terms. He wants to be committed like Fahmi, yet he is not. Mahfouz attempts to show that it is not easy for this young boy to make up his mind about certain issues, while portraying him as a romantic idealist with a profound sensitivity to the human condition. He is in fact preparing for the second part of the trilogy, where Kamal appears to have created his own world of idealism but is unable to maintain or cope with it.

As the demonstrations continue and the casualties increase, the Sayyid discovers by sheer chance that Fahmi is deeply involved in the nationalists' struggle. As he and his sons are coming out of the mosque one Friday, an Azharite student points out Yasin and accuses him of being a British spy. Fahmi instantly retorts that Yasin is his brother and is not a spy. A young man steps forward and, recognizing Fahmi as one of the national fighters, asks the group to release his brother. The Azharite retreats with discomfiture, and the others apologize for the unfortunate incident. At home the Sayyid questions Fahmi and learns that he is a member of a committee of the national fighters and has been distributing nationalist circulars. He cannot believe that Fahmi, his favorite son, would expose himself to danger, when God has ordered the Muslims not to place their lives in jeopardy. Fahmi tries to justify his actions by saying that God urges the believers to engage in *jihad* (holy war). When his father objects that what God means by *jihad* is the struggle for his holy cause, Fahmi answers that fighting for the homeland and fighting for God are one and the same. But the Sayyid wants his son to cut his ties to the national movement and stop distributing circulars.

What should Fahmi do? He is too deeply committed to the national cause to retreat from it, yet he loves his father and does not want to displease him. He must choose between obeying his father and fulfilling his duty as a citizen. To join the revolution is noble, but to disobey his father is disgraceful. He decides to tell his father that he will give up his role in the national movement, while in reality he plans to continue the struggle. In other words, he will lie—and why not? All the family members have lied to his father at one time or another. Doing so is their only protection from his heavy-handed and unreasonable patriarchal authority. But Fahmi is deceiving himself. He is a moral and principled young man; deep in his soul, he does not want to give up the national struggle, but he cannot and will not lie to his father. Finally he tells his father he will obey his order. The Sayyid, wanting some assurance, asks him to swear on the Quran that he will give up his role in the national movement. Fahmi is astounded. Now his faith and his integrity are at stake. If he lies, he will compromise his moral standards. Seeing his hesitancy, his father suddenly bursts into rage, shouting that Fahmi is lying to him, like the rest of the family. Vowing not to be fooled, he insists that his son take an oath on the Quran. Fahmi refuses and says tearfully that he cannot let down the friends with whom he is working. He is no better than they, nor than those who were martyred by British fire. National principles and personal responsibility have finally overcome his father's authority.

Sayyid Ahmad is disappointed by his son's decision and shocked to find his patriarchal authority challenged and overthrown. He has long thought that by imposing harsh discipline he could raise a strong and moral family. Much to his chagrin, he discovers that his authority is not absolute, and that Fahmi, who represents the next generation, has an independent mind. Thus, Mahfouz succeeds in showing the intense conflict of morality and individual responsibility with traditional standards, which in some cases are not only unreasonable but conducive to duplicity. The Sayyid's family lies to him on many occasions to keep peace in the house although he thinks it is his own authority that has established peace and solved the family problems.

Mahfouz shows the British presence in Egypt as not only a denigration of national dignity but a source of humiliation to the people. Throughout the novel people complain about the behavior of the Allied troops, particularly the Australians. The humiliation of Sayyid Ahmad, however trivial it seems, is especially significant. This episode, which Mahfouz may have deliberately exaggerated to contrast the Sayyid's arrogance and his vulnerability, also reveals his nonchalant attitude toward the Egyptians' national struggle and exposes him as a self-centered person whose pleasure takes priority over moral or political principles.

While demonstrating students and others are dying, the Sayyid, sneaking out of Umm Maryam's house at midnight, is intercepted by a British soldier. He wonders why he has been stopped, since he is not a demonstrator or an agitator, or even active in politics. The soldier nearly knocks him to the ground, then takes him to a nearby building where many people from all walks of life are working in the yard. Suddenly alarmed, the Sayyid recalls the brutality of the British at the village of Dinshaway in June 1906. The villagers had asked some British officers hunting pigeons nearby to leave, and when they would not go willingly, drove them out. Unfortunately, a captain who was slightly wounded in the skirmish lost his way, wandered into the desert, and died of sunstroke. The British authorities accused the villagers of killing him in cold blood, tried them summarily, and hanged them in the village square. The Sayyid pictures himself meeting a similar fate. There is a deep hole in the building's yard, and the soldiers prod the detainees to fill it with dirt. One soldier pushes the Sayyid, ordering him to get to work or face severe punishment. What a humiliation for this authoritarian figure, feared by both family and friends! How could a businessman of his social standing and dignity be so humbled? He has never done a day of menial work in his life nor taken orders from anyone, and now a British soldier orders him to fill a hamper with dirt and carry it to fill the hole in the yard. He cannot believe that he and the others have been thus insulted. He wants to cry, but crying is not worthy of men. He wishes he were home in his comfortable bed, but home suddenly seems far away.

"Is this what the revolution is all about?" the Sayyid asks himself. The whole country is in a state of rebellion, and many people have lost their lives. "No," he decides, "this is sheer hell." But what does he know about the nature of revolution and the price of freedom? To him, Zubayda is more precious than the national revolution. Freedom is not Egypt's independence of British control; it is his individual freedom to pursue pleasure, which has been circumscribed by the British authorities. No one understands his thoughts better than Ghunaym Hamido, owner of an oil press in the Jamaliyya quarter and one of the pleasure companions who frequent Zubayda's house. He too is arrested and forced to work at the same location. Seeing the Sayyid in a miserable state, he says the reason for his predicament is that Zubayda has called down evil upon him. The Sayyid answers that maybe she did. Hamido asks, "Was not filling up Zubayda's crevice easier than filling this hole?" "No," says the Sayyid, "it was much more arduous." And when he later feels the need to urinate, he tells Hamido that doing so is more important than evicting the British from Egypt (520). This seemingly powerful man, whose word is law in his house, now stands with his dignity dragged to the ground, yet he does not grasp what the British have done to him and his country. Sadder still, he does not understand the noble ideas of his son Fahmi or the national cause for which he would give his life.

Eventually the Sayyid is released and returns to his home and work, but he cannot forget that Fahmi has for the first time challenged his authority. He wishes the revolution would end soon; he does not mind contributing money to the national cause but fears that someone close to him may become a casualty. Unwilling to show any sign of weakness, he refuses to admit to himself that when the British soldiers forced him to dig dirt, he wished Fahmi were there to save him from his plight.

His friend Shaykh Mutawalli Abd al-Samad, surprised that Fahmi would disobey such a disciplinarian, urges the Sayyid to admonish his son to stay away from trouble. Does Fahmi not know of the British atrocities in the villages of al-Aziziyya and Badrashin? Hundreds of armed British soldiers, he says, attacked the two villages at night, stormed the residences of their mayors, and violated their women, dragging them from their homes by the hair. They beat the men and pillaged everything they could put their hands on. Finally they set fire to the houses, made mostly of straw, and the villages went up in flames. He asserts that Fahmi should not become involved, for God alone can destroy the English, as in the past he destroyed nations that disobeyed him. Leaving the Sayyid's shop, he recites from the Quran, "The Rum have been driven to the end of the earth, but after their defeat they will become victorious" (30:1), implying that the Egyptians will someday overcome the British. Of course, we cannot expect a poor Muslim shaykh like Abd al-Samad to view the British presence as pragmatically as a politician; but he is like many Middle Eastern people, both Muslims and Christians, who believe firmly that a just, omnipotent God alone can avenge them against their enemies. To Westerners, his words sound not only absurd but pitiful. They reflect an obscurantist and abstract perception that contradicts the view, prevalent in the West, that man is the measure of all things and the master of his actions, responsible solely to himself.

The Sayyid and others, like his assistant Jamil al-Hamzawi, seem to see the nationalist movement and the demonstrations as primarily the activity of the younger generation. Reckless youths act irrationally, they say, and the adults suffer the consequences. Al-Hamzawi says these crazy days have so perverted the minds of youngsters that even his own son Fuad wants to join the demonstrations. These men of the older generation seek only a quiet life and see no benefit in defying the British, who nevertheless treat all the Egyptian people harshly and try to eliminate those who oppose them. Among their targets is Abd al-Hamid Bey Shaddad, the son of a leading dry goods merchant in the al-Abbasiyya quarter, deported from Egypt when the Khedive was deposed; we shall hear much of him in the second part of the trilogy.

When the British authorities saw that military force could not subdue the Egyptians, they released Zaghlul from exile on April 7, 1919. The news was received with great joy and high expectations, but no one was stirred more than Sayyid Ahmad, who shouted, "Allah Akbar!" (God is the greatest!) and "Victory to the believers!" He even hung Zaghlul's picture in his shop. Shopkeepers celebrated by giving soft drinks to passersby; women paraded in the streets, dancing and singing, "O Husayn, it was only an ordeal, and it is lifted!" (556).

The Sayyid cares less about Zaghlul's release than about Fahmi's safety. Now, he thinks, peace will come, and there will be no more casualties. But Fahmi, seeing Zaghlul's release as a surrender by the British, believes that Zaghlul will return from Paris with Egypt's independence, and April 7 will forever symbolize the victory of the revolution. His enthusiasm is contrasted with Yasin's passive attitude toward the national movement. Yasin says that he joined the students at his school in demonstrating joyfully; when Fahmi doubts this assertion, he protests that he is no less nationalistic. The difference between them, he says, is that he does not condone violence as a means of achieving national goals. He wants to harmonize his love of country with his desire for safety. When

Fahmi objects that this may not be possible, he says that then he will choose his safety, meaning that he loves his country but is not willing to sacrifice his life for it (557–58).

Kamal comments that some students at his school demonstrated peacefully in the schoolyard, while others took to the streets. When Yasin asks why he did not join them, Kamal says, "To hell with them." His answer reveals his indecisive attitude toward the national movement, which he cannot fully comprehend. Given his tender age, this response needs no apology, yet Mahfouz says rather lamely that Kamal made this statement without proper thought, and it does not express his true feelings. We can only conclude that although Kamal resents the presence of the British soldiers in his country, he looks upon them as superior to his countrymen.

Despite his expression of joy over the release of Zaghlul and hope for lasting peace with the British, the Sayyid is extremely unhappy. One of his sons has challenged his patriarchal authority, and this is no small matter. He imagined himself so powerful and important that lawyers and government officials would shrink in his presence, and now Fahmi has taken away this illusion. Fahmi, sensitive to his father's feelings, does not wish to disobey him, but his patriotic duty comes first. Believing that the national movement has achieved its goals, he seeks to make peace with his father, explaining that he was simply serving his country's interest. After some remonstration, the Sayyid tells him to cease his foolishness and not involve himself in national affairs.

But Fahmi is committed to the national cause and eager to see what Zaghlul's mission to Europe will achieve. Indeed, his greatest wish is to meet Zaghlul personally and be inspired by his courage and magnanimity. He decides to enjoy the fruits of his labor by joining a demonstration to celebrate Zaghlul's release, assuring his father that it has been approved by both British and Egyptian authorities. He makes his way to the Azhar and is put in charge of the secondary school students who will take part. Once he had wished that his national struggle might be crowned by martyrdom. Now, having put this thought behind him, he joyfully joins the demonstration, feeling proud that he has been designated to represent the National Fighters' High Committee. This is an honor he will forever cherish.

Cairo is filled with masses of demonstrators moving like waves from one square of the city to another. When they reach the Azbakiyya garden, suddenly and without the slightest provocation British soldiers open fire. Fahmi is one of those killed. The Sayyid is sitting in his shop when some national fighters call on him with the sad news. He cannot believe it; he thought that the time of killing was gone forever and peace was established. For the first time, this man who has spent his life pursuing pleasure feels the merciless pangs of grief. He is even more shocked to learn how his son died, having thought that he only distributed nationalist circulars. How can he go home, and what will he tell his wife? Will he have the strength to tell her that Fahmi is gone forever, and she will never see him again? Not only is he dead; the hope of his brilliant future has vanished, and with it the dream of a liberated and dignified Egypt. "How can anyone in the family fill the vacuum caused by his death?" the Sayyid wonders to himself on the way home. As he arrives, he hears Kamal singing, "Visit me once a year. It would be a shame if you should forget me completely." Thus ends *Bayn al-Qasrayn* (579).

The novel's conclusion is appropriate and impressive. Just as Fahmi has fallen, Kamal sings an appeal not to be entirely forgotten, as if he had a premonition about the death of his brother. Although he does not know what has happened, the song he is innocently singing applies perfectly to the situation. Its words and Fahmi's death are welded together. The ending is neat and economical, without a trace of sentimentality.

Qasr al-Shawq

The second part of the trilogy, *Qasr al-Shawq* (published in English as *Palace of Desire*) takes its title from the street where Yasin's house is located. He inherited this house from his mother and moved there after some disagreement with his father.[39] The novel opens in 1924, five years after the close of *Bayn al-Qasrayn*, and ends with the death of Zaghlul in August 1927. The Sayyid's family has experienced many changes since 1919. He and Amina, now in their fifties, are grandparents several times over; Yasin is twenty-eight, and Kamal, a recent high school graduate, is seventeen. Khadija and Aisha live with their sibling husbands and mother-in-law in al-Sukkariyya, not far from their parents' home. Khadija has two sons, Abd al-Munim and Ahmad. Aisha has two sons, Muhammad and Uthman, and a daughter, Naima. Yasin has a son, Ridwan, already seven years old, by Zaynab, whom he has long since divorced. Mahfouz again portrays the family's life in minute detail, mixing into the narrative internal monologues that he handles dexterously. His chief purpose is to show the clash of traditional values and concepts with those imported from the West, especially as it affects Kamal, who has the central position in the novel. He also describes political change, showing that the national movement has deteriorated into petty squabbling between the palace and the politicians, and the cultural changes resulting from the onslaught of Western ideas, including the slow decline of patriarchal authority.

Sayyid Ahmad's daily routine has changed little, but he is more conscious of his age and seems deeply affected by the loss of his son. During the past five years he has not touched a drink nor heard a song. Most of all, he has stopped womanizing. How could he return to his old wanton ways with Fahmi in the grave? He continues his compartmentalized life between the marketplace and the mosque, between his nightlife and his life at home. He still prays and accompanies his sons to the mosque, but his desire for pleasure is as feverish as ever. He longs for his boon companions and their orgies. Though part of him died when Fahmi was killed, he realizes that grieving will not bring him back and finds himself one night partying aboard a houseboat on the Nile with his cronies. Whether because of guilt or because he finally senses his age, he does not indulge in sex and drinking. Should he repent or resume his old life-style? He chooses the latter but discovers to his sorrow that he is not the same; indeed, nothing is the same—not his family, his friends, nor the country.

His choice between repentance and his old ways is made one Friday when, on the way to prayer services, he spots his old friend Zannuba entering the shop of the goldsmith Yaqub. With the sight of her voluptuous body seizing his mind, he passes by the mosque and follows her. He hopes to resume their relationship, but to his chagrin she greets him coolly and pays little attention to him. Having once fulfilled his lust for her, however, he wants her back, and so prevails upon his crony Muhammad Iffat to arrange a meeting between himself and Zannuba on the houseboat, without her knowing about it. After professing his love, he promises to rent a private houseboat for her and support her, provided that she be exclusively his. Zannuba agrees, and the Sayyid joyfully resumes his former life of dissipation. Infatuated, he ignores the warnings of his assistant Jamil al-Hamzawi that he is squandering his money, defending his expenditures by saying that God alone is perfect.[40] As in the past, he convinces himself that he should make up for the pleasures he has long missed, and that the forgiving God can wait for him to repent. But fate has something else in store for him. Zannuba, whom he considers his own, is soon to teach him a painful lesson in humility.

It has never occurred to Sayyid Ahmad that Zannuba may one day confront him with the drastic choice between marrying her and losing her forever. He goes to see her at the houseboat, intending to rebuke her because he suspects that she has been cheating on him. He argues that he has met all her demands, and she must honor their agreement. He further contends that he has made her a lady, and her aunt Zubayda would be jealous of her. Like a lioness, Zannuba roars that God created her a lady, and that she agreed to live with him only because of his insistence; she is not his slave, and if he does not like her behavior, he should leave her alone. The Sayyid cannot believe that she has dared to defy him and humiliate him. This lecherous man, who regards women solely as sex objects, cannot understand that despite having slept with all his cronies, she still has some human dignity left. The squabble comes to a show-down when she tells the Sayyid that she has been seeing a young merchant who is very serious about marrying her. She gives him an ultimatum: marry her or leave her alone.

The Sayyid suggests that the young man has deceived Zannuba, intending to take advantage of her, but she says her only desire is to be married and live a quiet, decent life. She can no longer endure the life of sin. Sayyid Ahmad is stunned and humiliated. It is unthinkable that he, a respectable member of society, should marry a woman like Zannuba. How could he face his friends and family when she is known to have slept with other men, including the young merchant, with whom she was in bed just the night before? This is sheer social and moral suicide. In a long but intense internal monologue, Mahfouz portrays the forceful conflict between the Sayyid's conscience and his self-image as he agonizes over his decision. Indeed, he lusts after Zannuba and wants to marry her but fears that doing so will bring him disgrace both at home and in society. Having often rebuked Yasin for his wanton life-style, he wonders how he could face his son after marrying a woman like Zannuba. Torn between his desire and his false sense of dignity, he tells her that marrying her would be incompatible with his honor. When she repeats her ultimatum, he tells her to gather her possessions and leave the houseboat. She answers that the lease is in her name, and she has every right to remain; if he protests further, she will call the police to remove him. The Sayyid looks at Zannuba with contempt but finally leaves to avoid a scandal.

Sayyid Ahmad may well terminate his relations with Zannuba here rather than suffer further humiliation, but desire overcomes dignity. He visits his cronies to ask their advice, although there is no reason to expect this will help. As Muhammad Iffat admits, all of them have slept with Zannuba, but none ever considered establishing a long-term relationship with her (334). The Sayyid is not outraged by Iffat's words; he and his friends are hypocrites, hiding beneath a veneer of social respectability, to whom adultery is normal and acceptable, but an intimate association with a whore is not. The truth is that the Sayyid is infatuated. He is not repulsed by her wanton life-style, but he is outraged and dejected when he learns about his younger rival. He suddenly realizes that he is old and can no longer impress women with his sexual prowess. How can a powerful man like himself, whose favor and companionship Zubayda and other woman seek, be humiliated by a mere youth?

Anxious to know who his rival may be, he returns to the houseboat to play detective. On seeing Zannuba leave, he follows her to Qasr al-Shawq—where, to his utter amazement, she knocks at the door of Yasin's house. Incredibly, his own son is the young rival who has promised to marry Zannuba. The earth seems to shake under his feet. Does Yasin know of his own amorous relationship with her? When and how did they meet? How many times did they betray him? Trying to make sense of his discovery, Sayyid Ahmad finally convinces himself that he is not jealous, reasoning that it is better to be defeated by his own son than by a stranger. Realizing for the first time that his role in life has faded, he simultaneously laments the waning of his power and envies Yasin, whose turn it is to carry on the life of pleasure. He must face life with a new determination. The rules of the game have changed, and there is no returning to the old days. Though he accepts the fact that he has lost Zannuba forever, he is troubled because Yasin has flouted his patriarchal authority. Lamenting his loss of control, he attempts to shift the blame for his failure by accusing his son of acting recklessly. He deludes himself into thinking that he has provided his sons with an excellent upbringing, and they have responded with disobedience (359–60, 362).

Mahfouz previously has portrayed Yasin as preoccupied with sex, largely due to heredity, but there is more to the matter. As we have seen already, he is an insignificant clerk in an obscure elementary school, typical of many government employees who were victims of a rigid administrative system and a repressive regime that determined their livelihood and careers and kept them forever at its mercy. Thus, Yasin must feel deep frustration and suppressed emotions. Sex is his means of release. His anxiety leads him to seek instant gratification, although he yearns for a quiet, stable family life. It is thus no surprise that his marital relations are troubled. Yet Mahfouz also portrays him as a tender person who truly wants to love and be loved, not merely as a despicable rake whose life is filled with cheap sex. But his lack of a mother's compassion and his father's hypocritical life greatly influence his conduct. He loves Maryam, the girl Fahmi wanted to marry; because she is his chosen mate, not forced upon him by his father, he is optimistic about the prospect of life with her. He even believes that Ridwan, his son by Zaynab, will be happy with Maryam as a stepmother.

Is Yasin sincere about settling into a quiet married life, or is he driven solely by his sexual desire? Mahfouz seems to forget that what he says about a character in one place does not harmonize with what he says about him elsewhere. We are told more than once that Yasin is lecherous by nature and cannot control his sexual behavior. To him, marriage is merely a convenience, and women are sex objects. Later we receive the impression that Yasin has tired of dissipation and cherishes love for its own sake. Chapters 5 and 16 detail his craving for a settled married life with Maryam and his determination to marry her despite his family's objection. Yet in chapters 25 through 27 he again becomes involved with Zannuba, marries her, and divorces Maryam. Nothing reveals his true nature so much as his internal monologue at the start of chapter 5, in which we are told that he has always been licentious, and that marriage to Maryam cannot ease his deep-seated frustration or satiate his sexual hunger. He says emphatically that no woman can quench his burning desire for sex, nor can his heart learn how to settle down. Better he should have been like his father, having one woman to bear and raise his children, while he was free to play around with others (295).

Yasin meets Maryam on the rooftop, where he professes his love and his desire to marry her. Initially unconvinced, she finally believes him when he persists. But he still needs his father's approval. Not surprisingly, the Sayyid objects, claiming that Maryam has a tarnished past and is unworthy to be his daughter-in-law. The real reason for his objection, of course, is his own affair with Umm Maryam, about which Yasin knows nothing. Unwilling to tell his son the truth for fear of scandal, the Sayyid must find another reason to convince him not to marry Maryam—for instance, the fact that she has been previously married and divorced on unknown grounds. He and the rest of the family argue that Yasin's marriage to Maryam would be a betrayal of Fahmi, who loved her. But before he was killed, Fahmi had heard about her flirtation with the English soldier Julian and given up the idea of marrying her. Thus, Yasin does not see himself as dishonoring the memory of his late brother.

The only impediment is the Sayyid's patriarchal authority. If his father insists on blocking the marriage, Yasin will have no alternative but to leave home. He tells Kamal that Maryam never broke

Fahmi's heart; when Fahmi wanted to marry her, his father objected, just as he is doing now. To avoid conflict with the family, Yasin immediately moves to his mother's house in Qasr al-Shawq, openly rejecting his father's authority over him. Sayyid Ahmad finally gives his blessing to the marriage, very much against his will. He believes that his son has made a big mistake and should bear sole responsibility for it (187–88). The Sayyid's daughters also agonize over accepting Maryam as a member of the family. Khadija, ever contentious, reminds Aisha of Maryam's dalliance with Julian. She wonders why Yasin cannot see the truth about her, but she prudently does not mention her concern to her husband and finally accepts reality, telling her mother that whether they like it or not, Maryam will become one of the family.

In depicting the impact of Sayyid Ahmad's warped sense of values and hypocrisy on Yasin's behavior, Mahfouz points up the conflict between the Egyptian lower-middle-class morality and the desire for social respectability. How can the Sayyid, having had illicit relations with Umm Maryam, give sound moral advice to Yasin, who differs from his father only in that he admits the sinful nature of his actions? Umm Maryam, as obsessed with sex as the Sayyid, considers it normal to covet Yasin as his father coveted her. When he calls on her to ask her daughter's hand in marriage, he is suddenly aroused by her full figure, especially her enormous, domelike behind, and wishes that Maryam were similarly endowed. He even cites the Quran (83:26), albeit out of context, as proof that ambitious men will compete for a luscious body like that of Umm Maryam (140). Yasin finds her more appealing than her daughter or his father's mistresses, Zubayda and Jalila. She reciprocates his lust, whispering to herself ironically, "Help the one who came to ask the daughter's hand in marriage, but fell into her mother's trap." Umm Maryam and Yasin soon find themselves passionately engaged in amorous pleasure. She begins to visit him clandestinely at Qasr al-Shawq, under the cover of darkness and without her daughter's knowledge. Within a week, however, Yasin tires of having sex with this middle-aged woman who acts like a teenager. He hopes she will call off this game and let him concentrate on his future bride, but she persists. On learning that Yasin has met with Maryam to plan their marriage, she flies into a rage, cursing him as the lecherous son of a dissolute woman. After a brief altercation in which she slaps him, he leaves (chapters 11–12).

Having lost Yasin, Umm Maryam seeks to renew her relationship with his father. She visits the Sayyid at his shop, ostensibly to ask whether he has approved of the marriage. She tries flattery, telling him that he is still young and should not give up his old ways. But the Sayyid tells her that he has aged, and the past is gone forever. Having already lost Fahmi, and with Yasin soon leaving and Kamal rebelling against him, he is not interested in Umm Maryam, although he concedes that she is still luscious, despite traces of age in her face. Thus ends her relationship with the Sayyid and his son. Two weeks after Yasin's wedding, the Sayyid's family and friends are stunned to hear that Umm Maryam has married Bayyumi al-Sharbatly, a lowly shopkeeper. Sayyid Ahmad flies into a rage, declaring he cannot tolerate such a socially unacceptable person as Yasin's father-in-law. Worse still, Bayyumi is already married, and when his wife learns that he has married Umm Maryam, she attacks him both verbally and physically. A few days later, Umm Maryam dies after a brief illness, without time to enjoy her marriage (189–92).

Yasin's sexual and marital problems seem endless. For all intents and purposes, he seems committed to sex as others are committed to ideological causes. Except for reading Western fiction and an occasional piece of light Arabic literature, Yasin has no other interest in life. He even associates work with sex. At one time he wanted to have a shop of his own, like his father, rather than work in the bureaucracy, mainly because he believed that independent work would give him more opportunities for sexual liaisons.

Unhappy in his marriage to Maryam, Yasin decides to replace her with another woman who will satiate his craving for sex (294–95). Unexpectedly he meets Zannuba, whom he has not seen for a long time. She tells him she is single and looking for a husband; he responds that he is married, but looking for another wife. He invites her to have a drink, and she accepts. Zannuba has changed; her manners are more polished than before. She tells him that she has become a real lady, abandoning her country dress for Western attire, although in fact it appears she has simply become a more sophisticated whore. But he does not care whether she is a whore nor whether she is sophisticated. He is interested only in her body. He finds her more ravishing than the day he left her. As before, she calls him a bull, but he does not mind. He is obsessed with the thought of seeing her dance naked.

After drinks and small talk, he takes her to his home at Qasr al-Shawq, where their continued carousing awakens Maryam. She becomes angry and curses him for daring to bring a whore into their house. Yasin in turn calls Maryam and her mother whores and, recalling her flirtation with Julian, laments that he did not heed the advice of good people who warned him not to marry her. If she is a whore, Maryam retorts, then he is a pimp; he should marry Zannuba, because they are two of a kind. The altercation reaches a climax when Yasin tells Maryam that she is divorced; under Islamic law, she must leave the house. He awakes in the morning to find Zannuba in Maryam's bed and realizes what he has done. Zannuba tries to coax him into marrying her, saying he should not worry too much about her past. Having branded Maryam a whore, she asks, why should he not marry another? She tells him she is the mistress of a rich merchant who seeks to marry her, but she is hesitant because he is already married, with children; in truth, of course, her paramour is Yasin's father.

Sayyid Ahmad, no longer the authoritarian father who controls the lives of his sons, has no idea that Yasin has divorced Maryam, thinking that she has simply moved out, probably to her mother's house. He learns of Yasin's marriage to Zannuba only from his friend Muhammad Iffat and is relieved to hear that she has not revealed their own relationship to his son. The Sayyid is angry because Yasin's failure to inform him of his marriage constitutes an egregious violation of his authority, and he worries about Ridwan, now seven, growing up with Zannuba as his stepmother. Grieving over the situation, he rejects Yasin's claim that he lacked the courage to tell him of his plans and rebukes him for acting wholly selfishly. Yasin, he says, has compromised the honor of the whole family by marrying a disreputable woman whose aunt is equally notorious. The Sayyid, mindful that Zannuba tried to trap him into marriage but failed, asks his son to divorce her before she can conceive and disgrace the family forever. When Yasin objects, the Sayyid reminds him that he is duty bound to obey him and insists he mend his ways. Obviously, he is more concerned about people's opinion of himself and his family than about his son's marriage. Mahfouz implies that an amoral man like Sayyid Ahmad cannot offer his son sound moral advice, nor can he be a good example. Perhaps he is jealous, feeling that Yasin not only has stolen Zannuba but exposed his old age and loss of sexual power. He finally forces his son to allow Ridwan's grandfather Muhammad Iffat to take custody of the child (chapter 32).

Yet Yasin, consistently portrayed as a lewd person with no willpower, defies his father's authority not only by marrying Zannuba but by refusing to divorce her. He senses that she represents his last prospect for success in marriage. She is tougher than his former wives. Unlike Zaynab, who was imposed upon him by his father, Zannuba is his own choice; unlike Maryam, she treats him like a man and fulfills his sexual desires. She knows he thinks of marriage in terms of passion, not true love, and she accepts the fact that he may soon be cheating on her. Indeed, Yasin regards women as all alike, made for sex. He tells Kamal that the ideal woman does not exist, adding that like their father, he appreciates women with large behinds, and an angel with a desirable figure would not be able to fly. Yet he tries to convince Zannuba that she will be the only woman in his life. Eager to believe him and aware that arguing with him would be pointless and destructive, she leaves him to his own conscience (403–6, 416–17).

Inevitably, Yasin's decision to marry Zannuba affects his social status and his job; the Ministry of Education plans to transfer him to a remote place in upper Egypt. When the Sayyid asks why, Yasin says the principal has accused him of endangering the good name of his school. The father reminds him of his warning that Zannuba is not socially acceptable, but Yasin says that she is his lawful wife and he expects people to treat her accordingly. When Yasin asks him to use his influence to annul the transfer order, the Sayyid calls on the principal, feeling that he must either defend his son or see him humiliated. He argues that it is unjust to punish someone for marrying badly because this is a personal matter. The principal replies that there are other complaints against Yasin, including his fight with a whore on Tayyab street, and charges that he is lazy. The Sayyid refuses to let Yasin down and, with help from his friends in the parliament, manages to have him reassigned to the ministry's records office. At the same time, he insists that Yasin divorce Zannuba and return home, and he promises to find him another decent, compatible wife. But Zannuba is already pregnant, says Yasin, and he does not want to add another divorce to his earlier sins. The Sayyid, enraged to learn that Zannuba is carrying his grandchild, swears that Yasin is nothing but a curse (chapter 39). He does not raise the issue again. Presumably, he finally accepts the idea that Zannuba will be his son's wife for life.

Indeed, the Sayyid must amend his own life before he can demand the same of his son. Still yearning for the life of pleasure, he visits his cronies on Zannuba's houseboat and drinks and joins in the merriment, hoping to renew his relations with Zubayda. But alas, times have changed, and he is no longer young. Zubayda remarks sarcastically that Sayyid Ahmad has become her kinsman by marriage, and she seems angered because her niece Zannuba has failed to maintain contact with her. One of the Sayyid's friends suggests that he and Zubayda reenact their "wedding" scene. But despite the lively, wide-ranging conversation and the convivial atmosphere, these longtime companions are forced to recognize that they have aged and changed, and the pleasure they seek is not the same as it was years ago. They all complain of one ailment or another, including Sayyid Ahmad, who has developed high blood pressure. When Muhammad Iffat asks whether he still rules his household with an iron rod even in these democratic times, the Sayyid answers that democracy is for the populace, not the family. He asks in jest whether it means that if he wants to make a decision, he must ask his wife and children what they think. Zubayda reminds him sarcastically to ask Zannuba's opinion too (chapter 41).

Soon afterward, Sayyid Ahmad becomes seriously ill and is confined to bed. In keeping with the old belief that high blood pressure results from an increased amount of blood in the body, he is bled. His illness shocks his children, who believe that he is stronger than illness or pain, and that life without him is worthless. Indeed, he is the very heart of the family, keeping it cohesive and intact. Although he curtails the freedom of his wife and children, he is always ready to support them. But like many men of his generation, he does not know how to express his love for them. He acts tough to maintain his authority and elicit their respect, but he has no real understanding of their thoughts or needs. He is content to be a good father and provider.

After his illness the Sayyid appears to seek repentance, thinking that to postpone it is a denial of God's grace. He asks God to protect him from the wiles of the devil. He takes his children to the mosque of al-Husayn, who he believes will intercede on their behalf with the Prophet Muhammad on the day of judgment. The aged Shaykh Mutawalli Abd al-Samad visits the ailing Sayyid and asks him, as an act of penitence, to feed the poor and perform the pilgrimage to Mecca. Yet there is no clear indication that he regrets his actions and will not return to his dissolute ways. He appears to repent not because he has sinned against God and his laws but because his illness has curtailed his life of pleasure. Even Yasin, to whom the question of his father's repentance is very important, is uncertain about his intentions.

Although Mahfouz depicts the morality of the Egyptian lower middle class chiefly through Sayyid Ahmad and Yasin, we should not conclude that everyone in this class is immoral. Rather, Mahfouz seeks to expose the hypocrisy of those who profess faith and claim respectability, but whose inner lives are tarnished by moral weakness. Focusing on the human condition, he gives an accurate, detailed picture of the social, economic, political, and religious aspects of life in the first half of the twentieth century and of the extensive changes in the family structure during that period. In presenting the saga of a family much like his own, he appears to be a committed writer with an almost mystical relationship with and understanding of his characters. Reading him is like contemplating a gigantic mural that embodies social themes in panoramic scenes.

Mahfouz spends several chapters examining the problems arising when many people live together under one roof, as did Aisha and

Khadija, together with their husbands, children, and mother-in-law. Aisha is amiable, tolerant, and fun loving. She smokes and occasionally drinks with her husband, parties with friends, and enjoys singing and dancing. She even allows her young daughter Naima to dance. Khadija, however, is contentious and intolerant and quite critical of her sister, who she thinks has overstepped the bounds of social decorum. She also does not get along with her aged mother-in-law, who asks the Sayyid to resolve their dispute. He calls on them, feeling that being asked to mediate is a great honor, a recognition of his social status and authority within the family. He finds most of their complaints insignificant. The mother-in-law claims that Khadija is disrespectful, calling her *Tiza* (aunt) rather than *Nina* (mother), and has taken over the part of the rooftop where she raised chickens and forced her to move them into the yard. Finally, she complains, Khadija prepared a *sharkasiyya* (chicken dish) for her husband's guests, falsely claiming it was a family specialty, when it came from Yasin's ex-wife Zaynab. Khadija takes this remark as an insult and calls her mother-in-law a liar. Sayyid Ahmad, outraged by his daughter's insolence and disrespect, tells her to kiss the old woman's hand and call her Nina or lose his support, and she reluctantly complies. Khadija also complains to her mother about Aisha's behavior, but like her husband, Amina gives her a lesson in tolerance and compassion (182–83). To a contemporary Western reader, such family disputes may seem trivial and silly, but to a Middle Eastern reader, they are still part of the human condition even to this day.

Unlike his father and Yasin, who seem plain, mediocre, and static, Kamal is a vibrant, charming, and intelligent seventeen-year-old with a bright future. Mahfouz devotes a great portion of the novel to him as representing a more propitious aspect of the family and of society interested more in the life of the mind than in sensuality. Like his late brother Fahmi, Kamal is educated with a penchant for intellectual pursuit. He is the brain of the family, the only one interested in ideas. In this second volume of the trilogy, the unfocused curiosity of the ten-year-old Kamal is transformed into genuine intellectual activity. He wants to learn about the origins of things, especially man, God, and the universe. He seeks the truth, and his quest motivates him, like Mahfouz, to study literature and philosophy. He is not, like the rest of the family, interested in mundane subjects, but rather (like Fahmi) in human precepts. He even spends his summer vacation reading, while his classmates, having finished high school, are content to rest (26–27).

His father wants him to undertake a career like law, medicine, or engineering, which will bring him wealth and prestige, but Kamal hopes to enroll in the Teachers' College and study literature and philosophy. He wants to live "the life of the mind," which he finds difficult to explain to his father. Their disagreement over which school he should attend parallels that between Mahfouz and his father. Mahfouz's first inclination was toward engineering or medicine, and when he decided to study philosophy, his father was quite angry. His high school teachers, especially Bishara Baghus, were unhappy about his decision, feeling that he was weak in the humanities. But when he began reading philosophical treatises by some Egyptian writers, he found he was inclined more toward philosophy than other disciplines, believing it could answer his questions about the mysteries of human existence. His father, unable to understand his motive, thought the study of law or medicine would serve the same end just as well.[41]

Kamal's talk with his father about his education and career underscores the gap between the old and new generations. The Sayyid is reluctant to let his son enroll in the Teachers' College, for to him teaching is a miserable profession, neither prestigious nor lucrative. A teacher stands between the respected effendi and the despised *mujawir* (an Azharite student who lives in the Azhar mosque and depends on other people's charity, even for food). The Sayyid asks Kamal why he cannot emulate Fuad al-Hamzawi, his assistant's son, who plans to enter the law school. He points out that Fuad, to whom Kamal once gave his old suits out of charity, will someday be a rich, respected member of society, while he, having chosen teaching, will be poor and despised.

Kamal cannot understand why his father disparages his chosen field. He argues that knowledge is more honorable than money or prestige. Are there not learned Azharites, like Sa'd Zaghlul and the esteemed writer Mustafa Lutfi al-Manfaluti? Why then does his

father despise teachers and their profession? The Sayyid acknowledges the eminence of both men; if his son believes he has God-
given talents, he says, let him be like al-Manfaluti. Kamal tries hard
to convince his father that literature and philosophy are highly
respected, even hallowed by Europeans. His father retorts that they
live in Egypt, not Europe, and he wants him to have a respectable
and secure future. But Kamal insists that teaching is the way that
leads to the life of the mind.

"And what is the life of the mind?" asks the Sayyid. What is
mysterious about it? There is nothing new under the sun. Life began
with Adam, he observes philosophically, and people will go either
to paradise or to hell. Frustrated, he tries to focus on his son's
future, while Kamal tries unsuccessfully to convince his father that
the life of the mind represents a sublime human goal, largely
because he himself is not clear about what it is. We can hardly blame
Sayyid Ahmad for feeling as he does. He is simply a semiliterate
shopkeeper who wants his son to have a secure position and not
dabble in some gibberish people call literature and philosophy.
These abstract disciplines, he thinks, will afford Kamal only an
unenviable, underpaid position teaching in an obscure elementary
school. There are many parents like him, even in the United States,
who could not care less about the study of humanities but want
their children to attend school, specialize in a useful discipline, and
assure themselves a good living. As Mahfouz explains, in the 1920s
many Egyptian families were concerned about basic human needs
and not abstract concepts, which could not put food on the table.
Many young men aspired to become writers but had to struggle
very hard just to make a living; Mahfouz himself, for instance,
received no remuneration for what he wrote.

Mahfouz points out that the Egyptian people were coming to
look with increasing favor on government employment. In a country where farming was in the hand of lowly and ignorant *fallahin*,
industry was of little consequence, and small business was not very
prestigious or lucrative, people began to view government work as
quite respectable, offering power and prestige among the mass of
illiterate and ignorant people. Moreover, it was a more secure

livelihood than, say, farming or small business. For these reasons, Sayyid Ahmad tries to convince Kamal to seek a government position and suggests that he try the military or police academy if he persists in refusing to enter the law school. But Kamal rejects the idea.[42]

Why did the Egyptians view government employment as more respectable than teaching or working in the private sector? In the West, government employees are considered civil servants whose duty is to serve the people, not be served by them. Indeed, the institution of civil service is based on the democratic principle that state powers are vested in the people, not in functionaries. But in Egypt, as in all the Middle Eastern countries, the concept of civil service is upside down. The powers of the state are vested in the government, not the people. In other words, the government is regarded as the master, and the people are expected to obey its dictates. Government employment offers the civil servants (or rather, civil masters) prestige and power. Furthermore, it is clean work, compared to that of the *fallahin*, and thus brings popular respect. This is why Sayyid Ahmad wants Kamal to be, say, a judge, and not an elementary school teacher. When he cannot convince Kamal that attending the Teacher's College is not in his best interest, he calls him an ignorant fool.

Kamal is understandably distressed because his father does not see his point of view, and even more upset because Yasin sides with his father. But Yasin is not an intellectual, merely a semiliterate elementary school clerk who has little respect for the teaching profession. Drawn to the carnal and mundane, he has no use for abstract ideas. He voices surprise at Kamal's ignorance of the real values in life, declaring that the life he ought to live does not exist in the books of al-Manfaluti. Kamal must deal with the vicissitudes of daily life, with real people. Although some people regard the teacher as an apostle (as the poet Ahmad Shawqi states), to Yasin this view is an illusion. He tells Kamal to accompany him to the Nahhasin School and see for himself how many of the teachers deserve to be called apostles. If by the life of the mind Kamal means the study of literature and history, he says, these are made for mere entertainment, not for practical living. He warns Kamal not to let the opportunity to build a successful career slip away, as he himself did.

Having failed to win over his father and Yasin, Kamal hesitates to turn to his mother, fearing she cannot comprehend the issue at hand. He finds her surprisingly sympathetic and understanding. Although she is illiterate, she seems to have more common sense than her husband and stepson. When Kamal tells Amina the knowledge he seeks is rooted in religion, morality, and contemplation of God's attributes and the mysteries of his creation, she says enthusiastically that this is the best of knowledge, the same kind that her grandfather and father pursued. No one should scorn the teacher, she adds, using the aphorism popular in the Arab world, "He who taught you one letter has in reality made you his slave." When Kamal reminds her that his father says teaching is not lucrative, Amina cites the words of her own father, that knowledge is more important than money. She shows good common sense, but because she lacks education he finds it difficult to take her opinion seriously.

Neither parent seems to realize that he does not want to enter teaching for its own sake. His purpose in studying the humanities is to write a book, possibly a voluminous work like the Quran, with copious commentaries and marginal notes. He is uncertain what he should write about, because the Quran contains everything known to man. Nevertheless, he believes that the book he dreams of writing will be monumental and bring him lasting fame, which no government position can give him. After all, he reasons, every educated person knows who Socrates was, but no one remembers his judges' names (66).

We see here the inchoate reasoning of an immature adolescent, dealing with profound philosophical concepts that are beyond him. According to Aristotle, it is axiomatic that man desires knowledge, but does he seek it for its own sake, or for mundane purposes? Knowledge is useless unless it leads to a better, more meaningful life. Seeking knowledge in order to put it in a book is futile and in fact ignoble. One's objective in acquiring knowledge should be to know the truth about life, or rather to know life in truth. Kamal has no concrete understanding of knowledge or its significance. The life of the mind, which he praises to his father and others but cannot articulate, is what makes man cognizant of the real world in which he lives. It is the essence of his existential being. Kamal has not yet defined his priorities. He seems to be a rationalist, equating the life of the mind with the life of reason, and something of a dreamer. Only his mother shares his enthusiasm for knowledge, and he does not take her seriously. He lives in a society that is concerned not with his idealistic life of the mind but with the brutal reality of everyday life.

Shocked to realize his father is preoccupied with the externalities of life, he is even more stunned to find that his friend Fuad al-Hamzawi shares his father's outlook, although he expresses it in more sophisticated terms. Mahfouz appears to set up Fuad as a foil to contrast Kamal's idealistic dreams. Though he has not had the same educational opportunities as Kamal, he is an intelligent and assiduous student. He is also pragmatic, realizing that to survive in a materialistic society, he must choose a career that will ensure him a good living. Aware of Kamal's plans to enroll in the Teachers' College, Fuad urges him to think seriously about his future and attend the law school to secure a respectable position and then pursue the intellectual life. He considers his own choice a rational one and sees no difference between the study of law and the life of the mind, which Kamal insists is the study of human values and concepts that transcend purely material considerations. Fuad appreciates Kamal's lofty values but questions whether they are appropriate to the environment in which he lives. Kamal responds that if Sa'd Zaghlul had thought the circumstances were wrong, he would not have gone to the high commissioner to press for independence. The truth is that in their ideas and outlook on life, Kamal and Fuad are miles apart. Although we may be inclined to regard the idealist Kamal as altruistic and tolerant, in his encounter with Fuad we detect evidence of contempt and envy—contempt because Fuad is not his social equal, and envy because he is a smart, realistic young man who has clearly defined objectives in life (78–81).

Kamal's quest for the life of the mind, which has developed from his youthful curiosity, is but one side of his character. He is also a romantic idealist, as is manifested in his falling instantly in love with Aida, the daughter of Abd al-Hamid Bey Shaddad. For four years he idolizes her, seeing her as the embodiment of absolute perfection. For a seventeen-year-old to fall in love is normal, but in Kamal's case love becomes an obsession, a kind of chronic disease affecting his being and outlook on life. It is an ill-fated love that ends not (like Romeo's love for Juliet) in loss of life, but in loss of being, in nothingness. Like his plan to write a classic book, it is a manifestation of his ambitious quest for immortality. It is a mystic love that causes Kamal much anguish and suffering, but he has no capacity to handle suffering, simply because he is no mystic. True love, which ought to bring him closer to God, instead drives him into stultifying skepticism.

Mahfouz uses Kamal's love of Aida to show the gap between the lower and upper classes in Egyptian society. Aida comes from a rich, aristocratic family living in a sumptuous villa in the Abbasiyya district, enjoying the comforts and amenities befitting the upper class—a car and private chauffeur, a special cook, and servants. When the Khedive was deposed in 1914, Abd al-Hamid Bey Shaddad settled with his family in Paris; after the war they returned to Cairo. Kamal, a schoolmate of Aida's brother Husayn, occasionally visited his home, and on meeting Aida, he instantly fell in love with her (21). This love appears to have a basis in Mahfouz's own life. When he was twelve, his family moved to the Abbasiyya district, which was not so aristocratic then as it is today. In his teens he became taken with a neighbor girl who was two years older than himself; it was a romantic love that never grew into a lasting relationship because of the disparities in ages and social status.[43]

Kamal's friendship with Husayn Shaddad may suggest wrongly that there were no substantial differences between the upper and lower classes. Although friendship between young men was common, when the relationship between a young man and woman from different classes became serious, the social scales were tipped. Husayn has other friends from the lower middle class, among them Ismail Latif, who knows that Kamal is in love with Aida but recognizes the social gap that separates them. The importance of social differences is driven home when the class-conscious Aida decides to marry Hasan Salim, another of Husayn's friends who, like him, is from an aristocratic family. His father, Salim Bey Sabri, is a judge on the court of appeals, with all the social privilege the almost hallowed title of Bey conveys. Inclined toward the Liberal Constitutionalists, the opponents of Sa'd Zaghlul, he is influential in politics and judicial affairs.

A conversation among Husayn and his friends reveals their aspirations and their prospects. More important, it shows the powerful effect of social status in determining the individual's career. When Ismail Latif asks Hasan Salim what he plans to do after graduating from law school, Husayn says Hasan will surely find a judicial or diplomatic position, because of his excellent performance. Ismail observes accurately that his father's influence outweighs his own intelligence or success in law school in helping him find an appropriate position. Obviously Hasan knows the truth, but in self-defense he asks sarcastically, "And you yourself, have the efforts of those with connections helped you?" Ismail laughs aloud, exposing sharp, smoke-stained teeth, and says, "Not much. I was rejected by the schools of medicine and engineering for poor grades, and there was nothing for me except the schools of commerce and agriculture. I chose commerce."[44] Mahfouz seeks to show that young men of the lower middle class had far fewer educational opportunities than their upper-middle-class counterparts. Husayn Shaddad could at any time leave the law school and continue his studies in France, but Kamal and Ismail Latif could not afford to do so.

The conversation also makes clear that knowledge pursued for its own sake, as Kamal intends, is not a worthwhile goal in a society which does not value it, and that the teaching profession is not highly respected by young people because it entails no prestige, money, or power. Ismail Latif thinks Kamal is crazy. Husayn, sounding apologetic, observes that several prominent men are graduates of the Teachers College. Hasan politely but pointedly asks Kamal, "Do you really want to become a teacher?" When he says that he does, Ismail replies, "What a calamity" (166–67). The question of whether the primary objective of education is to provide job training or to impart knowledge persists to this day. Many students perceive education as a means of finding work, while the parents who have provided for their education want them to have a rewarding, secure future. Acquiring knowledge for its own sake is left to idealistic dreamers like Kamal.

There is no indication that Kamal is thinking of class differences when he fails in love with Aida. He knows only that as a friend of Husayn, he can visit the family and satisfy his feverish desire to see her. Indeed, he feels so much a member of the family that he freely embraces and kisses her three-year-old sister Budur as if she were Aida herself. Poor Kamal! He is simply infatuated. To him Aida is no longer a human being of flesh and bones but a goddess, an abstract symbol transcending this material world. He cannot think of her acting like other people, eating, drinking, making love, and having children. Even her laughter is divine. He loves her for love's sake, not with an eye to marriage, which he considers a degeneration of love. He sees no fault in her; she is an adored symbol, above human frailties.

Kamal is living in a make-believe world created by his wild imagination. He is able to perceive reality but simply refuses to accept it. He places Aida above Aphrodite and resents the fact that she is not worshipped as the goddess he imagines her to be. He cannot see that in social status, education, and outlook on life she is quite different from himself. He is finally shocked out of his dream-world and back to reality when Husayn Shaddad invites him to visit the pyramids along with Aida and Budur. Looking at the pyramids and the vast desert stretching before them, Husayn exclaims how beautiful the sight is. Then Aida says something in French, and Kamal assumes that she is translating Husayn's words. Thinking that in Egypt she should speak Arabic, he explains away her use of French as intended to offset his own partiality toward his native tongue and to display her feminine graces (199). But in fact it brings into focus the belief of the Egyptian aristocracy that conversing in French was a sign of cultural polish. As we saw in *al-Qahira al-Jadida*, it was one of many practices by which the aristocracy set themselves apart from the common Egyptians, whom they scorned as uncouth peasants. Aida jabbers away in French simply to show that she belongs to a more sophisticated social class. Kamal senses her intention but, blinded by love, tries to overlook it.

The gap between the aristocracy and the lower middle class is real, even if Kamal ignores it. Husayn knows his family has wealth and prestige yet questions why people seek these ends. His father believes any activity that is not conducive to more wealth is pointless and in fact cultivated a friendship with the deposed Khedive in order to obtain the honorable title of Pasha. Husayn complains about his family's money and status but does not reject the benefits they bring; on the contrary, he hopes someday to travel around the world. He says hypocritically that he hates having to ingratiate himself with the aristocracy, yet he has no use for people of lower social standing, whether they be political leaders like Sa'd Zaghlul or schoolmates like Kamal.

Aida's preference for the aristocracy is nowhere more explicit than when she rebukes her brother for criticizing their family's wealth and position. She sees nothing shameful in pursuing money and titles, which she considers lofty goals. She defends her father's lavish spending to entertain the Khedive's brother on the grounds of friendship, loyalty, and above all honor, which no prudent person can overlook. When Husayn objects to their father's friendship with prominent politicians like Adli, Rushdi, and Tharwat, she denies that it is selfishly motivated. Seeking favor with such men, she says, is ignoble for ordinary people but absolutely essential for her own family. In sum, the life of the aristocracy, embodied in the Shaddad family, depends not on hard work and high ethical standards but on influential connections and hypocritical behavior.

Cultural and religious differences also separate Kamal and Aida. She has become Westernized, and Kamal sees her as more refined than his mother and sisters. Her speech, her attire, even her table manners are different. She reads French fiction and listens to Western music. She and her brother are Muslims only in name. Aida knows more about Christianity and its rituals than she knows about Islam. At the Mère de Dieu School she studied the Christian religion, sang hymns, and prayed at chapel. Although she is Muslim by birth, she has read little of the Quran and remembers even less. She and Husayn drink beer and eat pork, contrary to the strictures of Islam. She scarcely fasts during the month of Ramadan, which her family observes out of social necessity rather than religious conviction. Her conduct shows the growing influence of Western ideas and civilization since Egypt's occupation by Napoleon in 1798 and the subsequent reign of Muhammad Ali (1804–49).

But Kamal, who knows nothing of foreign countries beyond what he has read in Western writings, is decidedly the product of his Muslim upbringing. As a child he believed in the miraculous attributes of al-Husayn and was greatly disappointed when a teacher declared that al-Husayn is not buried in the mosque that bears his name. Apparently an upright, devout young man who obeys the religious laws, Kamal refuses Fuad al-Hamzawi's invitation to meet some girls for sexual sport because he does not want to stain his body with sin and then face God in prayer (81). He is so idealistic that Husayn says he and his family are pagans by comparison. Although Aida asks Kamal not to consider her irreligious, plainly she does not take religion as seriously as he does; indeed, she and her brother are almost agnostics. Yet Kamal tries to ignore the disparities between himself and Aida, whom he adores despite her shortcomings. If she does not take her faith seriously, what does it matter? Love covers a multitude of sins (204–5).

A conversation between Aida and Kamal reveals the impact of Western literature on the Arab world. Knowing that Kamal wants to write a book, she asks whether he has read French fiction. He says he has read some stories in translation, but his French is not good enough. She says he will never become a writer until he has mastered the language and read Balzac, George Sand, Madame de Stael, and Pierre Loti. Kamal states scornfully that fiction is not a significant intellectual undertaking, and he intends to produce a serious work. When Aida protests that fiction is serious, Husayn agrees, declaring that it has brought many European writers immortality (205). Kamal's attitude reflects that of many people in Egypt and throughout the Arab world who considered fiction literary trash and a detriment to public morality. They objected especially to translations of Western fiction, often hastily done without the literary subtlety and stylistic polish they cherished, and full of amorous adventures and detective plots that some readers found offensive to their taste and tradition.[45] Nevertheless, in the

1920s a new generation came under the influence of Western ideas, and especially Western fiction.

Kamal wants to write a serious book yet has no subject in mind. He is a disillusioned young man with no clear literary direction and objective, and when the novel ends, he still has not written his book. He continues to read traditional and modern Arab writers, with a smattering of translated Western works, but is more systematic than before. Like Mahfouz, he spends hours at the national library (Dar al-Kutub), broadening his intellectual horizons and attempting to write on philosophical subjects.

Mahfouz presents Kamal not only as an idealist but as a conservative young Egyptian, so much so that he wears the traditional fez even on the trip to the pyramids, when he ought to relax and be less formal. When Husayn remarks that he is a model of the conservative man and Aida asks him why he has not let his hair grow out, Kamal does not know how to react. If they are not actually mocking him, they make it clear that his narrow views do not mesh with theirs, and principles are in total disharmony with the modern world. They feel sorry for this "backward" young man who has not freed himself from the shackles of conservatism and who observes religious laws they consider superfluous and objectionable.

Kamal feels more deeply hurt when Husayn tells him that he was born to be a teacher.[46] To the Western reader, this comment seems innocuous. But to the Middle Eastern reader, who knows that Egyptians in the 1920s viewed teaching, especially below the university level, as less respectable than other professions, it demeans Kamal's career choice. If he had aspired to be a judge or to join the diplomatic corps, Husayn and Aida would have praised him for his prudence, for then he would be their equal. But he has chosen a career that entails no power or prestige and thus does not share their values or fit into their social class. Although they are friendly and hospitable, he is still socially inferior. His preoccupation with the life of the mind and writing a book cannot be taken seriously. Aida appears refined, but in essence she is a shallow person who cares less for knowledge and values than for the comfortable life of the upper class. Perhaps Kamal senses that she and her brother do not genuinely care for him, but he is too infatuated to accept reality. His friendship with them recalls the relationship between Kamil Ali and Ahmad Bey Yusri in *Bidaya wa Nihaya*—friends, but not equals.

The romantic idealist Kamal refuses to believe that Aida is using him to attract his friend Hasan Salim, whom she considers more suited to her. Hasan know that Kamal loves Aida but does not understand that his feeling is purely platonic and not intended to culminate in marriage. So he resorts to calumny to win her affection, declaring Kamal has said she tries to trick young men into believing she is in love with them, hoping to be every young man's dream girl. Moreover, he says, Kamal accuses her of becoming totally Westernized and abandoning her heritage (245–46). The strategy works; Aida treats Kamal harshly and refuses even to see him. He then rebukes Hasan for telling utter lies, but Hasan contemptuously responds, "Let Aida decide between what the son of the merchant and the son of the superior court judge said" (249). Kamal feels wounded. Hasan Salim has drawn the social line between them, and Kamal finally sees that his supposed friend looks down on him. Husayn, Hasan, and Aida have been friendly, but this does not mean that he is their equal. When the veil concealing social discrimination is removed, Kamal suddenly feels persecuted. He compares his case with that of Sa'd Zaghlul, who was caught in the machinations of treacherous so-called friends like Ziwar Pasha, who betrayed him to become prime minister; as Egypt deserted Zaghlul, he thinks, so Aida has deserted him (253).

Kamal seeks to prove his innocence, but Aida tells him what happened has happened, and she does not want to see him any more. For the first time he finds the courage to declare his love; he expects her to react with pride and pleasure, but she asks disdainfully, "And what is beyond love?" He says that the end of love is permanent union. Whether she understands or even pays attention to his words, she must consider him an immature adolescent captivated by fantastic ideas, with no grasp of real life. Indeed, she has never loved Kamal nor thought of loving him. She is too pragmatic to bind herself to a young self-styled philosopher who talks about love for love's sake. She is concerned about her own life and happiness, which depends on marrying a young man from her own social class; she has no time for dreams. Soon she becomes engaged to Hasan Salim, who is accepted in the diplomatic corps and assigned to the Egyptian embassy in Brussels. Poor Kamal is left with a broken heart and a dream that someday he will be a prominent writer.

Having revealed much about the aristocracy through Kamal's friendship with the Shaddad family, Mahfouz expands on class differences. Kamal seeks to know more about the aristocrats, especially those who appear to run the government and stand as a separate caste. He has an opportunity to do so at the wedding of Aida and Hasan, which is in itself painful but at least allows him to see his adored Aida once more. The orchestra plays Western music; Kamal thinks that it should rather play a mournful tune as he buries his love. The reception, graced with champagne and a sumptuous dinner that befits the high status of the Shaddad family, is entirely different from his sisters' wedding parties. This should not surprise us, for the Shaddads consider themselves Parisians and look down on celebrating the wedding according to the native Egyptian custom. As Mahfouz says elsewhere, Aida's father lavishes money only for selfish interest, and this party is meant to impress the rich and influential.

When the ceremony begins with chants from the Quran (more for social pomp than religious conviction), Kamal wonders aloud whether a *madhun* (an official authorized to perform marriages according to Islamic law) will officiate. Ismail Latif answers wittily that what is needed is not a *madhun* but a priest. Among the guests are prominent political figures, some of them members of the Wafd party. Kamal seems awed, but Ismail says they are just people like themselves, though many are old and merit little attention. If they are so ordinary, he wonders, why the disparity between himself and Hasan, one of whom worships the goddess while the other marries her? He decides that these aristocrats are cut from a different cloth, although he should realize that essentially they differ from others only in their values and ethics. Like aristocrats the world over, they love money, power, and prestige. To stay in power, they must dominate and manipulate other people, especially the lower class.

Kamal sees Aida's marriage as an unbearable calamity, the end of his dreams and his life. He cannot envision her making love and laments that she must leave her heavenly state; to him love is more sublime than marriage, which culminates in copulation. He is unable and unwilling to understand that Aida never reciprocated his feeling nor even shared his vision of love. She ridiculed his attire, his hairstyle, and especially his wish to write a book, then used him to prompt Hasan Salim to ask for her hand in marriage. Kamal loved her for love's sake but, perhaps realizing that he could not have her, built an image of her in his mind and worshipped it. His love is so strong, vibrant, and unselfish that he not only tolerates Aida's ridicule but even forgives Hasan for slandering him to win her heart.

Kamal falls in love to no selfish end. He does not aspire to marry Aida to gain money or prestige or even to rise to her social level. He loves her because of what he understands love to be—pure, sincere, and selfless. He seeks in her a symbol of something profound that he himself cannot fathom, and when he does not find it, his world collapses. When he discovers that Aida, her brother, and other friends have ridiculed his love, which they do not understand, he is merely saddened. But when he thinks of her making love and becoming pregnant, he sinks into despair. Tarnished by carnality, his immaculate spiritual idol is lost forever. He did not set out to find an ideal; rather, he created her out of his romantic temperament and his need for absolutes, which comes from his strict, conservative upbringing. Finally realizing he cannot live in a nonsensuous world of romantic idealism, Kamal abandons it altogether and turns eventually to drinking and wenching. But even here his intellectual curiosity is very much alive; he constantly questions what he has done and still seeks to live the life of the mind.

Before turning to the life of dissolution, however, Kamal is profoundly influenced by Darwin's theory of evolution and the descent of man. The loss of Aida has shaken his faith in those close to him and in society. He feels he is a victim of the combined forces of fate, heredity (his massive head and nose, which Aida made fun of), and social injustice. Kamal, who started as a believer, becomes a skeptic. His dream of an intellectual life seems more real when he publishes an article entitled "The Origins of Man," just as the young Mahfouz, influenced by Salama Musa, began by writing on various philosophical and scientific subjects. Kamal's article, a summary rather than a scientific treatment of Darwin's theory, contains nothing new but shows the encroachment of Western ideas on a traditional Middle Eastern society. It also precipitates an intense confrontation between Kamal and his father. The Sayyid, unable to understand why evolution should be taught in the schools as science, objects vigorously to its contents. What sort of science, he asks, declares that man is descended from an animal, when Jews, Muslims, and Copts all believe that God created Adam from the dust of the earth? He voices the utter outrage of traditional Muslims against this theory, which to them is sheer blasphemy. His questions have already crossed Kamal's mind, and he has sought rational answers to them, asking himself whether the Quran is or is not the true word of God. But he cannot explain Darwin's theory to his uneducated father, who assails science to defend a myth. He lacks the courage to admit that he regards evolution as a scientific reality and thinks it can be used as the foundation for a general philosophy of existence.

For two years Kamal has been struggling with doubt, especially after encountering the ideas of two Muslim skeptics, the poet Abu al-Ala al-Ma'arri and Umar al-Khayyam. He maintains that he still believes in God, but belief in God is permanent, while belief in religion has vanished from his mind, along with the legend of al-Husayn. Kamal has liberated himself from the strictures of religion, yet feels he will be nearer to God than before. To him, science is the only true religion. It holds the keys to the mysteries and majesty of the universe. If prophets were sent into the world today, he thinks, they would choose science as their message. Kamal feels as if he has awakened to discover the true religion of science, goodness, and beauty, which he believes lead to God. He must draw the line between a past based on fables and a present filled with the light of science, and bid farewell to his false hopes and suffering (347).

Even if, as Mahfouz says, Kamal reflects his own intellectual crisis, it is not easy to equate them. Is Mahfouz a skeptic, convinced that science is the only true religion? Does he accept Darwin's theory of the descent of man, and how does he reconcile it with the Quranic doctrine of creationism (already stated in the Old Testament)? What is the nature of science, and how can ordinary men understand the reality of the universe if science alone holds the keys to its mysteries? Kamal's absolute glorification of science seems to belittle the meaning of life and man's desire to live happily. It is not clear that science can account for the formation of the universe and the origin of life without relying on fantastic hypotheses and speculation presented as scientific knowledge. And how can we explain human phenomena, even Kamal's love, in purely scientific terms?

In his earlier novels, Mahfouz stresses the importance of science but fails to define it; he does so here too, just as Kamal fails to define the life of the mind. The irony is that Kamal has been influenced by a Western theory totally alien to a traditional Muslim society. Darwin's theory is not the product of a Christian mind but rather of scientific rationalism, which has rejected religious explanations of the origin of life as implausible. Although the Western mind is sufficiently latitudinarian to accommodate doctrines considered contradictory and offensive to a religious belief, in a Muslim fundamentalist society that tolerates no doctrine contrary to those contained in the Quran Darwin's theory is wholly anathema. Muslims may study and analyze it, but they cannot accommodate it in their culture and will always look with great suspicion upon the faith of the person who accept it.

Thus, if Kamal reflects Mahfouz, it will be difficult for Mahfouz to justify his profession of Muslim belief. It is unclear whether Kamal really represents Mahfouz or is a purely fictitious character in a fictitious milieu. The fact remains that Mahfouz came under the influence of science early in life and believed that free thinking is conducive to the truth. As we shall see, in the third part of *Thulathiyya* he again uses one of his characters to proclaim that every age has its own prophets, and the prophets of this age are the scientists.

Kamal's intellectual curiosity has finally led him to skepticism. He no longer believes in the metaphysical; everything must be subject to reason and verifiable by the senses. Yet, confusing the life of reason with science, he never realizes that science satisfies man's intellectual needs but not his hunger for truth, beauty, and other lasting values. Indeed, science does not address man's spiritual needs. What then is this rational truth he seeks, and how can he harmonize it with the reality of life? Kamal's vague dream of writing a book surfaces again, but he puts it aside; since he has lost his faith and Aida, nothing seems meaningful. The prophets who had a spiritual message are no more, and heaven and hell are not so important as he once thought. He now sees the science of man as merely an extension of the science of living things, including animals. Nothing has really changed, and he must find another subject to write about (379).

Kamal (and by implication Mahfouz himself) appears to have substituted science for religion and reason for faith. He seems convinced that to be a rational man seeking beauty and truth means one must be an unbeliever. The more pragmatic Ismail Latif challenges him to explain why, if both reason and religion seek the same ends, he embraces one and rejects the other. But Kamal already has decided the issue, and there is nothing left for him but to descend from his world of idealistic dreams to the "real" sensual world. Having lost Aida and his faith, he feels alienated, ill at ease in a world that can no longer satisfy his spiritual needs. Psychologically estranged from his own being, he regains his sense of reality and discovers painfully that only a thin line divides the ideal and the concrete.

Kamal begins drinking and chasing women. Ismail Latif becomes his alter ego, teaching him that real life is the life of sensual pleasure, not that of books and reason. And since Kamal has deserted his faith, there is no reason for him not to indulge in the carnal. Ismail takes him to a bar and then to a brothel, where he meets Ayyusha, a brunette prostitute. At first repulsed when he sees her lying on the bed naked, rubbing her lower abdomen with henna-tinged fingertips, he seeks to escape. Sensing his hesitancy, she puts out the light and entices him into sex. Kamal is stunned at what he has done. When he regains his composure, he whispers to himself, where is Aida? Where is reason, where is philosophy, and most of all where is beauty? All his sublime values come tumbling down as he lies with Ayyusha. He feels a sense of guilt. His experience with a common prostitute is painful and even humiliating. He yearns for the idealistic love for Aida, despite all the suffering it caused him, but now he has no symbol to worship. Sensuality is the only reality he can contemplate (392–95).

Kamal's agonizing does not seem to purify his body and soul from the stains of sin. The idealistic young man who for religious reasons abstained from wine becomes an avid drinker. Likewise, having earlier declined Fuad al-Hamzawi's invitation to pleasure with the daughters of Abu Sari, he now engages in cheap sex with a prostitute. His idealism turns out to be as shallow as his dream of writing a great book, and his faith is shallower still. He lacks the intellectual and moral stamina to comprehend the tragic sense of life. Because of his tender age and lack of experience, he falls under the heavy burden of an idealism he has created but cannot bear. He begins with high moral ideals and ends in abject immorality, no better than his father or Yasin.

Indeed, Yasin, who once caught his father with Zubayda, by chance finds himself face to face with Kamal at the brothel, where he too is waiting for his turn with Ayyusha. Here we should laud Mahfouz as a master at creating plausible coincidences that turn ordinary incidents into fascinating, even dramatic events. To Yasin, seeing his upright, deeply religious brother in a brothel is a momentous event worthy of celebration; the night of Thursday, October 30, 1926, will remain in his memory. Shocked and embarrassed to find his married brother waiting for Ayyusha, Kamal decides to pay her without having sex, then goes with Yasin to a bar. They realize that they are no different from one another or from their father in seeking sensual pleasure; in fact, Kamal says, they were born to be like him. He can finally accept Yasin's claim that he saw their father with Zubayda. The Sayyid is no longer that serene, dignified man who imposed his moral values on his family, but a brazen, shameless libertine.

Yasin, having already discovered this reality, felt encouraged to keep his dissolute life-style. But Kamal was shocked and bewildered, uncertain what is real and what is not. Since then, he has doubted the meaning of everything, even questioning who he is and why he cannot overcome his deep mental confusion and anguish, caused by his inability to harmonize between abstract, idealistic love and the largely physical attraction that leads to marriage. Does Kamal, as some writers suggest, represent the mental paralysis of the petty bourgeoisie of his time because of a lack of freedom and backwardness?[47] Mahfouz particularizes Kamal so minutely that it is hard for me to accept such a premise. Kamal is too individualistic, even eccentric, to stand for a whole social class. If indeed he does, then the typical Egyptian of this class should be considered romantic, idealistic, intellectually curious, and skeptical—which is hardly the case. Kamal may reflect Mahfouz's intellectual agony and that of others in similar situations, but he does not typify the young men of his class and time.

Kamal's strict, conservative upbringing is largely responsible for the shattering of his romantic ideals and his belief in absolutes. He grew up in a strongly Muslim family that observed the Islamic religious duties of praying, fasting, and visiting holy shrines. His father was an authoritarian tyrant; everything in the home revolved around him and was done to please him. Sayyid Ahmad may have loved his children in his own way, but he did not show it. The children grew up to fear him rather than genuinely love him. In a doleful monologue, Kamal laments his father's tyranny and lack of affection but does not blame him. He pledges that if he ever marries and has children, he will first be their friend rather than their provider. Kamal loved his father and craved his love in return; he respected him not as a loving person, but as a righteous and God-fearing man. But now he loses faith in his father, unable to understand why he treated his family as he did while he lived two different lives, one at home and another away. He also realizes that his mother, though kind and loving, filled his head with fables that he must now unlearn. He feels that he is the victim of a repressive home environment and parents who have never understood him or his ideas and of a heredity (reflected in his physical features) that he cannot control.

What is left for him, now that he has lost Aida, God, and his father? He is like a country without a history, a life without a past. He tries to love his parents and life itself, but the situation has changed. Suddenly, all the bad things in life seem not so bad as he thought; even Ayyusha, who at first repulsed him, seems appealing. He sees himself as the embodiment of a humanity suffering from a hangover and nausea. Having failed to win his father's love, and later to win Aida's love, Kamal sees his dream world fall apart. He replaces it with the sensuous world, apparently the only one he can perceive. It is unpleasant, even repulsive, but it will at least cater to his basic needs.

Kamal, who values freedom as he does love, unrealistically dreams of living in a world free from fear and compulsion. He is still fettered by his father's authority. No sooner does Sayyid Ahmad recover from his illness than he takes his sons to pray at al-Husayn's shrine. Kamal, no longer a believer, yields to his father's command while recognizing his own hypocrisy. As they pass along the road, people greet the Sayyid and shopkeepers rise to their feet; thus Kamal discovers that while his father is no aristocrat, he is still highly respected by people of his own class. In acknowledging this fact Kamal signals that he has no desire to climb the social ladder. As he nears the shrine, he realizes that he has changed, and so has his faith. What once impressed him as a symbol of spiritual majesty is now simply a structure of massive stones, steel, and timber. He goes through the motions of prayer to please his father. He doubts the importance of shrines and prayer, thinking they only remind people of the end of time, as if they should believe in such an illusion. He wonders whether this world, which seems utterly unfamiliar, was created just yesterday. He looks at his father and brother and silently asks why all people cannnot be one family. Kamal sounds like the pantheistic Sufi mystic martyr Abu Mansur al-Hallaj (d. 922), who said in a poem that his heart has accepted every form of worship. Yet he has neither the audacity nor the will to refuse to pray at al-Hysayn's shrine, and so he approaches his tomb with pangs of skepticism and a tormented heart.[48]

Kamal's patriotism, like his love, is more romantic than empirical. He is an ardent nationalist, so much so that his friend Husayn Shaddad considers him obsessed (199). He joins the Wafd party at an early age, espouses its goals, and becomes a devoted follower and admirer of Sa'd Zaghlul. His involvement in politics parallels that of Mahfouz, who joined the Wafd in 1926 and says that it was indisputably the nation's party, and that the Egyptian people loved Zaghlul with a fierce passion. Mahfouz was so devoted to the Wafd that he abhorred its opponents, like the Muslim Brotherhood, which he felt sought to weaken a formidable political force.[49] But Zaghlul's popularity drew the envy of many opportunistic, self-seeking politicians who opposed him and even sided with the British, while many wealthy upper-middle-class people scorned him because of his humble *fallahin* origin.

While Kamal considers the Wafd the central force in the national struggle against the British, an idea he inherited from Fahmi, Hasan Salim disparages Zaghlul and praises his Liberal Constitutionalist opponents, Adli Yagan Pasha, Tharwat Pasha, and Muhammad Mahmud, whom Kamal rightly dismisses as traitors or British lackeys. Hasan calls Zaghlul a "popular clown" who uses bombastic speeches not to serve the nation but to captivate the people, and he cites as evidence his momentous words after negotiations with the British government in 1924 failed to settle the Egyptian national question: "They invited us to commit suicide, but we refused to do so."[50] Kamal retorts that it is unfair to judge Zaghlul by his words alone, because he is a man of action too. But surprisingly Ismail Latif ridicules Zaghlul's words, saying that he could best serve Egypt by committing suicide. This negative attitude demonstrates that some members of the disadvantaged lower middle class did not support Zaghlul, perhaps because they worked for the aristocracy or in some way depended on their protection and favor (170–71).

Predictably, Husayn Shaddad doubts that Zaghlul's policies will succeed in ousting the British from Egypt. After the assassination of Sir Lee Stack, the commander-in-chief of the Egyptian army and governor-general of the Sudan, by a Wafdist fanatic, Lord Allenby, the British high commissioner, retaliated by demanding an apology from the Egyptian government, punishment of the assassin, payment of a large fine, and, worst of all, extension of the irrigated land in the Gezira district of the Sudan, which would require the diversion of high quantities of precious Nile water. This outrageous demand led Zaghlul to resign, whereupon Ziwar Pasha, a British lackey, became prime minister and quickly accepted all of Allenby's conditions. Husayn mockingly offers his condolences, while Husan Salim accuses Zaghlul of gratuitously arousing animosity against the British. This charge enrages Kamal, who says it sounds like the opinion of the British authorities, frequently echoed by Zaghlul's Liberal Constitutionalist opponents (200).

Although this second volume of the trilogy does not put much emphasis on politics, it shows the divergent attitudes of the lower and upper middle classes. It suggests strongly that members of the upper class, particularly politicians, lacked moral strength and national commitment. Consequently, the Egyptian government was one of individuals rather than institutions. Zaghlul alone could unite the people against British imperialism. His death in August 1927 left the nation's destiny in the hands of petty, dishonest men who were more often engaged in futile squabbles than in constructive political action.

Qasr al-Shawq ends with Zaghlul's death. Kamal grieves for this man, who endured persecution and exile for the sake of freedom and the constitution. He has lost his brother Fahmi, his beloved Aida, his friend Husayn Shaddad, and now Zaghlul; it seems there is no end to his suffering. Sayyid Ahmad has regained his health, but has lost much of his virility and his patriarchal authority. Still saddened by the loss of Fahmi, he is soon to lose hope in Kamal and his future. Yasin still pursues pleasure but seems well matched with Zannuba, who ironically is due to give birth on the day of Zaghlul's death. Just as ironically, tragedy strikes Aisha on the same day; her husband and their two sons die of typhoid fever, and she and Naima move in with her parents. As for Kamal, his behavior indicates that he is totally estranged from his own culture, out of place in a society he cannot identify with. He is homeless in a land controlled by foreigners and whose political leaders lack direction and vision.

Al-Sukkariyya

Al-Sukkariyya (literally, The Sugar Bowl, translated into English with the title *Sugar Street*,) named for the street where Khadija and Aisha lived with their families, covers the period from January 1935

to the summer of 1944.[51] In this part of the trilogy Mahfouz concentrates not only on Kamal but on Yasin's son Ridwan, Khadija's two
sons, and other characters representing the third generation. He
also looks closely at politics, examining the rift within the powerful
Wafd party, the emergence of new parties, and the base conduct of
some politicians who collaborated with the British, putting their
personal advantage ahead of Egypt's national interest. He dexterously shows the conflict between Western ideologies, especially
socialism, and the Muslims' traditional beliefs. He also shows the
impact of World War II through his characters' reactions. The
modern era is heralded by the radio, which brings entertainment,
news, and even religious services. Another sign of the times is the
shifting of social position: while Fuad al-Hamzawi rises to upper-
middle-class status, Aida's family sees its standing decline.

The family of Sayyid Ahmad Abd al-Jawad has experienced
many changes, not all for the better. As the novel opens, the Sayyid,
in his mid-sixties, has lost weight and cannot drink or indulge in his
old pleasures. So feeble that he needs a cane, he cannot perform his
daily prayer or even go to the bathroom unaided. He has had to
close his shop; sometimes, passing by and seeing the sign that once
bore his name and his father's, he laments the changes time inflicts
on people. He realizes that the years of his youth are gone forever,
and he must accept old age with all its problems. Some of his old
friends have died; others are bedridden or seriously ill. Occasionally he attends prayer services at al-Husayn's mosque, but he still
yearns for the life of pleasure, indicating he has not truly repented
or prepared for the world to come. Yet he experiences moments of
spiritual revelation that raise his soul to high heaven and fill him
with a sense of happiness whose source he cannot fathom. He gets
some pleasure from the radio, which lets him listen to the news or
his favorite traditional Egyptian music. He has lost his patriarchal
authority but still seeks to have his granddaughter Naima stay
home instead of attending school. He no longer argues with his
children and is less strict with his wife, allowing her to visit al-
Husayn's mosque and other holy places, although she still has to
treat him as master of the house. Sayyid Ahmad is again suffering
from high blood pressure. During a German air raid on Cairo he

makes his way to a shelter and collapses; Kamal carries him home, where he loses consciousness and breathes his last. The patriarch of the family whose saga is the focus of the *Thulathiyya* plays only a minor role in this final volume.

Yasin, the Sayyid's eldest son, still drinks and stays out nights but is less of a womanizer. He spends most evenings at coffeehouses and bars, meeting men from every walk of life, some of them government employees who talk mostly about politics or their work. He is given to exaggeration and describes his role in the anti-British demonstrations and Sa'd Zaghlul's walking in Fahmi's funeral procession. He treats his children more gently than his father treated him. Returning home after midnight, he plays the gramophone to entertain Ridwan, who is busy doing homework, or rouses his daughter Karima from a sound sleep for some nocturnal play. This behavior, which seems immature and imprudent, may be meant to compensate for the lack of compassion he associates with his own childhood.

Yasin was a minor employee at the Ministry of Education, seemingly destined to remain at the bottom of the administrative ladder. But through the efforts of his son Ridwan and a shady politician, Abd al-Rahim Pasha Isa, he rises to head an administrative office at the ministry, bypassing several more qualified employees. This is of course a side issue, which Mahfouz uses to show government corruption. Yasin and Zannuba seem to have a stable, happy marriage. She catches him flirting with a new female tenant, but this appears to be an isolated incident, and he protests his innocence. He is, unlike his father, no hypocrite, and appears to be genuinely contrite in confessing his misdeeds. He tells friends that some members of his family regard themselves as religious yet consistently violate Islamic laws and will have to repent before facing judgment. Plainly, he has a sense of morality and would rather acknowledge his sins than hide them under a veneer of self-righteousness.

Yasin also cherishes his individual freedom. When a policeman stops him on the street one night and orders him to cease his loud singing, he argues that he has every right to sing; after all, he is no noisier than the bombs that fall on Cairo after midnight. Although he is living in a strict society, he understands his rights and obligations. He is fully aware that a nation like his cannot be called civilized while it is ruled by British military power. Like his country, he himself has no freedom; his life is run by his wife at home and his boss at work. Indeed, he will have no freedom even in death, for according to Islamic tradition, every Muslim is examined at death by two grotesque-looking, brutal angels, Munkar and Nakir. If he is found righteous, he will be rewarded with quick admission to paradise, but if he is found sinful and hence not a true Muslim, they will punish him severely.

Amina, not yet sixty when the novel opens, typifies the traditional wife and mother of the older generation. Trying to hold the family together, she has endured her husband's tyranny with saintly patience and is faithful to him till the end. There is nothing exciting about her monotonous life, but she has more freedom of action than before and seems to enjoy it. She is not very impressed by the radio; she listens to it for news and the chanting of the Quran rather than entertainment. She seems to know little of events outside the home but excitedly informs the family that Hitler has attacked Poland and World War II has begun. Near the end of the novel Amina, totally paralyzed because of high blood pressure and pneumonia, slips into a coma as death approaches.

Aisha's case is tragic. Having lost her husband and two sons, she has only her teenaged daughter Naima and has changed both mentally and physically. Just thirty-four, this once beautiful, merry young woman has aged rapidly. She is so thin that her cheekbones protrude and her eyes sink deep into their sockets. She begins to lose her hair, and her doctor recommends that she have her teeth removed. To assuage her grief, she drinks coffee and smokes. She loses interest in everything. Her mother urges her to busy herself to forget her sorrow, while the Sayyid begs her to join her mother in visiting sacred shrines. Nothing can comfort her, however, and she becomes totally withdrawn. She finds nothing useful about her life and wishes that God would take her and end her agony. Sometimes she becomes delirious, talking to herself or to her lost loved ones. She even begins to see extraordinary phenomena. One day she rushes from the rooftop to report that she saw a window open in heaven, and that an extremely bright light shone from it and filled the whole earth. This vision apparently results from Aisha's constant remembrance of her loved ones and her desire for consolation. But tragedy seems to be her lot, for she soon loses Naima, who dies while delivering her first child.

Her sister Khadija, a voracious eater, has grown fat but is proud of her heaviness because it is a sign of beauty. Contentious as ever, she bosses the other family members around, especially after the death of her mother-in-law. She credits the success of her sons Abd al-Munim and Ahmad to her discipline and sound upbringing. After they marry, when their wives do not immediately conceive, she complains that a married woman without children is useless, thus pointing up a very sensitive and practical concern in Egypt and throughout the Middle East. When one son marries a working woman, she laments that such women are not fit wives, highlighting the then prevalent view that wives should simply take care of their families rather than work outside the home.

Zubayda, once Sayyid Ahmad's favorite mistress, the beautiful, powerful woman called the Sultana, ends in sheer poverty and misery. After falling in love with a cart driver who took her money and deserted her, she became a cocaine addict and wound up living in a small room on the roof of a friend's house. In dire need, she appeals to the Sayyid to lend her money or even buy her house, but without success. Later she passes by the coffeehouse Kamal and his friends frequent, but she has changed so physically that he does not recognize her. Realizing he is the Sayyid's son, she begins to reminisce about the good old days, and she shows genuine sorrow on being told of his passing. Zubayda represents those unfortunate women caught up in the carnal life as they struggle to survive. Men like Sayyid Ahmad and his cronies use them to satisfy their lust, then discard them after they lose their looks. She fully understands the way things are but cannot remedy her situation.

In complete contrast stands her niece Zannuba, who began as a lutist in Zubayda's ensemble. After marrying Yasin, she becomes a respectable wife and mother. Yasin, unconcerned about her past, does not seek to save her soul or even to reform her. He marries her partly because her personality and nature are suited to his own, but primarily because he is captivated by her body. Moreover, after two failed marriages he seeks a quiet, peaceful life with a wife of his own choosing. Indeed, this woman who has wallowed in the depths of immorality turns out to be decent and moral. Although his family at first will not accept her because of her past, eventually her conduct gains her the respect of all who come in contact with her. She stands in contrast to women like Ihsan in *al-Qahira al-Jadida* and Hamida in *Zuqaq al-Midaqq*, who plunge into the life of sin and meet with disaster. The presentation of Zannuba appears intended to show that no matter how much society condemns and despises such women, they have merit, but men must stop exploiting them and give them the chance to prove their worth.

Some tragicomic relief in the novel comes from a familiar character, the mystic Shaykh Mutawalli Abd al-Samad. He is senile; his memory has gone, and naughty boys make fun of him. Walking through the Ghorya quarter with a cane, he suddenly lifts his head and asks where the road to paradise is, and a passerby answers that it is the first turn to the right. He appears at the funeral of Sayyid Ahmad and asks whether the deceased was someone from his quarter. When Kamal tries to remind him who his father was, sadly the old man remembers no one. The shaykh and other secondary characters may appear superfluous, but they still represent an integral part of the human condition, revealing various aspects of social behavior and reminding us of the vicissitudes of life.

Kamal and his nephews Abd al-Munim, Ahmad, and Ridwan dominate this final part of *Thulathiyya*. Kamal, twenty-eight when the novel begins, teaches English at the Silahdar Elementary School and contributes articles on philosophy to the magazine *al-Fikr* (The Intellect). Ridwan, after graduating from law school, received an important post as secretary to the minister of education. Abd al-Munim, also a law school graduate, works in the same ministry and also acts as legal consultant to the Muslim Brotherhood (*al-Ikhwan al-Muslimun*). His brother Ahmad, who attended the College of Arts, is a translator/writer for Adli Karim's magazine *al-Insan al-Jadid* (The New Man). Interestingly, they have espoused two

opposing ideologies, Abd al-Munim joining the Muslim Brotherhood and Ahmad becoming a communist; thus, the battle is joined
between traditional religious values and irreligious materialism.

Mahfouz presents Kamal as a cohesive but complex personality
who merits careful in-depth analysis. He is still self-conscious about
his massive head and nose, which his students ridicule as his
beloved Aida did years before. But, determined to have respect
rather than pity, he rises above matters by showing compassion,
understanding, and effectiveness as a teacher. He bears comments
on his appearance patiently, and simply changes the subject to
national affairs or his memories of the Egyptian revolution of 1919.
But his main concern is to harmonize his work teaching English
with his writing on philosophy. He is worried that his colleagues
and principal may misread his monthly articles as contradicting
accepted moral standards. Fortunately the magazine has a small
circulation, and none of his coworkers read it.

A more serious problem is that Kamal does not really like his
work. Although he is an excellent teacher and the principal often
entrusts him with additional responsibilities, he considers teaching
a chore. But he hides his dissatisfaction, especially from his father,
and endeavors to make the best of his situation. He still aspires to
live the life of the mind, and teaching elementary English, although
unsatisfying, can at least help him attain that goal. The Sayyid,
feeling that he spends most of his time in unprofitable pursuits,
urges him to take up private tutoring to earn extra income. When
Kamal rejects the idea, his father thinks he is imprudent, but his
mother believes he simply places knowledge above money.[52] His
parents do not understand him. They want him to find a respectable, secure position in life like other men his age, but he is unlike his
contemporaries in outlook and objectives. Why does Mahfouz present this character as he does, and to what extent does Kamal
represent him? We have previously touched upon these questions,
but we must answer them more thoroughly to understand
Mahfouz's view of Egyptian society.

Kamal has chosen to become an elementary school teacher. Although this position is neither respected, lucrative, not intellectually stimulating, it satisfies his idealistic view that knowledge is

more important than money or prestige. Like thousands of other teachers, he finds his routine tedious; he does his chores in the morning and spends the rest of the day tending to his personal needs. But Kamal is different in that he appreciates the life of the mind, and especially philosophy. He spends time in his library reading Bergson's *The Two Sources of Morality and Religion*, Spinoza's pantheism, or Schopenhauer's triumph of the will. He studies Leibnitz's explanation of evil in order to empathize with Aisha's misery, for philosophy gives him solace. He also reviews his monthly article on pragmatism for the magazine *al-Fikr*, published by Abd al-Aziz al-Asyuti. Here he parallels Mahfouz, who began his literary career by writing articles on philosophy for Abd al-Aziz al-Islambuli's periodical *al-Ma'rifa* (Knowledge). The similarity of the two publishers' names is too close to be coincidental; moreover, in 1934 Mahfouz contributed an article on pragmatism to Salama Musa's *al-Majalla al-Jadida* (The New Magazine).[53]

Kamal's articles, like those of Mahfouz, do not reflect any particular view; they are simply general surveys presenting the ideas of philosophers to a limited audience unfamiliar with the subject. Even those who read them, like Ismail Latif and Fuad al-Hamzawi, cannot fully understand or appreciate them. When al-Hamzawi asks why he does not write about literature, Kamal replies that that is not his field. Pressed further, he says he is neither a man of letters nor a true philosopher, merely an elementary school teacher exploring the world of ideas. He picks materials from various sources, puts them together, and submits the result for publication. He says he is like a tourist in a museum, owning nothing in it, or like an historian without history. Al-Asyuti tries to justify his efforts, arguing that producing general surveys of philosophical themes is a good start for a beginning writer like Kamal, who may someday develop a new philosophy.

Kamal has no time for literature, especially fiction. Unlike Mahfouz, he does not feel compelled to choose between philosophy and literature; even at the end of the trilogy, he has not chosen one over the other. As Mahfouz did, he appears to believe that philosophy is more important than fiction, and that Egyptian readers are more interested in substantive subjects. But when several friends urge him to write about more popular subjects to attract a wider audience, Kamal, who previously felt insulted by such advice, seems more inclined to accept it. He was motivated to write on philosophy by his quest for knowledge, truth, and adventure in the world of ideas and by his desire to find solace for his grief and loneliness. Now he is uncertain not only about the worth of his writings, but about his own ability. He writes enthusiastically about rational and materialistic ideas, but his spirit is tempered by skepticism. Philosophy no longer satisfies his hunger for the truth, yet he keeps on writing about it.[54]

Plainly Kamal is suffering from mental anxiety. Having long since lost faith in God, he now doubts the validity of science and philosophy. He feels locked up in a tight world from which there is no exit. One day he meets a young Copt, Riyad Qaldas, a translator at the Ministry of Education who writes short stories and summaries of well-known plays. Qaldas is a skeptic who rejects religion, contending that no one can understand its essence except perhaps the prophets. He believes in science and aesthetics, calling one the language of reason, the other the language of all mankind. He says science is the magic of mankind, its miraculous guiding force, and above all the religion of the future. Although Kamal considers him somewhat pompous, he is happy to have found this wonderful friend who shares some of his ideas and can alleviate his loneliness. Qaldas, quick to sense Kamal's anxiety, chides him gently, implying that by immersing himself in the world of books (and especially those that present ideas incompatible with the traditional values of his society), Kamal has cut himself off from reality, and he will never be able to live normally until he escapes his abnormal situation.[55]

Kamal seems to have lost interest in everything in life, even politics. His support of the Wafd party is merely symbolic; he is not committed in the way his friend Qaldas is. He still voices a belief in the inherent rights of the Egyptian people but has no idea whether this means the rights of man in general or the right of survival of the fittest, that is, the politicians who manipulate the masses for their own ends. Kamal's political sentiment is as strong as when he participated in the revolution of 1919, but he is saddened by the chaos resulting from the death of his idol Sa'd Zaghlul. Increasingly despondent and perplexed, he feels he must find the true meaning of life or abandon it altogether. His friends perceive his difficulty and try to help him overcome it, but with little success. Riyad Qaldas recognizes that he is experiencing a personal mental crisis and attributes it to his attempt to fathom the mysteries of life. But Kamal's agony is caused mainly by his espousal of Western ideas; unable to harmonize them with those inculcated in him by his Eastern upbringing, he is lost between East and West.

Kamal reflects the mental anxiety Mahfouz himself experienced as a young man. Mahfouz admits that he gave Kamal such a prominent role in the *Thulathiyya* not haphazardly, but "because he is an integral part of myself."[56] Both were voracious readers and productive writers, influenced by Western scientific ideas. Both glorified science and considered it the cure for the ills of their society. Both were Wafdists who participated in the national revolution against the British and sought independence for their country. Yet it is unrealistic to maintain that Kamal represents Mahfouz in every trait, idea, or action. We do not know, for example, that Mahfouz lost his faith in God or expressed his doubt of religious traditions, nor whether he so despaired of life as to consider suicide. But in his novel *Awlad Haratina*, he appears suspicious of religious superstition, fanaticism, and parochialism, which oppose scientific inquiry.

But we can infer from the *Thulathiyya* and the other contemporary novels that Kamal represents the hopes and frustrations of Mahfouz's generation in the 1930s and 1940s. The greatest problem of the Egyptian intelligentsia was to balance the spreading Western ideas with their traditional values. To be sure, Western concepts had influenced Egyptians since the beginning of the nineteenth century. But their impact was greatest after World War I, as a new generation of young men and women, better educated than their parents, came to cherish independence and freedom of thought. What Mahfouz calls "the middle generation" had to deal seriously with the forceful challenge of new ideas. Unfortunately, most of Kamal's contemporaries knew these ideas only through reading rather than personal experience such as travel or study in foreign countries. Indeed, Mahfouz's only visit to the West took him to Yugoslavia for a few days on official business. Thus, it was inevitable that Western ideas should effect many substantive changes in the thinking of this middle generation. Their impact was increased by the political infighting after Zaghlul's death, the lack of economic opportunities, and the general breakdown of public morals, all of which exacerbated the spiritual crisis of Kamal's generation.[57]

Yet there is more to Kamal's confusion and despair. His main problem is spiritual; having disavowed God and his traditional faith, he looks to science for the meaning of life, but science, which deals with life's causes and effects, cannot answer his questions. Kamal, having been raised in an essentially theistic society, should understand that only God gives meaning to life. Instead, he places his faith in science without understanding its nature and its impact on his own life. Although later he begins to question its value, he cannot find anything to replace it and give him peace of mind. Kamal has lost his heart and soul and can no longer think or act straight. He does not have a sound view of himself. He is left with no moral rules to follow, no meaningful life to live, no reason for being. Without hope, he feels he must find another reality or end his life. His feelings fluctuate wildly; at one point, he decides that if life has no meaning, he must give it meaning, but then he concludes the task is impossible.

Kamal's emotional emptiness and his incapability of joy, tranquility, and certitude, are manifested most clearly in his avoidance of marriage. Mahfouz devotes much of this volume to the question of whether Kamal will marry, appearing almost obsessed with the subject, perhaps because he did not marry until late in life. Like Kamal, Mahfouz fell in love at an early age with a young woman who was socially beyond his reach. Like Kamal, too, he believed that marriage stood in the way of his literary career. And like Kamal, he was reluctant to undertake the great responsibility of being a husband and father. But while Mahfouz eventually married and had two daughters, Kamal remains a bachelor.[58]

Indeed, Kamal suffers so severely from moral confusion and existential emptiness that he is no longer capable of love, so emotionally paralyzed that he cannot imagine taking care of a wife and children. Al-Asyuti astutely calls him a bachelor in life and thought. His comment stimulates Kamal to explore the relationship between his views on life and his single status. Is his bachelorhood the result of his state of mind, or is it the other way around? Riyad Qaldas tries to assure him that he will not stay single forever, but he turned out to be wrong. Other than his writing on philosophy, the solitary life—from which he finds relief in alcohol and carnal pleasure—is the only reality Kamal has.

In emphasizing Kamal's single status, Mahfouz tries to portray the fear, confusion, and irresoluteness of many young men of the middle generation in facing the realities of life. In a conversation with Fuad al-Hamzawi, Kamal observes wistfully that they are almost thirty and still single. Indeed, their generation is filled with unmarried men, but he does not know why. Muhammad Iffat, his father's old friend, offers a partial explanation. Girls today, he says, are more liberated than those of the older generation and exhibit loose behavior, which makes them less attractive. Moreover, the economic crisis precipitated by the 1929 stock market crash has limited job opportunities. Even a university graduate has trouble finding work, and if he manages to do so, he cannot hope to earn more than ten pounds a month, which is hardly adequate to support a family.[59]

At first Kamal avoids even discussing marriage, partly because of his dissatisfaction with the social and political conditions in Egypt, and partly because of his own idealistic philosophy of life. His father, who believes marriage is the destiny of every man in Egypt, mentions several compatible young women from respectable families and points out that his friend Ismail Latif is happily married with children, while Riyad Qaldas is engaged; so why shouldn't Kamal marry? Qaldas and Ismail Latif frequently urge him to marry in order to alleviate his loneliness, contending that by staying single he has missed his chance to understand the reality of life. Yet he still shuns marriage, partly because he does not want to bear the responsibility of a family, but also because he harbors a destructive sense of failure. He believes he is without real worth. He compares his sad state to that of Aisha; she has lost her husband and sons, who were once flesh and bones, while he has lost his hopes, which were nothing but false dreams.

At one point he meets Aida's sister Budur, whom he used to play with when visiting her family. In another flight of fantasy, he suddenly feels a desire to marry her but abandons the idea because she is much younger than he and already engaged, and because he fears he will repeat his experience with Aida. He still believes that marriage is the debasement of true love. Riyad Qaldas tries to find out how Kamal can separate love and marriage. He says Kamal's aversion to marriage implies that he does not love Budur; if he loves her but does not want to marry her, then he is mentally unstable and should consult a psychiatrist. Kamal retorts that he has already written an article on psychoanalysis, as if to say that he does not need treatment. Qaldas tells him, "You have really baffled me." To this Kamal answers, "I am the one who is baffled forever" (325).

Qaldas has put his finger on Kamal's emotional problem, a deep-seated anxiety that tends to neurosis. It is caused partly by his loss of faith, his uncertainty about the meaning of life, and his fear of accepting his responsibilities as a member of society. More important, he does not know what role to pursue in life and what principle of action to follow. He is right when he says he is forever bewildered, for he has no idea where he is going. Should he seek material success as his father wants him to do, or simply be a good human being, as Khadija's husband Ibrahim Shawkat believes he is? Should he marry and have children to perpetuate his family's name? Kamal desires immortality, but not through such mundane means. Should he keep the moral values he held as an adolescent or bury his anxiety in the bosoms of prostitutes? Kamal's basic problem is lack of goals and values. Genuine religious faith no longer influences or sustains his perceptions of life. If he still had his faith, he might not hesitate to marry and have a family. Fuad al-Hamzawi urges him to follow the example of the Prophet Muhammad, whose marriage did not prevent him from pursuing a spiritual life, then hastily apologizes for citing the Prophet as an example. Kamal answers that although he calls himself an atheist, he doubts atheism, and this doubt is a step toward faith. But his comment is simply another manifestation of his perplexed state; there is no evidence that he has regained faith.

Kamal's lack of definite goals and his chronic bewilderment are clear when his actions are compared with those of his nephews Abd al-Munim and Ahmad. Like him, they are educated and face similar problems in choosing a career. But they have the will and determination to pursue their goals in life. They do not suffer from the confusion and irresoluteness that beset Kamal. Although they have diametrically opposed political views, they remain true to their ideological objectives, and each marries a young woman of his own choosing.

Ahmad's case is of special interest because, like Kamal, he falls in love with a young woman from the upper middle class and is rejected because he does not have sufficient financial means to support her. But Ahmad does not despair, retreat into fantasy, or make his beloved an idol of worship. Instead, he finds another young woman better suited to him and marries her. Kamal envies his strong resolve but also admires his courage and judgment, as if they compensate for his own passivity and indetermination. He begins to wonder why marriage is such a difficult step for him, while others take it in stride. Why should he not marry Abu Sari's daughter Qamar, who truly loves him? The unpleasant truth is that he is very conscious of her lower-class status and the accepted norms of his society, which he cannot ignore, no matter how ugly and callous they may seem. Yet he contemplates marrying Aida's sister Budur, who could give him upward mobility, until he learns that her family has fallen in status.

Kamal's class consciousness comes to the fore when he hears that Fuad al-Hamzawi seeks to marry Naima, the only surviving child of his sister Aisha. Naima is now a beautiful sixteen-year-old, while Fuad, who graduated from the law school, has become a prosecuting attorney. The news of their prospective engagement stirs the family members to debate whether Fuad is an acceptable suitor for Naima. While Kamal defends him as an excellent young man, Amina and the others contend that without the assistance of the Sayyid, who employed his father, he would never have risen to his present position of prominence. Fuad visits Kamal and discusses a variety of topics with him but makes no mention of marrying Naima. After he leaves, Kamal and his mother argue heatedly over his intentions. Kamal asserts that Fuad's father initiated the discussion of marriage without his knowledge, and that Amina and the others are trying to condemn him for something for which he is not responsible.

But afterward Kamal retires to his room, ostensibly to contemplate the situation. Rather self-righteously, he asks himself whether Naima should be the wife of a man "who, despite his humble origin, could be the life partner of a young woman who has an excellent education, beauty, wealth, and more honorable origin." He impugns Fuad's motives, thinking that although he is honest, intelligent, and upright, perhaps he acts assertively to maintain his pride or to compensate for his sense of inferiority. Moreover, he seems immodest; he sat before the Sayyid with his legs crossed, signifying utmost disrespect. Yet such behavior is not his fault, but rather the result of his social background; having risen from the depths of poverty, Fuad seeks to show that he is of a higher social standing than Kamal and his father. This internal monologue reveals that Kamal envies Fuad's success but considers him inferior by birth. He decides Fuad is not suitable for Naima, although he exaggerates her education and wealth. Only sixteen, she has no education, and her wealth comes solely from her grandfather, Sayyid Ahmad (112–13).

Perplexed and irresolute, Kamal seeks solace in carnal indulgence. He begins to frequent the brothel run by Jalila, once his father's mistress. She receives him warmly and tells him that it was in this very house that his father first had sex outside marriage. Sayyid Ahmad soon learns from his cronies that Kamal is visiting Jalila and fears that she will tell him about his past amorous adventures with her—as indeed she does, deriving special pleasure from the fact that the son is taking his father's place. Yet Kamal feels no moral outrage on hearing of his father's actions; he cannot condemn his father without first condemning himself. He finally concedes that his life is not so straight as his family thinks. Although his brother-in-law Ibrahim Shawkat once called him a respectable and upright man who would be an ideal husband, he sees himself as nothing but an infidel and a drunkard, a lecher and a hypocrite. He is a bewildered man trying to bury his anxiety in self-indulgence, and he has found exactly the place to ease his cares.

His favorite among Jalila's girls is Atiyya, a divorcée who apparently became a prostitute to support her children. Mahfouz here implies that many such women, mostly illiterate and lacking job skills, saw prostitution as the only solution to their problems, because there were no government social services or training programs for them. Kamal appears to show concern for Atiyya, especially on one occasion when she cannot entertain him because she must care for her sick son. In fact, however, his primary concern is that he has missed an opportunity to be with her, and as soon as her son recovers, he returns to her.

Nothing reveals Kamal's moral confusion more clearly than the time he spends in Jalila's brothel. Here he contemplates his achievements and place in life, and here he seeks the meaning of existence in the company of Jalila or in the embrace of Atiyya. Of all the places in Cairo, he can quench his thirst for knowledge only here, where other men quench their lust. Here too Kamal finds that his family has sunk into obscurity since his father died, though no one seems to care. And here he comes to realize that his cherished life of the mind cannot help him avert a personal problem. Kamal is utterly stunned when administrators at the Ministry of Education order his transfer to the remote town of Asyut. He mistakenly thinks they have appreciated his intellectual contributions enough to realize that he belongs in Cairo. He asks Fuad al-Hamzawi, now a judge, to intercede on his behalf, but his old friend says he cannot compromise his position by interfering in such cases. Finally Kamal turns to his nephew Ridwan, who through the offices of his homosexual partner, Abd al-Rahim Pasha Isa, has the transfer rescinded. He feels embarrassed that Ridwan must rescue him when he, a teacher and writer, is helpless. What is the use of philosophy, he wonders, and what is the value of his writings, which merely summarize the ideas of philosophers? Any graduate of the College of Arts can write as well or better. Intellectual achievements are less useful than unscrupulous and immoral means in this effete society. Kamal's frustration reaches a peak when he decides that he cannot write the book he has so long dreamed of. It is pointless even to publish a collection of his articles, because so many books are published every day. Such is the bewilderment of Kamal as he sits in the brothel and contemplates his life.

When he returns to reality, he asks Jalila for a drink and then has sex with Atiyya. Life seems to him utterly purposeless and absurd, except for wine and sex. The world is topsy-turvy. Fuad al-Hamzawi, whose family got by only because of his father's charity, has risen as he himself slid down the social scale. His nephew Ridwan, whom he used to carry on his shoulders, took up his burden and averted his transfer, though Kamal forgets that Ridwan was able to do so only through his immoral relationship with a cabinet minister in a decadent society where integrity and intellectual achievement count for nothing. Yet what strikes him as most absurd is Jalila's statement that she is tired of her profession and wants to retire and repent (in the manner of Defoe's Moll Flanders). When he wonders who will look after him, she tells him not to worry, for if she retires, Atiyya will see that he is well taken care of. What irony! Jalila seeks repentance, while he looks for a new house of pleasure. If she wants to change her life, he thinks aloud, why should he not follow her example? As a drowning man will grasp at anything to save his life, he must do the same. Having long ago concluded that life has no meaning, he must strive to give it meaning. Naturally Jalila, unable to make sense of his mutterings, thinks he is drunk. Predictably, he laughs and apologizes, asking when Atiyya will come home. Since he has not yet found the meaning of life, the best way to give it meaning for the time being is through sex.

Oddly enough, Kamal yearns to marry, settle down, and end his carnal indulgence—but only if he can find a woman with Atiyya's body and Riyad Qaldas's spirit. Budur could satisfy his emotional needs, but she is engaged and will soon vanish from his life as her sister did. Atiyya is attractive, but he wants more than sex. Visiting her at her new brothel in Muhammad Ali Street, he remarks how compatible they are; thinking he is drunk, she does not take him seriously. He persists, saying what a happy couple they would make, but she points out that she has children to support, and if she asked for more than her usual fee, he would refuse to pay. Kamal sarcastically says that like Jalila, he is thinking of repenting, and once he has done so he will leave his wealth to her. Atiyya responds smartly that the day Kamal repents, their relationship will end. She is right. He has no desire either to repent or to marry her. Lonely and frustrated, he is completely confused about himself, about life, and particularly about their relationship (339–40).

Because Kamal has no clearly defined objective, his life is purposeless and painful. He needs to know himself in order to be rescued from his agony. Watching children play, he wishes he could regress to discover whether he was a happy child. He yearns to find a meaning for life, yet how can someone so thoroughly alienated fulfill such a monumental task? He has abandoned God and moral law, and he has lost his self-esteem. He has tried drinking and sex, but they do not satisfy his hunger for something he cannot define. His life is monotonous, slowly leading him nowhere. Feeling isolated from life's purpose, he strives to discern it, as a host of philosophers have done since antiquity. Perhaps, like Jean Paul Sartre in *No Exit*, Kamal is really trying to understand how one functions in a meaningless world. After all, finding the meaning of existence will not alter his life, mitigate his suffering, or dissuade him from entertaining false dreams. One could justify his search if he were suffering pain, but this is not so; indeed, he fears and avoids pain (231).

One of Kamal's problems is that he is weary, not from pain but from pleasure. He seeks relief not through marriage and a decent, normal life, but through sensual pleasure, which brings him no closer to the meaning of life and instead generates a feeling of futility. Kamal's negative attitude and his quest for peace of mind in Atiyya's arms deprive his life of real meaning. The only thing that can save him from his mental turmoil and give his life direction is a genuine return to God. After all, he is the product of a society that cherishes the sovereignty of God. Atheism, which is alien to Islam and all its traditions, has gripped Kamal's mind and robbed him of the most precious hope his faith can offer, total dependence (*tawakkul*) on God's providence. If God is truth, then he alone can give life purpose and meaning. In short, Islam pervades every aspect of Kamal's culture and is the foundation of its social, political, and

religious institutions. He cannot reject any one of these underpin-
nings without rejecting the whole structure; thus, his renunciation
of his faith attests to his belief in the absurdity of his entire culture.

Kamal is aware that his life is leading him toward self-destruc-
tion. Having lost faith and spirit, he walks through life with his
head down. In a monologue, he admits that there is a conflict within
him between sensual pleasure and a mystical life of austerity and
righteousness. He knows that he cannot continue his debauchery
but is reluctant to give it up because he regards the alternative as a
passive escape from reality. Yet he yearns for this mystical life;
indeed, he appears to be seeking God, for the very essence of
mysticism is the sublimation of the soul and its ultimate union with
God or, as Sufis (mystics) believe, the final annihilation of the self in
God. It is his desire for something more substantive than pleasure
that keeps him from committing suicide. After vacillating between
carnality and commitment, Kamal chooses the celibate life, much as
Ahmad chooses communism and marries a young woman who
shares his conviction. Ahmad, having cast his lot, does not agonize
over a conflict between faith and atheistic ideology. Kamal, however, remains confused, irresolute, and intellectually paralyzed. He
fails to find meaning in life, but seems to accept the notion that his
uncertainty is a small price to pay for survival (18).

In contrast to the second volume of the trilogy, *al-Sukkariyya*
concentrates heavily on politics, particularly the events following
Zaghlul's death and the efforts of the autocratic King Fuad to
weaken the power of the Wafd. Under Zaghlul's leadership the
Wafd had tried to unite Egyptians, regardless of their religious
affiliation or station in life, under the nationalist banner. It enjoyed
great popularity among the masses, especially among the Christian
Coptic minority. Zaghlul was its moving spirit and deservedly the
most trusted political figure in Egypt. An inspiring orator and a
man of great integrity, he could identify with the lower classes
because of his peasant origin. It is no wonder that under him the
Wafd became the national party par excellence. So powerful was its
popular appeal, says Mahfouz, that anyone who was not a Wafdist
was looked on as an infidel.[60] Zaghlul's death gave the opposition
parties, especially the Liberal Constitutionalists, who represented

wealthy landholders and supported Fuad, an opportunity to run the government and manipulate national policy. Behind them stood the British authorities, who used both the king and the politicians to control Egypt.

Mahfouz depicts the Egyptians as almost obsessed with politics, their primary topic of conversation at home, at work, or in the marketplace. The people have placed their trust in Zaghlul's heir, Mustafa al-Nahhas, and the Wafd and are suspicious of opportunistic politicians who support the king or collaborate with the British. Kamal is no less interested in politics than his countrymen, but he avoids becoming actively involved.

Mahfouz uses the Jihad national festival (November 13, 1935) to depict the political sentiments of common Egyptians. As Kamal rides a packed train to the festival, the passengers focus on Sir Samuel Hoare's recent statement against the national movement. One says that Hoare should be refuted at the festival. Another, noting that he advised the Egyptians not to restore the 1923 and 1930 constitutions, asks what business he has offering advice. A third remarks that Hoare claims he has given advice only when asked by the Egyptian government—but who asked him? If anyone wants an answer, another says, let him ask about political panderers like Tawfiq Nasim (a politician of Turkish origin, hand-picked as prime minister in May 1920 by then-Sultan Fuad in order to further his own autocratic rule).

Kamal, here representing Mahfouz, listens attentively and then offers a lengthy monologue on the tribulations he and his countrymen have shared. He has endured the era of Muhammad Mahmud, a Liberal Constitutionalist prime minister who suspended the constitution three times yet held the favor of the British because he supported their policies. He has suffered through "the years of terror and political prostitution" under Ismail Sidqi (prime minister for the first time from June 1930 to January 1933). Through this lackey, whom he had chosen to curb the popularity of the Wafd and al-Nahhas, King Fuad suspended the 1923 constitution, proclaimed a new constitution, and called for elections. Lacking popular support, Sidqi formed a new party, ironically called *al-Sha'b* (the People's party) and rigged the election to increase his backing in the parliament. (Earlier, Sayyid Ahmad recalled the bitter days of Sidqi, whom he called Satan, when government agents clubbed people and forced them to vote for his party, and whole families suffered economic ruin.)[61] A severe constitutional crisis arose in June 1931, when Sidqi suspended the parliament for a month, prompting al-Nahhas to urge the people to revolt. As in 1919, demonstrations erupted throughout Egypt, and the government responded by firing on the demonstrators, killing hundreds. The political situation was made worse by the depression. The government could not sell its cotton crop, and bales of cotton began to pile up and rot in warehouses. When the people despaired over the troubled situation, they grew cynical and avoided active involvement in politics, weakening the Wafd's power and leaving national policy to opportunistic, compromising men. As Ahmad notes, there was an unlimited number of treacherous men like Mahmud and Sidqi (once Wafdists and supporters of Zaghlul) who sought to punish the Wafd, and who would hypocritically pose as nationalists to accomplish their political objectives. The Egyptians have always looked for trustworthy men to govern them and solve their problems, Kamal says, but they end up with detestable executioners protected by British clubs and rifles. The British excuse for controlling the people this way is that the Egyptians have not yet matured politically and need their guidance (115).

When Kamal reaches the festival site near Bayt al-Umma, he sees British soldiers guarding the site and the access roads. Bursting with nationalist sentiment, he is moved by the sight of the crowd to shout the praises of the Wafd. Mahfouz describes Kamal's mental agony as he strives to harmonize the political situation in his country with his idealistic life of the mind. In his personal library he can communicate with a few excellent friends of consummate intellect, mostly Western philosophers, whose ideas have deeply influenced him. Here the pavilion teems with thousands of other friends, well intentioned but evidently not so gifted. Yet he considers them no less important than Western thinkers, because both play a role in the making of history. The conflict between intellect and emotion is most perplexing, but he is resigned to the fact that life is fraught with perplexities. When he hears al-Nahhas deliver a fiery speech urging revolt against the government, Kamal wonders whether he can trust this man. And when he hears the Quranic verses wherein God admonishes Muhammad to entice the believers to fight for his cause, he is reminded that he was once a staunch believer. Kamal is thrust back into reality when he leaves the pavilion and sees British constables shooting at the demonstrators. More tragically still, Egyptian soldiers also open fire and kill many of their countrymen, including young students. He finds shelter, and when the shooting stops he returns home, recalling how as an elementary school student he sought refuge under similar circumstances. He cannot recall the shopkeeper's name but vividly remembers the events of that day, especially the whizzing of the bullets and the cries of the fallen.

Mahfouz continues to focus on the struggle between the Wafd and Fuad, who by 1935 was a sick old man. A conversation among the Sayyid's cronies reveals the people's unwavering trust in al-Nahhas, whom they consider even more adamant than Zaghlul in defending constitutional rights. Once, they say, the king put his hand on al-Nahhas's shoulder and tearfully asked him to form a coalition cabinet, hoping at least to dilute the Wafd's power, but he would not comply unless the king restored the 1923 constitution. Though the people trusted al-Nahhas more than any other leader, some simply despaired of the political situation. They could not believe that the British, having occupied Egypt since 1882, would readily leave. They were everywhere, controlling the army, the police, and various government departments. They still held the privileges known as Capitulations, granted to foreigners since Ottoman times. Even so, they seemed eager to normalize their relations with Egypt. The king restored the 1923 constitution in December 1935, apparently finding it in his interest to join with the Wafd in forming a so-called national front. But this rapprochement did not last long; Fuad died on April 28, 1936, and the throne passed to his sixteen-year-old son Farouk, who assumed his full rights the following year. Buoyed by a resounding victory in the May 1936 election, al-Nahhas formed an all-Wafd cabinet, which immediately proposed to renew negotiations with the British. When the British agreed, al-Nahhas led a delegation to London to meet with the high commissioner, Sir Miles Lampson. Their efforts culminated in the signing of the Anglo-Egyptian treaty on August 26, 1936.

Showing considerable interest in these developments, Kamal's nephew Ahmad comments that Farouk is still young and lacks his father's political finesse, and that the Wafd's resurgence will eventually bring additional successes. He expresses similar views soon after his graduation from high school, in a conversation with Adli Karim, the owner-publisher of *al-Insan al-Jadid*. Asked about the political orientation of the students, he replies that like himself the great majority are Wafdists, though some are attracted to other groups like *Misr al-Fatat* (Young Egypt), also called the green-shirts. He hastens to add that the students want more political gains; thus the Wafd is most favored not as an end in itself but as a means to national goals. Karim agrees, calling the Wafd a natural and significant evolutionary step. Unlike the reactionary, religious, and pro-Turkish *al-Hizb al-Watani* (National Party) founded by Mustafa Kamil (d. 1908), it has crystallized and purified Egyptian nationalism. As a starting point, it is preferable to *Misr al-Fatat*, a fascist, reactionary, criminal group whose ideology echoes German and Italian militarism, which worships power and rejects traditional human values. But, says Karim, the people need a new social school of thought. Independence is not the end; it is a means for the people to gain constitutional guarantees of economic and human rights (106–8).

Adli Karim's viewpoint becomes clearer if we realize that he represents the socialist Salama Musa, who greatly influenced Malfouz's thinking and published many of his articles in *al-Majalla al-Jadida*. What is significant here is that Karim/Musa is not satisfied with the political gains made by the Wafd. He sees the Anglo-Egyptian treaty and the establishment of Egypt's independence as only the first steps in building a new society based on socialistic principles. What he seeks is essentially social democracy, which suits a country whose people have been deprived of social justice. Ahmad is clearly impressed by Karim's ideas, and years later he reiterates them in a conversation with his brother Abd al-Munim, contending that the Wafd is the heart of the national movement, and that Egyptian independence should be the primary consideration. But nationalism must assume a fuller meaning, he adds, perhaps intending that it should deliver full constitutional rights to the people. Here he seems to share the view of Riyad Qaldas, who tells Kamal that national independence is not everything, for the people have a sacred right to enjoy full sovereignty and live in dignity as free men, not slaves (175).

The conversation between Adli Karim and Ahmad reveals much about Musa's intellectual orientation. Musa, who studied in England at the turn of the century and returned home before World War I, was thoroughly imbued with Western socialistic and scientific ideas. He regarded science as the only answer to religious fanaticism and reactionism. Karim tells Ahmad that every age has its prophets, and the prophets of the present age are the scientists. He prefers science to literature as a means of liberation, saying literature can easily be used to support reactionism, as is clear from the example of al-Azhar and Dar al-Ulum, which for many generations have produced morbid writings which froze reason and killed the human spirit. So it is necessary for men of letters to acquire some knowledge of science. No one ignorant of science belongs to the twentieth century, and no man can be truly educated unless he espouses science, which must replace ancient divination. Karim's ideas are so similar to those voiced by Musa in his autobiography *Tarbiyat Salama Musa* (The Education of Salama Musa) that we are convinced the two men are one and the same.[62]

The signing of the Anglo-Egyptian treaty gave the Wafd and al-Nahhas confidence that they could control the government and keep popular support for a long time, but this feeling vanished after Farouk assumed full power in July 1937. In accordance with the constitution, al-Nahhas resigned and the king asked him to form a new government. But no sooner had he named his cabinet than the king criticized him for having excluded certain loyalist politicians. Al-Nahhas also outraged public opinion by omitting Mahmud Fahmi al-Nuqrashi, respected as a strong nationalist and loyal Wafdist. He further angered Farouk and his supporters by refusing to allow his coronation in a civil ceremony. Thus, he was beset simultaneously by the king, the Liberal Constitutionalists, and the Saadists (disaffected Wafdists), with whom al-Nuqrashi aligned himself.

Mahfouz devotes much of chapter 21 to the public outcry protesting al-Nuqrashi's exclusion, the main topic of conversation at a gathering hosted by Abd al-Rahim Pasha Isa. One guest says al-Nahhas has done himself irreparable political damage by this action. Another blames Makram Ubayd, a Christian Copt and staunch Wafdist, charging that he seeks to gain control of the party by eliminating effective leaders like al-Nuqrashi. Some guests wonder whether al-Nuqrashi will join with opposition parties to form a new government and whether the Wafd itself will be divided, while others argue al-Nahhas has offended the king by constantly attacking him. These comments all have some merit. Ubayd, a brilliant and forceful politician who had won Zaghlul's unwavering trust, was popularly called "Sa'd's first-born son" and "the great combatant," and rose swiftly to become the Wafd's general secretary. It is no wonder that al-Nahhas included him in every cabinet until inevitably they collided, causing a disastrous rift within the party. At the same time, al-Nahhas differed with al-Nuqrashi over the implementation of the 1936 treaty and believed that he had already joined ranks with the opposition.

Al-Nahhas's actions gave Farouk an opportunity to remove him and curb the power of the Wafd. Backed by the Liberal Constitutionalists, the Saadists, and Shaykh al-Maraghi, the rector of al-Azhar, the king dismissed al-Nahhas in December 1937 and appointed Muhammad Mahmud, who formed a non-Wafdist cabinet. This action outraged many people, especially the Coptic minority. Riyad Qaldas calls it a setback for the Egyptian people in their struggle with the royal palace. He says the dismissal of al-Nahhas was concocted not by Farouk alone, but also by enemies of the people like Muhammad Mahmud and Ali Mahir, although the British apparently were not involved. If the country were purged of such treacherous men, he says, no one would back the king's unjust actions. The people must now oppose him and fight for their rights.[63]

Mahmud's cabinet, dominated by personalities rather than ideology, had no parliamentary base and little popular support. To remedy the situation, the king on January 3, 1938, dissolved the parliament and set new elections for April. Meanwhile, the prime minister began purging Wafdists from office and replaced them with men who were loyal to him. By collaborating with the king and the opposition parties, he managed to rig the election so that the Wafd won only twelve seats. Even al-Nahhas and Ubayd were defeated.

As the election is held, Aisha's daughter Naima, now married to her cousin Abd al-Munim, is about to have her first child. Her fragile health has deteriorated during pregnancy. Kamal and other family members are there as she goes through delivery. Ahmad, the committed communist, takes perverse delight in a radio report of the Wafd's defeat. His father remarks smartly that although the Wafdists thought the era of rigged elections was past, their opponents have turned out to be worse than ever. He uses the popular saying, "Shihab al-Din adratu min akhihi," (Shihab is a worse farter than his brother) to compare Muhammad Mahmud unfavorably with the inept Ismail Sidqi. Ahmad cannot believe the election was so blatantly rigged and says Egypt must be roused from her comatose state. But no one reacts with more outrage than Kamal, who says "these dogs" (Mahmud and other opponents of the Wafd) are restoring autocratic rule to Egypt, and Farouk will be more despotic than his father. Everyone knows what they did, yet the government affirms that the elections were legal. Thus, the people will believe that the members of parliament and cabinet officials have stolen their positions, the government is a sham, and thievery and deception are countenanced as legal. Should the common people be blamed, then, if they renounce moral principles and embrace such practices? Ahmad remarks that these men should be allowed to rule; it is better for the Egyptians to suffer this disgrace than to be ruled by men whom they trust and cherish, without investigating whether they can fulfill their hopes. Having pondered the matter, he can accept the rule of tyrants like Mahmud and Sidqi, since the Wafd has not met the people's desires. But this response is to be expected; Ahmad would probably reject any government, regardless of who leads it (183–89). Sadly, Naima dies in childbirth, just as

the Egyptians' hopes for democratic rule and national independence have died with the Wafd's election defeat.

Mahfouz explores the sensitive question of the Coptic minority in
the conversation between Kamal and Riyad Qaldas following al-
Nahhas's dismissal. Riyad states that the Copts see themselves first
and foremost as Egyptians, not as a Christian minority expecting to
be treated differently from the Muslims. For this reason they back
the Wafd, which embodies their national hopes and transcends
parochial considerations, rather than religious or ethnic interest
groups such as al-Hizb al-Watani. They deeply resent their persecution under Sidqi, who, unlike the Wafd, treated them as a minority.
Kamal, who is too wrapped up in his self-contained world to think
of the world outside, cannot understand Qaldas's complaint. His
failure to see the plight of the Copts is not surprising; in almost
every society, minorities are considered of little importance. Kamal
naïvely supposes that Qaldas, like himself, is a freethinker whose
interest in the arts and sciences is greater than his concern for
political affairs. Qaldas tells him that as a Copt, he is a free man who
considers Christianity not his religion but his birthright. His faith
forces him to divide his loyalty between his Coptic nation and
Egypt, the land of his birth. But this problem, he says, will immediately vanish when his people feel that they and all the Egyptians are
united by the bond of nationalism, as Zaghlul intended. He cites
al-Nahhas as living proof that his cause transcends religion; he is a
Muslim by birth and upbringing, but also an Egyptian nationalist in
every sense.

Watching Riyad Qaldas as he talks, Kamal is impressed by his
authentic Egyptian features, which remind him of the portraits of
ancient pharaohs. (Thus Mahfouz indirectly acknowledges the
Copts as the descendants of the pharaonic Egyptians.) Although he
admires Qaldas's argument, he cannot comprehend the distinction
drawn between the majority and the minority. Qaldas does not
believe that a minority can survive living amidst a society that
persecutes it harshly, although every sublime human doctrine supports the persecuted and promises happiness for all people. Kamal,
meanwhile, cannot believe that the Copts are persecuted while
living alongside the Muslim majority. This sectarian problem is

entirely new to him. His mother taught him from the beginning to love everybody, and he grew up during the Egyptian revolution, which transcended religious differences. But Qaldas dispassionately asserts that both groups harbor feelings of sectarian fanaticism. The Muslims regard the Copts as accursed infidels, and the Copts consider the Muslims usurpers of their homeland; indeed, when the Muslims invaded their country, they were able to preserve their Christian faith only by paying a poll tax.

Kamal cannot decide whether this conflict has its origins in religion or human nature, but he seems to lean toward the latter. If it were based on religion, he thinks, one would expect to see conflict between Shiites and Sunnites, or between Hijazis and Iraqis. (Indeed, fighting between Shiites and Sunnites is a historical reality.) Qaldas acknowledges the conflict but says it is a thing of the past. The Copts' problem today is the problem of all Egyptians; they will be enslaved or liberated together. Gone are the days when a fanatic like Abd al-Aziz Chawish (d. 1929) could propose that Muslims make shoes out of the skins of Copts. Mahfouz likewise concedes the existence of a Muslim-Copt conflict but seems to be neutral and objective, not blaming either side for its strong position. In his view, nationalism transcends sectarianism, and all Egyptians suffer alike from petty political infighting and British control of their national destiny (175–78).

Toward the end of the novel, Mahfouz describes two other political developments: al-Nahhas's return to power with British support, and the growth of a rift within the Wafd that culminated in the ouster of Makram Ubayd. After Farouk dismissed al-Nahhas, the Wafd remained out of power for nearly five years, during which time several opposition politicians headed the government. One of them, Ali Mahir, who succeeded Mahmud just before the outbreak of World War II, strongly supported the king against the British, who saw any internal political disturbance in Egypt as detrimental to their interests. After Italy declared war on the Allies in June 1940, the British urged Mahir to declare war on Italy; when he refused, they pressured him into resigning. His successors likewise refused to declare war but partly placated the British by severing diplomatic relations with the Axis. With the entry of German troops under General Rommel in April 1941, which jeopardized the British position in Egypt, Mahir continued to agitate against the British but was eventually placed under house arrest. The sentiment of the Egyptian people, however, was decidedly pro-Axis. The British authorities were especially alarmed when on February 2, 1942, crowds shouting Rommel's praises demonstrated in Cairo. Seeing that the Wafd was still powerful and enjoyed popular support despite the king's antagonism, they sought to pacify the situation by reinstating al-Nahhas as prime minister, but Farouk adamantly refused. Thus two nights later, with British armored units surrounding the royal palace, the British ambassador, Sir Miles Lampson (later Lord Killearn), offered him an ultimatum: accept al-Nahhas's appointment or abdicate and leave the country. The king yielded, in what has come to be known as the February 4 affair. Having for many years kept the Wafd from power because they considered al-Nahhas their foe, the British in a complete reversal of policy managed to spare themselves political trouble in Egypt for the duration of the war.

The controversy engendered by the February 4 affair is apparent in a discussion among Riyad Qaldas, Ismail Latif, and Kamal. Latif suggests that al-Nahhas collaborated with the British to retaliate for his dismissal, but Qaldas says he would not have conspired with the British just to return to power, and he instead blames Mahir for betraying the Wafd and the people to side with the king. Kamal reaffirms his belief in the integrity of al-Nahhas, who may have erred but certainly did not conspire with the British or betray the national trust. He doubts that al-Nahhas acted solely out of a desire for power but is not sure his motives were altogether altruistic. Nevertheless, he says, the king's compliance with the ultimatum shows Egypt's independence is a sheer illusion. Latif says cynically that al-Nahhas retaliated as any politician would but agrees that independence is an empty word. Why, he asks, should Farouk be replaced by a military governor? He thinks the British authorities simply used al-Nahhas for their own purposes and will force him out as soon as they no longer need him (284–86). Clearly the controversy remains unsettled, and the circumstances surrounding al-Nahhas's return to power are not fully known. Mahfouz, however, does not mention the great service al-Nahhas rendered to the British by subduing their opponents, cracking down on spies and saboteurs, and marshaling domestic labor to help in the many work projects needed for the British war effort.

An equally momentous political development was the rift within the Wafd marked by the expulsion of the Christian Copt Makram Ubayd, one of its most influential members. He served in al-Nahhas's first five cabinets but was dropped from the sixth in May 1942, partly because of the jealousy of al-Nahhas's wife Zaynab al-Wakil, who believed that Ubayd had become too powerful, and the party and her husband would be better off without him. Ubayd might have thought that joining forces with the king would eventually make him prime minister, but most likely his estrangement from al-Nahhas resulted from a personality conflict. Be that as it may, he was ousted not only from the cabinet, but from the parliament. On March 31, 1943, he presented a petition to the king, later expanded and published as *The Black Book*, in which he exposed corruption and immoral practices within the Wafd. Joined by a number of disgruntled Wafdists, Ubayd formed a new opposition party called al-Kutla (The Bloc). The split cost the Wafd popular support and encouraged the king to play off other parties against it. When al-Nahhas brought the Wafd to power for the last time in January 1950, it was a severely weakened party, easily manipulated by the king.

Mahfouz offers opposing view of Ubayd's downfall through Riyad Qaldas and Kamal. Qaldas, speaking for the Copts, calls it a national catastrophe. Although Ubayd may be ambitious and difficult to control, he says, the corruption he revealed could not be covered up. (We should note here that the Wafd was known for its patronage system.) Ubayd must have thought it his duty to expose the Wafd, even if doing so cost him his position. Kamal, however, feels he was motivated less by the Wafd's corruption than by his own ambition and fear of losing his position. The rift, he says, will be welcomed by the king, and Ubayd's only chance for political survival is to join forces with the opponents of the Wafd.

Although Kamal is affected little by Ubayd's departure, Qaldas fears that because the Copts have lost their staunchest defender, even the Wafd and al-Nahhas will turn on them. If the Wafd persecutes them as other parties do, he asks plaintively, what will become of them? Kamal replies that by identifying Ubayd with the Copts, Qaldas has distorted the whole issue. He is only one man; his presence in the Wafd is of no great consequence, but the national ideology the party represents is indispensable and lasting. Qaldas, unconvinced by this rationalization, feels that by expelling Ubayd the Wafd has expelled the Copts. This affair has stirred a conflict between his reason and his feelings. If he says he is a Wafdist, he must deny his emotions; and if he claims he is an enemy of the Wafd, he rejects common sense. Kamal, who feels as if all mankind is acting out a comedy with a tragic ending, tries to convince him that what he sees as a problem will disappear if only the Copts will look at Ubayd not as their representative, but simply as a politician. When Qaldas asks whether the Muslims look at Ubayd this way, Kamal answers that he himself does so, but Qaldas objects that he has renounced his faith. Kamal says he sees no difference in their positions, but Qaldas retorts that there is one difference; Kamal does not belong to a minority group (294–96). By this he means the Muslim majority, which has always looked on the Copts with suspicion, if not contempt, has little or no comprehension of their problems. Perhaps Ubayd does not personify the ethos of the Coptic people, but his role in the government signified that they are a political force to be taken seriously. Fearing that his dismissal of Ubayd may alienate the Copts, al-Nahhas appointed another Copt, Kamil Sidqi, as minister of finance. Although Sidqi was not quali-fied for the post and proved to be a liability to the Wafd, al-Nahhas could not get rid of him, for fear of offending his people.[64]

The veteran minister Abd al-Rahim Pasha Isa exemplifies the corruption and immorality of many Egyptian politicians. Through him Mahfouz shows that the government was one of personalities rather than laws, and that powerful men could manipulate its processes to suit their own interests. Yasin's son Ridwan, for exam-ple, manages to rise to the top of the administrative scale through the Pasha's influence rather than his own personal qualifications. And the Pasha, considering al-Nuqrashi's dismissal disastrous be-cause of his political skill, supports him in his split with the Wafd and encourages student demonstrations promoting him to replace al-Nahhas as prime minister.

Abd al-Rahim Pasha Isa calls politics merely a pastime, a diversion from his loneliness. A bachelor, he lives in a lovely villa in Hulwan, with a doorman, driver, and valet. Yet he is hardly lonely, for there are several young men with whom he has intimate relationships. We soon gather from his life-style that he is homosexual. One of his regular companions is Ali Mihran, ostensibly his business agent, although their conversations make it clear he is one of the Pasha's sex partners. Another is Hilmi Izzat, a law school classmate of Ridwan who introduced him into the Pasha's circle of friends. Indeed, it is through the Pasha that Ridwan becomes secretary to the minister of education, arranges Yasin's promotion, cancels Kamal's transfer, and finds a position for his cousin Abd al-Munim.

The Pasha distinguishes between private and public morality, saying his personal life has no bearing on his actions as a judge or politician. He takes pride in having been an honest judge but claims love of his country forced him to abandon the law and take up politics. Yet the very case he cites to prove his honesty betrays his hypocrisy. Shortly before he was to hear an inheritance case, a friend introduced him to a handsome young man with Ridwan's fair face, Hilmi Izzat's shapeliness, and Mihran's grace. The Pasha befriended this young man, not knowing his true identity, and on the day of the trial discovered to his surprise that he was the attorney for one of the litigants. Naturally, he withdrew from the case and broke off relations with the young man because of his lack of morality. This self-praise does not amuse Mihran, who remarks sarcastically that the Pasha has kept him as a companion because of his good character. That the Pasha sees no connection between his private life and his conduct as a public figure is hardly surprising, for most politicians in our time have a similar affliction.

The Pasha's spiritual life resembles that of Sayyid Ahmad. Like every Muslim, he hopes to perform the pilgrimage to Mecca, which he believes will wash away his sins and assure his salvation. But his concept of sin seems shallow, for he asserts, "Our sins are like innocent childish amusement" (356). Similarly, he sees repentance not as an internal religious experience that involves renunciation, but a change in outward conduct, shown by visiting Mecca and approaching the tomb of the Prophet. Ali Mihran reminds him that there is as much temptation in Mecca as in Egypt. Hilmi Izzat says it will be difficult to find a fair face like Ridwan's there, prompting the Pasha to reply that there is no face like that even in paradise. His companions do not take his intention to repent seriously. Ali Mihran, who has been associated with him for many years and perhaps best knows his true nature and all the secrets of his degenerate life, is confident that as soon as the Pasha returns from his pilgrimage, he will resume his usual ways.

Mahfouz devotes much of the novel to the third generation, represented chiefly by Abd al-Munim and Ahmad and their cousin Ridwan, together with secondary characters like Hilmi Izzat, Alawiyya Sabri, and Susan Hammad, and others of less importance. He uses the cultural growth of these people to illustrate the changes in Egyptian society between the two world wars.

The Wafd began to lose its supremacy after Zaghlul's death, and for the first time the nationalists had competition from extremists groups—the communists on the left and the Muslim Brotherhood on the right. This rivalry is manifested in the thoughts and actions of the two brothers, Abd al-Munim and Ahmad, who espouse diametrically opposed ideologies. How could such political philosophies appeal to young men from a very conservative Muslim family? Clearly the members of the new generation have more freedom of thought and action than their predecessors. Unlike Kamal, they have the will to make up their minds about what course of action they will take. Not motivated by self-interest, they have moral courage and determination and believe deeply in principles for which they are ready to suffer and sacrifice. This new generation felt frustrated by the moral paralysis of their leaders, who were mere puppets of the British authorities. Fully aware of the degeneration of the political process, they lost faith in the existing parties and sought different ideologies that could offer action instead of rhetoric and real answers to Egypt's problems. Thus, it is fair to say that Ahmad's and Abd al-Munim's commitment to their causes represents their generation's revolt against the prevailing political, social, and economic conditions.

But other young Egyptians accepted the status quo and manipulated it to suit their selfish interests. Thus, instead of espousing an ideology, Ridwan becomes a votary of Abd al-Rahim Pasha Isa. At the other end of the social spectrum from his cousins, he is an ambitious young man whose self-interest transcends values or principles. His main objective is to rise to the top by associating with powerful men, even if this means accepting pederasty and other forms of immoral conduct. Ridwan's cousins understand his ambitions, but they are young men of moral conviction, committed to their causes rather than personal success. He in turn is fully aware of their position but lacks the courage to acknowledge his homosexual behavior. It is a secret he keeps buried deep in his soul, a constantly haunting nightmare. He feels like a stranger, isolated from the mainstream of his generation. He can understand his cousins' conflicting ideologies, yet he cannot distinguish between normal and aberrant behavior; he is baffled by the human condition, wondering why men like himself act as they do in spite of themselves.[65]

Both communism and the Muslim Brotherhood emerged in Egypt during the 1920s. The Communist party of Egypt was founded in 1922 by Joseph Rosenthal and later financed by Henri Curiel, a bookseller and son of a Jewish millionaire. It was an illegal party whose members were mostly foreigners. By the 1940s it gained great prestige because of Soviet successes and the opening of a Soviet legation in Cairo in 1942. Although small (membership peaked around 5,000), it had a great appeal and strong influence among educated younger Egyptians. The Muslim Brotherhood was founded in 1928 at Ismailiya by Hasan Ahmad al-Banna, a teacher who came to be known as the Murshid (Guide or Grand Master). At first religious in nature, in time it grew politicized. It often used terrorism to achieve its goals; among its victims was Prime Minister al-Nuqrashi, assassinated in December 1948. The Muslim Brotherhood was then outlawed by the government, and in February 1949 al-Banna himself was killed in front of its headquarters. As a movement defending the tenets of Islam and sworn to support the Palestinians in their struggle to restore their country and national identity, it permeated Egyptian society and had tremendous appeal in many Arab countries. The teachings of both communism and the Muslim Brotherhood even penetrated the high schools, as we see in the case of Ahmad and Abd al-Munim.

As he watches the funeral of King Fuad in 1936, Ahmad remarks that he does not like tyrants, whatever the political circumstances are. Likewise, he detests fanatics like the Muslim Brotherhood. His nascent socialistic views are shown in an argument with his mother over the rent owed by the tenant of an apartment his parents own. When Khadija complains that the tenant has asked to delay payment for a month, Ahmad remarks that the family will not starve if he cannot pay on time. She asks sarcastically whether he believes people should rent houses without paying. Ahmad retorts that he is not sure people should own homes privately. His response plainly reflects the ideas of Adli Karim, who encourages Ahmad and Susan Hammad (whom Ahmad later marries) to study Marxism. But he reminds them that although Marxism is a historical necessity, its determination exists only through men's will and effort. Their duty is not to philosophize but to make the proletariat conscious of the historic role it must play to save itself and the world.

But why should Mahfouz portray Adli Karim (who represents Salama Musa) as influencing Ahmad rather than Kamal (who represents Mahfouz himself)? The answer is that in thought and deed, Kamal has reached the point of no return in his life. He has entered a blind alley with no exit. His life has become meaningless, vacuous. He has abandoned his faith and rejected marriage and has come to doubt virtually everything, including his own being. He can neither progress nor regress. He is not only static but sterile. Mahfouz has no choice but to let Ahmad, who is active, determined, and committed, carry the novel to its logical end.

Abd al-Munim encounters the teachings of the Muslim Brotherhood while still in high school. After watching King Fuad's funeral, he and Ahmad go to the coffeehouse of Ahmad Abduh, Kamal's favorite haunt. There the bearded Shaykh Ali al-Manufi, principal of al-Husayn Elementary School, stands amid young men, to whom he explains the brotherhood's principles. He greets and embraces Abd al-Munim, signifying that he is one of the group. Ahmad refuses to join the circle, but al-Manufi calmly tells his audience that many men initially shun the brotherhood but are finally led by God to join it. From his speech we learn that the main objective of the Muslim Brotherhood is to restore Islam to its pristine state. Its motto, proclaimed by the Murshid Hasan al-Banna, is "return to the Quran." Al-Manufi emphasizes that Islam has declined because the people today are Muslims only in name and need to become Muslims in action. The brotherhood, he says, possesses spiritual treasures that it must uncover and spread throughout the world. He tells the young men around him they are the army of God, over whom Satan has no dominion. It is incumbent on them to spread the light of God and fight his foes. Their sharpest weapon is faith. The Europeans rely on materialistic civilization, he argues, but the brotherhood relies only on faith in God. He rejects the proposition that despite their true faith the Egyptians are weak and cites the example of the Prophet, who conquered Arabia as later the Arabs conquered the whole world by faith. Mahfouz shows that the Muslim Brotherhood's teachings are not confined to religion but extend to politics, for to its members the two are wholly insepara-ble. Al-Manufi stresses this point by asserting that Islam is a doc-trine, a law, and politics. God is too compassionate to leave the believers without law or guidance, he says, citing evidence from the Quran and the traditions of the Prophet (98–100).

Because it called for a return to the roots of Islam, the brother-hood appealed to the lower class as well as to the educated younger generation. It was a religious society whose members covered the political spectrum, but when it accused al-Nahhas of collaborating with the British, Mahfouz felt that its actions would weaken the Wafd. Obviously he disliked the Muslim Brotherhood for its politi-cal orientation, not its religious beliefs.[66] Nevertheless, he appears to be fair and objective in portraying it as a movement to be taken seriously because of its impact on young Egyptians.

Abd al-Munim's involvement with the Muslim Brotherhood sparks a lively discussion among his peers. When one of them wonders whether marriage will interrupt his studies, Hilmi Izzat says that is unlikely to happen to a member of the brotherhood. Ridwan, unfamiliar with the group, is told that it is a religious society seeking to return to the original doctrines of Islam. Abd al-Munim adds that its objectives is not just to educate and train character but to promote Islam as a religion, a way of life, and a government. Some of his fellow students do not understand the beliefs of the organization, while others consider them too reactionary to suit the times. One comments that its ideology has simply created more confusion for the Egyptians, who have no idea whether to embrace democracy, fascism, or communism. Another considers it an oppressive movement and asks whether its members stone their opponents (according to the laws of Islam). Abd al-Munim explains rather angrily that although present-day young Muslims deviate from the tenets of Islam and have become morally degenerate, stoning is not an appropriate punishment; members of the brotherhood try to win people to their cause through proper education, spiritual guidance, and sound advice. But Hilmi Izzat objects that although members of the brotherhood are tolerant, so are the Wafdists, as evidenced by the fact that the chief counselor to the party's leader is a Christian Copt, Makram Ubayd. What, then, makes the Muslim Brotherhood more attractive than the Wafd? Strictly for Muslims, it is far from being an open movement striving for equality for all Egyptians; it promotes religious sectarianism rather than social equity. The students' discussion reveals the confusion of the younger generation about the many political choices facing them. It also indicates their fear that the Muslim Brotherhood may jeopardize the Wafd's efforts to achieve independence.[67]

The debate shifts from the objectives of the Muslim Brotherhood to the sensitive question of equality between men and women. In the 1930s and 1940s, the number of female students attending the university increased. Many of them entered the College of Arts, intending to teach high school after graduation. Yet, Ahmad contends, the question of equality cannot be settled by these facts. Abd al-Munim objects that Islam has established the equality of women with men except in the case of inheritance (according to the Quran, 4:10, the male receives twice the share of the female). Ahmad sarcastically interjects that Islam has made women equal with men even in slavery, since the Quran (4:3) gives a man the right to take four legal wives and an indefinite number of slave girls as mistresses. If women are mere slaves to men, he asks, where is the equality his brother speaks of?

The conversation turns to another sensitive and controversial topic, the conflict between religion and science. Abd al-Munim epitomizes religious faith and adherence to the principles of Islam, while Ahmad and Hilmi Izzat represent liberal thinking and belief in science. Their argument indicates Mahfouz's own perplexity over this conflict, which apparently became almost an obsession for him. He injects it into his earlier novels and makes it a central point of *Awlad Haratina*. Here he seems to be objective and neutral, leaving the reader to draw his own conclusions.

Abd al-Munim is outraged by his brother's statement that Islam has not established equality between the sexes, and that women are mere slaves to men. It is tragic, he says, that men like Ahmad do not understand Islam. This unspecific response does not satisfy the liberal-minded Hilmi Izzat, who counterattacks by asking what Abd al-Munim himself knows about Islam. The debate degenerates into an altercation that seemingly is going nowhere until Ahmad says he knows only that Islam is merely a religion, and he does not believe in religion. Abd al-Munim asks resentfully,

> "Do you have proof of the invalidity of religions?"
> "And do you have proof of their validity?" answers Ahmad.
> "Yes, I have proof, and so does every believer. But let me ask how do you live?"
> "I live by my faith in science, humanity, and the future. I live by my commitment to duties whose long-range purpose is to prepare the world for a new order," says Ahmad.
> "You have destroyed everything that qualifies a man to be a real man," retorts Abd al-Munim. (160)

Ahmad remains unconvinced. The fact that Islam has existed for over a thousand years, he says, is evidence not of its strength but rather of the weakness of that segment of mankind which resists development and change. What suited him as a child does not suit him as an adult, and he must try to change things. As long as man is slave to nature and to other people, he must strive to overcome his enslavement—in one case through science and inventions, in the other through progressive doctrines. Clearly he believes that Islam is not a progressive social force and that Muslims are hostile to innovation. Abd al-Munim understands him to mean that religion cannot solve mankind's problems, and only science and progressive thinking can deliver men from bondage. He is repulsed by his brother's ideas and calls atheism merely an easy solution, an escape from man's commitment to his God, his people, and himself. There is no proof that atheism is stronger than faith, he says, because people choose one or the other less through reason than because of their moral inclination. To Hilmi Izzat, this talk of faith, mankind, and the future is sheer nonsense. He believes only in the social order based on science and says that mankind must work to eradicate every trace of weakness and establish a new standard for human conduct (159–62).

The brothers' argument continues at home, arousing comments from their elders. Their father thinks they are wasting valuable time in worthless dispute and in associating with unimportant men like al-Manufi and Karim. He does not understand the principles of these ideologies, let alone their cultural significance and their impact on individuals and society. Like the Sayyid, he has become inured to political corruption and accepts the notion that neither his generation nor the next can remedy the country's maladies. His feeling of frustration and hopelessness is accentuated by Yasin, who says, "A sultan is he who stays away from the real Sultan," meaning that the man who wants to live in peace and control his destiny should keep his distance from politicians and other powerful men. Like Ibrahim Shawkat, he has no confidence in the political process and chooses to turn his back on it. Kamal, who has spent his life dabbling in intellectual pursuits, feels his two nephews may lack the intellectual maturity to comprehend the weighty and profound principles of religion and communism, or the strength of heart to adhere to them. Whether he is right about their intellectual capacity or not, plainly he lacks their determination and commitment. Although he questions the existence of absolutes, their devotion to their ideologies attests to their belief in lasting values (108, 208).

Mahfouz depicts both brothers as moral characters who adhere to different values. Abd al-Munim believes in God as the ultimate reality and truth and puts his faith into practice. He shuns the advances of a neighbor girl who tries to seduce him, believing that fornication is sinful and God wants him to keep himself pure. In order to maintain his virtuous life he even marries while still a student, despite his family's objection. Ahmad too is a moral young man, not a pleasure-seeker like his peers. But, believing only in science and communism, he tries to live according to dialectic materialism, which offers no spiritual guidance. Interestingly, many Egyptians today live by moral law, while scientific socialism has disappeared. However much the secularist Ahmad decries his brother's religious convictions as evidence of theocratic despotism and dangerous fanaticism, the fact remains that Abd al-Munim's faith offers a moral system suited to the traditions of Muslim Egyptians. But what can Ahmad's materialistic beliefs offer the Egyptians except disillusionment? History seems to be on Abd al-Munim's side, especially now that we have seen the collapse of scientific socialism in the former Soviet Union and Eastern Europe.

Like his brother, Ahmad seeks to marry at a young age. But his first love, the art student Alawiyya Sabri, does not share his socialistic beliefs. Like Kamal's Aida, she comes from a well-to-do upper-middle-class family. Looking not for love but for security, she rejects Ahmad because she thinks he will not be able to support her comfortably. But he accepts this development philosophically and finds another young woman whose ideas are compatible with his own. While he translates and contributes articles for *al-Insan al-Jadid*, Susan Hammad helps in various capacities to prepare it for publication. Although she comes from a working-class family (her father supervises the magazine's printers), she and Ahmad share the same ideology. She is only a high school graduate, while he is university educated, but she is proud of what she has learned from Adli Karim, which she considers no less important than formal schooling. Susan is a hard-line Marxist, more radical than Ahmad. She believes a writer should be committed to an ideology and should not write only to entertain. She urges Ahmad not to confine his efforts to translating Western works but to try serious writing, even poetry. When he says he is more inclined toward writing essays, she comments that considering the political situation in Egypt, the essay should be considered risky, because it is direct, candid, and often read by the authorities. But fiction, she says, is an intriguing art with unlimited subtleties. The story has become a popular genre and will soon predominate over other forms of literature. Moreover, every major writer is trying to establish a place for himself by undertaking fiction. Susan feels that it is safer for free writers (i.e., Marxists) to disseminate their ideas through secret publications. Indeed, this is exactly what communist writers in Egypt and elsewhere in the Middle East did, especially after the party was widely outlawed.

To Susan Hammad, literature is not an intellectual luxury or a form of entertainment; it should have the specific objective of motivating mankind to progress until the world becomes free in the Marxist sense. She does not like the writings of Riyad Qaldas or Kamal. She thinks Kamal is totally involved in abstract metaphysical subjects like the spirit and epistemology, mere intellectual diversions. Although he has read about nazism, democracy, and communism, he, like most bourgeois writers, has no empathy with oppressed people. He may be able to feel pain, but he is indifferent to the pain of true sufferers. Even Riyad Qaldas, who in his short stories portrays the peasants and the working class, confines himself to describing their state. His literary work, she says, does nothing to confront the real battle in life, that is, the conflict between communism and capitalism. He and Kamal must address themselves to this struggle and support the proletariat.

Ahmad is stunned by her attitude toward literature and writers. "What a woman," he thinks to himself, "not only serious, but ready to fight!" He had expected to meet a fine and gracious young woman who might become his life partner, not an ideological indoctrinator. Susan queries him to learn what he knows about communism, asking whether he has read modern Soviet writers, particularly Maxim Gorky. Ahmad, whose chief interest is the social sciences, says little, but she insists that he should read Soviet literature and promises to lend him some books on the subject. She contends it is not enough for the free man to be a reader or writer;

principles are connected with man's will, which is preeminent. Although he is taken aback by Susan's forceful and pugnacious attitude, he finds her charming and attractive in a natural way. He sees in her qualities which other young men often ignore. He is careful not to antagonize or offend her, having suffered enough pain when Alawiyya Sabri rejected him. Fascinated and impressed by Susan's strong personality, intelligence, and industriousness, Ahmad soon begins to emulate her and busily translates pieces from magazines around the world.

Susan Hammad exemplifies perfectly those Egyptians who truly believed in communism as the ultimate solution to the ills of their society. She distrusts the bourgeoisie and their values, even doubting Ahmad when he wants to marry her. Because he comes from a bourgeois family, she thinks he is not a true communist like herself. She says she and her family lived in poverty, which caused her to lose a sister, and wonders whether Ahmad has experienced its pangs. She wants to be sure that he is sincerely devoted to communism as she is, and that he will continue delivering speeches to the workers, regardless of the consequences. She knows that he loves her, but her commitment to her cause transcends such considerations. He understands her viewpoint but contends that his family is not so rich as she thinks, and that there is no shame in being bourgeois. To him, what is opprobrious is to be culturally stagnant, out of tune with the Zeitgeist (Ruh al-Asr). The progressive Ahmad believes in the principles of communism, but he also loves this young woman and cannot relinquish her. He wants to marry her without feeling he must assume all of mankind's burdens. When she protests that love is incompatible with the struggle for communist principles, Ahmad points out that multiple marriages did not prevent the Prophet of Islam from fighting for his cause. Saying he sounds just like his religious brother, she states that Marx left his wife and children in poverty to write Das Kapital; but, Ahmad retorts, the fact remains that Marx was married.

Genuinely in love with Susan, Ahmad is equally committed to Marxist principles, although they may make him a target for government persecution. He shares her belief that capitalism has run out of objectives and is dying, and that the proletariat must take advantage of the process of economic evolution. The communists' duty is to make the working class aware of their momentous role in this process, but this is a hard task when German troops are approaching Cairo and King Farouk may soon toast Rommel's victory. Susan cannot understand why the people love the Germans. They do so, Ahmad says, because they detest the British; it is ridiculous for the peasants to believe that Rommel will distribute the land among them. Susan declares that Russia never will be defeated, and that the hopes of mankind are safer beyond the Ural Mountains. She realizes that the Egyptian communists have external enemies (the Germans) and internal enemies (the Muslim Brotherhood and the reactionaries).

Her comment points up the conflict between the Communist party and the Muslim Brotherhood, both of which sought to supplant the government. Plainly her view would not please Abd al-Munim, who claims the Muslim Brotherhood's progressive ideology puts materialistic socialism to shame. Indeed, some Muslim writers in Egypt and elsewhere have argued that Islam is a socialist religion, and that Muslim societies can be reconstructed on socialistic principles. But to hard-line communists such an opinion is anathema. Susan concedes that there is a seed of socialism in Islam, but it is a utopian socialism like that of Thomas More, Louis Blanc, and Saint Simon. Islam seeks a solution to social injustice in man's conscience, she says, while the solution is to be found in the evolution of society. Because Islam is concerned with individuals rather than social classes, it has no relation to scientific socialism; its teachings, based on metaphysical myths, cannot solve the present problems. But the communists detest the Muslim Brotherhood mainly because they believe its members use hypocritical means to propagate their cause. To the educated they present Islam as a progressive ideology, while to the uneducated they talk about heaven and hell. Thus, they spread their ideals in the name of socialism, nationalism, and democracy. To some extent Susan's ideas resemble those of Riyad Qaldas, who says communism can create a world free from racial, religious, and class conflict. When Kamal answers that Islam has already created such a world, Qaldas retorts that Islam is merely a religious myth, while communism is a science (chapter 43, and 179–80). One can only guess what Qaldas and Susan Hammad—or for that matter Mahfouz himself—would say about the collapse of communism in our time.

Susan is apprehensive not only about Ahmad's devotion to communism but about his parents' view of her as a future daughter-in-law. She loves him and wants to marry him, but because she comes from a working-class family, she fears they may reject her as a woman of inferior social status. Her apprehension is well founded. No sooner does Ahmad declare his intentions than he encounters vehement objections. Khadija cannot believe her son is involved with such a low-class woman. She thinks that no woman works unless she is socially worthless, ugly, or unfeminine. It is not enough that her own son has chosen journalism, a contemptible profession; now he wants to marry a woman who has made the same choice. Mahfouz here shows the low status of the *journalji* in Egypt, due largely to the fact that most of them were semiliterate young people who could not find a more substantial means of making a living. Susan Hammad is one of these, having no formal education beyond high school. Khadija, investigating personally, is shocked to learn that Susan's family lives in a one-bedroom apartment on a street filled with Jews, and that her mother looks more like a domestic servant than a genteel lady. She cannot imagine why Ahmad would want to marry Susan, a rather plain woman in her thirties. Perhaps the most sensible view is that of Yasin, who tells Khadija it is pointless to condemn her son. Parents cannot properly judge their children because of the cultural gap between them. If Ahmad wants to marry, let him do so and bear the consequence of his decision, and Kamal agrees.

Ahmad is well aware that his mother objected earlier to the marriage of his brother Abd al-Munim to Yasin's daughter Karima because Karima's mother had a tarnished past. He listened to his mother's argumentative pronouncements with dismay, whispering to himself that the bourgeois class is fraught with complexes and needs treatment by a skilled psychiatrist. With luck, he thought, he would marry before his brother, but then he was rebuffed by the bourgeois Alawiyya Sabri. He cannot be sure now that his mother will not create problems for him as well, but he finally ignores his family's views and marries Susan, showing that the new generation is wholly different from Kamal's in its determination and single-mindedness.

Perhaps the most dramatic part of the novel is Mahfouz's portrayal of the parallel activities of the Muslim Brotherhood and the communists. Abd al-Munim becomes a bona fide active member of the brotherhood, serving as its legal counselor and contributing articles to its periodical. He is a zealot, ready to sacrifice money and effort to serve its ends. He believes in it as a *Salafiyya* movement, fashioned after the one founded by Muhammad Abduh (d. 1905), a Muslim reformer who sought to return to the pristine principles of Islam. He also regards the brotherhood as a Sunni *tariqa* (religious order), a Sufistic reality, a political organization, a group bound by science, an economic association, and a social doctrine. By night his apartment, a more suitable venue than Ahmad Abduh's coffee-house, is an assembly where Shaykh Ali al-Manufi can meet his disciples and expound on the tenets of the brotherhood. Al-Manufi tells them the laws and teachings of Islam completely regulate man's activities in this life and the life to come; Islam is a dogma, a mode of worship, a homeland, a religion, a state, a nationality, a spiritual entity, a book (the Quran), and a sword. A young listener says that today the Muslims are stagnant, doing nothing while men of no faith rule over them. Al-Manufi answers that the brothers must spread their principles and gain as many followers as possible. When the war is over and Egypt is ripe for revolt, they should rise to a man with arms and the Quran. Abd al-Munim agrees, adding that the Quran must become the constitution of all Muslims. Al-Manufi stresses that Islam is a religion for all mankind, and that the brotherhood will not achieve complete success until all the Islamic countries adhere to its principles. Thus, Mahfouz shows the brotherhood as a militant Islamic movement whose objective was to create a theocratic state dominant not only in Egypt but throughout the Muslim world. Not surprisingly, the Egyptian government viewed it as dangerous and subversive. Although it was rumored that King Farouk subsidized the Muslim Brotherhood and used it to counterbalance the popularity and political power of the Wafd, this speculation had no basis in fact.

Meanwhile, every night in the lower apartment in the same building, Ahmad and Susan meet with a small group of friends, mostly journalists, to study and discuss Marxism. They are frequently joined by Adli Karim, who declares that although it is commendable to study Marxism, translate books on communism, and give speeches to indoctrinate the workers, this is not enough. Their priority should be to win over the uneducated, as a first step toward gaining seats in parliament and ultimately taking control of the government. Ahmad objects that because communism renounces metaphysical myths, that is, religion, it is difficult to convince educated people that their faith is utter nonsense, useful only as an anesthetic. Likewise, it is difficult to discuss communism with ordinary Egyptians, who regard it as an atheistic ideology. Karim says the communists must first fight people's submissiveness and indifference. As for religion, it will be overcome only by free rule. Generally, poverty prevails over faith, and it is wise to talk to people at their level of understanding. When Ahmad complains that their movement attracts opportunists and unbelievers who seek only wages or personal gain, Karim says he is aware of the problem but notes that the Umayyads, who embraced Islam hypocritically, spread it even to Spain. Thus the communists should use such people, for time is on their side. He agrees that the Muslim Brotherhood is the chief impediment to communism, but he says it is not so formidable as Ahmad thinks. Its members often refer in their speeches to the socialism of Islam, and even if they effect a coup d'état, it will be partly a victory for communist principles. The brotherhood cannot stop the inexorable progress of communism toward its goal; the dissemination of science will drive out its teachings as surely as light expels bats (350–55).

Mahfouz offers a vivid picture of the government's crackdown on both the communists and the Muslim Brotherhood. Late one night, Abd al-Munim is arrested for distributing anti-government publications. Ironically, the officer in charge is Hasan Ibrahim, who years earlier sought Aisha's hand and was rejected by Sayyid Ahmad. Khadija reminds him that they are the nephews of her brother Fahmi, who was once Hasan's friend, but to no avail. The police also search Kamal's house, and he too finds that old friendships count for nothing.

Nothing in this whole episode is more compelling and saddening than the reaction of Amina, now a sick old woman. This pathetic figure from a dying generation, a peaceful and deeply religious woman who respects the government as a defender of the faith, asks why her grandsons have been arrested and is told they are suspected of acting against the government. She tells Kamal she has been given to understand that Abd al-Munim is under arrest because he is a Muslim, but this makes no sense. If the government claims to be Muslim, why does it oppress the Muslims, who are bound by brotherhood to support one another? He says this is simply her view of what Islam should be, not that of the Egyptian government. When she asks why Ahmad has been arrested, Kamal says it is because he is a *shuyui* (communist). Obviously bewildered, she asks whether these *shuyuis* are the "Shiites of our Lord Ali," and is told they are a party opposed to both the government and the British authorities. Sadly she wonders why the government has targeted her family.

Awaiting trial, Abd al-Munim and Ahmad are held in a dingy underground jailhouse packed mostly with college students and political activists, two of them law students charged with passing out publications advocating the distribution of agricultural wealth in Egypt. Abd al-Munim, unable to bear the humidity and discomfort, asks in a whisper why he should be thrown into this dungeon just because he worships God. Ahmad wonders why he has been thrown into the same place for not believing in God. The point Mahfouz is making is that the government could not care less about what people believe unless they become a threat to its authority, and then it uses any measures and any pretexts to maintain its power. In this dirty dungeon are lumped together the political activist, the Muslim brother, the communist, the drunkard, and the thief, all victims of a brutal government that does not represent the people but in fact is their enemy. Thus Mahfouz protests against the corruption of the Egyptian government, its subservience to the British, and especially its persecution of those who desire reform, whether or not they worship God. The government, he says, sees itself as the master and the people as slaves. It has no respect for law nor constitution, and it does not treat the Egyptians as human beings.

Mahfouz forcefully presents the new generation's philosophy of life in a conversation between Kamal and his nephews shortly before they are moved to the Tur concentration camp. Ahmad, who seems to view his situation quite realistically, tells Kamal that life consists of action, marriage, and the universal human duty of carrying on an eternal revolution. He believes in life and people and declares himself committed to follow communism's high ideals, which he regards as true; to do otherwise would show cowardice and escapism. By the same token, he is committed to revolt against these ideals if he finds them false; not to do so would be treachery. Interestingly, Abd al-Munim approves of what his brother says about true and false ideals and seems equally committed to his cause. He is a Muslim zealot, convinced that Islam is the right ideology to challenge a corrupt government and docile people who are Muslims only in name. They need total rejuvenation, and they need the Muslim Brotherhood to rouse them and prod them into action. Both brothers are active and committed, and both have suffered for their beliefs. They must become involved and serve a cause bigger than themselves or they will stagnate. To them life is service and action. If they do not use life, they will surely lose it. What they believe in matters less than putting their principles into practice.

Kamal appears to be stirred by Ahmad's remarks, but he refuses to act, to serve, or to commit himself to a cause and instead continues to brood over himself. He correctly understands that Ahmad has given him a call to faith; he must either come out of his isolation and become active in life or face death. Tormented by his conscience, he feels that he has selfishly betrayed himself and society. He desperately needs some faith but has no idea how to acquire it. He realizes his internal struggle is not yet over and, indeed, may never be resolved. This confused man, still living in a totally closed world of his own fancy, has become incapable of faith and thus is doomed to utter oblivion and nothingness. Life has passed his generation by; now it is the turn of the new generation to save Egypt from a corrupt system and push it toward a better, more dynamic future.

That Kamal has become spiritually empty and incapable of feeling is shown by his reaction to Aida's misfortune and death. Her brother Husayn has unexpectedly returned from Paris after many years' absence. He tells Kamal that after a few years of marriage, Hasan Salim, who was assigned to the Egyptian embassy in Tehran, divorced Aida to marry a woman employed at the Belgian legation. Aida returned to Egypt in 1943 and remarried but died a few months later. Ironically, Kamal attended her funeral without knowing that it was his once-beloved Aida who was being buried. When he learns the truth, he finds he cannot genuinely grieve over her death and the past, which now is forever lost. He has become too insensitive to life. If she had died in 1926, when he was madly in love with her, he would have committed suicide. But now it is 1944, and the symbol of love has become a vanishing memory. His only response is a vague feeling of sadness (370–71).

Husayn further details his family's misfortunes. His father became bankrupt, losing his wealth and villa. (Husayn omits mentioning that his father, incapable of enduring this loss, took his life.) His mother and Budur moved to a humble apartment in the Abbasiyya district. Husayn himself fared no better. When World War II broke out he was in Paris, married to a Parisian woman, but unemployed and dependent on his father-in-law. He too returned to Egypt but could not find suitable work and finally, desperate, accepted a minor position as a translator at the Censorship Bureau. When he learns that Kamal has attained his lifelong objective of becoming a teacher and writer, Husayn cannot conceal his envy, for he himself has done nothing in life. What irony! The wealthy aristocrat who with his sister once scorned Kamal for choosing teaching as a career and ridiculed his literary ambition now envies him for his achievements. What is even more deplorable is that Husayn, who could have had a position befitting his family's high status, now has had to accept a minor government appointment suitable for someone from the lower class. Mahfouz seems to imply that social status based on wealth alone is ephemeral and will vanish as soon as the wealth vanishes. Husayn, no longer the vain aristocrat Kamal knew in 1926, seems humble and subdued, like a member of the lower middle class, although he still hopes one day to restore his family's wealth and prestige (chapter 51).

The novel's action ends in 1944. The older generation is almost gone; Sayyid Ahmad and his cronies are dead, Amina is paralyzed and comatose, and the aged Shaykh Mutawalli Abd al-Samad has lost his memory. Seeing him, Kamal recalls when the shaykh visited his father in his shop. Suddenly realizing that the black tie he has worn to mourn his father's death is torn, he stops to buy another, for his mother's passing is imminent. Despite the adversity that has affected so many of his family and friends, life goes on as usual. Abd al-Munim's wife Karima is expecting a baby who represents the next generation of the Sayyid's family. The novel ends with Kamal and Yasin walking home together, anticipating Amina's death.

Five

Awlad Haratina

AWLAD HARATINA (literally, Children of Our Quarter, translated into English with the title *Children of Gebelawi*) is a radical departure from Mahfouz's previously published works. In fact, this historical allegory deviated so drastically that the uproar it created in conservative Islamic circles has not abated more than thirty years later. When it first appeared in serialized form between September and December 1959, it met with vehement opposition from the Muslim establishment. As a consequence it was never published as a novel in Egypt, and it was not until 1967 that it first appeared in book form in Lebanon.[1]

After Mahfouz was awarded the Nobel Prize in literature, he was again attacked. An extremist group issued a *fatwa* (juristic opinion) condemning Mahfouz—this time even going so far as to call for his death. Most of the criticism was focused on Mahfouz's apparent disregard for the Islamic belief that the prophets are infallible and, because of the divine message entrusted to them by God, should not be the subject of criticism by mere men. Further, the traditionalists objected, the representation of God in any human form is blasphemy according to Islamic belief. Lastly, they accused Mahfouz of stripping God and the prophets of their spiritual qualities. Many fair-minded critics, however, supported Mahfouz and condemned the *fatwa* for its fanaticism and disregard for freedom of speech.[2]

The writing of *Awlad Haratina* is directly connected to the 1952 revolution in which Jamal Abd al-Nasir, the head of a group of junior army officers, overthrew Egypt's King Farouk and announced with typical revolutionary hyperbole the dawning of a new day. For seven years afterward, Mahfouz watched, waited and remained silent. He had held the same high expectations as everyone else when the palace coup succeeded. But by 1959 he had waited long enough. He saw little improvement in the condition of the Egyptian people, but what he did see was the replacement of one inefficient and unresponsive regime by another; he saw the enrichment of Nasir's fellow officers, just as he had seen deep corruption in the circle of Farouk. Disillusioned by the outcome of the revolution, Mahfouz decided to write *Awlad Haratina* as a specific comment upon the Egyptian situation within the more encompassing context of the human condition.[3]

Because of the controversial nature—in his society—of the social, political, and religious issues, the story is told in the book in simple parablelike language. Mahfouz deliberately chose a stylistic anachronism, the simple, repetitive phrasing of the fable spinner, to surround his message with a web of allegory and symbolism.

Divided into five separate yet related chapters, each named for its hero, the book follows a loose chronology from the beginning of history to the present and is reminiscent of Shaw's *Back to Methuselah*. The first chapter is a barely disguised retelling of the story of Adam and Eve and their sons Cain and Abel; the second parallels the life of Moses; the third chapter, that of Jesus; the fourth, Muhammad; and the last and most important chapter introduces Arafa, who symbolizes modern science. All of the characters and the people who surround them live in the alley of history, or *hara*. Immediately contiguous to it, the house of the powerful and enigmatic Gebelawi dominates not only this "alley," but the historical vision of man as well.

Mahfouz's *awlad* (children) experience history as an endless cycle of hope and despair. Although men have from time to time attained fame and promised much, the world has always sunk back into "misery and death." Those in the alley have always sought freedom from tyranny, yet they have been able to escape its cold grip only for short periods. The hope inspired by Moses, Jesus, and Muhammad has been blunted by time. And the tyranny of forgetfulness has led men to fall under the control of one sort of worldly tyrant or another. Paradise was always lost.

Although the first four chapters parallel the lives of famous figures in the history of religion, Mahfouz is not particularly concerned with religion but rather with social and political issues and the role science plays in them. A careful reading shows that Mahfouz sees no inherent contradiction between faith and science.[4] This fact, however, did nothing to avert misinterpretation by overzealous Muslims who publicly attacked him and labeled him a blasphemer and apostate.

A brief look at the structure of the book reveals how the chapters are chronologically related and thematically unified. The author establishes a palpable historical framework for the spinning of his allegorical tale. We encounter the terrible Gebelawi in the first chapter and learn that he is the father of Adham (Adam) and his brother Idris (Iblis, or Satan), the father-in-law of Umayma (Eve), and later the grandfather of Qadri (Cain) and Hammam (Abel). Adham and Umayma inhabit Gebelawi's large house, enjoy his idyllic garden, and share the fruits of his large estate. Unfortunately, their sublime happiness is not to last. The peace of their lives is destroyed by the duplicity of Idris, the manipulation of Umayma, and the compliance of Adham. Adham and Umayma are expelled from Gebelawi's house, cut off from the estate (*Waqf*), and condemned to a barren existence in the desert beyond. Although he is rarely seen or heard from, Gebelawi's presence dominates the emotions and actions of the characters.

There is some ambivalence throughout the work concerning the nature of Gebelawi. The reader may find himself asking, Is this a real father who punishes his disobedient son and daughter-in-law? A distant grandfather who reassures Gebel (Moses)? A great-grandfather who encourages Rifaa (Jesus)? An unimaginably old man who conveys his will to Qasim (Muhammad), and whose decrepit existence is finally extinguished by Arafa (Science)? And indeed, Gebelawi may be all of these, but in reality he is the God who exists in the minds of men and whose name is endlessly repeated on the tongues of many generations—not always with love and understanding. Again and again he is characterized in less than friendly fashion by the people in the alley. They curse him for his lack of compassion, for his distance, and for his indifference in allowing tragedy to burden history. They regard him as a tyrant, not so much for his misdeeds as for his failure to prevent misfortune. There is apparently a direct relationship between men's religious faith and the worldly favors granted by or expected from Gebelawi. The division of the "estate" is always on their minds. This kind of attitude ensures the rise of new tyrants, power-hungry men who claim to be the representatives of God and the succorers of the people but who in reality rob them blind. Gebel is the enemy of these interlopers.

The story of Moses in the second chapter is familiar. Mahfouz does not wander far from its well-known line. The chapter opens with the *hara* under the rule of the effendi (pharaoh), who terrorizes it with his ubiquitous thugs. The happiness that Adham and Umayma were forced to relinquish is nowhere to be seen. Believing that he is carrying out the will of Gebelawi, Gebel comes to the rescue and temporarily restores material well-being and justice to the *hara*. But it is a limited dispensation of beneficence, for Gebel concerns himself only with the Jews (the children of Hamdan). He feels justice will have to be dispensed not by Gebelawi himself but by those who believe they are his agents. Gebelawi is nowhere to be seen, despite the dark and brooding presence of his massive house overshadowing the alley. For most of poor, benighted humanity his face will be forever hidden and his voice forever silent.

When we encounter the story of Rifaa (Jesus) in the third chapter, the *hara* has again sunk into oppression, poverty and inequity. Once more the people lament their abandonment by Gebelawi, asking, "Why does he shut himself in his big house surrounded by an impregnable wall, far removed from the world of the *hara?*" Rifaa's father, the carpenter Shafii, mourning the dolorous state of the *hara*, cries out, "Why has Gebelawi forsaken us?"[5] The tyranny of forgetfulness, on the part of both Gebelawi and the people, is a recurring reality throughout the novel.

Of the four historical figures Mahfouz portrays, Rifaa is the least accurately done. The chapter has a confusing disjointedness that leads to a lack of clarity and contributes to some historical inaccuracy. One thing is clear, however; Rifaa is completely devoid of interest in the material world. He believes that Gebel, who saw his mission as that of equitably redistributing Gebelawi's "estate," mistakenly thought true happiness would result from success in that mission. "The estate is such a petty thing," he tells his followers. "It is possible to attain true life without it, and anyone who wants to can. . . . The estate is nothing . . . ; the happiness of a contented life is everything. Only the demons of sin come between us and happiness" (249). Rifaa, then, is a true prophet, concerned solely with the realm of the spirit. Because of his emphasis on sin and spirit, he believes that he is not a threat to the secular powers and their henchmen; he will not be harmed. How wrong he is! To those who rule by force and fear, even one such as Rifaa, who is unmaterialistic and innocent, constitutes a threat. Because of their insecurity and paranoia, Rifaa is killed. The only true ascetic in the book dies believing himself a failure. His fame and influence come only after his death. Mahfouz is at pains to show that greatness is often bestowed upon men after they die by the half-truths, legends, and wishful thinking that rise like fog from the fallow ground of men's understanding. Similarly, Gebelawi no longer represents an objective, concrete, transcendent God but rather one who has been fashioned over time in man's image. The irony is that the very history that men proclaim as the theater of truth and the raison d'être of all their actions is no more a representation of the objective manifestation of God than their fashioning of the figure of Gebelawi. Thus, men languish under the tyranny of their own self-inflicted ignorance!

The most fully realized chapter in terms of the development of character, contextual reality, and clear motivation is the fourth, whose hero is Qasim. The story line faithfully follows Muhammad's life, relating how he was taken into his uncle's house, how he became a merchant and married a rich older woman, how he was visited by the angel Gabriel, how he had difficulty in gaining supporters, how he was opposed by the merchant-class rulers of his society; and how he left his native city to return triumphant at the head of a formidable force. Mahfouz emphasizes the fact that Qasim advocates force and leads the reader to believe that without it those who want to be successful reformers, religious or otherwise, can never succeed—at least not in their lifetime. We are forced to ask, Are arms needed to counteract arms? It appears that Mahfouz would have us believe so. Of course, this idea seems contradictory to what a prophet should stand for. On the other hand, only a strong man who is willing to use the ways of the world can make headway in a world dominated by raw power. Qasim is that man.

All well and good. But one wonders why Mahfouz spends so much time in this chapter on the brutal details of fighting and violence—especially since they serve no real purpose in illuminating the greater truths of the work. It remains a puzzle why, in a book that has a serious message to deliver, he describes at length acts of violence designed to appeal more to the imaginative adolescent than to the sober and intelligent reader.

At the opening of the chapter the world is, of course, once again in the hands of self-serving tyrants. Despite Gebelawi's promises, Adham's penance, Gebel's leadership, and Rifaa's exalted work, men's affairs are back to normal: Gebelawi is absent, tyrants hold sway, and the long-dead prophets are forgotten. The cycle continues. If Mahfouz believes in progress at all, it is understood only in terms of time passing, a kind of accretive chronology. Human society doesn't make much headway. Additionally, one may expect that as a Muslim, Mahfouz would somehow portray Qasim and his accomplishments in a much better light. Such is not the case.

In fact, a particularly interesting highlight of this chapter is that Qasim and his circle are portrayed as consistent users of the hashish pipe. When hashish (and alcohol) appear on the scene, people, as may be expected, begin to talk a bit fancifully about a new and better future. Is Mahfouz reminding us of what has often been pointed out as the social and political naïvete of the religious prophets, whose promises and claims in these areas are akin to the disappearing smoke of the hashish pipe and exist in the luminous air of imagination or in the drunken affirmation of illusion? We know that Mahfouz had socialist sympathies; Marx's aphorism, "Religion is the opiate of the masses," hangs too heavy in the air to be ignored—even though Mahfouz certainly does not agree with this in precisely the way Marx meant it.

These chapters devoted to Adham, Gebel, Rifaa, and Qasim are a mere prelude to the last chapter, where Mahfouz reveals at last where he has been going and why. Naturally, we find the world once more mired in misery. The *hara*, despite the strong vows and good intentions of Qasim and his followers, has once again succumbed to the natural order of things: forgetfulness has returned, and, hence, tyranny. There is much violence, misery, and hatred and little love in the *hara* when Arafa, the hero of this culminating chapter, makes his appearance. "Nothing seems to have changed. . . . The people have become as they were in the bad old days, without honor or dignity. They were eaten up with poverty, threatened by cudgels, pushed and punched. Filth and flies were everywhere, and the place swarmed with beggars, cripples, and swindlers. Gebel, Rifaa and Qasim were only names in songs sung by drugged storytellers in the cafes. Each faction was proud of its hero, of whom no trace remained" (448–49). Despite all this, there is still a severely weakened but nonetheless persistent hope that God and religion will deliver men from their wretched state. "It is not impossible," murmurs the inner voice of men, "that what happened yesterday will happen tomorrow and the dreams of the storytellers will come true again and the darkness will lift from our world" (448–49). It is this world that the magician, Arafa, hopes to change with his "magic." Boldly confident of his powers, he declares that if the people of the *hara* do not heed him, the darkness will never lift.

We first encounter the would-be illuminator, Arafa, returning after a long absence to his native quarter, the *hara* of Qasim. He is the illegitimate son of Jahsha, a fortune-teller whose identity is symbolically linked to the Western world. Arafa and his brother Hanash, a dwarf, are made to feel unwelcome in the *hara*. Enduring sarcasm, mockery, and insults, they finally find quarters in a cellar with a single barred window, symbolizing Mahfouz's conviction that Islamic society has little regard for science and its companion, technology. Placed under society's feet, they are separated from the people of the *hara* by the iron bars of neglect, ignorance, and cultural disdain. Arafa and his brother nevertheless humbly accept their lot.

This does not keep Arafa from lamenting, "Everything I do is for the people's good, but all my life I have only been abused." To this Hanash replies, "Success will repay you for all the harm that has been done to you—or to our poor mother" (455). The West is obviously the source of the most advanced understanding and applications of science. Although science has contributed to a vastly improved and more comfortable way of life, it has also been applied to the creation of destructive instruments of war as well as negative techniques of oppression. Science has not solved all the West's problems, but it has given the West social, economic, and political advantages seen nowhere else. Arafa will have a difficult task balancing these two disparate sides of science and working his magic on a stagnant society, unnecessarily suspicious of everything that seems to contradict its concept of "truth" and impregnated as it is by the misty thinking of religious millenarianism.

Betrayed by tyrants and condemned by superstition, the masses see nothing but the present. Mahfouz attacks this present-mindedness and believes that the last hope of mankind is to fashion a more lasting and better future without the use of violence—not a future based on the shaky foundations of justice laid by prophets, but a very desirable material prosperity brought into being by the clear light of science. It does not seem to be the cold, unfettered instrumentality of science that Mahfouz has in mind but rather a science that needs to be wed to human feeling, sentiment, and understanding. To accomplish this, Mahfouz introduces into Arafa's life a woman, Awatif ("human sentiment"), who attempts to soften Arafa, that is, mitigate the power of science. Science and technology need to be devoted to purely good human ends. It must, to paraphrase an old idea, have a human face. Considered thus, science has the power to change the world more than Gebel, Rifaa, and Qasim ever could. Initially carried away by his claims of knowledge, Arafa gloats, "I have wonderful things which give me a power ten times that of Gebel and Rifaa and Qasim put together" (471). But, after meeting Awatif, he gives up all thought of using his power to seek revenge on the tyrants of the alley. He believes, as all men of science must, that the light of truth must always triumph.

If in the practice of science, that is, magic, there is power, it must not only reveal the truth but emancipate men from the darkness of existence. Rebuffed by his fellow *hara* dwellers, who insist that this existence is "the will of God," Arafa adamantly responds, "Oh yes, your father talks about Qasim and Qasim talked about our ancestor; that is what we hear; but all we see is Qadri and Sa'd Allah and Ajjaj and Santouri and Yusuf [thugs]. We need power to deliver us from the torment; what use are our memories?" (468). The collective memories of men, corrupted by time, have failed to mitigate the sorry acquiescent state of men in the present.

Arafa sees himself as having a kind of messianic mission; he too preaches a new religion. He too wants to promise the imminent advent of the millenium. But his salvation is concerned more directly with worldly aims and material interest. The clarifying force he represents can define the structure of reality objectively in contrast to the half-forgotten dreams that imprison men. Arafa does not deny the existence of God, nor does he attempt to arrogate what is properly God's business for his own. He concedes that "God is all-powerful" but also insists, "It is the same with magic; it is all powerful" (483).

Arafa's appearance, mission, and significance can be interpreted on two levels. First, there is a general delineation of the history of science; in its nascent stage, men believed—as Arafa believed—it was capable of accomplishing everything. But its original purpose was soon channeled into uses that did not always serve the best interests of society. Arafa's "magic" is indeed usurped by the powerful to be used against the weak.

On the second level, Mahfouz traces the episodic career of science in his own society. Arafa has returned as the bastardized offspring of the West and when the magician appears in the *hara*, he is jeered at because of his illegitimacy. He is neither understood nor trusted. In turn, Arafa curses the ignorance, the cultural and religious parochialism that have led the people to a destructive contempt for a "magic" that is identified with the West. "They appreciate a mere trifle like the present [a box containing an aphrodisiac potion that Arafa gave to the thug, Ajjaj]," Arafa grumbles, "but that present is not everything . . . the fools do not realize the true value of Arafa.

Perhaps they will someday, and then will have to ask God's mercy on my mother and not insult her as they do now" (461).

In the West, however, there has been less of a problem reconciling faith and science. It has long been understood that science deals strictly with matter, with the diverse physical phenomena of material being. God transcends the material world and has little to do with the proofs or disproofs of his existence by science. Science does, however, serve to exorcise unworthy attitudes and superstitious beliefs from men's minds. It has never been—nor could it ever be—the intent of science to "kill" God.

To be sure, Arafa believes that he has inherited the mantle of and must follow in the difficult footsteps of Gebel, Rifaa, and Qasim. Reflecting on the contempt of the people of the *hara*, he is determined to forge ahead: "I am not the first man to choose hardship. Gebel could have stayed in his job with the trustee; Rifaa could have become the *hara's* chief carpenter; Qasim could have been content with his wife and her property. . . . But they chose other paths" (487). Because of this determination, Arafa believes he cannot "escape" investigating the "big house" and its occupant, the long-absent and silent Gebelawi. Arafa sets off on a quest to see, hear, and identify Gebelawi. He wants to clarify men's ideas about God once and for all. He wants to cast light on the shadowy, insubstantial wraith that exists in men's minds. Arafa covertly enters the house of Gebelawi, whose shadowy presence has for centuries darkened the life of the *hara*. After tunneling under the mansion wall and making his way through the untended garden, he enters the ancient house and stealthily moves through darkened rooms in quest of Gebelawi and the book that contains the secrets of the universe. He has no success and manages only to blunder into a frail old servant—a Nubian as dark as the rooms of the house—whom in a panic he unintentionally kills. Accomplishing nothing but the unfortunate death of the servant, he makes his escape. Not long after, the *hara* is abuzz with the news that Gebelawi is dead—dead from shock and grief upon discovering the lifeless body of his faithful slave.

Why is the servant killed directly and Gebelawi "killed" indirectly? Perhaps the answer can be found in the idea that science is no threat to the real Gebelawi. It is, however, a threat to the traditional protectors, holders, and representatives of his "estate." Thus, science does not kill God but rather kills the idea of God in men's minds, perverted by their earthly focus and maintained by his so-called representatives on earth. God remains inviolable. He has not been killed by Arafa directly, nor could he have ever been. The crude, anthropomorphic Gebelawi is an image fashioned out of men's ignorance. He is a God made in man's image. In the true Islamic sense, God does not exist in human form on earth; further-more, God's concern and men's religious duty are not to be identi-fied solely with the division of some earthly estate. Religion places God in the transcendent realm of the spirit, where he belongs.

Chastened by the belief that he has indeed killed Gebelawi, Arafa assumes a new sense of responsibility. He must now give the *hara* something to fill the void created by Gebelawi's death, which he points out to his companion can serve another purpose. "His death is more powerful than his words; it makes it necessary for the good son to do everything, to take his place, to be him" (503).

There is, however, a note of caution sounded. Because of the ways of the world and the baseness of men, science can be and has been made to go astray. Unreconciled with the better human impulses and higher concerns, it can become dangerous as well as arrogant. In an impulsive moment, Arafa unrestrainedly exclaims, "I have something no one else has, not even Gebelawi: I have magic, which can bring about things that Gebel, Rifaa, and Qasim together could never have achieved. . . . Magic will become the music that Adham dreamed of" (498).

Science holds mixed blessings. If on the one hand it offers the cornucopia, on the other lurk the dangers of Pandora's box. Science without a sense of responsibility, unguided by conscience, can be as great a danger as any dictator. In fact, modern governments have always been quick to utilize the destructive potential inherent in science while often underplaying its advantages. The same prob-lems can attend its intended dissemination as those which plagued and eventually corrupted the work of the religious prophets.

A responsible science recognizes its duty. If it destroys the an-thropomorphic God who burdens the superstition-sotted minds of men, then it must show it can replace this corrupt creation with something purer and more enduring. Science, consequently, does not replace religion but illuminates the darkness that has always surrounded the *hara*. Where there is willingness to seek the truth, no matter what the consequences, there is freedom. And where truth and freedom are, there is at last justice. Science is thus conceived as an instrument not only of empirical truth but freedom of thought and expression. These latter are the foes of intellectual stagnation, religious fanaticism, and one-dimensional party-line thinking.

The hashish addiction of one of the guardians of party-line thinking, the alley boss Sa'd Allah (whom Arafa summarily kills), reminds the reader once again of the sense of unreality and corruption that exists where the "founder's" so-called representatives are to be found. Moreover, there is a harsh sense of irony attached to this practice because "Gebelawi was killed in his house while round about it the mighty chiefs were taking hashish" (502). Fantasy and falsehood are as real a threat to belief as the people of the *hara* believe science to be. Science has no quarrel with Gebelawi; its real enemy is irrational thought and behavior.

Later, summoning Arafa before him, the "trustee" shocks him by telling him that he has learned from his spies that Arafa has killed both the old servant of Gebelawi and his underboss, Sa'd Allah. But he has something much more important to discuss. He wants the magic bottles, that is, the modern weapons he knows Arafa possesses. Indeed, the crafty hypocrite goes so far as to tell the hitherto despised Arafa, "You needn't bother to work for pennies; you'll have your time free to work magic for my defense, and you'll have everything you desire" (513). History seems to be on the verge of repeating itself. It is not such an easy task to change the world as Arafa had first thought. It is not the benefits that follow upon the pursuit of truth that will win out, he begins to understand, but rather the dark side of science, the side that aids and abets the powerful and the power hungry. Mahfouz is under no delusions. The gathering of destructive weaponry into the hands of those who govern has led to the age of the modern dictator.

The agonizing reality of Arafa's position becomes glaringly clear to him: "Qasim could win a strong following by a single kind word, but it will take me years and years to train one man in my work and make him into my follower" (516). It takes time for something as different and difficult as rationalism and science to become a commonplace and integral part of life. The liberating qualities of science are much more difficult to develop than the simple beliefs that are rooted in prophetic promises. The irony is that men are more willing to believe, even to sacrifice their lives for, a doubtful doctrine than a verifiable methodology and concrete ends.

Thanks to Arafa's magic bottles, the trustee soon disposes of his enemies and cows the people into submission. He then magnanimously announces: "Happiness and peace have been granted to you, by grace of his honor . . . long may he live! From today there are no chiefs to humiliate you and steal your money" (520). And the people, sheepish and gullible as ever, fill the blood-stained air of the *hara* with cheers for their "redeemer."

From this time forward, Arafa and his family are watched closely. Of course, the dictator is not worried about Arafa but about the power he possesses. The modern world has often seen science "imprisoned" by powerful leaders who use its destructive power without hesitation while dispensing its potential benefits in niggardly fashion. Arafa catches the irony of the situation when in anguish he cries, "You wretch, you made me your prisoner! I wanted to use magic to destroy you, not to serve you. Now those I love and wish to free hate me." The devil's pact has been made. "Don't be afraid; your life is in no danger from me," replies the tyrant. "As you know, if one of us betrays the other he betrays himself" (524). The people, as ignorant as ever about Arafa's magic, now hate him, and the estrangement between science and the *hara* deepens.

Not surprisingly, Arafa and the tyrant now puff on the hashish pipe regularly. Consequently, the magician becomes more and more inclined to indulge the dictator's fantasies, vis-à-vis science. At times even he babbles in the same phantasmagorical gibberish as the hashish addicts do.

This indulgent behavior leads to another estrangement. The happy union with Awatif is soon destroyed. Corrupted by hashish and compromised by the trustee, the confused and guilt-ridden

Arafa is unfaithful to Awatif, and she abandons him. Science becomes estranged from human feeling in serving the narrow political
interests of the few. Justice, freedom, love, and peace can be established on a sustained basis only by men of human understanding
and religious goodwill. Science and technology divorced from faith
and humanism can serve no good ends.

There is in all this travail a positive note. An old woman claiming
to be Gebelawi's servant delivers a message from Gebelawi: "Tell
[Arafa] that his grandfather died pleased with him" (538). Incredu-
lous, he insists that it is impossible for someone he killed to be
pleased with him. With equal incredulity she replies, "No one killed
Gebelawi. No one could have killed him" (538). The point is once
again affirmed: the true God, the transcendent God, can never be
killed. The paradox is that men need no help from science; they
killed God long ago with their misty, earthbound ideas, enveloping
an already flawed anthropomorphic figure of Gebelawi.

The chapter abruptly ends with the deaths of Arafa and his wife
at the hands of the trustee. The "killer" of Sa'd Allah and Gebelawi
is now himself killed. As is to be expected, the people of the *hara*, the
"children" of Gebelawi "take pleasure" in the news of the magician's death. They do not understand that the source of the tyrant's
weapon may also be the spring of their salvation.

As time goes on, however, true to the fickle nature of man as well
as the tricky nature of history, the people have a change of heart.
"The rumor spread from one hashish den to another that Hanash,
who had escaped death, would finish what Arafa had begun and
would take a terrible revenge on the trustee" (551). Thus it is
implanted in the ever-hopeful minds of the people of the *hara* that as
long as Hanash lives and has possession of Arafa's magic book,
there is something to look forward to. Hanash, the disciple, will
save them. Arafa's martyrdom has engendered the mystical belief
that what was once contemptible can now be the means of their
salvation. "They longed to help Hanash in his stand against the
trustee, to make his victory their own and secure a life of justice and
peace" (551).

This whole work reflects a very pessimistic view regarding the
ability of any society to maintain justice for long. It is clear, how-

ever, that Mahfouz does not believe religious figures have been totally ineffective: Gebel establishes peace and retributive justice for the Jews; Rifaa goes beyond Gebel and teaches forgiveness; Qasim is presented as a true "internationalist," bridging the narrow concerns and limited impact of both Gebel and Rifaa. Nevertheless, nothing can stop their memory from being perverted by ensuing generations. The people of the *hara*, who are supposed to inherit the "estate" of Gebelawi, remain powerless and miserable. Mahfouz's philosophy of history is not so much a negative view of man but, rather, a conclusion afforded by the unavoidable facts.

Obviously, Mahfouz views science as the last great hope of mankind, but he leaves us in doubt as to whether it can overcome human tyranny. He understands that it can be used as an instrument for either good or evil, and that it brings no relief to man unless man himself changes. Therefore, one cannot really say that Mahfouz yearns for the death of God or believes that religion is a hindrance. Rather, religion, if freed from fanaticism, parochialism, superstition, and tyrants, can lead men's rulers to use this benign instrument for the good of all. Certainly we can understand that science and its handmaiden technology can be used as instruments of power and suppression or as vehicles for enlightenment and freedom. Mahfouz, too, understands this yet remains both ambivalent toward and naive about science—as naïve, in fact, as those who believe in the social fixes of the past.

Finally, there seems to be an intimate connection between the Spanish-Arab philosopher Ibn Rushd (Averroes, 1126–98) and Arafa. Averroes was a devotee of the "scientific sage" of the ages, Aristotle, on whose works he wrote copious and intelligent commentaries. He came to the conclusion that there was no personal immortality and affirmed the eternity of the world. This, of course, was antithetical to accepted Islamic orthodoxy. Averroes thus presented an argument to defend himself from Muslim conservatives.

There are and must be, he said, two kinds of truth: philosophical and theological. The former, though not in strict accordance with the Quran, is nevertheless not incompatible with an allegorical interpretation of it. Theological truth, on the other hand, has demands that can be satisfied only by "probabilities." It is grasped by simple religious faith and satisfied with imaginative pictures and symbols. An example of this may be the Quranic assertion that the universe had a beginning (*muhdath*), that is, it was created in time by God. In this way minds confined within the limits of religious symbology and theological assertiveness are able to represent or "image" the religious "truths." This double-truth mechanism used by Averroes seeks to justify "heretical doctrines" on the grounds that they are the conclusions at which reason must necessarily arrive and that in fact all thinking men would accept were it not for the other "truth," the Islamic verities revealed in the Quran.

William of Occam (d. 1349), a renowned medieval scholastic philosopher, also recognized the efficacy of the "double truthfulness" of things and advanced the idea a step further. When presented with two hypotheses, both of which account for a given fact, he advised, give preference to the simpler. These men, Averroes and Occam, as well as other thinkers of like mind in the West, are important because they helped to secularize reason by freeing it from the superstitions of a religious establishment bent on maintaining dogma. The acceptance of this coexistent relationship freed men to pursue a philosophy that would justify the double-truth idea of Averroes and ultimately establish the foundations of modern science.

Because of theological squabbles in northern Europe, the works of Averroes and Occam did not find fruition there for another century and a half. But in Padua, Italy, there developed empirically oriented schools that were vigorous and enterprising. The Averroist philosophical tradition of Padua allowed for empirical action and investigation without the undue restraints of religion. The foundations of the modern world are to be found in this atmosphere of scientific inquiry that, beginning in Italy, eventually spread to all of Europe; and in this atmosphere the outright suppression of truth by theological dogmas that insisted on identification with and interpretation of the natural world was tolerated less and less.

Speaking through the character of Arafa, Mahfouz no doubt sees this double truth as the means for creating an opportunity for independent investigation within the bounds of orthodoxy—something that could never occur until the authority of Islamic conservative thinkers was shattered. Therefore, perhaps the best way to approach Arafa and describe his purpose is in Averroist and Occamist terms. Certainly Mahfouz's philosophical background would seem to indicate this. Consequently, as far as the sciences go, one's attitude and approach have to be secular. Only in this way can the human race get on without divine assistance in the way of special illuminations, by way of the prophets. Moreover, this point of view follows from Arafa's determination to separate the two spheres of reason and revelation. If they are separate, reason will reach its own kind of truth in its own kind of way. This, in turn, leads to the idea of the acquisition of scientific truth through the scientific method.

Arafa's insistence on a knowledge that is truthful and complete was disruptive of the Islamic position insofar as it encouraged men to explore the finite world and to track down the truths it contains. The "dangers" to the conservatives lies in the fact that this "razor" (to use Occam's term) is capable of destroying the theological and metaphysical basis of the Islamic approach to reality. Not the least of the problems encountered by Arafa is that science, guided by reason, gives a much simpler account of what occurred in the phenomenal world than can be derived from the historically accepted and tenaciously held hidden purposes, occult forces, and divine motivation that dominate the world, that is, the *hara*. "Do not multiply being unnecessarily," advises Occam.

Averroes, like Arafa, was concerned with reconciling his philosophical ideas with orthodox Islamic theology. Accordingly, the double truth theory did not imply that there is a true and a false theory, but rather that one and the same truth can be understood clearly in philosophy and allegorically in theology. The rightness of the allegorical approach of the Quran and, by direct attribution, the approach Mahfouz takes in *Awlad Haratina* is that it expresses the truth in a manner intelligible to the ill-educated masses. On the other hand, philosophy strips away the exterior "packaging" and comes to grips with truth unhampered by the historical and religious clutter of men's minds. Thus, theology becomes, in a sense, subordinate to philosophy. This leads to the viewpoint that Mahfouz obviously holds, that the rational philosopher decides what religious doctrines need allegorization, and determines the format of *Awlad Haratina*.

In the West, after initial resistance, the Averroist/double-truth approach came to be preferred. Sir Francis Bacon's *Novum organum*, which was rooted in Averroist/Occamist "heresy," strongly advocated a position that was soon adopted everywhere: the wedding of science and rational thought was useful. This understanding soon resulted in scientific improvements and new inventions. The flowering of the scientific establishment depends on the separation of reason from theology, revelation from empiricism. This was not the case when Mahfouz wrote *Awlad Haratina*; it is not the case today in most of the Middle East.

It is easy to see why the acceptance of this double-truth theory incited the wrath of Islamic theologians. They interpreted Averroism as suggesting that theological doctrine was nonsense. And indeed, it is nonsense to Arafa when it stands in the way of any approach to the truth of the real world other than that of religious sentiment. Perhaps this was Averroes's position. If we follow the logic of the double truth, if A is true in the theology of the conservatives, then A is true in the camp of the enemies of science, that is, it is *false*. Averroes, Arafa, and by direct implication Mahfouz had no use for traditionalists who rejected the reasoned demonstrations of philosophical inquiry. The uproar surrounding the ideas of Averroes led to the direct prohibition of philosophy and the burning of philosophical works. Mahfouz has fared no better in the twentieth century. His *Awlad Haratina* has continued to be attacked in most of the Islamic world.

Mahfouz, then, is not in the mainstream of Muslim thought and religion. It is difficult to understand how he could be, given the extent of his exposure to Western ideas and ideals. He himself has acknowledged in several interviews that the two formative ideas of his life were science and socialism. This is not the only work in which he emphasized their potential benefits to a society that is openly receptive to the methodology and discoveries of science as well as the theories of socialism. In his chief work, *Thulathiyya*, Mahfouz often has his characters muse about the necessity of deepening the effects of science on their society. In fact, they almost believe in the idea of science as a redeemer. Mahfouz has more than once admitted that there is a great deal of him in Kamal, and that Kamal's nephew Ahmad is greatly influenced by Adli Karim, who is modeled after Salama Musa, the advocate of science and socialism. In *Khan al-Khalili,* the astute and sophisticated attorney Ahmad Rashid is also portrayed as being an ardent devotee of socialism and science.

It is hard to avoid concluding that Mahfouz not only sees science as necessary for human progress but believes it will help reveal the true transcendent God, who is much more than Gebelawi, a god fashioned out of men's minds, a tyrant whose motives are mysterious, and whose intermittent and seemingly arbitrary intervention leaves men to struggle alone most of the time. Thus, the fashioning of God in the image of man and the superstitions, myths, false hopes, and fantasies that arise from belief in this earthbound "God" have no place in the vision of Mahfouz. Words and rituals without the transcendent God, and without peace and justice residing in the hearts and souls of those who say the words and perform the rituals, are meaningless.

Notes

1. The Formative Years

1. See the interview of Mahfouz by Abd al-Tawwab Abd al-Hayy, "Asir Hayati," 126–34; Jamal al-Ghitani, *Naguib Mahfouz Yatadhakkar*, 9 and 14–15; Ghali Shukri, *al-Muntami: Dirasa fi Adab Naguib Mahfouz*, 26–27; Sabri Hafiz, "Naguib Mahfouz: Masadir wa Mukawwinat Tajribatih al-Ibda'iyya," in the anthology *Naguib Mahfouz: Atahaddath Ilaykum*, 78–82, first published in *al-Adab*, 1973, 34–44; Abd al-Muhsin Badr, *Naguib Mahfouz al-Ru'ya wa al-Adat*, 82–83; Mahmud Fawzi, *Naguib Mahfouz: Za'im al-Harafish*, 9; Sami Khashaba, "Naguib Mahfouz wa Iskaliyyat al-Hadatha," 99. On how Mahfouz received his name, see the postscript by Said Jawdat al-Sahhar appended to Naguib Mahfouz's novel *al-Baqi min al-Zaman Sa'a*, 1, n. 1.

2. Fuad Dawwara, "Al-Wujdan al-Qawmi fi Adab Naguib Mahfouz," 102; Muhammad Sabri al-Sayyid, "Naguib Mahfouz," 93; Sasson Somekh, *The Changing Rhythm: A Study of Naguib Mahfouz's Novels*, 42; "Naguib Mahfouz wa Harat Mikhail Jad aw Ilaqat Naguib bi Salama Musa," *al-Jumhuriyya* (December 1, 1960); and al-Ghitani, *Naguib Mahfouz Yatadhakkar*, 39.

3. Adham Rajab, "Safahat Majhula min Hayat Naguib Mahfouz," 92–99.

4. Ibid., 89–99; "Shullat al-Harafish," *al-Sharq*, 18: 103–106; Muhammad Afifi, "Naguib Mahfouz Rajul al-Sa'a," 1970, 137–41; and al-Ghitani, *Naguib Mahfouz Yatadhakkar*, 88.

5. Dawwara, "Rihlat al-Khamsin ma al-Qira'a wa al-Kitaba," 12, reprinted in his book *Ashrat Udaba Yatahaddathun*, 265–92.

6. Ibid., 13.

7. Ghali Shukri, *Naguib Mahfouz min al-Jamaliyya ila Nobel*, 12.

8. Dawwara,"Rihlat al-Khamsin," 7; Sasson Somekh, *The Changing Rhythm*, 44; Hafiz, *Naguib Mahfouz*, 93.

9. Dawwara, "Rihlat al-Khamsin," 7–11; al-Ghitani, *Naguib Mahfouz Yatadhakkar*, 41–42.

10. Hafiz, "Naguib Mahfouz," 93.

11. Ibid., 93–96.

12. Ibid.; Mahmud Kushayk, "Hiwar ma Amid al-Riwaya al-Arabiyya Naguib Mahfouz," 140.

13. Shusha, "Ma al-Udaba: Naguib Mahfouz," *al-Adab* (June 1960): 18–21, reprinted in *Naguib Mahfouz: Atahaddath Ilaykum*, 51–52; Muhammad Hasan Abd Allah, *al-Waqi'iyya fi al-Riwaya al-Arabiyya*, 465.

14. Abd Allah, *al-Waqi'iyya fi al-Riwaya al-Arabiyya*, 542; Shukri, *Naguib Mahfouz min al-Jamaliyya ila Nobel*, 40–41; and al-Ghitani, *Naguib Mahfouz Yatadhakkar*, 70.

15. See Mahfouz's vignette "Hanan Mustafa" in *Naguib Mahfouz, al-Maraya*, 77–83.

16. Most of his articles appeared in periodicals like *al-Majalla al-Jadida* (owned by Salama Musa), *al-Thaqafa, al-Ma'rifa, al-Jihad* and *Kawkab al-Sharq*. See Anis Mansur, in *Naguib Mahfouz: Atahaddath Ilaykum*, 14–15; and Hafiz, "Naguib Mahfouz bayn al-Din wa al-Falsafa," 116–27. For his rewriting of short fiction, see al-Ghitani, *Naguib Mahfouz Yatadhakkar*, 25–26.

17. Rajab, "Safahat Majhula min Hayat Naguib Mahfouz," 96–97; and al-Ghitani, *Naguib Mahfouz Yatadhakkar*, 94.

18. *Naguib Mahfouz: Nobel 1988, A Memorial Book*, 185; and Hafiz, "Naguib Mahfouz bayn al-Din wa al-Falsafa," 121.

19. Ahmad Muhammad Atiyya, "Katib wa Mawqif," in *Naguib Mahfouz: Atahaddath Ilaykum*, 31; and Badr, *Naguib Mahfouz*, 35–36.

20. Atiyya, "Katib wa," in *Ma Naguib Mahfouz*, 31; Dawwara, "Al-Wujdan al-Qawmi fi Adab Naguib Mahfouz," 104; Hafiz, "Naguib Mahfouz," in *Naguib Mahfouz: Atahaddath Ilaykum*, 87–88; and Mahfouz's interview with Ahmad Said Muhammadiyya in *Naguib Mahfouz: Atahaddath Ilaykum*, 199–200. For a list of the early short stories of Mahfouz, see al-Nassaj, *Dalil al-Qissa al-Misriyya*; Badr, *Naguib Mahfouz*, 494–98, gives the titles of short stories Mahfouz wrote between 1932 and 1946, according to their dates of publication. For a general study of Mahfouz's short stories see Evelyn Farid Yarid, *Naguib Mahfouz wa al-Qissa al-Qasira*.

21. Rajab, "Safahat Majhula min Hayat Naguib Mahfouz," 94.

22. Mahfouz, "Ihtidar Mu'taqadat wa Tawallud Mu'taqadat," 1468–70; Shukri, *al-Muntami*, 46; Badr, *Naguib Mahfouz*, 43–44.

23. See *al-Ayyam*, November 30, 1943, 8; and Badr, *Naguib Mahfouz*, 58.

24. Raja al-Naqqash, "Bayn al-Wafdiyya wa al-Markisiyya," 40–41, and "Al-Wajh al-Alami li Naguib Mahfouz," in *Naguib Mahfouz: Nobel 1988, A Memorial Book*, 87.

25. Dawwara, "Rihlat al-Khamsin ma al-Qira'a wa al-Kitaba," 12; cf. Somekh, *The Changing Rhythm*, 41.

26. For these articles see *al-Ayyam*, November 30, 1943; December 7, 1943; and January 4, 1944.

27. Badr, *Naguib Mahfouz*, 57.

28. See the list of Mahfouz's articles on Bergson ibid., 47–49 and 492–93; Abd al-Rahman Yaghi, *al-Juhud al-Riwa'iyya min Salim al-Bustani ila Naguib Mahfouz*, 93–95.

29. See Mahfouz, "Ma'na al-Falsafa," *al-Jihad*, August 21, 1934; and Badr, *Naguib Mahfouz*, 52.

30. Mahfouz, "Falsafat al-Hubb," 79–82; Hafiz, "Naguib Mahfouz bayn al-Din wa al-Falsafa," 119; and Badr, *Naguib Mahfouz*, 55–56.

31. Mahfouz, "Allah," 43–46; and "Fikrat Allah fi al-Falsafa," 33–40; Hafiz, "Naguib Mahfouz bayn al-Din wa al-Falsafa," 118–19; Badr, *Naguib Mahfouz*, 52–55.

32. Mahfouz, *Qasr al-Shawq*, 372–75. Cf. Hafiz, "Naguib Mahfouz bayn al-Din wa al-Falsafa," 124–25; and Abd Allah, *al-Islamiyya wa al-Ruhiyya fi Adab Naguib Mahfouz*, 189–210.

33. Shukri, *al-Muntami*, 8; *Mudhakkirat Thaqafa Tahtadir*, 261–62; "Al-Hiyad al-Fanni Tariqan li al-Inhiyaz al-Fikri," in *Naguib Mahfouz: Atahaddath Ilaykum*, 62–63; Atiyya, *Ma Naguib Mahfouz*, 33–34; Latifa al-Zayyat, "al-Shakl al-Riwa'i ind Naguib Mahfouz," 73; and al-Ghitani, *Naguib Mahfouz Yatadhakkar*, 68.

34. Atiyya, *Ma Naguib Mahfouz*, 24; and al-Ghitani, *Naguib Mahfouz Yatadhakkar*, 68.

35. See Mahfouz's responses to the Kuwayti newspaper *al-Qabas* in *Rose El-Youssef*, no. 2486 (February 2, 1976): 87; and "Hiwar ma Naguib Mahfouz," *Afaq Arabiyya*, no. 6 (February, 1976): 101; Badr, 74; and al-Shatti, "Naguib Mahfouz: Rihlat al-Hara min al-Mu'anat ila al-Masarrat," 65. Originally, Mahfouz made this statement to Muhammad Hasan Abd Allah in *al-Bayan* (March 1973).

36. Hafiz, "Naguib Mahfouz," in *Naguib Mahfouz: Atahaddath Ilaykum*, 98–99.

37. Dawwara, "Rihlat al-Khamsin," 9–10, and Kamal al-Najmi, "Ma al-Ghina wa al Mughannin fi Adab Naguib Mahfouz," 130.

38. See the interview of Mahfouz and his wife in the magazine *al-Musawwar*, reproduced in the literary quarterly *al-Sharq*, no. 4 (1988): 94, 117; *al-Ayyam*, (December 21, 1943): 7; Badr, *Naguib Mahfouz*, 60, 84; and al-Ghitani, *Naguib Mahfouz Yatadhakkar*, 97.

39. See Mahfouz, "Al-Ruju ila Methuselah," 592–95; and Badr, *Naguib Mahfouz*, 63.

40. Shukri, *Mudhakkirat Thaqafa Tahtadir*, 259.

41. Mahfouz, "Thalatha min Udaba'ina," 65–66; and Badr, *Naguib Mahfouz*, 65.

42. Al-Aqqad, *Fi Bayti*, 27–28.

43. Ibid., 28.

44. Ibid., 30–31.

45. Mahfouz, "al-Qissa ind al-Aqqad," 952–54. Cf. Badr, *Naguib Mahfouz*, 65–67.

46. Matti Moosa, *The Origins of Modern Arabic Fiction*, 179.

47. Dawwara, "Rihlat al-Khamsin," 12.

2. The Historical Novels

1. Fuad Dawwara, "Rihlat al-Khamsin," 13–17, and "al-Wujdan al-Qawmi fi Adab Naguib Mahfouz," 102–103; Abd al-Muhsin Badr, *Naguib Mahfouz*, 90–91, 151; Ghali Shukri, *Naguib Mahfouz min al-Jamaliyya ila Nobel*, 10, 98; Sasson Somekh, *The Changing Rhythm*, 60–64; Muhammad Amin al-Alim, *Ta'ammulat fi Alam Naguib Mahfouz*, 26–32; in an interview by Mamun Gharib in *al-Bayan* (January 1989), 193, Mahfouz admits that he read only one story by Scott and was not influenced by him.

2. Ahmad Haykal, *al-Adab al-Qisasi wa al-Masrahi fi Misr*, 256.

3. For a full analysis of Salim al-Bustani's novels, see Matti Moosa, *The Origins of Modern Arabic Fiction*, 122–46.

4. For a detailed discussion of Jurji Zaydan and his novels, see ibid., 157–69.

5. Ibid., 158–59.

6. Mahmud Hamid Shawkat, *al-Fann al-Qisasi fi al-Adab al-Misri al-Hadith 1800–1956*, 143.

7. For further analysis see Ibid., 180–86.

8. Al-Alim, *Ta'ammulat fi Alam Naguib Mahfouz*, 27; Taha Wadi, *Madkhal*

ila Tarikh al-Riwaya, 87; Badr, *Naguib Mahfouz,* 151–52; and Sulayman al-Shatti, *Al-Ramz wa al-Ramziyya fi Adab Naguib Mahfouz,* 35–40.

9. Naguib Mahfouz, *Abath al-Aqdar,* 1966. See Somekh, *The Changing Rhythm,* 200–201; Muhammad Hasan Abd Allah, *Al-Islamiyya wa al-Ruhiyya fi Adab Naguib Mahfouz,* 31–34; Badr, *Naguib Mahfouz,* 156–63; and Matityahu Peled, *Religion, My Own: The Literary Works of Najib Mahfuz,* 29–36.

10. Baikie, *Ancient Egypt* (1912), trans. by Naguib Mahfouz as *Misr al-Qadima* (1932), 5–8, 32–33; Mahfouz, *Abath al-Aqdar,* 5–25; Fatima Musa, *Fi al-Riwaya al-Arabiyya,* 35.

11. James Henry Breasted, *A History of Egypt from the Earliest Times to the Persian Conquest,* 122–23; see also Baikie, *Ancient Egypt,* 36–37; Badr, *Naguib Mahfouz,* 154.

12. Mahfouz, *Abath al-Aqdar,* 23; Badr, *Naguib Mahfouz,* 157–58.

13. Mahfouz, *Abath al-Aqdar,* 255.

14. Abd Allah, *Al-Islamiyya wa al-Ruhiyya fi Adab Naguib Mahfouz,* 31–38.

15. Farouk Shusha, "Ma al-Udaba: Naguib Mahfouz," 19–20.

16. Mahfouz, *Abath al-Aqdar,* 5–24. See this tale in Wallace Everett Caldwell and Mary Francis Gyles, *The Ancient World,* 75.

17. Badr, *Naguib Mahfouz,* 184.

18. James Henry Breasted, *A History of Egypt from the Earliest Times to the Persian Conquest,* chap. 5, describes the official and private life of the Pharaoh, especially Khufu, and shows particular interest in the development of the hieroglyphic script, the rise of a class of educated scribes, and the establishment of a library that housed numerous papyrus documents on every discipline of learning known at that time.

19. Mahfouz, *Abath al-Aqdar,* 10.

20. Breasted, *A History of Egypt,* 74.

21. Mahfouz, *Abath al-Aqdar,* 112–13.

22. Ibid., 61–62.

23. Ibid., 74, 78.

24. Ibid., 151; Breasted, *A History of Egypt,* 97–98, 222–34. For other inaccuracies, see Somekh, *The Changing Rhythm,* 61, n. 3.

25. Dawwara, "Rihlat al-Khamsin," 22.

26. Mahfouz, *Radobis.* For a detailed analysis, see Badr, *Naguib Mahfouz,* 189–229, and Peled, *Religion, My Own,* 41–50.

27. Badr, *Naguib Mahfouz,* 190.

28. Breasted, *A History of Egypt,* 143, 598; Barbara Mertz, *Temples, Tombs and Hieroglyphics* (reprint, Peter Berdick Books, 1990), 112.

29. Mahfouz, *Radobis*, 84–85.

30. Ibid., 74, 77; Badr, *Naguib Mahfouz*, 215–16.

31. Mahfouz, *Radobis*, 122.

32. Ibid., 20–21. Cf. Shawkat, *al-Fann al-Qiasi, fi al-Adab al-Misri al-Hadith*, 201; and Abd Allah, *al-Islamiyya wa al-Ruhiyya fi Adab Naguib Mahfouz*, 50–53.

33. Sabri Hafiz, "Naguib Mahfouz," in *Naguib Mahfouz: Atahaddath Il-aykum*, 90–91.

34. Hamdi Sakkut, *The Egyptian Novel and Its Main Trends, 1913 to 1952*, 72–73; Somekh, 62; Dawwara, "al-Wujdan al-Qawmi fi Adab Naguib Mahfouz," 103; al-Alim, *Ta'ammulat fi Alam Naguib Mahfouz*, 27; Ahmad Muhammad Atiyya, *Ma Naguib Mahfouz*, 125, 158; Fatima Musa, *Fi al-Riwaya al-Arabiyya*, 37; Wadi, 88; Badr, *Naguib Mahfouz*, 189–90; and Abd Allah, *al-Waqi'iyya fi al-Riwaya al-Arabiyya*, 200.

35. Badr, *Naguib Mahfouz*, 189–90.

36. Musa, *Fi al-Riwaya al-Arabiyya*, 39.

37. Mahfouz, *Kifah Tiba*. See also Peled, *Religion, My Own*, 57–66.

38. Hafiz, "Naguib Mahfouz," in *Naguib Mahfouz: Atahaddath Ilaykum*, 86–87.

39. Ibid., 88–89; Sakkut, 73–74.

40. Mahfouz, *Kifah Tiba*, 82.

41. Ibid., 76.

42. Ibid., 157, 171.

43. Moosa, *The Origins of Modern Arabic Fiction*, 54–56.

44. Badr, *Naguib Mahfouz*, 257, 276.

45. Mahfouz, *Kifah Tiba*, 32.

46. Hafiz, "Naguib Mahfouz," in *Naguib Mahfouz: Atahaddath Ilaykum*, 86–87.

47. Mahfouz, *Kifah Tiba*, 156–157, 162–171; Badr, *Naguib Mahfouz*, 252, 258, 268–269.

48. Mahfouz, *Kifah Tiba*, 15–16, 194; Badr, *Naguib Mahfouz*, 260–61; Abd Allah, *Al-Waqi'iyya fi al-Riwaya al-Arabiyya*, 57–59.

49. See Mahfouz's address to the Nobel Prize Committee in no. 59 (January 1989): 10–14; and Milton Viorst, "Man of Gamaliya," 33.

3. The Contemporary Novels

1. Sabri Hafiz, "Naguib Mahfouz," in *Naguib Mahfouz: Atahaddath Il-aykum*, 92.

2. Naguib Mahfouz, *al-Qahira al-Jadida*, 5–10; Ali B. Jad, *Form and Tech-*

nique in the Egyptian Novel, 1912–1971, 151–52, 171, 174; Hamdi Sakkut, *The Egyptian Novel,* 115–19.

3. Abd al-Muhsin Badr, *Naguib Mahfouz: al-Ru'ya wa al-adat,* 291.

4. Mahfouz, *Al-Qahira al-Jadida,* 24, 29; Hilary Kilpatrick, *The Modern Egyptian Novel: A Study in Social Criticism,* 73–75, 213–14.

5. Mahfouz, *al-Qahira al-Jadida,* 216. Cf. Muhommad Hasan Abd Allah, *al-Islamiyya wa al-Ruhiyya fi Adab Naguib Mahfouz,* 146, 149; and Badr, *Naguib Mahfouz,* 312–13.

6. Mahfouz, *al-Qahira al-Jadida,* 45–46; Shukri, *al-Muntami Dirasa fi Adab Naguib Mahfouz,* 200, 207.

7. Mahfouz, *al-Qahira al-Jadida,* 217; Ahmad Muhammad Atiyya, *Ma Naguib Mahfouz,* 146–47.

8. Badr, *Naguib Mahfouz,* 279, 285.

9. Ibid., 283–284.

10. Fatima Musa, *Fi al Riwaya al-Arabiyya,* 50.

11. Atiyya, *Ma Naguib Mahfouz,* 153.

12. Mahfouz, *Khan al-Khalili,* 10–11; Sayyid Qutb, *Kutub wa Shakhsiyyat,* 159, 165; Jad, *Form and Technique,* 151, 164, 172.

13. Al-Ghitani, *Naguib Mahfouz Yatadhakkar,* 64–65; Kilpatrick, *The Modern Egyptian Novel,* 76, 78, 215–216.

14. Mahfouz, *Khan al-Khalili,* 35–40.

15. Musa, *Fi al-Riwaya al-Arabiyya,* 75.

16. Badr, *Naguib Mahfouz,* 356.

17. Farouk Shusha, "Ma al-Udaba: Naguib Mahfouz," in *Naguib Mahfouz: Atahaddath Ilaykum,* 18.

18. Mahfouz, *Khan al-Khalili,* 41, 44, 59–60, 88; and Sami Khashaba, "Naguib Mahfouz wa Ishkaliyyat al-Hadatha," 104–105.

19. Mahfouz, *Khan al-Khalili,* 46.

20. Ibid., 47–48, 73; Badr, *Naguib Mahfouz,* 344, 347.

21. Abd Allah, *al-Islamiyya wa al-Ruhiyya,* 84.

22. Al-Ghitani, *Naguib Mahfouz Yatadhakkar,* 18, 93; and Mahmud Fawzi, *Naguib Mahfouz Za'im al-Harafish,* 120.

23. Mahfouz, *Khan al-Khalili,* 50, 61.

24. Abd Allah, *Al-Islamiyya wa al-Ruhiyya,* 87–88.

25. Mahfouz, "Allah," 43.

26. Abd Allah, *Al-Islamiyya wa al-Ruhiyya,* 88–89.

27. Mahfouz, *Khan al-Khalili,* 127.

28. Mahfouz, *Hams al-Junun,* 231, 242. Cf. Musa, *Fi al-Riwaya al-Arabiyya,* 74.

29. Mahfouz, *Zuqaq al-Midaqq.*

30. Ibid., 1, 8; Jad, *Form and Technique,* 151, 164, 170; Roger Allen,"Najib Mahfuz: Nobel Laureate in Literature, 1988," *World Literature Today,* 63 (1989): 6; Kilpatrick, *The Modern Egyptian Novel,* 70–80, 215–16; Sakkut, 119–24.

31. Mahfouz, *Zuqaq al-Midaqq,* 312; Badr, *Naguib Mahfouz,* 409–10; and al-Shatti, *al-Ramz wa al-Ramziyya fi Adab Naguib Mahfouz,* 118.

32. Mahfouz, *Zuqaq al-Midaqq,* 6, 13.

33. Ibid., chap. 3, esp. 27, 32; Kilpatrick, *The Modern Egyptian Novel,* 80–81.

34. Mahfouz, *Zuqaq al-Midaqq,* 42–49.

35. See *Sahih Muslim* 8, 44, 51. In the Middle East one often hears it said of a prostitute, "Allah qaddara alayha," meaning that God has predestined that she will become what she is. When I began practicing law in the courts of Mosul, Iraq, in 1946, a Muslim woman asked me to help retrieve the belongings of her late sister, whose house had been pillaged by thieves after her death. She was hesitant to tell me what her sister had done for a living, and when I insisted, the woman whispered, "Allah qaddara alayha."

36. Mahfouz, *Zuqaq al-Midaqq,* 49, 53, 79, 122–24, 224, 229.

37. Ibid., 60, 67.

38. Yusuf al-Sharuni, *al-Ushshaq al-Khamsa,* 51, 56.

39. Mahfouz, *Zuqaq al-Midaqq,* 18, 21, 180–84, 213, 241, 246, 249.

40. Musa, *Fi al-Riwaya al-Arabiyya,* 43.

41. Abd Allah, *al-Waqi'iyya fi al-Riwaya al-Arabiyya,* 486; Nabil Raghib, *Qadiyyat al-Shakl al-Fanni ind Naguib Mahfouz,* 199; Sasson Somekh, *The Changing Rhythm: A Study of Najib Mahfuz's Novels,* 100, 105; al-Ghitani, *Naguib Mahfouz Yatadhakkar,* 65.

42. Muhammad Amin al-Alim, *Ta'ammulat fi Alam Naguib Mahfouz,* 42; Badr, *Naguib Mahfouz,* 366, 369.

43. Badr, *Naguib Mahfouz,* 370–71, 375.

44. Mahfouz, *al-Sarab,* 7, 18–19, 102; Jad, *Form and Technique,* 161–62, 166, 172, 174–75; Kilpatrick, *The Modern Egyptian Novel,* 216, 218; and Matityahu Peled, *Religion, My Own: The Literary Works of Naguib Mahfouz,* 151, 154.

45. Mahfouz, *Bidaya wa Nihaya.*

46. Ibid., 1, 12; Jad, *Form and Technique,* 171; Kilpatrick, *The Modern Egyptian Novel,* 218, 219; and Peled, *Religion, My Own,* 141, 150.

47. Mahfouz, *Bidaya wa Nihaya,* 11, 38; al-Shatti, *al-Ramz wa al-Ramziyya,* 98.

48. Mahfouz, *Bidaya wa Nihaya*, 32; al-Shatti, *Al-Ramz wa al-Ramziyya*, 99.

49. Badr, *Naguib Mahfouz*, 449–51.

50. Mahfouz, *Bidaya wa Nihaya*, chap. 70; Mahmud Hishmat Abd al-Zahir, "al-Nihaya fi *Bidaya wa Nihaya*, 44."

51. Mahfouz, *Bidaya wa Nihaya*, 170–71.

52. Abd al-Zahir, "al-Nihaya," 44.

53. Mahfouz, *Bidaya wa Nihaya*, 180, 182, 185, 190–91, 234–35; Abd al-Zahir, "al-Nihaya," 44.

54. For more elaboration on the subject, see Moosa, *Extremist Shiites: The Ghulat Sects*, 147–148.

55. Mahfouz, *Bidaya wa Nihaya*, 374–375.

56. Ibid., 381–82. Cf. al-Sharuni, *Dirasat fi al-Adab al-Arabi al-Mu'asir*, 92.

57. Mahfouz, *Bidaya wa Nihaya*, 381.

58. Ibid., 71.

59. Al-Shatti, *Al-Ramz wa al-Ramziyya*, 99.

60. Mahfouz, *Bidaya wa Nihaya*, 68–72.

61. Ibid., 141, 163–169.

62. Musa, *Fi al-Riwaya al-Arabiyya*, 61.

63. Mahfouz, *Bidaya wa Nihaya*, 229–30.

64. Ibid., 9, 11, 24, 31; Badr, *Naguib Mahfouz*, 470–71.

65. Mahfouz, *Bidaya wa Nihaya*, 17.

66. Musa, *Fi al-Riwaya al-Arabiyya*, 64–65.

67. Jacques Jomier, *Thulathiyyat Naguib Mahfouz*, 6–7.

4. Thulathiyya (Trilogy)

1. Jamal al-Ghitani, *Naguib Mahfouz Yatadhakkar*, 68.

2. Ibid., 63–64; Sakkut, 125–42.

3. See the postscript by Said Jawdat al-Sahhar to Mahfouz's novel *al-Baqi min al-Zaman Sa'a*, 2.

4. Al-Ghitani, *Naguib Mahfouz Yatadhakkar*, 59.

5. Ibid.

6. Al-Sahhar states his suggestion that Mahfouz divide the novel into three separate parts (*Al-Baqi min al-Zaman Sa'a*, 2–3).

7. Roger Allen, "Najib Mahfuz: Nobel Laureate in Literature, 1988," 5.

8. Jacques Jomier, *Thulathiyyat Naguib Mahfouz*, 11, 15; and Muhammad Amin al-Alim, *Ta'ammulat fi Alam Naguib Mahfouz*, 64–65.

9. Naguib Mahfouz, *Bayn al-Qasrayn*.

10. Ibid., 23.

11. Ibid., 13, 22–24, 32–34.

12. Ibid., 26, 33, 36.

13. Abu Hamid al-Ghazzali, *Ihya Ulum al-Din*, 2:58, n. 3.

14. See Hans Wehr, *A Dictionary of Modern Written Arabic*, 402.

15. Mahfouz, *Bayn al-Qasrayn*, 8–9.

16. Ibid., 10.

17. Ibid., 49, 94.

18. Al-Ghazzali, *Ihya Ilum al-Din*, 2:55–57. I personally witnessed an instance of this tradition recently when I was the guest of a strict Muslim religious leader who not only forbade his wife to leave the house without his consent, but also would not allow her to join us while he and I were relaxing in the evening. When I protested that we were living in the United States, not some remote Middle Eastern village, he said bluntly that he was following the dictates of his religion and that I should not interfere in his affairs.

19. Mahfouz, *Bayn al-Qasrayn*, chap. 27, esp. 190, 193.

20. Ibid., 222–23.

21. Ibid., 147.

22. See Ali's speech in Ibn Abi al-Hadid, *Sharh Nahj al-Balagha*, 2:76–77, and another edition of the same work by Muhammad Abduh, 1, 125–26.

23. Mahfouz, *Bayn al-Qasrayn*, 179.

24. Jomier, *Thulathiyyat Naguib Mahfouz*, 26.

25. Yusuf al-Sharuni, *Dirasat fi al-Adab al-Arabi al-Mu'asir*, 67.

26. Louis Awad, *Maqalat fi al-Naqd wa al-Adab*, 359–65.

27. Mahfouz, *Bayn al-Qasrayn*, 51.

28. Wehr, *A Dictionary of Modern Written Arabic*, 713.

29. See 2d Timothy 3:5.

30. Mahfouz, *Bayn al-Qasrayn*, 92.

31. On this subject see Moosa, *The Origins of Modern Arabic Fiction*, 79.

32. Mahfouz, *Bayn al-Qasrayn*, 66–67.

33. Al-Ghitani, *Naguib Mahfouz Yatadhakkar*, 88.

34. Mahfouz, *Bayn al-Qasrayn*, 387.

35. Al-Ghitani, *Naguib Mahfouz Yatadhakkar*, 68.

36. *Bayn al-Qasrayn*, 59–60.

37. Al-Ghitani, *Naguib Mahfouz Yatadhakkar*, 14.

38. *Bayn al-Qasrayn*, 396–99.

39. Mahfouz, *Qasr al-Shawq*, 132, 138.

40. Ibid., 150–51.

41. Al-Ghitani, 26–27.

42. Mahfouz, *Qasr al-Shawq*, 63–64.

43. Ghali Shukri, *al-Muntami: Dirasa fi Adab Naguib Mahfouz*, 57; al-Ghitani, *Naguib Mahfouz Yatadhakkar*, 17, 21.

44. Mahfouz, *Qasr al-Shawq*, 162.

45. See Moosa, *Origins of Modern Arabic Fiction*, chap. 4.

46. Mahfouz, *Qasr al-Shawq*, 203.

47. Shukri, *al-Muntami*, 57, 68.

48. Mahfouz, *Qasr al-Shawq*, 454–56.

49. Al-Ghitani, *Naguib Mahfouz Yatadhakkar*, 76–77, 79.

50. Mahfouz, *Qasr al-Shawq*, 170.

51. Mahfouz, *al-Sukkariyya*.

52. Ibid., 13–17.

53. Shukri, *al-Muntami*, 50.

54. Mahfouz, *al-Sukkariyya*, 124–25.

55. Ibid., 126–28.

56. Al-Ghitani, *Naguib Mahfouz Yatadhakkar*, 68; and Shukri, *al-Muntami*, 7.

57. Al-Ghitani, *Naguib Mahfouz Yatadhakkar*, 68; and Anwar al-Ma'addawi, "Malhamat Naguib Mahfouz al-Riwa'iyya," 21.

58. Shukri, *al-Muntami*, 57.

59. Mahfouz, *al-Sukkariyya*, 54.

60. Al-Ghitani, *Naguib Mahfouz Yatadhakkara*, 76.

61. Mahfouz, *al-Sukkariyya*, 40.

62. Ibid., 108–9. In Salama Musa, *Tarbiyat Salama Musa*, 236, 268–69, the author expresses the view that in the civilization of the future, technology would replace religious doctrines and even socialism.

63. Mahfouz, *al-Sukkariyya*, 173–75.

64. Yunan Labib Rizq, *Tarikh al-Wizarat al-Misriyya 1878–1952*, 451.

65. Ibid., 93–94, 161–62.

66. Al-Ghitani, *Naguib Mahfouz Yatadhakkar*, 79.

67. Mahfouz, *al-Sukkariyya*, 155–57.

5. Awlad Haratina

1. Naguib Mahfouz, *Awlad Haratina*.

2. Abd al-Sattar al-Tawila, "Mu'amarat al-Samt ala Fatwa al-Shaykh Umar," *Rose El-Youssef*, no. 3177 (May 1, 1989) 12–14; and ibid., Karam Jabr, "Ana wa Salman Rushdi," 14–16. Shaykh Umar Abd al-Rahman, a member

of the extremist Islamic group al-Jihad, is the one who issued a *fatwa* (juristic opinion) that Naguib Mahfouz should repent or be killed. For further attacks against Mahfouz see Anwar al-Jundi, "Riwayat Salman Rushdi wa Naguib Mahfouz," *al-I'tisam*, no. 1 (April 1989) 5–7; and al-Shaykh Abd al-Hamid Kishk, *Kalimatuna fi al-Radd ala* Awlad Haratina, 227–61, which contains articles by Mustafa Adnan against *Awlad Haratina* published in the newspaper *al-Nur* in 1988.

3. Shukri, *al-Muntami*, 231; and Haim Gordon, *Naguib Mahfouz's Egypt: Existential Themes in His Writings*, 87.

4. Nabil Faraj, *Naguib Mahfouz: Hayatuh wa Adabuh*, 80, 92.

5. Mahfouz, *Awlad Haratina*, 216.

Selected Bibliography

Abd Allah, Muhammad Hasan. *Al-Waqi'iyya fi al-Riwaya al-Arabiyya* (Realism in the Arabic Novel). Cairo: Dar al-Maarif, 1971.

———. *Al-Islamiyya wa al-Ruhiyya fi Adab Naguib Mahfouz* (Islamic and spiritual Elements in the Literature of Naguib Mahfouz). Cairo: Maktabat Misr, 1978.

Abd al-Hayy, Abd al-Tawwab. "Asir Hayati" (The Essence of My Life). *Al-Idha'a*, December 21, 1975, 126–34.

Abu-Haidar, Jareer. "*Awlad Haratina* by Najib Mahfuz: An Event In The Arab World." *Journal of Arabic Literature* 16 (1985): 119–31.

Abd al-Zahir, Mahmud Hishmat. "Al-Nihaya fi Bidaya wa Nihaya" (The End in the Beginning and the End). *Al-Adab*, November 1960, 43–47.

Afifi, Muhammad. "Naguib Mahfouz Rajul al-Sa'a" (Naguib Mahfouz, Man of the Hour). *Al-Hilal*, February 1970, 137–41.

Alim, Muhammad Amin al-. *Ta'ammulat fi Alam Naguib Mahfouz* (Contemplations in the World of Naguib Mahfouz). Cairo: al-Haya al-Misriyya al-Amma li al-Talif wa al-Nashr, 1970.

Allen, Roger. *The Arabic Novel: A Historical and Critical Introduction*. Syracuse, N.Y.: Syracuse University Press, 1982.

———. "Najib Mahfuz: Nobel Laureate in Literature, 1988." *World Literature Today* 63 (1989): 5–9.

Aqqad, Abbas Mahmud al-. *Fi Bayti* (At My House). Cairo: Dar al-Maarif li al-Tibaa wa al-Nashr, Silsilat Iqra, 1945.

Atiyya, Ahmad Muhammad. *Ma Naguib Mahfouz* (With Naguib Mahfouz). Damascus: Manshurat Wizarat al-Thaqafa, 1971.

Awad, Louis. *Maqalat fi al-Naqd wa al-Adab* (Essays on Criticism and Literature). Cairo: Maktabat al-Anglo-al-Misriyya, n.d.

Badr, Abd al-Muhsin. *Naguib Mahfouz: al-Ru'ya wa al-Adat* (Naguib Mahfouz: The Vision and Technique). Cairo: Dar al-Thaqafa li al-Tibaa wa al-Nashr, 1978.

Badri, Uthman. *Bina al-Shakhsiyya al-Riwa'iyya fi Riwayat Naguib Mahfouz* (The Structure of Character in the Novels of Naguib Mahfouz). Beirut: Dar al-Hadatha, 1986.

Baikie, James. *Ancient Egypt*. London, 1912. Translated into Arabic by Naguib Mahfouz under the title *Misr al-Qadima*. Cairo: Matbaat al-Majalla al-Jadida, 1932.

Battuti, Mahir Hasan al-. "Kamal Abd al-Jawad al-Lamuntami" (Kamal Abd al-Jawad the Outsider). *Al-Adab*, June 1963, 30–32.

Beard, Michael, ed. *Naguib Mahfouz From Regional Fame to Global Recognition*. Syracuse, N.Y.: Syracuse University Press, 1993.

Breasted, James Henry. *A History of Egypt from the Earliest Times to the Persian Conquest*. 2d ed. N.Y.: Charles Scribners' Sons, 1912.

Bullata, Isa J., ed. *Critical Perspectives on Modern Arabic Literature*. Washington, D.C.: Three Continents Press, 1980.

Caldwell, Wallace Everett, and Mary Francis Gyles. *The Ancient World*. 3d. ed. New York: Holt, Rinehart and Winston, 1966.

Darwish, al-Arabi Hasan. *Al-Ittijah al-Ta'biri fi Riwayat Naguib Mahfouz* (Expressional Orientation in the Novels of Naguib Mahfouz). Cairo: Maktabat al-Nahda al-Misriyya, 1989.

Dawwara, Fuad. *Ashrat Udaba Yatahaddathun* (Ten Men of Letters Converse). Cairo: Dar al-Hilal, 1965.

———. "Al-Wujdan al-Qawmi fi Adab Naguib Mahfouz" (National Consciousness in the Writings of Naguib Mahfouz). *Al-Hilal*, February 1970, 100–109.

———. *Naguib Mahfouz min al-Qawmiyya ila al-Alamiyya* (Naguib Mahfouz from Provincialism to Universal Recognition). Cairo: al-Haya al-Misriyya al-Amma li al-Kitab, 1989.

———. "Rihlat al-Khamsin ma al-Qira'a wa al-Kitaba" (The Journey of Naguib Mahfouz in his Fiftieth Years of Age with Reading and Writing). *Al-Katib*, January 1963, 5–23.

Enany, Rasheed El-. *Najib Mahfuz: The Pursuit of Meaning*. New York: Routledge, 1993.

Faraj, al-Sayyid Ahmad. *Adab Naguib Mahfouz wa Ishkaliyyat al-Sira bayn al-Islam wa al-Taghrib* (The Writings of Naguib Mahfouz and the Problem of the Conflict between Islam and Westernization). Al-Mansura: Dar al-Wafa, 1990.

Faraj, Nabil. *Naguib Mahfouz: Hayatuh wa Adabuh* (Naguib Mahfouz: His Life and Writings). Cairo: al-Haya al-Amma li al-Kitab, 1985.

Fathi, Ibrahim. *Al-Alam al-Riwa'i ind Naguib Mahfouz* (The Fictional World of Naguib Mahfouz). Cairo: Dar al-Fikr al-Muasir, 1978.

Fawzi, Mahmud. *Naguib Mahfouz: Za'im al-Harafish* (Naguib Mahfouz: The Leader of the Common People). Beirut: Dar al-Jil, 1989.

Ghazzali, Abu Hamid al-. *Ihya Ulum al-Din* (The Revival of the Sciences of Religion). Vol. 2. Cairo: al-Maktaba al-Tijariyya al-Kubra, n.d.

Ghitani, Jamal al-. *Naguib Mahfouz Yatadhakkar* (Naguib Mahfouz Remembers). Beirut: Dar al-Masira, 1980.

Gordon, Haim. *Naguib Mahfouz's Egypt: Existential Themes in His Writings.* New York: Greenwood Press, 1990.

Hadid, Ibn Abi al-. *Sharh Nahj al-Balagha* (Commentary on the Path of Eloquence). Vol. 2. Beirut: Dar al-Huda al-Wataniyya, n.d.

Hafiz, Sabri. "Naguib Mahfouz bayn al-Din wa al-Falsafa" (Naguib Mahfouz between Religion and Philosophy). *Al-Hilal,* February 1970, 116–27.

———. "Naguib Mahfouz: Masadir wa Mukawwinat Tajribatih al-Ibda'iyya" (Naguib Mahfouz: Sources and Constituents of his Creative Ability). In *Naguib Mahfouz: Atahaddath Ilaykum,* 75–123.

Hawari, Ahmad Ibrahim al-. *Al-Batal al-Mu'asir fi al-Riwaya al-Misriyya* (The Contemporary Hero in the Egyptian Novel). Baghdad: Dar al-Huriyya li al-Tibaa, 1976.

Haykal, Ahmad. *Al-Adab al-Qisasi wa al-Masrahi fi Misr* (The Story Writing and Theatrical Fiction in Egypt). Dar al-Maarif fi Misr, 1971.

Id, Raja. *Dirasa fi Adab Naguib Mahfouz: Tahlil wa Naqd.* (A Study in the Writings of Naguib Mahfouz: Criticism and Analysis). Alexandria: Manshurat al-Maarif, 1974.

Jad, Ali B. *Form and Technique in the Egyptian Novel, 1912–1971.* London: Ithaca Press, 1983.

Jomier, Jacques. *Thulathiyyat Naguib Mahfouz* (The *Trilogy* of Naguib Mahfouz). Translated from the French by Dr. Nazmi Luqa. Cairo: Maktabat Misr, 1959.

———. "Roman à clef et contestation: Awlad Haretna de Naguib Mahfouz." *Institut Mélanges Dominicain de l'Etudes Orientales* 11 (1972): 265–72.

Jundi, Anwar al-. "Riwayat Salman Rushdi wa Naguib Mahfouz" (The Novels of Salman Rushdi and Naguib Mahfouz). *Al-I'tisam,* no. 1 (April 1989): 5–7.

Khashaba, Sami. "Nagiub Mahfouz wa Ishkaliyyat al-Hadatha wa Shakh-siyyatuha fi al-Riwayat al-Ijtima'iyya al-Ula" (Naguib Mahfouz and the Problem of Adolescence and Characters in His Early Social Novels). *Al-Bayan*, January 1989; 97–114.

Kilpatrick, Hilary. *The Modern Egyptian Novel: A Study in Social Criticism.* London: Ithaca Press, 1974.

Kishk, al-Shaykh Abd al-Hamid. *Kalimatuna fi al-Radd ala* Awlad Hara-tina (Our Word Against *Awlad Haratina*). Cairo: al-Mukhtar al-Islami, 1989.

Kushayk, Mahmud. "Hiwar ma Amid al-Riaya al-Arabiyya Naguib Mahfouz" (Interview with Naguib Mahfouz, Doyen of the Arabic Novel). *Al-Thaqafa al-Jadida*, April 1988, 136–45.

Le Gassick, Trevor, ed. *Critical Perspectives on Naguib Mahfouz.* Washington, D.C.: Three Continents Press, 1991.

———. "Trials of the Flesh and of the Intellect." *The World and I*, February 1992, 424–31.

Ma'addawi, Anwar al-. "Malhamat Naguib Mahfouz al-Riwa'iyya" (The Fictional Epic of Naguib Mahfouz). *Al-Adab*, April 1958, 18–22, and May 1958, 11–16.

Mahfouz, Naguib. "Ihtidar Mu'taqadat wa Tawallud Mu'taqdat" (The Death and Birth of New Doctrines). *Al-Majalla al-Jadida*, October 1930, 1468–70.

———. "Thalatha min Udaba'ina" (Three of Our Men of Letters). *Al-Majalla al-Jadida*, February 1934, 65–66.

———. "Falsafat al-Hubb" (The Philosophy of Love). *Al-Majalla al-Jadida*, October 1934, 79–82.

———. "Al-Ruju ila Methuselah" (Back to Methuselah). *Al-Maarif*, April–May 1934, 592–93.

———. "Allah." *Al-Majalla al-Jadida*, January 1936, 43–46.

———. "Fikrat Allah fi al-Falsafa" (The Idea of God in Philosophy). *Al-Majalla al-Jadida*, March 1936, 33–40.

———. *Kifah Tiba* (The Struggle of Thebes.) Cairo: Lajnat al-Nashr li al-Jami'iyyin,1947.

———. "Al-Qissa ind al-Aqqad" (The Story Writing with al-Aqqad). *Al-Risala*, August 27, 1945, 952–54.

———. *Abath al-Aqdar* (Ironies of Fate). Cairo: Maktabat Misr, 1966.

———. *Awlad Haratina* (Children of Our Quarter). Beirut: Dar al- Adab, 1967. Translated into English by Philip Stewart from the serialized version (*al-Ahram*, 1959) under the title *Children of Gebelawi*. London: Heinemann, and Washington, D.C.: Three Continents Press, 1981. Reprinted by Three Continents Press in 1988, revised and published by the same press in 1990.

———. *Al-Maraya* (Mirrors). Beirut: Dar al-Qalam, 1972.

———. *Radobis.* Cairo: Maktabat Misr, 1977.

———. *Al-Qahira al-Jadida* (New Cairo). Cairo: Maktabat Misr, n.d.

———. *Khan al-Khalili.* Cairo: Maktabat Misr, n.d.

———. *Zuqaq al-Midaqq* (Midaqq Alley). Cairo: Maktabat Misr, n.d. Translated into English by Trevor le Gassick under the title *Midaq Alley.* Beirut: Khayat, 1966. A corrected edition was published by Heinemann in 1975, and reprinted in 1977 and 1980 and by Three Continents Press in 1989.

———. *Al-Sarab* (The Mirage). Cairo: Maktabat Misr, n.d.

———. *Bidaya wa Nihaya* (The Beginning and the End). Cairo: Maktabat Misr, n.d. Translated into English by Ramses Awad under the title *The Beginning and the End.* Cairo: American University of Cairo Press, 1985.

———. *Bayn al-Qasrayn* (Between Two Palaces). Cairo: Maktabat Misr, n.d. Translated into English by William Maynard Hutchins and Oliver E. Kenny under the title *Palace Walk.* New York: Doubleday, 1990.

———. *Qasr al-Shawq* (The Palace of Desire). Cairo: Maktabat Misr, n.d. Translated into English by William Maynard Hutchins, Lorne Kenny and Olive E. Kenny under the title *Palace of Desire.* New York: Doubleday, 1991.

———. *Al-Sukkariyya* (Sugar Bowl). Cairo: Maktabat Misr, n.d. Translated into English by William Maynard Hutchins and Angele Botros Samaan under the title *Sugar Street.* New York: Doubleday, 1992.

———. *Al-Baqi min al-Zaman Sa'a* (What Is Left of Time Is an Hour). Cairo: Maktabat Misr, n.d.

———. *Hams al-Junun* (The Whisper of Madness). Cairo: Maktabat Misr, n.d.

Mertz, Barbara. *Temples, Tombs and Hieroglyphics.* New York: Coward McCann, 1964. Reprint, Peter Berdick Books, 1990.

Mikhail, Mona. *Studies in the Short Fiction of Mahfouz and Idris.* New York: New York University Press, 1992.

Moosa, Matti. *The Origins of Modern Arabic Fiction.* Washington, D.C.: Three Continents Press, 1983.

———. *Extremist Shiites: The Ghulat Sects.* Syracuse: Syracuse University Press, 1988.

Mousa, Nedal al-. "The Nature and Uses of the Fantastic in the Fictional World of Naguib Mahfouz," *Journal of Arabic Literature* 23 (March 1992): 36–48.

Musa, Fatima. *Fi al-Riwaya al-Arabiyya* (On the Arabic Novel). Cairo: Matbaat al-Anglo-Misriyya, 1971.

Musa, Salama. *Tarbiyat Salama Musa* (The Education of Salama Musa). Cairo: Muassasat al-Khanji, 1962.

Naguib Mahfouz: Atahaddath Ilaykum (Naguib Mahfouz: I Converse with You). Beirut: Dar al-Awda, 1977.

Naguib Mahfouz: Nobel 1988, A Memorial Book. Cairo: Matabi al-Haya al-Misriyya al-Amma li al-Kitab, 1988.

Najib, Naji. *Qissat al-Ajyal bayn Thomas Mann wa Naguib Mahfouz* (The Story of Generations between Thomas Mann and Naguib Mahfouz). Cairo: al-Haya al-Misriyya al-Amma li al- Kitab, 1977.

Najmi, Kamal al-. "Ma al-Ghina wa al-Mughannin fi Adab Naguib Mahfouz" (Singing and Singers in the Writings of Naguib Mahfouz). *Al-Hilal,* February 1970, 130–35.

Naqqash, Raja al-. "Bayn al-Wafdiyya wa al-Markisiyya" (Between Wafdism and Marxism). *Al-Hilal,* February 1970, 40–41.

Nassaj, Sayyid Hamid al-. *Dalil al-Qissa al-Misriyya* (A Guide to the Egyptian Story). Cairo: al-Haya al-Amma li al-Kitab, 1972.

Nawfal, Yusuf Hasan. *Al-Qissa wa al-Riwaya bayn Taha Husayn wa Naguib Mahfouz* (The Story and the Novel between Taha Husayn and Naguib Mahfouz). Cairo: Dar al-Nahda al-Arabiyya, 1977.

Nobel Prize Annual, 1988. IMG, New York: 1989, 69–77.

Peled, Matityahu. *Religion, My Own: The Literary Works of Najib Mahfuz.* New Brunswick, N.J.: Transaction Books, 1983.

Qasim, Siza Ahmad. *Bina al-Riwaya: Dirasa Muqarana li* Thulathiyyat *Naguib Mahfouz* (The Structure of the Novel: A Comparative Study of the *Trilogy* of Naguib Mahfouz). Beirut: Dar al-Tanwir, 1985.

Qutb, Sayyid. *Kutub wa Shakhsiyyat* (Books and Personalities). Beirut: Dar al-Shuruq, n.d.

Raghib, Nabil. *Qadiyyat al-Shakl al-Fanni ind Naguib Mahfouz* (The Question of Aesthetic Form with Naguib Mahfouz). Cairo: al-Haya al-Amma li al-Kitab, 1988.

Rajab, Adham. "Safahat Majhula min Hayat Naguib Mahfouz" (Unknown Aspects of the Life of Naguib Mahfouz). *Al-Hilal,* February 1970, 89–99.

Rizq, Yunan Labib. *Tarikh al-Wizarat al-Misriyya: 1878–1952* (History of the Egyptian Cabinets: 1878–1952). Cairo: Matabi al-Ahram, 1975.

Sahih Muslim (Genuine Collection of Traditions by Muslim). Cairo: Matbaat Muhammad Ali Sabih, A.H. 1334 (Vol. 8,1915).

Said, Fatima al-Zahra Muhammad. *Al-Ramziyya fi Adab Naguib Mahfouz* (Symbolism in the Writings of Naguib Mahfouz). Beirut: al-Muassasa al-Adabiyya li al-Dirasat wa al-Nashr, 1981.

Sakkut, Hamdi. *The Egyptian Novel and Its Main Trends, 1913 to 1952.* Cairo: American University in Cairo Press, 1971.

Samaan, Angele Botros. *Dirasat fi al-Riwaya al-Arabiyya.* (Studies in the Arabic Novel). Cairo: al-Haya al-Misriyya al-Amma li al-Kitab, 1987.

Sayyid, Muhammad Sabri al-. "Naguib Mahfouz," *al Qissa,* January 1989, 90–99.

Sharuni, Yusuf al-. *Al-Ushshaq al-Khamsa* (The Five Lovers). Cairo: Matabi Rose El-Youssef, 1954.

———. *Dirasat fi al-Adab al-Arabi al-Mu'asir* (Studies in Contemporary Arabic Literature). Cairo: al-Muassasa al-Misriyya al-Amma li al-Talif wa al-Tarjama wa al-Tibaa wa al-Nashr, 1964.

———. *Al-Riwa'iyyun al-Thalatha: Naguib Mahfouz, Abd al-Halim Abd Allah wa Yusuf al-Siba'i* (The Three Novelists: Naguib Mahfouz, Abd al-Halim Abd Allah and Yusuf al-Siba'i). Cairo: al-Haya al-Amma li al-Kitab, 1980.

Shatti, Sulayman al-. *Al-Ramz wa al-Ramziyya fi Adab Naguib Mahfouz* (Symbol and Symbolism in the Writings of Naguib Mahfouz). Kuwait: al-Matbaa al-Asriyya, 1976.

———. "Naguib Mahfouz: Rihlat al-Hara min al-Mu'anat ila al-Masarrat" (Naguib Mahfouz: Journey of the Hara 'Quarter' from Suffering to Happiness). *Al-Arabi,* January 1989, 65–67.

Shawkat, Mahmud Hamid. *Al-Fann al-Qisasi fi al-Adab al-Misri al-Hadith 1800–1956* (The Art of Story Writing in Modern Egyptian Literature: 1800–1956). Cairo: Dar al-Fikr al-Arabi, 1956.

Shaykh, Ibrahim al-. *Mawaqif Ijtima'iyya wa Siyasiyya fi Adab Naguib Mahfouz: Tahlil wa Naqd* (Social and Political Positions in the Writings of Naguib Mahfouz: Analysis and Criticism). Cairo: Maktabat al-Shuruq, 1987.

Shukri, Ghali. *Al-Muntami: Dirasa fi Adab Naguib Mahfouz* (The Insider: A Study in the Writings of Naguib Mahfouz). Cairo: Matbaat al-Zunnari, 1964.

———. *Mudhakkirat Thaqafa Tahtadir* (Memoirs of a Dying Culture). Beirut: Dar al-Talia, 1970.

———. *Naguib Mahfouz min al-Jamaliyya ila Nobel* (Naguib Mahfouz from the Jamaliyya Quarter to Nobel). Cairo: Wizarat al-Ilam, 1988.

"Shullat al-Harafish" (The Gang of Countrymen). *Al-Sharq,* September–December 1988, 103–6.

Shusha, Farouk. "Ma al-Udaba: Naguib Mahfouz" (With Men of Letters: Naguib Mahfouz). *Al-Adab,* June 1960, 18–21; reprinted in *Naguib Mahfouz: Atahaddath Ilaykum,* 43–56. Beirut: Dar al-Awda (1977).

Somekh, Sasson. *The Changing Rhythm: A Study of Najib Mahfuz's Novels.* Leiden: E.J. Brill, 1973.

312 Selected Bibliography

Steppart, F. "Gott, die Futuwwat und die Wissenschaft: *Awlad Haratna*," *Mélanges d'Islamologie*. Vol. 2, *Correspondance d' Orient no. 13*. Center pour l' Études de Problemes du Monde Musulman Contemporain, Brussels, 1975.

Stewart, Philip. "*Awlad Haretna:* Its Value as Literature and the Public Reaction." M. Litt. diss., Oxford University, 1963.

———. "An Arabic Nobodaddy: The Gebelawi of Naguib Mahfouz," in Alan Jones, ed., *Arabicus Felix: Luminosus Britannicus, Essays in Honor of A.F.L. Beeston.* Ithaca Press, Reading for the Board of the Faculty of Oriental Studies, Oxford University, 1991, 213–20.

Tadros, Khalil Hanna. *Naguib Mahfouz al-Ustura al-Khalida* (Naguib Mahfouz the Immortal Legend). Cairo: Matbaat al-Nasr, 1989.

Tarabishi, George. *Allah fi Rihlat Naguib Mahfouz al-Ramziyya* (God in the Symbolic Journey of Naguib Mahfouz). Beirut: Dar al-Talia li al-Tibaa wa al-Nashr, 1973.

Tawila, Abd al-Sattar al-. "'Mu'amarat al-Samt ala Fatwa al-Shaykh Umar" (The Conspiracy of Silence Regarding the Juristic Opinion of al-Shaykh Umar). *Rose El-Youssef*, no. 3177 (May 1, 1989). 12–14.

Vatikiotis, J.P. "The Corruption of the Futuwwa: A Consideration of Despair in Awlad Haritna." *Middle East Studies* 7/(1971): 169–84.

Viorst, Milton. "Man of Gamaliya." *The New Yorker*, July 2, 1990, 32–53.

Wadi, Taha. *Madkhal ila Tarikh al-Riwaya, 1905–1952* (Introduction to the History of the Novel, 1905–1952). Cairo: Maktabat al-Nahda al-Misriyya, 1972.

Wa'il, Aziz. *Al-Haqiqa al-Gha'iba Wara Fawz Naguib Mahfouz bi Ja'izat Nobel* (The Unrevealed Truth Behind the Success of Naguib Mahfouz in Winning the Nobel Prize). Cairo: Dar al-Haqiqa li al-Ilam al-Arabi, 1989.

Wehr, Hans. *A Dictionary of Modern Written Arabic.* Edited by J. Milton Cowan. Ithaca: Cornell University Press, 1961.

Yaghi, Abd al-Rahman. *Al-Juhud al-Riwa'iyya min Salim al-Bustani ila Naguib Mahfouz* (The Efforts of the Writing of Fiction from Salim al-Bustani to Naguib Mahfouz). Beirut: Dar al-Awda, 1972.

Yarid, Evelyn Farid. *Naguib Mahfouz wa al-Qissa al-Qasira* (Naguib Mahfouz and the Short Story). Amman Jordan: Dar al-Shuruq li al Nashr wa al-Tawzi, 1987.

Zayyat, Latifa al-. *Naguib Mahfouz al-Sura wa al-Mithal: Maqalat Naqdiyya* (Naguib Mahfouz, The Image and the Symbol: A Critical Study). Cairo: Jaridat al-Ahali, 1989.

———. "Al-Shakl al-Riwa'i ind Naguib Mahfouz min *al-Liss wa al-Kilab* ila *Miramar*" (Fictional Form in the Writings of Naguib Mahfouz from *The Thief and the Dogs* to *Miramar*). *Al-Hilal*, February 1970, 73–74.

Index